Barack Obama's Post-American Foreign Policy

Barack Obama's Post-American Foreign Policy

The Limits of Engagement

Robert Singh

BLOOMSBURY ACADEMIC

First published in 2012 by

Bloomsbury Academic
an imprint of Bloomsbury Publishing Plc
50 Bedford Square, London WC1B 3DP, UK
and
175 Fifth Avenue, New York, NY 10010, USA

CIP records for this book are available from the British Library and the
Library of Congress

ISBN 978-1-78093-038-1 (hardback)
ISBN 978-1-78093-037-4 (paperback)
ISBN 978-1-78093-113-5 (ebook)

This book is produced using paper that is made from wood grown in managed,
sustainable forests. It is natural, renewable and recyclable. The logging and
manufacturing processes conform to the environmental regulations of
the country of origin.

Printed and bound in Great Britain by MPG Books Group, Bodmin, Cornwall.

Cover image: © Jason Reed/Reuters/Corbis

www.bloomsburyacademic.com

To Alia

Advance Praise for *Barack Obama's Post-American Foreign Policy: The Limits of Engagement*

Outstanding. This is the single best book to grasp and assess the international priorities and overall foreign policy record of the Obama administration. Rather than simply taking for granted the superiority of the president's distinctive foreign policy approach, Singh subjects it to a genuinely sophisticated, nuanced, and critical analysis. He finds that Obama has transformed US foreign policy much less than might have been expected, and that an emphasis on diplomatic engagement has run up against its own limitations. Systematic, intelligent, and thoroughly convincing.

— Colin Dueck, George Mason University, USA

Rob Singh has two big things exactly right: Barack Obama's hope to transform American foreign policy is truly audacious, but his struggle against past American strategic culture and habits of international leadership is, at best, incomplete. And he offers not just an analysis of the story to date, but a way to understand what a second Obama term would mean.

— Thomas Donnelly, Director, Marilyn Ware Center for Security Studies, American Enterprise Institute, USA

Singh has done the debate over the Obama presidency a great and necessary service. He has managed to depoliticize the assessment of one of the most polarizing presidents of the recent past and offer a preliminary judgement devoid of the rancour and eulogising that accompany contemporary Obama studies. I can think of no book that 'gets' Obama in the manner Singh does here. This book is a seminal accounting of what promised to be a transformative international agenda and yet became a misunderstood reworking of the Bush Doctrine. You don't have to like this interpretation; you do have to deal with it.

This book is required reading for everyone – American and non-American – that in 2008 invested the Obama presidency with too much hope or too much cynicism. Singh avoids the delusions of both and offers a portrait of a foreign policy that is compelling, critical and historically-informed.

— Timothy J. Lynch, editor of the *Oxford Encyclopedia of American Military and Diplomatic History*, University of Melbourne, Australia

The co-author of the prescient and groundbreaking *After Bush* now focuses his considerable expertise on President Obama's foreign policy. The result is a highly informative, thought-provoking and important work that challenges much of what passes for conventional wisdom on the subject. A must-read for all those interested in contemporary international affairs.

— Rory Miller, Director of Middle East and Mediterranean Studies, King's College London, UK

Covering a wide swathe of issues, Singh presents a well-rounded exposé of the strengths and weaknesses of Obama's foreign escapades, ensuring this is a must-read for anyone seeking to comprehend the direction of US foreign policy in the post-Bush years.

— James D. Boys, Richmond University, London and the Global Policy Institute, UK

Contents

Tables

Preface and Acknowledgments

As part of his State Visit to the United Kingdom, Barack Obama delivered the first ever speech by an American president in Westminster Hall to Members of both Houses of Parliament on May 25, 2011. I was fortunate enough to be part of the audience, as a guest of the United States Embassy in London. The great state occasion was also a rather curious one, with a mixture of Members of the House of Commons and the House of Lords, former prime ministers and the great and the good of British public life assembled together (not to mention assorted UK academics, the Archbishop of Canterbury and Tom Hanks). After a tour of the Palace of Westminster, President Obama was unfashionably late in arriving – prompting certain former PMs unused to such treatment to look askance at their watches – and provided a curiously unengaged speech, his gaze only rarely wavering from the teleprompter and his words only once interrupted by a spontaneous round of applause. Nonetheless, the president was received in a by now familiar combination of reverence and awe, entering and exiting to standing ovations and numerous attempts by star-struck Brits to gain a presidential handshake or a have a brief word with the world's most powerful leader and hottest celebrity. In the presence of this particular American president, the normally unemotional, stoic and sceptical British exhibited tingles of which MSNBC's Chris Matthews would have been deeply envious.

At the time, what was striking to me about the speech was less its predictably enthusiastic reception than its rather formulaic content. If one closed one's eyes and listened intently, the kinds of themes that the president articulated were ones not so different from those of his much-unloved predecessor in the White House: the crucial partnership between America and Britain, through history and down to today; the set of shared values that underpinned this, and their export through the wider world; the necessity of opposing tyranny, if necessary with military force; and the importance of market democracies. An academic colleague commented to me at its conclusion that it "sounded quite neo-con in places" and, certainly, George W. Bush would surely have been excoriated for delivering the same speech for which Obama was loudly applauded. That seemed to me to confirm the peculiar state of flux affecting transatlantic relations in 2011–12 and the profound confusions that continue to surround Washington's approach to international affairs. It also encouraged me to try to complete an assessment of Obama's foreign policy, even if his term was not yet complete; one that sought to reconcile the aspirations for transformative change that had so strongly informed the 2008 presidential campaign with the more prosaic and conventional features that appeared to characterize his grand strategy in office.

Long before his speech to Westminster Hall, the original genesis of this book occurred during a year of very high – and in retrospect, as some of us argued at the time, far too high – expectations, back in 2008. In June of that year, shortly after then Senator Barack Obama of Illinois had secured the Democratic Party's nomination after a protracted and fractious campaign against the initial frontrunner, Hillary Clinton, but prior to the two major party conventions and the political and economic upheaval brought about by that fall's devastating financial crisis, I spent some three weeks in Washington, D.C. Promoting a book that I had co-written with my then University of London friend and colleague, Timothy Lynch, entitled *After Bush: The Case for Continuity in American Foreign Policy* (New York: Cambridge University Press, 2008), the historic 2008 campaign partly framed our mixed reception in the nation's capital.

Our book's central argument was that, despite the very serious and costly errors in its execution, the key principles and policies that had informed what had come to be known variously as the "Bush Doctrine" and the "war on terror" would, and should, continue to shape US foreign policy after January 2009 – regardless of who won the 2008 election. That was, at the time, a highly controversial thesis, as we were well aware when we wrote the book, and as we were regularly reminded on both sides of the Atlantic – with varying degrees of doubt, disdain and indignation – after its publication. Especially coming from two Brits, the highly contentious notion that, after seven years of an extraordinarily controversial and divisive presidency, key elements of Bush's foreign policy were essentially correct, and therefore should continue, was a claim that few Americans other than Republican partisans, stalwart conservatives and immediate members of the extended Bush family could entertain (never mind Europeans, for whom Bush was marginally less popular than the bubonic plague and avian bird flu combined).

What was perhaps more surprising than the normative and prescriptive disagreements about the Bush Doctrine, the war on terror and other foreign policies, however, was the more predictive aspect: that regardless of its merits and demerits, Bush's successor in the White House *would* likely continue much of the foreign policy that the forty-third president had initiated. In touting our contrarian speculative wares around various of the many think tanks and research councils that make Washington such an intellectual powerhouse as well as an unmatched political hotbed – the American Enterprise Institute, the Brookings Institution, the Hudson Institute, the World Affairs Council and so on – what became strikingly apparent was how hostile all sides of the pronounced partisan and ideological divide were to the very idea of continuity in US foreign policy after Bush.

Although moderate conservatives such as David Brooks, Christopher Buckley and Colin Powell ended up supporting him as the better choice for president, for many conservatives Barack Obama represented one of the most radical and disturbing national figures to have arisen in recent American politics, whose recent national emergence and potential control of the White House – particularly with supportive congressional Democratic majorities – promised extensive and fundamental discontinuity with his predecessor. Indeed, to many on the right, an Obama presidency promised a clear break not simply with George W. Bush, but also with all of his modern-era predecessors, along with the broad bipartisan commitment to maintaining and enhancing American primacy that had guided presidents of both parties from Harry S. Truman onwards. For many conservatives, Obama was not only so radical in his political views but also so self-consciously "cosmopolitan" in his background and demeanour that he represented something of a "post-American" – or even "un-American" – quantity. On this conception, much as he pledged to spread some of the wealth around domestically, so an Obama foreign policy seemed likely to spread some of the power around globally – to America's lasting damage and international stability's long-term detriment.

For progressives, by contrast, while Obama was as all-American as any other candidate – perhaps more so, in personally symbolizing the changing demographic dynamics and mixed heritage of the quintessential immigrant nation – the notion of Obama maintaining continuity in foreign policy was equally as distasteful as to those on the right, owing to the strategic shambles that Bush had presided over as Commander-in-Chief. After years of seemingly irreparable damage that the Toxic Texan had wrought upon Washington's international relations, Obama would effect the decisive "change" that he relentlessly campaigned on and finally restore rationality, realism and pragmatism – not to mention "hope" alongside humility – to US foreign policy, in place of ideology, dogma and hubris. If American relations with the wider world were indeed about to take a decisive break from the status quo, then for those on what Howard Dean liked to refer to as the "Democratic wing of the Democratic Party," this was to be warmly welcomed. For both Obama's critics and his supporters, then, the one commodity that would not be distinctive of his administration was essential continuity.

Perhaps I was naive to experience some surprise at the strongly bifurcated reactions to our case. But even for an experienced scholar, it is one thing to read in dry, abstract and regression-equation-heavy academic books and political science journal articles of the intense polarization of recent American politics. It is another entirely to experience this at first hand. What struck me forcefully during the summer of 2008 was not that the thesis of essential continuity in US foreign policy could be doubted; conservatives and progressives alike advanced a lot of carefully reasoned and well-made points that showed up important weaknesses in our central argument and that undeniably held a lot of critical weight. At minimum, as David Frum – then a high-profile denizen of AEI – helpfully suggested, there is a distinction worth making between weak and strong versions of the continuity thesis. But to encounter some of the nation's leading intellectuals as if one were addressing paid-up affiliates of party committees was an interesting phenomenon, to say the least. Another book probably deserves to be written about that, and the extent to which – in marked contrast to the United Kingdom, for instance – the stakes of politics inside the Beltway are in part so high because many of the hard-working intellectuals in research institutes and think tanks are so heavily, and persistently, involved and invested personally in partisan politics. Their career trajectories are married, at least to an extent, on whether the party they support is in power or not, and their prospects for government office – and hence the opportunity to actually make or influence policy, the holy grail for many policy wonks – likewise hinge on brute party politics and election outcomes. But that is not for this volume.

Instead, I was left wondering about the next American president, the quixotic international environment awaiting his attentions, and the extent to which the arguments of partisans on the left and the right would likely be vindicated by events. Some shifts in foreign policy were almost certain to occur, at least at a declaratory if not a substantive level. There could, after all, be little doubt that Candidate Obama was committed to some major departures from Bush-era foreign policy. Moreover, as the summer of 2008 turned to autumn, it became increasingly clear that he would win the presidential election with relative ease and take up office in January 2009.

On the one hand, with a decisive victory in the presidential election, strong partisan majorities in both houses of Congress, and a huge stock of national pride and international goodwill, Obama seemed set to dominate the American and world stages in ways no president since Reagan, and perhaps even FDR, had done. On the other, the deeply inauspicious economic climate, combined with the many vexing international problems facing Washington, established a very high bar for presidential success, international breakthroughs and enduring foreign policy achievements. At least as significant, the far-reaching structural changes affecting the world order promised a new and challenging environment that would probably hamper any occupant of the Oval Office. In that sense, it appeared to me, some American conservatives seemed to get the argument precisely wrong, both analytically and politically. The "post-American" aspects of Obama's foreign policy would derive less from him personally than from the inhospitable international climate into which the US had already forcefully emerged long prior to his arrival in D.C. By casting Obama as wedded to a transformation in American foreign policy because of his personal identity, upbringing and "exotic" background, rather than his considered agreement with a body of prevailing literature on world politics and Washington's declining ability to navigate its turbulent new currents, some of the right's critique missed its target – and cost its proponents intellectual credibility and political mileage to boot.

Beyond the prescriptive elements, though, lay the more prosaic empirical questions about the new political realities at home and abroad. As president, could Obama achieve the ambitious changes that he promised in line with the strategy of American renewal that he espoused? Would either the international environment or politics at home place insuperable constraints on the exercise of presidential leadership by a man who, for all his prodigious personal assets, was still a political novice at the highest level? Could an obviously gifted and charismatic individual who entirely lacked executive experience transition from being a South Side Chicago community organizer, part-time law professor and neophyte legislator to being the dominant world figure of an increasingly fissiparous international community? Or, as *After Bush* had argued, would the combined realities of certain enduring features of both the international and US landscapes powerfully inhibit Obama – as they would any successor to Bush, whether Democrat or Republican – from making truly decisive departures in US foreign policy?

That is the central subject of this book, which, in a certain sense, serves as a quasi-sequel, update and corrective to *After Bush*, albeit that it is my interpretation alone herein (Tim now having departed London for the sunnier environment of the University of Melbourne in Australia, fine wines and an inferior national cricket team). Inevitably, an author feels some fidelity to his prior work(s) and arguments, but I have tried as much as possible to do justice to the evolving Obama foreign policy without the undue influence of partisan or ideological lenses, something perhaps easier at least to attempt as an outsider than an American author. For, as the comments above suggest, while partisanship has its many virtues, it also has its vices as far as dispassionate scholarship and fair commentary is concerned. As readers will see, while I share many of the reservations about the foreign (and domestic) policies that Obama has followed as president, I depart from much of the conservative critique of Obama, which seems to me to be at times unfair, excessive and intemperate (and, even worse, politically self-defeating).

The book has been composed over 2009–11, the writing completed in December 2011. I gained an immeasurable amount from a series of open-ended interviews in London, Madrid and, especially, Washington, with scholars, researchers and staff on Capitol Hill. I have also benefited greatly from a series of formal interviews and many informal conversations with individuals, colleagues and friends on both sides of the Atlantic. In that regard I should particularly thank Lisa Aronsson, Carly and James D. Boys, Howard Burdett, Julia Capps, Paula Clemett, Mick Cox, Devon Cross, Jamie Davis, Eric Edelman, Douglas Eden, Douglas Feith, Bob and Nancy Lieber, Michael and Anne Mandelbaum, Rory Miller, Pietro Nivola, Hazel Nyandoro, Andrew Rudalevige, Gary Schmitt, Barak Seener, Adam Steinhouse, Bill Tompson, Christopher Williams, Keith Willis, and Jonathan Vickery. Tim Lynch kindly read two chapters and offered invaluable insights and corrections. I'm grateful, too, to the constructive criticism of the anonymous reviewer of the manuscript. I owe a debt of thanks to the administrative staff in the Department of Politics at Birkbeck, especially Christopher Leigh and Irene Breckon, for their assistance.

I should also thank Caroline Wintersgill and the staff at Bloomsbury for taking the project on and seeing it to completion and, especially, my wonderful copy-editor, Hilary Lissenden.

Above all, I owe a huge debt of particular thanks, as always, to my father, Shiv, and my brother, Neil, for their love, encouragement and support. Errors of fact and interpretation are entirely and exclusively my responsibility, as ever.

RS

1

A Post-American Foreign Policy for the Post-American World

The day I take the oath of office, the world will look at us differently.
—US Senator Barack Obama, 2006[1]

If there's just Roosevelt and Churchill sitting in a room with a brandy, that's an easier negotiation. But that's not the world we live in.
—President Barack Obama, 2009[2]

Whether intellect is the crucial attribute for a leader; whether less cerebral traits, such as courage or honesty or diligence, are more important; and whether brains can get in the way of these – these are ancient arguments all republics face. Richard Nixon had the best raw intellect of any president since Woodrow Wilson and look where it got him. The former editor of the Harvard Law Review who sits in the White House shows signs of being in over his head.
—Christopher Caldwell[3]

If he goes down in history as a poor leader, it will be a sad outcome for a man deemed to be a transformational figure at the start. Obama began his presidency intending to set the agenda and so much more. He was, by definition, a historic president – the first African-American, vanquisher of a hapless and aging opponent. Some saw him as the next FDR, and he seemed to buy into his own press when he promoted ambitious plans to stimulate the economy and remake health care. Now we're left to contemplate one of the enduring mysteries of this presidency: how a man who came from nowhere in 2008 to dominate the national agenda – much as Reagan did – lost control of it so completely once he entered the Oval Office.
—Michael Hirsh, "The Decider?"[4]

Introduction

Four years after a momentous victory in the 2008 presidential election that was celebrated around the world, Barack Obama's foreign policy excites little of the passionate intensity or global animosity of his controversial and polarizing predecessor, George W. Bush. Instead, as President Obama seeks a second term in the White House in 2012, domestic matters dominate the American public's evaluation of his stewardship of the United States. Popular attentions remain resolutely focused on the Great Recession and the multiple manifestations of a seemingly precipitous national decline since the financial crash of 2008: a fragile and faltering economy, a projected budget deficit for 2011–12 of $1,580 billion, a $14.6 trillion (and increasing) sovereign national debt, a downgraded national credit rating, and a myriad of disconcerting domestic discontents from a stubbornly persistent 9 percent unemployment rate (and near 20 percent "underemployment"[5]) to home foreclosures, mortgages in negative equity and 46.2 million Americans – one in six – with incomes below the official poverty line.[6]

Since President Obama took office in January 2009, the US unemployment rate has risen from 7.6 percent to 9.1 percent (by August 2011), the number of people out of work has grown from 11.6 million to 14 million, the national debt has soared from $10.6 trillion to $14.6 trillion, and the number of Americans without health insurance has increased to 49.9 million.[7] Amid such a plethora of dismal economic indicators, both a double-dip recession and a "new normal" of high unemployment, falling incomes and long-term economic stagnation appeared a real and disturbing possibility for a United States unaccustomed to economic dystopia – the rudest of awakenings from the American Dream. So much, apparently, for the once potent promise of "Obamanomics" to spread the wealth and replace trickle-down economics with "bottom-up economic prosperity."[8]

Over the same time-frame, the president's job approval ratings have fallen precipitously, from 65 percent after his first 100 days in office to an all-time low of 40 percent in opinion polls taken during the autumn of 2011.[9] By then, no less than 43 percent of Americans strongly disapproved of the role Obama was performing as president,[10] 62 percent disapproving of his handling of the economy[11] and 77 percent thinking that things generally in the US were moving in the wrong direction under his leadership.[12] Obama still has good reason for confidence that he can yet, Lazarus-like, triumph over his Republican Party opponent in 2012 despite such ominous economic indicators. But no US president with unemployment above 7.2 percent and job approval ratings as low as 40 percent has been re-elected since World War Two. What was once inconceivable a few short years previously is now eminently conceivable: Barack Obama as a one-term American president, his presidency assessed not as an historically "great" or "near-great" transformative one but instead an ignominious and ineffective failure. Obama appears to be teetering on the precipice of an early retirement – denied his preference to be a great one-term president, rather than a mediocre two-term one; with a mediocre (or worse) one-term presidency becoming his premature political obituary.[13]

With the economy front and center for Americans, international affairs appear to be forcefully eclipsed as a major presidential election concern for 2012. Although an international crisis, war or "October Surprise" could yet re-focus voter attentions on foreign affairs, this seems improbable, given the breadth and depth of America's economic malaise. Still, to the extent that they impinge positively on his re-election ambitions – even at the margins – Obama's central foreign policy achievements strongly underscore his claims to have been a successful Commander-in-Chief: the killing of al Qaeda leader Osama Bin Laden; the final withdrawal of all US troops from Iraq; the overthrow of Libya's Colonel Qaddafi without a single American casualty; the beginning of the end of the protracted campaign against al Qaeda in Afghanistan – America's longest war; and the emphatic restoration of American prestige and respect around the world. After being handed a metaphorical shovel rather than a magic wand to dig America out of its various deep global holes in January 2009, Obama can seek re-election on the basis of having set out carefully defined international commitments that he mostly delivered – and having clearly passed what his one-time opponent, Hillary Clinton, famously dubbed the "3am test" of successful crisis management.

But, to survey the voluminous outpourings of US foreign policy observers over Obama's leadership since 2009, one could be forgiven for believing that Obama's foreign policy remains less a methodical, prudent and effective grand strategy for America than an on-going, *ad hoc* and tentative work in uncertain progress – not so much the audacity as the opacity of hope. In the commentariat sweepstakes to identify an "Obama Doctrine" to replace and repudiate that of his Republican predecessor – the much-dissected, misunderstood and mis-underestimated "Bush Doctrine" – no analyst has yet succeeded in attributing a definitive worldview to America's forty-fourth president. While some on the American right continue to bitterly excoriate Obama as at best a weak, naive and feckless Commander-in-Chief, others on the left appear to exhibit a disheartened "buyer's remorse" about a president whose once great appeal to enlist hope in order to effect transformative change ("yes we can") instead seems to have foundered on the rocks of international resistance or – even worse – to have been cynically abandoned for the sake of short-term domestic electoral politics. After all, who now – beyond his immediate family and the president's more light-headed partisan supporters – continues to herald Obama's arrival in the White House as "the moment when the rise of the oceans began to slow and our planet began to heal"?[14]

In relation to foreign affairs, the central question this book seeks to answer is whether such widespread expectations of transformation proved correct, and why. To address this core question, three subsidiary themes are explored in the chapters that follow:

i.   What was/is Barack Obama's view of America's appropriate role and influence in the world?

ii. To what extent has the president successfully implemented this strategic vision and, thereby, departed from the foreign policies of his immediate predecessor (and perhaps prior US presidents as well)?

iii. How effective has Obama been in terms of securing the ultimate policy results that his strategy sought to achieve, and what best explains this?

The book's core argument is that the widespread expectations of transformative change associated with Obama's election have not been realized – despite the administration's best efforts to do so.

As the following pages contend, the divisions and dissensus about Obama that have marked his meteoric rise from community organizing in Chicago's South Side through the Illinois state legislature to the US Senate and the Oval Office are part and parcel of his unique historic achievement, distinctive personal character and particular political time as US president. Yet, arguably, although observers may differ sharply on the details, a reasonably clear framework to Obama's approach to international affairs is identifiable.

Obama's foreign policy can best be understood as adhering strongly to a "post-American" conception of world order – one in which American primacy is steadily but inexorably ebbing, with the US president's task being not to stem and reverse, but rather to gracefully manage, that obvious and inevitable decline. Contrary to those American conservatives who – inaccurately and sometimes irresponsibly – depict Obama as a dangerous, unpatriotic and even un-American radical, Obama's belief in a post-American approach stems not from some Third Worldist, socialist, or anti-colonial identity. Rather, it emerges from a careful and judicious – though not necessarily correct[15] – assessment of America's commitments, resources and limits in an increasingly interdependent, networked and globalized international order.

In essence, Obama shares the influential analysis offered by Fareed Zakaria: that after the two major power shifts of the past 500 years – the rise of the West from the fifteenth century and the United States from the end of the nineteenth century – the "rise of the rest" represents the third great epochal change in the global distribution of power. The onset of once unimaginable economic growth, centered on but not confined to Asia, has given birth to a truly global order in which countries on every continent are now influential players in the international system, not just passive observers or objects. Combined with the diffusion of power from states to other, non-state actors, a new and multi-layered international system is emerging that is quite unlike those of prior centuries. In such a system, while the US still remains for the time being the sole superpower, the distribution of global power – industrial, financial, educational, social, cultural – is steadily shifting away from American dominance into a *post-*, if not necessarily an *anti-*, American world; one "defined and directed from many places and by many people":

> Functions that were once controlled by governments are now shared with international bodies like the World Trade Organization and the European Union. Non-governmental groups are mushrooming every day on every issue in every country. Corporations and capital are moving from place to place, finding the best location in which to do business, rewarding some governments while punishing others. Terrorists like al Qaeda, drug cartels, insurgents, and militias of all kinds are finding space to operate within the nooks and crannies of the international system. Power is shifting away from nation-states, up, down, and sideways. In such an atmosphere, the traditional applications of national power, both economic and military, have become less effective.[16]

With the world inexorably returning to something akin to its condition at the end of the nineteenth century, where no single country or economy is predominant, how should the United States respond to this disconcerting new order and the rise of the rest? While it would be politically suicidal publicly to declare a foreign policy of American renewal premised on a core assumption of "managed decline," as both presidential candidate and as president, Obama has sought consistently to alert Americans to the realities of a changing world order – while at the same time sustaining the notion that America can nonetheless maintain its leading position in that order. From his 2011 State of the Union speech declaring that, "This is our generation's Sputnik moment,"[17] to his address to a joint session of Congress on September 8, 2011 – "Building a world-class transportation system is part of what made us an economic superpower. And now we're going to sit back and watch China build newer airports and faster railroads? At a time when millions of unemployed construction workers could build them right here in America?"[18] – Obama has held America up to unflattering international comparisons in order to proclaim the continuing imperative of change.

While they may not represent irreconcilable impulses, squaring the circle of preserving Washington's primacy in a post-American era – adapting to an international order in transition while renewing America's leading role within that order – has been the abiding predicament of Obama's foreign policy since January 2009. The watchwords of America's emerging role and place within this shifting order – retrenchment, lowered ambitions, restraint, balance, prudence, patience – at once reflect and reinforce Obama's post-American approach. Rather than merely reconfiguring the deckchairs, as "captain of a shrinking ship," the president has instead attempted to perfect "the art of declining politely" in order to navigate the American ship of state into less turbulent waters and narrower straits.[19]

But however reasonable the Obama diagnosis of a changing international order, the prescriptive elements informing his foreign and national security policies have proved highly problematic in achieving the ambitious goals that the president has set out to accomplish. Central to Obama's approach to international affairs have been two particular tensions that the president has thus far been unable fully to resolve. The result has been that, much as his domestic presidency has encountered intense opposition and obstruction, so profound limits have circumscribed the Obama administration's ability genuinely to exert effective, meaningful or sustained international leadership: strategically, to set a global agenda; and tactically, to persuade, cajole and coerce other actors into implementing that agenda.

The first tension, as Stanley Renshon anticipated, is between the international problems and foreign and national security policies that Obama inherited, on the one hand, and, on the other, the key premises of the president's own worldview – a tension that ultimately cannot endure if Obama is fully (or even substantially) to succeed on the world stage.[20] On the one hand, while repeating the standard liberal internationalist mantra about shared interests, mutual respect and common humanity that have characterized mainstream Democrats for at least three decades, Obama has adopted not so much a quintessentially realist statecraft (in the international relations sense of "realism") as an unrelentingly pragmatic, prudent and at times accommodationist approach to world affairs – one not so dissimilar, in important respects, to those of Dwight D. Eisenhower, Richard Nixon, and George H. W. Bush. Convinced that US power is ebbing, other states are embarked on an inevitable if uneven rise, and international goals must above all be sharply tailored to constrained national capacities, Obama has been doggedly intent on re-crafting America's foreign policy for the "post-American" world.

That does not mean that the US under his leadership will cease providing global public goods, opposing tyranny or rejecting the use of military force. Nor does it entail the complete abandonment of idealism or "American values." But it does entail their emphatic relegation to a secondary – even marginal – place. As a result, democracy promotion, human rights, and individual liberties (political and economic) have rarely received such muted public emphasis by a modern American president. Obama's contemporary reformulation of John F. Kennedy's famous 1961 inaugural address for our turbulent twenty-first-century times might declare that a cash-strapped America will only "pay part of the price, bear some of a modest burden, meet an occasional hardship, support the odd friend, oppose the odd foe" – not so much to assure the success of liberty in the world, but primarily to get the faltering foundations of America's own collapsing house in order. The tension between adhering to an internationalist approach while attending closely to the national interests of the US – especially in the context of his ambitious domestic agenda forming the political priority for Obama – has been acute and abiding.

The second tension derives from an important underlying assumption of the post-American approach; namely, that however much global relations are in flux, other countries – including other great powers on the rise – still anticipate, expect and demand American leadership of the international community. Obama's oft-touted means of achieving this has been an avowed grand strategy of "engagement." Since, in the president's view, globalization remains the key driver in international politics, the reality is that in an era of increasing interdependence, for both good and ill, even a strong America – let alone a frugal one maxed-out on its national credit card – cannot go it alone. Too many challenges that America is unable adequately to face and overcome on its own – from climate change to nuclear proliferation, pandemics to cyber-war, sovereign debt crises to people-trafficking – confront other states too.

Obama has therefore pursued a strategy of engagement that extends "respect" to civilizations, states and peoples alike, designed to replenish America's depleted stock of international capital and begin the process of realizing his vision of a more peaceful, stable and even, ultimately, a nuclear weapons-free world. Obama is, in terms of the American foreign policy tradition, an exemplarist, not a vindicationist.[21] His particular version of American nationalism believes strongly in America leading by the force of example and exhortation, not that of intervention and imposition. By eschewing coercion and bellicosity for outreach and diplomacy, embracing the United Nations and international legalism instead of pursuing "coalitions of the willing" and power politics, emphasizing America's past culpabilities and present openness rather than uncritically celebrating its divinely ordained and righteous exceptionalism, Obama's Washington can exert the kind of consensus-oriented global leadership that will both reassure and cajole other states into cooperative action in a consortium of like-minded actors. Leading the changing international order still remains necessary, desirable and feasible for the US.

The sharp irony of the president's first term, however, is two-fold. Firstly, abroad, the basic premise of strategic engagement has simply been rejected out of hand by many of Washington's key interlocutors. America may "objectively" share multiple interests with China, Russia, India, Brazil, Turkey and many other nations in the abstract. But that convergence in practice has proved to be much more limited, selective and contingent than the Obama administration first imagined. America remains, for the time being, the most important military, diplomatic and economic power on the planet – the sole superpower – even as China's steep ascent advances rapidly on most dimensions of national power. But in a globalized world, where power is more widely diffused and dispersed not just to other states but also to peoples, the assumption of either the expectation or the demand for American leadership of the international community is now inherently problematic and widely questioned – not least when the American president himself makes so forcefully clear his predominant focus on US domestic affairs.

If unmistakable signs of a waning of American leadership emerged strongly under George W. Bush, this became especially vivid during Obama's presidency. From the Copenhagen negotiations over climate change in December 2009 through Brazil and Turkey's interventions on Iran's nuclear program, from Islamabad's duplicitous "alliance" against terrorism through the largely autonomous Arab Spring of 2011 to Palestinian efforts to achieve statehood and on-going attempts to revive the ailing global economy through the G8 and G20, many nations and peoples were simply not looking to Washington any longer for leadership, influence or even advice. From being, as former Secretary of State Madeleine Albright once dubbed America, the "indispensable" – and even, to its critics, the inescapable – nation, the United States under Obama appears increasingly to resemble an irresolute, irrelevant and at times absent or invisible one.

Secondly, if Obama's transformative post-American "change" agenda has faltered abroad, so too has it encountered profound problems at home – ones with consequential foreign policy ramifications. Obama's post-American foreign policy has always been inherently linked to his transformative domestic goals. Not since Eisenhower has an American president so carefully and consistently linked the domestic and foreign aspects of his governing strategies. But, whatever the "post-partisan" rhetoric of candidate Obama in 2008, the president and his party – with the very active assistance of Republicans, movement conservatives and the Tea Party – have maintained, and in some respects deepened, a trend of intense partisan and ideological polarization in Washington that is now more than three decades old.[22] By reforming health care, stimulating and seeking to engineer a "green" political economy, Obama has appeared to his outraged conservative opponents – and to many moderate and conservative leaning independents, too – as apparently intent on "normalizing" America by effecting a more European-style social welfare economy at home and a more passive, reactive and accommodationist stance in the world at large, at least where the most vital of US national interests are not at stake. With perverse timing, such transformation has also been advanced at precisely the moment when the euro-zone threatens to implode in the face of Greek, Portuguese, Spanish and Italian sovereign debt crises and the entire European Union "project" craters under the severest political, social and economic strains.

Yet America remains, if public opinion polls are to be believed, an essentially center-right nation.[23] Even if Americans are "operationally liberal" – in accepting extensive government intervention and regulations – they mostly remain philosophically conservative: individualist, anti-statist, anti-government, and anti-Washington. Moreover, most Americans continue to resist the notion that there is nothing especially distinctive – or even unique and superior – about their nation, its history, values and appropriate role in the world.

One result of this post-American approach is that "No Drama Obama" – a serenely detached and un-emotive president for whom the populist "common touch" has proven persistently elusive – has partially eroded the very domestic support that is critical to an effective foreign policy over the medium to long term. With the downgrading of America's reliably pristine credit rating by Standard and Poor's, from AAA to AA+, on August 5, 2011, a decidedly unwelcome "end of empire" moment appeared finally to have been realized under Obama's post-American leadership.

The ultimate result of Obama's presidency has thus been a peculiar twist on the Declaration of Independence's pledge to evince a "decent respect to the opinions of mankind" (an historic term properly understood as endorsing US freedom of action, not – as is commonly thought – entailing its submission to prevailing international opinion). While the limits of his engagement strategy are very real and exacting, Obama's post-American foreign policy has neither restored US confidence at home nor won the hearts and minds abroad that it sought. The irony is that, while calibrating his foreign policies to the emergence of a much heralded "post-American" world, the president has done a great deal in America and internationally to bring precisely that world about – simultaneously advancing its arrival while failing to preside over the renaissance of US global leadership that, "fired up and ready to go," he consistently promised to deliver.

Hastening a post-American era, in which US power is seriously diminished, downgraded and declining, may not be the shining foreign policy epitaph that President Obama ultimately seeks for his administration. But it may well be the one that most aptly captures America's current trajectory under his controversial stewardship, where America can no longer entirely fulfil its traditional global responsibilities but from which it cannot fully extricate itself. To paraphrase the famous quip about the United Kingdom's downsized imperial status after World War Two, by Harry S. Truman's Secretary of State, Dean Acheson: while losing an "empire of liberty," Barack Obama's Washington has yet to discover a new world role.

Audacious no longer: from the fierce urgency of now to the timidity of "hope"

To the rapt attention and delight of much of America and most of the world, Barack Obama became the forty-fourth president of the United States on Tuesday, January 20, 2009. Rarely, however, has a modern American presidency so rapidly elated and disappointed in equal measure.

Although many of his fellow citizens entertained serious question marks over his beliefs, judgment and qualifications for the world's most important office

during the 2008 presidential election, for most Americans – not to mention
the overwhelming bulk of academics, citizens and the mainstream media in,
and especially outside, the United States – the historic campaign demonstrated
that Barack Obama's admirable temperament met in full the multiple criteria of
Rudyard Kipling's ideal "man." After twenty months of intense campaigning,
Obama – as *If* famously counselled – had waited and not been tired of waiting,
had been lied about but not dealt in lies, and had talked with crowds and
kept his virtue. If it was less clear that "all men count with you, but none too
much" – that not only excluded women (a major source of voting support) but
rather depended on which Electoral College state they occupied – the opinion
polls from the collapse of Lehmann Brothers on September 15, 2008 onwards
consistently predicted that "the Earth and everything that's in it" would soon
be his: a final definitive test of whether a formidably gifted politician with
an innate predisposition towards equanimity could, as President of the
United States, treat those two imposters, Triumph and Disaster, the same.[24]

But it was another, less admired Kipling poem – *The White Man's Burden* –
that had the potential to prove more telling, ironic and problematic for the
actual Obama presidency, especially with regard to American foreign policy.
Belying his reputation as the unofficial Poet Laureate of the British Empire,
and inspired by American intervention in the Philippines, Kipling's 1899 poem
(sub-titled "The United States and the Philippine Islands") instead pleaded
for the increasingly powerful United States to take up the so-called "white
man's burden." Steadily but inexorably, from William McKinley and Theodore
Roosevelt, through decisive interventions in World Wars One and Two and
the intra-European civil wars that exhausted the dominant colonial powers,
the US assumed the global leadership mantle that the United Kingdom
reluctantly but inevitably abandoned. By 1961, Kennedy famously declared
that the US under his leadership would indeed "pay any price, bear any burden,
meet any hardship, support any friend, oppose any foe" to ensure the success
of liberty during the Cold War. But post-Cold War, post-9/11, and post-George
W. Bush, the salient question on Barack Obama's entering the White House was
whether he would take up his, and America's, Sisyphean international burden
in turn, or instead – amidst myriad forces that were widely seen as hastening
a post-American world[25] – seek to transform or even relinquish it. And in
either case, would Obama's carefully constructed public identity help or hinder
the execution of an effective and enduring leadership role for Washington,
whatever the international constraints and burdensome costs?

As Obama asks the electorate for a second term as America's president, in
what promises to be one of the most ideologically charged election campaigns
in decades, those once heady days of "hope," "change" and "yes we can"
optimism now seem very much an artefact of the past; less an expression of
"the fierce urgency of now" than the rather empty promises of another era.
Obama's historic victory in the 2008 presidential election was greeted at

least as enthusiastically outside as within the United States; much more so, in fact. With a few, albeit significant, exceptions, the peoples of most nations outside America were considerably more united in their approval and anticipation of Obama than Americans were themselves; 46 percent of whom – of those who cast a ballot – voted for the Republican candidate, Senator John McCain (R-AZ), amidst the deepest recession since the 1930s, the end of a much despised and divisive Republican presidency, a "culture of corruption" that surrounded the congressional Republicans and their favored lobbyists, and an international environment of multiple challenges to US power and global order on every continent.

After one of the most controversial periods in the history of American foreign policy under George W. Bush, the Obama administration was generally expected to be the antithesis to Bush's thesis. Decisive and comprehensive changes for the better in the style, substance and results of US relations with the wider world were widely anticipated, for obvious reasons. In symbolism, not only had America seemingly confronted, at long last, its painful racial history in electing the first biracial president of both African and American descent. But the nation had also embraced a new phase of international leadership by a distinctive young progressive. Obama had spent his formative childhood years in Hawaii and Indonesia, and that pedigree facilitated his own self-definition as a "citizen of the world."[26] Such an unusual style of American internationalism offered a cosmopolitanism that openly displayed familiarity with how peoples outside America disliked "our tireless promotion of American style capitalism and multinational corporations" and resented America's "tolerance and occasional encouragement of tyranny, corruption and environmental degradation when it serves our interests."[27] As one account put it:

> Elected on a massive tide of discontent about America's role in the world and its own sense of worth, occasioned by the travails of Bush's global war on terror and horrific tales of systematic torture and kidnapping of terror suspects, held without charge, trial or the protections of the US constitution, Obama was the "new face" of American power, one that would steer America away from imperialistic hubris and war towards reconciliation, consultation and understanding: America under Obama would, once again, be a force for good in the world, and a power that would heal a divided society.[28]

Obama, too, strongly appreciated his own role in symbolizing historic change. Nor was he lacking in self-confidence about the transformative qualities that he would bring to the national and international stage: "The day I'm inaugurated, the country looks at itself differently. And don't underestimate that power. Don't underestimate that transformation."[29] Not only would America look at itself differently, but so too would the world. That self-confident prescience was subsequently confirmed by a series of opinion surveys during his first two years as president[30] and, even before the end of his presidency's first year, the award of the Nobel Prize for Peace (which, as Christopher Hitchens observed, was rather akin to "giving someone an Oscar in the hope that he would one day make a good motion picture."[31]) Rarely has a change of American administration generated such broad excitement or comparably high expectations both within and, especially, outside the US.

But by the latter stages of Obama's term, those stratospheric expectations had been effectively abandoned among widespread disillusionment about the authenticity of Obama's much-touted audacity of hope, which increasingly appeared more timid than audacious. Enthusiasm suitably curbed, the excitement of November 2008 appeared both eons ago, rather than merely the last presidential election cycle, and an aberrant rather than a rational moment.

The inexorable pull of political gravity occurred partly because the international problems confronting President Obama appeared decidedly more intractable than malleable – especially with the US stretched both economically, by the Great Recession, and militarily, in the midst of two protracted post-9/11 wars: Afghanistan continues to offer little hope for a secure and Taliban-free future for its citizens; despite the welcome and long overdue demise of Osama Bin Laden – or more precisely, as illustrated by its alleged duplicity in harboring him – Pakistan continues to offer the greatest state threat to regional and wider security from the potential nexus of nuclear weapons, Islamist terrorism, and a failing state; from the strait of Hormuz in the Gulf to the strait of Malacca in South-east Asia, the global economy remains under threat from piracy and terrorism designed deliberately to "bleed the West"; Israeli-Palestinian relations remain framed by pessimism and fraught with difficulties and mistrust, their irresolution reflecting and reinforcing broader Muslim extremism and threatening a new *intifada* and regional conflagrations; an increasingly embattled and paranoid Tehran steadfastly rejects compromise on its nuclear program, intimidating its regional neighbors while undercutting attempts to shore up the UN's creaking nuclear non-proliferation architecture; Russian-US relations remain less "reset" than in continual flux and mutual suspicion; rising powers China and India have been reluctant supporters of Washington; protectionist and nationalist pressures are on the increase from the European Union to China while trade liberalization faces major obstacles in Washington; Iraq's tentative experiment in democracy remains fragile and its security in question as US troops depart, sectarian rivalries thrive, and Iranian influence increases; and the Arab Spring that promised finally to bring states from Tunisia to Syria into the modern world instead threatens to bring to power a series of hostile, anti-Israeli, anti-Western and Islamist-influenced regimes in place of once reliable if authoritarian US allies.

Such inhospitable turns of diplomatic and geo-political fortune have cast something of a pall on the once-confident expectations of "hope" that accompanied Obama to the White House. In place of optimism, by the fall of 2011, almost three-quarters of Americans (71 percent) disapproved of

Obama's handling of the economy while a bare majority of Americans (51 percent) disapproved of Obama's handling of foreign affairs.[32] The heady American and international expectations of a new beginning for the US on the world stage, raised so extravagantly by the Obama campaign and abetted by an all-too-often credulous media, have for the most part been frustrated as Obama's foreign policy increasingly resembled an *ad hoc* exercise in damage limitation.

To be fair, admittedly, the president rapidly accomplished one important element in his ambitious foreign policy agenda virtually overnight: re-establishing much of the respect and international confidence in US leadership that was damaged, and some feared had been permanently eroded, during the Bush era. The Obama administration's approach, as executed by his widely respected team of foreign policy principals, was also welcomed as a return to the type of multilateral, consultative and pragmatically realist tradition that Bush's first term in office was generally perceived to have egregiously abandoned.

Yet, despite the new beginning and the symbolic penitence of the new administration's public diplomacy lending credence to Obama's election campaign promise of "hope," serious question marks remained in terms of policy substance and actual results. Substantively, the fiscal incontinence of the Bush years only intensified under the Obama administration, while signature elements of Obama's foreign policy reflected essential continuity with Bush rather than transformative change: more a not-so-subtle recalibration of the Bush Doctrine than an emphatic repudiation.

Moreover, in terms of concrete results, respected US foreign policy observers cautioned that, although it was too premature to declare the president an outright foreign policy "failure," Obama had – according to James Traub – "yet to bank a significant foreign policy success."[33] Other scholars graded him poorly, "O for 4 on the big ticket items that have defined his foreign policy agenda," according to Harvard's Stephen Walt.[34] While acknowledging Obama as an extraordinary communicator successfully altering international attitudes towards America, former national security advisor, Brent Scowcroft cautioned, "I'm still not sure, however, that he's the kind of chief executive that can take ideas, turn them into programs and initiatives, and then successfully execute and sell them."[35] A senior security advisor to the British prime minister, David Cameron – citing serious problems in Iran, Afghanistan, and Israel – even suggested that "There is a growing awareness that we are dealing with a weak American president who is failing to demonstrate effective leadership on a whole range of issues."[36]

The Navy SEALS' daring assassination of Bin Laden in Abbottabad, Pakistan on May 2, 2011 silenced such negative evaluations for a time. But while heavy in symbolism, the killing of the al Qaeda leader did little to still the broader criticisms of an American administration that, in the infelicitous but strikingly resonant words of one Obama advisor, was dedicated to pursuing a back-seat global leadership strategy of "leading from behind."[37] Partly reflecting this rearguard approach, and notwithstanding Bin Laden's death and Colonel Qaddafi's toppling and demise, by the time of the tenth anniversary of the 9/11 attacks, Obama's foreign policy was castigated as nothing less than "a study in confusion,"[38] while the once-towering president was memorably dismissed by Jeffrey Sachs as the "incredibly shrinking leader."[39]

In the light of such unflatteringly Jimmy Carter-esque evaluations, some analytical modesty and circumspection are surely merited. After all, no definitive or conclusive judgment can confidently be delivered on an entire presidential foreign policy before its term is fully complete; writing history while history is unfolding is a notoriously difficult exercise in speculative judgment, presentism and short-termism. As Bin Laden's death illustrated for Obama (albeit temporarily), volatile elements in the international system can unleash unexpected or momentous events, from Pearl Harbor and the Cuban Missile Crisis to the Iranian Revolution or the shock of 9/11. Unwitting or deliberate policy reversals and unanticipated innovations – such as the Nixon/Kissinger opening to China or the rapid victory in the first Gulf War for George H. W. Bush – can likewise reshape received evaluations overnight. "Rally-round-the-flag" events can bolster presidential credibility in foreign affairs (such as the Bay of Pigs) while "wag-the-dog" allegations can undermine it (think of Bill Clinton's cruise missile attacks on Afghanistan and Sudan amid the Monica Lewinsky scandal of 1998).

Moreover, the hyper-partisan, media-frenzied and sharply polarized nature of contemporary US politics generally hampers dispassionate assessments of presidential leadership, even by supposedly neutral, disinterested or dispassionate observers. Few of us have ready access to the key inside players in the US administration, and those fortunate few who do are, precisely in virtue of that, not necessarily guaranteed to receive unbiased information and provide balanced accounts. On top of all these reasons for caution, a long-standing scholarly tradition now also features revisionist accounts of the contemporary conventional wisdom regarding presidencies in general, and their foreign policies in particular, drawing attention to the inevitable errors of commission and omission that accompany "in time" historical judgments. Taken together, these all augur for caution in judging US foreign policy.

If we should therefore be mindful of the limits to our knowledge of the design and implementation of US foreign policy, at the same time, such understandable and legitimate reservations have rarely impeded scholars from offering critical reviews at a relatively early stage – often ones highly negative in character (nowhere more so than in the case of Obama's immediate predecessor, who attracted a remarkably large volume of antipathetic monographs in a very short time-frame). So it is important to be conscious that an interim assessment of Obama's foreign policy is by necessity just that: a provisional judgment based on an incomplete and still unfolding history. Nonetheless, despite its relatively

early days, it is also important to attempt a balanced appraisal of Obama's strategic choices and achievements thus far, and their future prospects; even if it represents at best a first draft.

Contextualizing Obama

Perhaps unsurprisingly, given the unique historic features of his candidacy, campaign and election – not to mention the left-of-center political leanings of most American and European social scientists – a voluminous and largely sympathetic literature has already arisen about Barack Obama: as an individual character;[40] as a campaigner;[41] as president;[42] and even as a pioneer "for any business seeking to prosper in the Web 2.0 world of the 21st century."[43]

Many of these works are immensely valuable, carefully reasoned, and contribute greatly to our understanding of the highly complex forty-fourth president of the United States – his ambitions, choices and the constraints on his leadership of the US at a time of profound domestic socio-economic upheaval, acrimonious political division and great international turmoil.[44] Some, it must be said, are less impressive, reflecting a glaring lack of critical balance, dispassion and even-handedness. A great deal of the literature is, inevitably, shaped by the sharp ideological and partisan leanings of the writers, not least those in the US. On the left, several books veer from uncritical adulation and virtual hero-worship to equally injudicious and sweeping condemnation.[45] On the right, hagiographies are not surprisingly absent in print, but a number of volumes venture comprehensive critiques that effectively cast Obama as some kind of cartoon presidential villain (the "Joker" of some Tea Party posters in 2009–12), apparently animated by an array of dark inner demons and dedicated to ruining America at home while reversing US influence abroad.[46] A more temperate assessment may, arguably, be a useful if modest addition to this literature, especially with regard to Obama's foreign policies.

For his supporters, the messages of "hope" and "change" that the Obama candidacy embodied as well as articulated together represented a powerful and overdue antidote to the two-term presidency of George W. Bush – as if an even more impressive real-life version of the *West Wing*'s President Jed Bartlet was finally riding to America's rescue with his own "Camelot" in retinue. Moreover, as his mobilization of the youth vote in 2008 indicated, Obama's election represented a generational changing of the guard on a par with Kennedy's in 1960; arguably more so, given the overt racial dimension. A relatively young candidate untainted by the divisions of the Vietnam era – who was only thirteen when the US withdrew its last military forces from Saigon in 1975 – could plausibly lead America beyond that era's pervasive culture wars, a task that had clearly eluded his two most immediate baby-boom-era predecessors in the White House. On a raft of domestic and international issues – from health care, education, job creation and housing, through climate change, cap-and-trade, to homeland security, Afghanistan, Iran and Israel – the Obama campaign symbolized and promised a new progressivism for the twenty-first century that emphatically repudiated Bush's supposedly "compassionate" conservatism.

For Obama's most fearful opponents on the right, the Illinoisan represented an unprecedented threat to much that they cherished most about the United States, as not simply another run-of-the-mill centrist or southern Democrat in the mould of a Bill Clinton, but as a committed progressive seeking to radically change America's domestic structures and the US posture and influence in the wider world. Possessing solid partisan majorities in both houses of Congress after the 2008 elections, the potential for dramatic and decisive presidential leadership was powerful. For good and ill, then, widespread expectation existed from left to right in January 2009 that an "Obama Effect" would usher-in major changes in both America's domestic and foreign public policies.

And President Obama has undoubtedly sought – doggedly, shrewdly and sometimes subtly – to effect significant shifts in US public policies, tailored to a much altered, and still rapidly changing, international environment. In some respects, the president has been undeniably successful. At home, most notably, the passage during 2009–10 of the $787 billion-plus budget stimulus, major health care overhaul and financial regulatory reform together represented substantial legislative achievements by the standard of any modern American presidency. The 2010 lame duck session of the 111th Congress – ratifying the New START arms control agreement with Russia, finally ending the "don't ask, don't tell" policy towards gays in the military, and extending the Bush-era tax cuts and unemployment relief – added further achievements to one of the most legislatively productive congressional sessions in modern US history.

Abroad, too, Obama initiated important changes in American foreign policies, from Afghanistan and Iran through non-proliferation and climate change to Russia. In terms of concrete achievements, most obviously, Obama effectively changed public perceptions of America and US leadership dramatically in large parts of the world, reviving the positive features of America's global image. The president's erudition and ease with the English language – "the armoury of the mind," as Samuel Taylor Coleridge once described it – at the teleprompter and in television interviews was the most striking personal contrast with his predecessor's frequent (mis)communication battles. But Obama's oft-repeated public commitment to renewed diplomacy, strategic engagement, multilateralism and mutual respect was likewise the echo and foundation of his principled counterpoint to Bush's belligerent, "bring it on" Texan swagger. Around the globe, Obama's analytical sharpness, articulate presentations and obvious ease with diversity in all its forms mitigated the legacy of his predecessor's "cowboy" image toxicity and, to some extent, moderated the global anti-Americanism that had experienced its own "surge" during the 2000s.

But that is only part of the story of Obama's presidency in foreign affairs and, in some ways, not remotely the most striking or consequential one. Whatever Obama's ambitious intentions, empathetic rhetoric about mutual interests, shared values and mutual respect, and dedication to serving as the "un-Bush" – self-consciously cerebral, erudite, informed, calm, cool, and cosmopolitan – the degree to which Obama as president achieved substantive changes in US foreign policies and international results has, thus far, been relatively modest. Leading from the rear rather than the foreground during an era of constrained internationalism, Obama's post-American foreign policy – tailored to the emergence of a more interdependent, complex and challenging international order – has instead exposed the profound limits of engagement as a strategy to enhance American interests, security and prosperity. Thus far, the execution of this approach – which often appears to comprise a default option of splitting the difference on issues from the Arab Spring to Mexico – has yielded only incremental results at best. Especially on some of the most pressing international problems and challenges – Afghanistan, Pakistan, Iran, China, Israel-Palestine, and relations with the Arab and Muslim worlds – Obama's presidency has not seen a material improvement in the dilemmas facing the US and has instead, in some regards, witnessed a troubling deterioration for American interests, values and security alike. Such light as exists at the tunnel's end all too often appears the headlamp of the oncoming train.

Moreover, despite a (partial) return to an enhanced multilateralism, reinvigorated diplomacy and a diminished emphasis on the "freedom agenda," many of the deep structural problems that were so graphically highlighted during the polarizing Bush years – from the operational limits and skewed contributions of NATO's European partners compared to the US, through the reliably problematic operation and utility to international security of the United Nations, to the difficult relations with other great powers such as Russia and China and emergent regional powers such as Brazil and Turkey – remain at least equally so today. Obama's more or less consistent search for the pragmatic middle way in domestic and foreign affairs alike, though admirable in many ways, has cost him important political support at home and abroad, while failing to make decisive foreign policy gains or important breakthroughs. As such, while calibrating his foreign policies to the emergence of a much-heralded post-American world, the president has ironically done much to hasten the arrival of precisely that world, while simultaneously failing to preside over the renaissance of US global leadership and transformative change that his presidency consistently promised to achieve.

That does not mean that Americans – still less the rest of the world – are wistfully pining for the return of George W. Bush. But while few would gainsay the dramatic personal contrasts between the forty-third and forty-fourth American presidents in many if not most respects, on several key dimensions of foreign policy, after three years in office the attention-grabbing aspect is less Obama's rejection of Bush-era principles and policies than the more general adherence – albeit that this continuity has often been forced upon the administration or been only reluctantly chosen. In ways that dismayed and even dejected his most ardent liberal enthusiasts, and which likewise surprised and pleased his most dedicated conservative critics, Obama has maintained, refined and, in some cases, aggressively expanded the central features of the post-9/11 Bush foreign policies – even while paying lip-service to contesting the central principles and values that informed their adoption. To the extent that this is the case, far from being a visionary, inspirational and transformative foreign policy presidency, Obama's has been muted, marginal and modest. That does not mean that such "change" as has occurred has been unimportant. But a combination of the heavy international constraints on Obama's room for international manoeuvre and some of his administration's strategic and tactical missteps have strongly limited the more ambitious dimensions that candidate Obama so confidently articulated for a new beginning and the securing of American renewal back in 2009.

Plan of the book

This, then, is the essence of the case set forth in the book: transformation has not happened on Obama's watch – at least, thus far. Making this argument clearly requires a detailed assessment of Obama's intentions, the transition to the presidency, and the evolving strategic and tactical approaches adopted by his administration in office as it was buffeted by dramatic events at home and abroad. The following chapters attempt to do this in a broadly sequential approach.

As a starting point, an important – and too often neglected – aspect of understanding Obama's foreign policies was what his initial approach actually comprised: the articulation of a post-American foreign policy better suited for a world in which US primacy was, on most if not all dimensions of power as classically understood, under challenge and eroding. In Chapter 2, by examining Obama as a candidate in the 2008 election – an election which, while it did not feature foreign policy prominently as a key voting issue for most Americans, nonetheless did see foreign policy contribute critically to Obama's confirmation as the Democratic Party candidate and also assist his ultimate victory over John McCain – the remarkable extent of interpretive division over Obama's approach to international affairs can be identified. Much of the disappointment about Obama, from supporters and critics alike, arguably stems from the many misperceptions that accompanied his election – or, more precisely, the extent to which the Obama campaign shrewdly allowed individuals to project onto their "human ink-blot" of a candidate whatever they wanted to perceive.

In Chapter 3, the attempts by the president and his key administration principals to mould a coherent foreign policy strategy aimed at American renewal – one conventionally termed "strategic engagement" – is appraised, along with the rapidly emergent conservative critique of its alleged flaws. In pursuing a prudent policy based on retrenchment and restraint, the nascent Obama Doctrine of "leading from behind" – while an unfortunate, singularly un-heroic and unusual conception of US leadership (one might as well term it "following from the front") – was an entirely apt term for the type of modest post-American approach championed by Obama in office.

Having thus established the kind of changes Obama sought to achieve in foreign policy, the extent of his success can then be considered in the light of five specific case studies. While it would be beyond the scope of this book to attempt an examination of every foreign policy area, the central argument necessitates an appraisal of the key priorities that the Obama administration has had to confront over 2009–12: Afghanistan, Pakistan and the war on terror; Iran; Israel, the Palestinian territories and the so-called "Arab Spring" of 2011; and great power relations with China and Russia. The book addresses these nation and region-specific challenges, rather than functional ones (such as non-proliferation, trade, and climate change) since these tend to be the focus for elite and mass attentions, while the functional issues tend to be subsumed under the rubric of bilateral or regional lenses and, notwithstanding the powerful forces unleashed by globalization, states (and, indeed, the lack of state capacity) remain in my view central to resolving many, if not most, transnational global threats. By not assessing Obama's policies through a purely functional lens, it may be the case that the account given here is not as full as it might otherwise be, but focusing on the key challenges facing Obama seems a more manageable and preferable course.

As both a candidate and as president, Obama set far-reaching aspirations for a new beginning in US foreign policy, one that his supporters and critics alike, international allies and – to a lesser extent – US adversaries around the world took very seriously. Moreover, Obama's analysis drew heavily on the notion that over 2001–09 George W. Bush had squandered US "soft power" – the ability to get others to admire and approve of you, and thence to follow your lead and/or agree with your goals – and that a key element in his foreign policy would be its steady recovery. A carefully calibrated marriage of hard and soft power resources ("smart power"), as recommended most prominently by Joseph Nye, was long overdue.[47] So, evaluating the extent and limits of change is intrinsic not only to gaining an accurate assessment of Obama's foreign policy leadership; it also sheds a powerful analytic light on a theory that is widely subscribed to by academics but that, arguably, has relatively meagre empirical support. If a post-American foreign policy has indeed increased America's soft power through changing global perceptions of the US, but without a commensurate gain in Washington's actual political influence, the implications for our understanding of international relations are at minimum worth exploring. It may, for example, raise the question of whether soft power really counts as power in any meaningful sense of the term, and whether there really exists any substantive meaning to the related term, "smart power."

Rightly or wrongly, Obama set stratospherically high public and international expectations of a dramatic shift in American foreign policy during his campaign, one historic in its dimensions and potential impact – only then to try steadily to temper those expectations in his election night acceptance speech of 2008, the Inaugural Address of 2009, and the many subsequent speeches and television interviews that punctuated his term in the White House. Whether the man whose first biography was entitled *Dreams from My Father* could abide by Kipling's sage advice, in office, to resist making dreams his master, looking too good or talking too wise, remained a very open question by 2012. But the heaviest burdens of his presidency – "waging savage wars of peace, filling full the mouth of Famine, to veil the threat of terror and bid the sickness cease" – remained a strategic necessity, not an optional extra, for the Obama administration. As this account attempts to show, Obama's efforts to re-create the romantic poetry of his campaigning amid the mundane but vital prose of government have proven only fitfully successful. But given the likely constraints on a potential Obama second term – should he achieve re-election – the "attractions" of foreign policy may yet only increase to a president likely to be strongly hampered in domestic affairs. As such, it is worth reminding ourselves exactly what, as a candidate for the presidency, Obama sought to achieve in crafting a post-American foreign policy for a post-American world.

2

The "Human Ink-Blot": Obama, Foreign Policy and the 2008 Election

*As a rooted cosmopolitan who has seen the US from the
outside, Obama has the potential to renew US foreign policy
for the Post-American Century.*
—Carl Pedersen, *Obama's America*[1]

*The truth is that my foreign policy is actually a return to the
traditional bipartisan realistic policy of George Bush's father,
of John F. Kennedy, of, in some ways, Ronald Reagan.*
—Barack Obama, presidential election campaign
event in Pennsylvania[2]

*Not to dampen any parade, but if one asks if there is a single
thing about Mr Obama's Senate record, or state legislature record,
or current program, that could possibly justify his claim to the
presidency one gets ... what? Not much.*
—Christopher Hitchens, "The Perils of Identity Politics,"
Wall Street Journal, January 18, 2008[3]

Introduction

The received academic wisdom on the 2008 US presidential election
described it, in John Kenneth White's words, as "The Foreign Policy Election
That Wasn't."[4] In a collection of academic essays on the 2008 campaign,
The Year Of Obama: How Barack Obama Won the White House, edited by
the distinguished American political scientist Larry J. Sabato, foreign affairs
barely merited even a passing mention, much less a separate chapter of its
own.[5] After three successive post-9/11 national elections – 2002, 2004 and
2006 – in which foreign policy figured prominently, with the on-going wars
in Afghanistan and Iraq and the wider war on terror dominating many voter
concerns, international affairs proved to be the "dog that didn't bark" in
2008. Eclipsed by the deepening recession from 2007, the financial shocks
of September-October 2008 that saw the Dow Jones Industrial Average fall
6,000 points from its peak of 14,000 one year earlier, and a loss of more than

$8 trillion in stock value in a matter of weeks, the 2008 election was – far more so even than that of 1992, a mild recession then also assisting the Democratic candidate for president – a question of "It's the economy, stupid." In a year during which all the key indicators reliably favored Obama for president, John McCain's fate was decisively sealed by the collapse of Lehman Brothers bank and all the convulsions that then ensued in the Great Recession.

It would be foolish to directly contest this interpretation (although the scholarly consensus points to economic developments prior to the autumn, rather than the financial collapse, as being determinative in the election[6]). But this orthodox view nonetheless requires some modest qualification, for three reasons.

First, as a growing body of influential academic literature argues, the relationship between domestic politics and US foreign policy is far more important, complex and subtle than many analysts of American politics and foreign policy either acknowledge or appreciate.[7] As Robert Saldin pointedly argues, "the elections literature is incomplete because it does not take foreign affairs seriously."[8] While much of the best political science is centered on voting behavior analyses, especially in the US, relatively little attention is generally devoted to the importance not just of international events, but also of public perceptions of the readiness of rival candidates to take up the unique burden of being Commander-in-Chief of the world's sole superpower. As Kurt Campbell and Michael O'Hanlon argued compellingly in relation to the 2000 presidential election between George W. Bush and Al Gore:

> Advisers to Vice President Al Gore, referring to public-opinion polls, counselled their candidate to avoid the defense issue. In so doing, they failed to appreciate what seems a truism to us: that when Americans choose a president, even when the polls do not predict or reveal it, they *always* [authors' emphasis] rate defense matters high. Even if Americans' security does not seem imminently imperilled, they understand the special place of America in the world as well as the special national-security powers entrusted by the Constitution to the chief executive. They also look to discussion of defense issues, which have a certain gravity and concreteness, as a way to assess the character and steadfastness of any would-be commander in chief.[9]

Second, despite the obvious dominance of economic concerns in the campaign and presidential vote, foreign policy did matter in 2008 – albeit in more subtle ways than many analysts conventionally conceded. In particular, foreign policy was crucial to Barack Obama's ultimately securing the Democratic Party nomination for president over the early frontrunner, Senator Hillary Clinton (D-NY); to his selection of Senator Joe Biden (D-DE) as his vice-presidential running mate; and also, in ironic ways, to effectively neutering traditional Republican advantages – and the obvious fact of Obama's own inexperience – on questions of national security in the general election. While McCain still held an edge over Obama on certain key foreign policy questions among American voters – most notably, dealing with the threat of terrorism – the proportion of voters who cast their ballot with international affairs as an important voting cue was modest. Critically, this was not simply a matter of the overwhelming salience of economic concerns, but also was a function of Obama's managing to convey sufficient strength on foreign affairs – despite the lightness of his resume and the political and media controversies over his relationships with William Ayers and Reverend Jeremiah Wright – that, even if he was without doubt untested, he could not plausibly be described to most US voters as "weak" on national security.

The third reason for qualifying the orthodox view of 2008 is perhaps even more subtle and extends far beyond the election itself. Obama's foreign policy platform, such as it was, not only helped to neutralize traditional Republican strengths on national security; more than this, it established a formidable set of expectations – in America and around the globe – as to what kind of innovative global leadership Obama would provide for a post-American world. Crucially, the Obama campaign deliberately raised public expectations extraordinarily – indeed, unrealistically – high. To take but one of multiple examples, Obama's peroration at St Paul, Minnesota after he had effectively won the Democratic nomination, memorably concluded:

> Because if we are willing to work for it, and fight for it, and believe in it, then I am absolutely certain that, generations from now, we will be able to look back and tell our children that this was the moment when we began to provide care for the sick and good jobs to the jobless ... this was the moment when the rise of the oceans began to slow and our planet began to heal ... this was the moment when we ended a war, and secured our nation, and restored our image as the last, best hope on Earth. This was the moment, this was the time when we came together to remake this great nation so that it may always reflect our very best selves and our highest ideals.[10]

Moreover, Obama's commitment to changing US foreign policy, and thereby altering the dynamics of international politics, exhibited a uniquely personal stamp. Aspirant presidential candidates inevitably promise much to their prospective voters. Who, after all, is rationally going to run on a platform of "elect me and nothing much will change"? But in Obama's case, the personalization was an inextricable and especially important aspect of his widespread appeal at home and, at least as significantly, abroad. As the Princeton historian, Sean Wilentz, later reflected, "There's something about a campaign that can lead to unreal expectations ... He had this among his supporters who, before he had even been sworn in, were already comparing him to Abe Lincoln and FDR. Some of his supporters thought he could transform the real world, but no one can transform the real world."[11]

The significance of this was sometimes obscured by the historic symbolism of Obama's candidacy and the sheer novelty of some of the campaign's developments. For example, never before had a US presidential candidate – note, not an incumbent president, nor a former president, but a then junior US senator and a neophyte aspirant to the office – addressed a mass gathering in a foreign nation's capital, as part of his own American election campaign: Obama's Berlin rally in June 2008 was entirely without precedent. Rarely in recent US history, moreover, had a candidate of either major party openly declared that he would meet with the leaders of noxious authoritarian US adversaries such as Iran, Venezuela, Cuba, and Myanmar "without preconditions"; Obama's commitment to do so during the Democratic Party internal debates – though it earned him trenchant criticism – was striking and novel. Never had a US presidential candidate openly described himself not simply as a US citizen, but also as a proud "citizen of the world"; Obama's cosmopolitanism was simply unheard-of in an American campaign for the highest office in the land. In short, too myopic a focus on the 2008 election itself obscures the more lasting political significance of one of the most historic and unprecedented campaigns for president that any candidate has mounted across the entire sweep of American history. Part of the explanation for the widespread disappointment felt about Obama's tenure in office also stems directly from the transformative undertakings that Obama promised to pursue.

What is additionally significant here – and, once more, somewhat neglected in most academic accounts of the election – is that exactly what an Obama foreign policy would look like remained essentially in the eye of the beholder even through Election Day 2008 and the inauguration of 2009. To some extent, this was a familiar and even reassuring feature of US presidential campaigns of both major parties. Few policy specifics are generally given, concrete commitments are mostly to be avoided, and broad thematic and rhetorical devices invariably prove preferable to policy minutiae, extensive detail, and premature undertakings. The historical record of broken presidential foreign policy promises – from FDR and LBJ pledging not to send American "boys" to war, in 1940 and 1964 respectively, through Bill Clinton's 1992 refusal to "coddle" dictators "from Baghdad to Beijing," to George W. Bush's 2000 commitment to lead America as a "humble," not an arrogant, nation – generally augurs well for candidate caution on the campaign trail. But the markedly opaque nature of the Obama grand strategy was arguably, in part at least, a function of this particular candidate's unprecedented distinctiveness. That is, the nature of the campaign that Obama ran, first to secure his party's nomination and then to win the general election, reflected and reinforced the opacity of his ideas about America's future course in the world. And that, in turn, was partly an artefact of the very cosmopolitan character that he deliberately, fully and skilfully embodied.

Contrary to conventional academic and popular interpretations that typically, and rightly, regard race as a powerful hindrance to the political fortunes of a prospective black presidential candidate, Obama wore – or rather, subverted – the burden(s) of racial politics relatively lightly in 2008. As far as foreign policy was concerned, especially, Obama's identity – or better, multiple overlapping identities – served as a perfect symbol for a newly cosmopolitan and transnational approach to America's evolving world role. Such an approach resonated powerfully with the knowledge class in the US and elsewhere. The approach can eschew specifics in favor of themes and generalities; claim multiple sources of inspiration; and tout on the basis of personally embodying diversity, rather than any particular set of concrete achievements or prior record of experience, a distinctive set of "qualifications" for political leadership: not just speaking for, but personifying, "change" (or, as one of his campaign slogans had it, "we are the change that we have been looking for"). This enticing appeal secured Obama substantial electoral support at home, and overwhelming political support and admiration abroad. As David Remnick noted:

> There was also little doubt that one large non-voting constituency favored Obama: the rest of the world. In a poll conducted by the BBC World Service in twenty-two countries, respondents preferred Obama to McCain by a four-to-one margin. Nearly half the respondents said that if Obama became President it would "fundamentally change" their perception of the United States.[12]

But this also obscured the extent to which, as Obama's campaign quote at the start of this chapter suggested, the impetus towards transformative change amid the "fierce urgency of now" ran against powerful pressures to adopt a more pragmatic or conventional approach to foreign affairs.

"I've got a confusion on Obama": Cosmopolitan, Liberal Internationalist, Realist, Reaganite, Leftist?

During the early stages of his campaign for the White House, "Obamagirl" famously developed a crush on the candidate from Illinois; one that came to be shared by many millions worldwide. But to judge by the many competing interpretations of Obama's foreign policy stance, while some observers evinced not dissimilar attitudes, the commentariat as a whole was anything but in agreement. Depending on one's perspective, it was a measure of either the shrewdness or the shallowness of the Obama campaign that, even by the day of the 2008 election, opinion as to what an Obama foreign policy promised was so divided both within and between broadly progressive and conservative camps. This was not simply a matter of the inevitably heated partisan nature of the election and the more ideologically driven forces on both the left and the right, but more with regard to mainstream analysts and commentators. Confusion, or at least disagreement, was more notable than consensus.

For example, for some analysts, such as Fouad Ajami,[13] the steady development of the Democrat's campaign increasingly suggested that Obama represented not only a decisive break from the George W. Bush years, but also "the sharpest break yet with the national consensus over foreign policy after WWII." Disaffected with American power and convinced of the utility of "soft power" – the ability to bend the world towards your view, through attraction rather than coercion – the Obama vision represented the embodiment of an elite liberalism which, in contrast with that of his erstwhile hero JFK and other Cold War hawks, had steadily become unmoored from traditional American nationalism and rejected entirely the notion that America was an exceptional nation-state:

> This is not only a matter of Senator Obama's own sensibility; the break with the consensus over American exceptionalism and America's claims and burdens abroad is the choice of the activists and elites of the Democratic Party who propelled Mr. Obama's rise.[14]

In heralding a "post-exceptionalist" foreign policy, Obama's securing the nomination of his party over the early frontrunner (albeit very narrowly, and after a protracted campaign) represented, on this view, more than ever the victory of the left in American politics over traditional liberals. Whereas, in 1960, Kennedy and Nixon occupied a similar generational and cultural milieu, and hence differed more on tactics than fundamental strategy in the Cold War struggle against communism, Obama and McCain occupied markedly different generational and cultural space in 2008. As a result, the election represented far more a choice than an echo. It heralded not simply a different occupant of the White House but an approach to America's place, role and influence in the world fundamentally at odds with all prior modern-era presidents, Democrat and Republican alike.

By contrast, rather than viewing Obama as a final victory for the left within the party, much foreign policy analysis – from the bulk of in-house journalists of the *Washington Post* and *New York Times* to *Time* and *Newsweek* and most pundits on CNN, ABC, NBC and CBS – accepted Obama as an emphatic return to a Bill Clinton-style liberal internationalism. The "radical," "rational" or "militant" center found vindication of such an interpretation in the vituperative attacks on the senator from both the activist left and the conservative right. On this basis, the selective shots that Obama had to endure from the *Huffington Post* and the Dennis Kucinich/John Edwards/Mike Gravel wing of the Democratic Party – from voting to confirm Condi Rice as Bush's Secretary of State in early 2005 to reversing position on immunity for telecommunications companies that assisted post-9/11 government eavesdropping on suspected terrorists in 2008 – testified to the senator's instinctive centrism, pragmatism and temperamental coolness: even a small "c" conservative disposition.

Similarly, the depiction of the McCain campaign, most conservative columnists and the right-wing blogosphere of Obama as a soft-headed, liberal idealist who believed that "soft power" alone, deployed with sufficient charm and erudition, could face down the threats and remedy the ills of a dangerous world, reinforced the notion that Obama represented a post-Bush "return to normalcy." Opposing "dumb" wars but not all wars, keeping all options on the table but being unafraid to negotiate directly with enemies, being supportive of open market democracies but recognizing the flaws in free trade, Obama represented the type of fresh, un-ideological and intelligent centrist Democrat cognisant of global interdependence that candidate Bill Clinton had previously in 1992.

The originator of the "post-American world" notion, Fareed Zakaria, by contrast, claimed that in terms of the framework foreign policy ideas that Obama elaborated during his presidential campaign, "What emerges is a worldview far from that of a typical liberal, much closer to that of a traditional realist."[15] The evidence for this? First, Obama was "strikingly honest" about his "inclinations and inspirations," not only repeating the Democratic foreign policy mantra of praising Harry S. Truman but also expressing "enormous sympathy for the foreign policy of George H. W. Bush." Second, Obama avoided moralistic speech, binary divisions, and a lack of complexity, viewing nations and sub-state actors as motivated as much by power, greed and fear as by ideology. Third, the Illinois senator "never" used soaring language like the "freedom agenda," preferring to speak of economic prospects, civil society and "dignity." Finally, Obama spoke admiringly of towering historic American foreign policy figures such as Dean Acheson, George Kennan and Reinhold Niebuhr. Acutely aware of the limits of both American idealism and American power, Zakaria concluded that "Obama seems – unusually for a modern-day Democrat – highly respectful of the realist tradition."

Still other Obama enthusiasts went even further. Eli Lake, for instance, dismissed conservative charges that Obama resembled a latter-day turbo-charged Jimmy Carter, instead suggesting that – at least in his approach to counter-terrorism – it would be Ronald Reagan's playbook on which he relied: eschewing a "one size fits all" approach to fighting terrorism, finding proxies to battle America's enemies, and aggressively seeking-out allies among the tribes co-mingling with terrorists while engaging and minimizing the corruption and brutality of local police and intelligence agencies.[16]

Such a view was of course anathema to many on the right, who viewed Obama's candidacy with a mixture of barely concealed fear and loathing. For many, Obama appeared a carefully calculated construction whose apparently moderate pedigree deceptively obscured a political trajectory typical of the far left. On this basis, from Obama's "exotic" personal journey through the associations with Reverend Wright and Ayers, to the community activism and Chicago machine politics, the senator's instincts were fundamentally far out of the mainstream of American politics. As the most notorious right-wing polemic put it, Obama possessed "at best only an intellectual understanding of foreign affairs," yielding a foreign policy that is "anti-war, anti-Israel":

> Obama's foreign policy appears predicated on an overconfidence that the power of his personality and his willingness to negotiate will somehow transform international politics to the point where we can pursue nuclear weapons disarmament, reduce our military, and withdraw from Iraq without adverse consequences, even for Israel. Obama talks as if he can transcend international

politics-as-usual simply by employing some of the listening skills he learned in Saul Alinsky's radical community-organizing methodology.[17]

Cosmopolitan, liberal internationalist, realist, Reaganite, leftist? Was this division in opinion more a function of the divisions within American politics more broadly or did it reflect a genuine interpretive problem on the Obama approach to world affairs? And, if so, where did the "real Obama" lie on foreign policy for the post-Bush and post-American worlds?

The stealth candidate: symbolism as strategy (hope) and substance (change)

The most oft-touted explanation for uncertainty as to Obama's foreign policy beliefs, cited by both defenders and opponents alike, was the normal dynamics of American presidential election campaigns. On this view, the infamous Nixonian advice of moving towards the partisan extremes to placate the activist base during the nomination battle before rapidly refocusing on the center ground for moderates and Independents in the general election adequately, and fully, captured Obama's foreign policy "refinements" over 2007–08. Faced by a principal, and formidable, intra-party opponent in then Senator Hillary Clinton, Obama exploited what limited differences existed between them on the substantive issues to appeal to the base of the party. In particular, his opposition to the Iraq war, and his criticisms of NAFTA and free trade, sought to distinguish his candidacy from hers and to pit his better judgment against her greater experience. Having ultimately succeeded in squeaking to the nomination, Obama's logical course was to reassure centrist opinion, which began as soon as June 4, 2008 with his first presumptive nominee speech to AIPAC.

But a deeper explanation for the more opaque aspects of his outlook on the world can be found in Obama's carefully crafted public image and his strategic political ambition. As his two memoirs make clear, Obama not only has been deeply preoccupied by the nature of his multiple overlapping personal identities since his early years, but has also carefully calibrated the public projection of this in his political life. In campaigning for the Illinois US Senate seat in 2004, Obama framed his life as "part of the great American narrative of rising above challenges, even though Obama benefited from many upper middle-class institutions, such as private schools."[18] He projected himself as "multicolored. He's everyone's candidate."[19] Obama stressed not only that he was genuinely African American, tracing half his heritage directly to Africa, but also that he belonged to the "community of humanity." His struggle to define his community encompassed not just race but class and geography, with a half-Indonesian sister married to a Chinese Canadian. While rooted in the

African American community, Obama stressed that, "I'm not limited by it."[20] As such, his persona served as an effective surrogate for actual positions. As two Illinois observers put it, Obama is "the literal embodiment of our cultural hybridity" and represents "whatever you want him to be."[21]

Such a capacious flexibility can constitute a burden as much as a boon, according to Obama, since "everybody's projecting their own views onto you."[22] But in fact, that opacity was something which, as one of only five African Americans ever to serve in the US Senate, and the first African American to mount a genuinely credible bid for the presidency, served Obama extremely well. As David Mendell put it in an early biography, in political terms, Obama "struck gold when it comes to race. Instead of being torn asunder trying to please each racial camp, he has strung a tightrope between the two and walked it with precision."[23] Moreover, Obama's calculated deployment of a trait that none of his African American predecessors shared, and which is applicable to very few American politicians even today, served partially to compensate for his slim resume and demonstrative lack of foreign policy experience or expertise. As Charles Krauthammer caustically observed:

> For no presidential nominee in living memory had the gap between adulation and achievement been so great. Which is why McCain's Paris Hilton ads struck such a nerve. Obama's meteoric rise was based not on issues – there was not a dime's worth of difference between him and Hillary on issues – but on narrative, on eloquence, on charisma.[24]

While Obama read and consulted widely on foreign policy as his presidential campaign progressed, and despite his much vaunted intellectualism, his familiarity with international affairs was limited and not especially distinctive. As Ryan Lizza recounted:

> As a student during the Reagan years, Obama gravitated toward conventionally left-leaning positions. At Occidental, he demonstrated in favor of divesting from apartheid South Africa. At Columbia, he wrote a forgettable essay in *Sundial*, a campus publication, in favor of the nuclear-freeze movement. As a professor at the University of Chicago, he focussed on civil-rights law and race. And, as a candidate who emphasised his "story," Obama argued that what he lacked in experience with foreign affairs he made up for with foreign travel: four years in Indonesia as a boy, and trips to Pakistan, India, Kenya, and Europe during and after college.[25]

That travel may well have broadened and even sharpened his mind. But, despite the efforts of some his more enthusiastic supporters to parse it otherwise – Martin Dupuis and Keith Boeckelman claiming that the Illinois senator had "established strong credentials on foreign affairs, especially with respect to nuclear disarmament,"[26] and John Wilson even suggesting that, prefacing a one-page summary of the senator's foreign policy achievements in the national legislature, "Obama's experience in foreign affairs may be his strongest attribute"[27] – Obama's foreign policy credentials were markedly meagre in 2008. Although he gained a seat on the (for established US senators, increasingly unattractive) Senate Foreign Relations Committee in 2005, his overriding focus was – understandably and entirely rationally – the domestic concerns of his Illinois constituents. Obama did travel to Russia, Eastern Europe and the Middle East, including Israel and Iraq, during his first year in the Senate.[28] In 2006 he also travelled to Africa, to visit South Africa and his father's homeland in Kenya, a prelude to the publication of *The Audacity of Hope* and, as even a sympathetic biographer noted, "much more successful as a major media hit than as a mission to imbue a first-term senator with greater knowledge about Africa."[29]

Compounding Obama's lack of foreign policy experience was a lack of legislative productivity, achievement or novelty. Again, while his defenders exaggerated his senatorial success, even a cursory examination revealed the hollowness of such claims. Wilson's one-page summary of his foreign policy record, for example, mentioned Obama writing a law signed in 2006 to provide $52 million to help stabilize Congo, and penning an op-ed with Sam Brownback (R-KS) in the *Washington Post*. The signal other achievements were working with Richard Lugar (R-IN) to secure dangerous conventional weapons in the former Soviet Union, penning an "incisive" chapter on foreign policy in his second book, and convincing "global experts" such as Samantha Power and Susan Hill to work for him. In their less hagiographic tome, Dupuis and Boeckelman's two-page review of Obama's work on international affairs also cited his work with Lugar and his 2006 trip to Africa. The latter was also stressed in Mendell's biography, where the senator symbolically took an HIV test in public and where his speech, "A Common Humanity Through Common Security," stressed that AIDS, nuclear proliferation, terrorism and environmental degradation should bind rather divide people across the globe – although Obama, typically, "offered few specifics as to how that should occur."[30]

In terms of his substantive policy views, Obama's senatorial record was one – unsurprising perhaps, as a junior senator with national ambitions – solidly in line with his party. He voted with his party 95 percent of the time in 2005, according to *Congressional Quarterly*, with just eight senators more consistently Democratic, and of his hundreds of votes he "agonized over a dozen or so."[31] According to *National Journal*, Obama's votes were more liberal than 76 percent of all fellow senators on foreign policy, and more conservative than 15 percent. He was rated as the most liberal senator of all one hundred on the basis of his 2007–08 voting record by *National Journal*. As Christopher Hitchens argued, the reality of Obama's foreign policy record, together with his inexperience of executive office, did not suggest a president bringing novel or transformative change to America's engagement with the world, even if his speeches and persona did.

Commander-in-Chief/Cosmopolitan-in-Chief

It was difficult, though not impossible (Al Gore, after all, ran for the presidency in 1988 and John Edwards first ran in 2004, at the end of his first full term in the Senate), to imagine a white American politician running for the presidency on the same meagre basis as Obama's bid: community organizer, state legislator, and barely two years in the US Senate before formally announcing a presidential campaign on February 10, 2007. With minimal foreign policy experience, and an entirely conventional liberal voting record, to present a campaign as "the new face of American politics"[32] also represented a truly audacious gambit. Its success relied on the deep unpopularity of the Bush years, the internal demographic battles of the Democratic Party's fractious base, and the ability of an exceptionally gifted, eloquent and distinctive candidate in Obama to connect with key elite officials, fundraisers and demographics – not least African Americans, the college educated, and the young – within the party.

In that respect, Obama almost certainly would not have won the party's nomination in 2008 without his unique position on the Iraq war. Among the leading candidates, only Obama was able to claim consistent opposition to the intervention. Clinton, Joe Biden, John Edwards, and Christopher Dodd had all voted for the Senate resolution to authorize the use of force in 2002, while Bill Richardson (then governor of New Mexico) had vocally supported it as well. By the time, in 2008, that almost no Democratic primary and caucus voters approved either of the war or of George W. Bush, only Obama was able to claim complete "purity." Not only did his good "judgment" thereby garner him early media attention, help his money-raising efforts and compensate for his lack of experience in foreign affairs – a key charge made against him by his opponents and, especially, Hillary Clinton – but he also made sure to note that he did not oppose all wars, only the "dumb" ones; crucial protection against subsequent Republican charges of softness on national security.

But in terms of specifics, the campaign's progression offered some more flesh on the relatively thin bones of Obama's foreign policy record. Drawing from his chapter in *The Audacity of Hope*, his *Foreign Affairs* campaign article of 2007, his campaign website, debate answers and public speeches, thirteen themes emerged as key templates of an emerging strategy to guide the US through a potentially treacherous post-American era:

i.   The war on terror, whether renamed or not, would continue, but with a more effective execution. Its central focus would return to Afghanistan, the real central front in the war on terrorism, and Obama would deploy two additional brigades (approximately 10,000 troops), made available by a 16-month draw-down from Iraq.

ii. Obama supported proposals by Joe Biden on pressuring Pakistan by tying US military aid more closely to Pakistani anti-terrorist actions, and to triple US non-military aid to Islamabad for education, health and infrastructure to $1.5 billion per year. Obama reserved the right to order unilateral US strikes on Pakistani territory.

iii.   American combat forces would be substantially drawn down, though not necessarily entirely removed, from Iraq by the end of Obama's first term.

iv.   Direct negotiations would occur with "rogue states" such as Iran and Syria.

v.   Efforts to end US oil dependence would be stepped up as an urgent national security priority.

vi.   Reinvigorating the "peace process" between Israelis and Palestinians would be a presidential priority from "day one."

vii.   92,000 additional Army and Marine Crops troops would be added to the Pentagon while the force structure was reassessed.

viii.   The US would recommit to the goal of ending not only nuclear proliferation, but also securing the reduction and ultimate elimination of nuclear weapons, as well as the prohibition of new types of nuclear weapons.

ix.   The US would amend NAFTA and use future trade agreements to raise labor and environmental standards.

x.   The US would seek a more level playing field on US-China trade relations.

xi.   Cap-and-trade proposals to cut US global warming pollution 80 percent below 1990 levels by 2050 would be advanced.

xii.   Oil drilling in Alaska's Arctic National Wildlife Reserve and new drilling on US coasts would be opposed. A windfall tax on multinational oil companies and tougher fuel economy standards on new cars and trucks would be imposed, to achieve a reduction of American oil use by 35 percent by 2030.

xiii.   The building of new nuclear reactors would be opposed until commercial nuclear waste can be disposed of safely, but the nuclear power option would be retained.

What these commitments amounted to in terms of gleaning any reliable sense of Obama's overall perspective on international relations remained rather unclear. For example, in *The Audacity of Hope*, he stated that, "We need a revised foreign policy framework that matches the boldness and scope of Truman's post-World War II policies – one that addresses both the challenges and the opportunities of a new millennium, one that guides our use of force and expresses our deepest ideals and commitments."[33] But in the next sentence he responded forcefully: "I don't presume to have his grand strategy in my hip pocket." What Obama did seem to reject was a mere set of traditional liberal goals, as might have befitted a Democratic candidate during prior decades. As he put it, the conventional objectives that liberals currently have – withdrawal from Iraq, stopping AIDS, working with our allies more closely – "have merit. But they hardly constitute a coherent national security policy" whereby "to make America more secure, we are going to have to help make the world more secure."[34]

Perhaps Zakaria's claiming Obama for the realist mantle therefore held better sway? After all, while excoriating the George W. Bush administration's "unilateralism," Obama argued that acting multilaterally, which is "almost always" in the US strategic interest when it comes to using force, did not mean giving the UN Security Council a veto power over the US. Instead, it "means doing what George H. W. Bush and his team did in the first Gulf War – engaging in the hard diplomatic work of obtaining most of the world's support for our actions, and making sure our actions serve to further recognized international norms."[35] Yet, the administration having done all of that hard work, most Democrats in the Senate voted against authorizing force in the Gulf in 1991 – including Obama's vice-presidential selection, Senator Joe Biden. What if the hard diplomatic work failed once more, as in 2002? Would Obama, like Biden later did in 2002, then endorse the "unilateral" deployment of US force?

Whether Obama – like Biden, Hillary, Tom Daschle and others – would have voted for the Iraq resolution had he actually been a sitting US senator in 2002 represented a "known unknown." But as a sitting senator, Obama did emphatically oppose the 2006–07 "surge" in Iraq, favoring instead the "realist" prescriptions of the Baker-Hamilton Study Group: he voted to deny funds to that surge; he insisted on a rigid timetable for withdrawal of troops; and he denied the centrality of the surge to the stabilization of Iraq in 2008. Thus, on the key question on which he could vote as a sitting legislator, his much vaunted judgment proved faulty and, as The Economist put it, "both wrong and dangerous"[36] – the surge being the key initiative bringing Iraq to a position in which, ironically, the war had receded sufficiently as an election issue that both Obama and McCain could commit to troop drawdowns. Indeed, just as Obama's opposition for the war sealed his advantage in gaining the nomination, so McCain's steadfast support for it (and especially for the surge when, at a time of deep demoralization among Republicans, the Arizona senator repeated his refrain that he would "rather lose an election than lose a war") was crucial to his obtaining the GOP candidacy.

But a similar predicament confronted Obama observers on other foreign policy issues. The strong campaign rhetoric that the senator deployed during the primaries and caucuses to tilt towards protectionism on trade he subsequently dismissed in the summer of 2008 as "overheated." Having argued for no preconditions for negotiations with Iran, he subsequently called for careful "preparations" before any such direct efforts. Having declared an undivided Jerusalem to be his position in his June 4, 2008 speech to AIPAC, his campaign retreated the next day to (re)state that the city's status was always to be part of a negotiated settlement between the Israeli and Palestinian parties. Having opposed it previously, Obama voted in the summer of 2008 for legislation to grant immunity to those telecommunications companies that cooperated with the federal government on counter-terrorist monitoring in the aftermath of 9/11. In sum, whether one followed an inductive or deductive method to ascertain Obama's core foreign policy philosophy, discerning where Obama stood on foreign policy specifics was a difficult enterprise.

Even in terms of his own party, the studied ambiguities, refinements of prior positions, and campaign emphasis on change together obscured rather than clarified where Obama's approach was best identified. In the useful typology of Kurt Campbell and Michael O'Hanlon,[37] four types of foreign policy tendencies are identifiable within today's Democratic Party: *hard power Democrats*, who view the flaw in the Bush Doctrine as its problematic execution, not its design; *globalists*, who focus on problems caused by globalization and broader definitions of security, and who are mostly uneasy with the use of military force; *modest power Democrats*, who would prefer America to retrench and refocus energies and treasure at home, regarding Bill Clinton-style Democrats as "Republican-lite;" and *global rejectionists*, comprising old-style leftists, labor unions and environmentalists, especially prevalent in the blogosphere and American academia. If one sought to place Obama within this particular typology, perhaps the only category from which one would confidently have excluded him was the last. But he could have fitted into the first three easily, and even the last – at least on the basis of his voting record – would have had something to commend it. "All and none of the above" was not an inappropriate assessment.

Some imprecision was perhaps inevitable. Ajami, pointing more to the personal story of Obama and the cultural milieu from which he emerged, put it thus:

> Samuel Huntington, in *Who Are We?*, a controversial book that took up this delicate question of American identity, put forth three big conceptions of America: national, imperial and cosmopolitan. In the first, America remains America. In the second, America remakes the world. In the third, the world remakes America. Back and forth, America oscillated between the nationalist and imperial callings. The standoff between these two ideas now yields to the strength and the claims of cosmopolitanism. It is out of this new conception of America that the Obama phenomenon emerges.[38]

Huntington's three-fold framework essentially reflected a realist/nationalist, neo-conservative/liberal interventionist, and a cosmopolitan/transnationalist trifecta. On the national model, America can neither become the world and remain America – the erstwhile cosmopolitan model; nor can it convert or impose "American values" abroad, however tempting the imperial impulse to do so has historically proven (the neo-conservative/interventionist model). But the cosmopolitan view, increasingly dominant in US universities, the mainstream media elites and among American judges and law professors, is one whereby the world in effect reshapes America:

> America welcomes the world, its ideas, its goods, and, most importantly, its people. The ideal would be an open society with open borders, encouraging sub-national ethnic, racial, and cultural identities, dual citizenship, diasporas, and led by elites who increasingly identified with global institutions, norms, and rules rather than national ones. America should be multiethnic, multiracial, multicultural. Diversity is a prime if not the prime value. The more people who bring to America different languages, religions, and customs, the more American America becomes ... The activities of Americans would more and more be governed not by the federal and state governments, but by rules set by international authorities, such as the United Nations, the World Trade Organization, the World Court, customary international law, and global treaties and regimes.[39]

In the hackneyed phrase, Americans should not act, as the late Richard Holbrooke described it, "with consistent disregard for what the Declaration of Independence called 'a decent respect to the opinions of mankind',"[40] – never mind that the actual meaning of the phrase was not about colonial Americans heeding foreigners' advice, but showing them the respect of declaring "the causes which impel them to the separation."

The dynamics and speeches of 2008 made it difficult, at that stage at least, to contest such an interpretation as being the most applicable to Obama's basic worldview. Obama's Berlin speech, while cultivated as much for Americans' eyes at home as for the ears of Europeans, certainly evinced the quintessential "world citizen" mode. Indeed, the speech serves as a model of Obama's cosmopolitanism – the quintessential product of "post-modern" multicultural politics. As Obama avowed in the speech, the West's triumph in the Cold War proved that "there is no challenge too great for a world that stands as one" (even though the world was, as tends to be the case in most wars, manifestly not as one). Much as Obama used his dual African and American heritages to appeal to an increasingly diverse black community in the United States during his campaigns for the state legislative and US Senate races – the product of immigration reform since the 1960s that has seen large-scale African and Caribbean immigration which has added to the community intra- as well as inter-racial tensions – to craft appeals as being rooted in but not limited by his identity, so the implicit message that Obama offered to the world was that he may be rooted in America, but he is not limited by that; unlike, most obviously, George W. Bush, Senator John McCain, and then Governor Sarah Palin. As Carl Pedersen suggested, Obama represented, much to their delight, a "rooted cosmopolitan" holding out the hope of bringing about a "post-American" foreign policy:

> A cosmopolitan American national identity actively promoted by a rooted cosmopolitan president will inevitably have an impact on notions of American exceptionalism that elide national differences in favour of an us-versus-them worldview ... Furthermore, cosmopolitanism can function as a bulwark against the cultural myopia that has plagued American foreign policy since 1898, by nurturing deep knowledge of other societies. Instead of seeing cosmopolitanism as a threat of disunion, Americans could regard it as an opportunity to become citizens of the world even as they maintain their allegiance to the US.[41]

Such an appeal carried obvious risks domestically, not least with the large swathes of America – small-town, provincial, nationalist, religious, gun owning, hunting – for whom the term "cosmopolitan" assuredly did not apply. Obama's prevailing in the presidential race owed at least as much to the burdens of elitism, class, and gender that he needed to triumph over as that of race. But the general election campaign also featured two important factors that assisted Obama strongly. First was the dominance of the economy – the most important issue to 63 percent of voters, 53 percent of whom supported Obama on it, compared to just 44 percent for McCain. But, second, it is important to note that exit polls showed Iraq to be the second most important issue to voters (at 10 percent) and terrorism tied with health care for third (9 percent each). Those citing Iraq as the most important issue to them favored Obama by 59 percent to 39 percent, while McCain carried those most concerned about terrorism by the huge margin of 86 percent to 13 percent.[42] The absence of another 9/11 terrorist attack on the homeland since 2001, and the relative stabilization of Iraq since the surge, had together muted the salience of foreign affairs to evaluations of the two nominees.

But the real burden of an approach that stressed the credentials of "Cosmopolitan-in-Chief" over Commander-in-Chief were always more likely to occur in office than on the campaign trail. Even with a Democratic House and Senate with large majorities, many of the "soft" security imperatives that Obama stressed need to be met – ending energy dependence, tackling the illegal narcotics trade and combating climate change – remained years, if not decades, away from significant reform, much less resolution. Convincing NATO allies to do more in Afghanistan was laudable, but quite how Obama proposed to succeed where Bush had failed was unclear. If the promised direct negotiations failed with Iran, as they did previously in more propitious times with the gifted diplomat Bill Clinton, what then? If a precipitate drawdown in Iraq plunged the nation back into instability, while failing to pacify Afghanistan or to meet the ever-growing security threats from Pakistan, how well would the rhetoric of "standing together" as one fare? And if Obama genuinely acted on his campaign promise to use military force within Pakistan if the US had actionable intelligence on al Qaeda and Islamabad refused so to do, what then of the attempt to reclaim America's legitimacy and respect in the Muslim world?

Moreover, finally, with a Democratic Congress and undivided Democratic control of the federal government for the first time since 1993–4, the dangers that the elected institution least susceptible to protectionist pressures (the presidency) would succumb to those most susceptible (the Senate and, especially, the House) remained very real and dangerous. Obama's trade record was a microcosm of the lack of clarity – or, for his supporters, the pragmatism – in his foreign policy more broadly.[43] He had stated that expanding trade and breaking down barriers between nations benefited the US economy and security. But Obama publicly supported yet then voted against the Dominican Republic-Central America-US Free Trade Agreement in 2005, voted for the Oman Free Trade Agreement in 2006, opposed the free trade agreement with Colombia – a key US ally – in 2008, and supported the Peru Free Trade Agreement in 2007 (only subsequently to miss the Senate vote). Obama's U-turns on NAFTA renegotiation, scepticism about the Doha Round, support for proposals to strengthen the renminbi, and advocacy of tax credits for US companies that kept their headquarters in America and that increased their US labor force relative to their overseas workforce together belied his "cosmopolitan" credentials and powerfully suggested that international relations under an Obama administration – particularly one backed by large Democratic congressional majorities – would be anything but straightforward for allies abroad.

Conclusion

As the 2008 campaign developed, Obama gained ever greater national and international admiration and support, while simultaneously posing an increasing enigma to more critical observers. Despite the rhetorical brilliance, self-conscious intellectualism and strongly charismatic appeals, the most audacious decision Obama made in his entire public life was to run for the US presidency. By virtue of being unknown and distinctive, Obama not only articulated but also symbolized the change which democratic politics is deliberately designed to facilitate. As critics such as Gerard Baker put it, "It is indeed audacious to think that hope – and not much else – is sufficient to run a great country."[44] And despite his campaign's tactical brilliance, its overall strategy was consistently cautious and risk averse. The change that Obama called for remained, for the most part, as reliably opaque as his voting record had been reliably conventional and his bipartisanship reliably rare. As previously enthusiastic Arab leaders increasingly realized, the black progressive African American senator increasingly appeared an American first, a progressive second, and an African American third. Whether this was so by calculation or conviction – or a carefully calibrated combination of the two – was not fully clear.

But Obama's victory was not because he was a black politician nor even a politician who "happened to be black" – one who, in Shelby Steele's formulation, was a "bargainer" rather than a "challenger" when it comes to dealing with the status quo.[45] Rather, it was because Obama embodied and exuded a cosmopolitanism whose symbolism overshadowed substance and was itself the story, the message, and – ultimately – the grand strategy. Obama's strongest supporters regarded him as not just a "change agent" but also a "transformational figure" who, largely by dint of who he was, could repair America's tarnished global image and bring closure, catharsis and redemption to the recent history of pain at home and abroad alike.

Obama's election certainly represented an historic symbolic development for America that had an impact at home and around the world. But, contrary to the forecasts of his most ardent supporters, for whom Obama's offer represented nothing less than "an end to US stupidity,"[46] there existed good reason to expect that in substance this would exacerbate, not ease, Obama's time in his office. As Krauthammer noted by way of historical comparison:

> The problem is that Obama began believing in his own magical powers – the chants, the swoons, the "we are the ones" self-infatuation. Like Ronald Reagan, he was leading a movement, but one entirely driven by personality. Reagan's revolution was rooted in concrete political ideas (supply-side economics, welfare-state deregulation, national strength) that transcended one man. For Obama's movement, the man *is* the transcendence.[47]

As Kathleen Hall Jamieson later reflected on the Obama campaign: "There's a tendency to overpromise and overestimate the power of the presidency. He made all those mistakes as a candidate. It helped him get elected. But it all but guaranteed he would fail to meet the expectations in his governance."[48]

Long before John McCain began stressing his admiration for "TR" during the 2008 campaign, Obama had characterized the Bush Doctrine as an extension of Theodore Roosevelt's more expansive corollary to the Monroe Doctrine ("the notion that we could pre-emptively remove governments not to our liking"[49]) from the Western hemisphere to span the entire globe. But the choice confronting Washington was, and remains, neither the starkly binary one of unilateralism versus multilateralism, realism versus idealism, nor war versus peace. Post-Bush, the next US president would confront a myriad of global challenges, a mix of reliable and unreliable allies, and a set of creaking institutions from the UN to NATO that, if not quite broken, were inadequate fully to meet the threats of a dangerous and changing world. President Obama, like all his predecessors since 1945, inherited an office at once of extraordinary power and extraordinary limitations. Priorities needed to be identified. Limited resources had to be deployed in a world of unlimited demands on American power. And a careful calibration of constraints as well as opportunities would necessarily condition American action with allies and against adversaries. How Obama sought to reconcile the harsh realities of office with the exuberant transformative hopes of his "change" campaign is the subject to which we turn next.

3

The Obama Doctrine: "Leading From Behind"

I hope that Obama will have as successful a term as I had in dealing with our nation's domestic and international affairs.
—Jimmy Carter, September 19, 2010[1]

... Barack Obama seems to have chosen Carter's ideological path over Clinton's pragmatic one. As his foreign policy appears more and more ideologically driven, erratic, uncertain and out of the mainstream, the president's response is to try to finesse the glaring contradictions in his initiatives by the power of his person. If there is no midcourse steering correction towards a more moderate appreciation of American interests, Obama might find that the people of this country will become disturbed by America's increasingly precarious position in the world and the messianic pretensions of their transnational commander in chief.
—Victor Davis Hanson, *How The Obama Administration Threatens Our National Security*[2]

I greatly admire his insights and understanding. I don't really think he has a policy that's implementing those insights and understandings. The rhetoric is always terribly imperative and categorical: "You must do this," "He must do that," "This is unacceptable" ... He doesn't strategize. He sermonizes.
—Zbigniew Brzezinski (National Security Advisor to President Jimmy Carter, 1977–81)[3]

Introduction

Scholars of US foreign policy, rather like Republican and Democratic Party lawmakers in the contemporary US Congress, are not well known for easily achieving lasting consensus. But even by the polarized and reliably fractious standards of today's political commentary, the breadth and depth of academic disagreement over Obama's foreign policy is striking. Obama's approach to international affairs since assuming the presidency has seen him defined and defamed variously as a foreign policy "realist,"[4] an "accommodationist,"[5] a "liberal internationalist,"[6] a "neo-conservative,"[7] an "isolationist,"[8] a "liberal-realist,"[9] and a "war addict."[10] Daniel Drezner raised the question of whether Obama actually followed a clear grand strategy in foreign affairs, only to conclude that his administration has pursued no fewer than two such strategies – "multilateral retrenchment" and, subsequently, "counter-punching."[11] The administration's central failure, for Drezner, has consisted principally in failing to articulate its latter-day pugilism sufficiently clearly to the American people.

Such dissensus seems to confirm Obama's own belief – and, arguably, as the last chapter suggested, his wilfully opaque self-definition – as a human Rorschach test: exactly what Obama thinks about the world seems to be strongly in the eye of the beholder. The originator of the term "post-American world," Fareed Zakaria, even responded to such critical tumult by concluding that the elusive search for a comprehensive "Obama Doctrine" was simply futile – the doctrinal approach to foreign policy no longer making sense in today's complex and multi-layered world – and should simply be abandoned as unhelpful to understanding the multifaceted nature of Obama's internationalism.[12]

In fact, fleshing-out the campaign commitments that he had staked-out as a candidate during the 2008 campaign, Obama's grand strategy became quite rapidly apparent in his early months as president, building on but clarifying those commitments and undertakings from his presidential campaign. Seeking to blend together a combination of the types of hard military and economic power employed by previous US administrations with a greater appreciation of the utility of soft power in an increasingly networked era, the administration's deployment of "smart power" was premised on the tough reality of rising powers, American decline, and power diffusion in an international order that was simultaneously changing and challenging Washington on multiple fronts around the globe. With an increasing range of rising powers competing for influence and resources, and the US quest to maintain primacy running directly against the opposition to such leadership in many parts of the world, the Obama approach resisted a one-size-fits-all dogmatism in favor of an eclectic mixture of instruments and tactics. What united them was a conviction in the need for Washington to calibrate its commitments carefully to its newly constrained capacities in order to maintain and maximize its potential still to lead a post-American world.

The fault-line of American foreign policy debates has for several decades fallen squarely between realists and idealists. Crudely put, this pits those primarily concerned with states' external behavior and relations – for whom "regime type" is simply an irrelevant black box – against those for whom the internal nature of states matters greatly, both as an intrinsic issue and as a guide to their external behavior (and for whom, therefore, the quest to shape that internal configuration, however difficult, should be a vital part of foreign policy). But Obama consistently sought to resist – or, more precisely, transcend – such traditional categories and conventional ideological tendencies. As one account put it, befitting a former editor of the *Harvard Law Review*, "Obama has emphasized bureaucratic efficiency over ideology, and approached foreign policy as if it were case law, deciding his response to every threat or crisis on its own merits."[13]

Keenly anti-ideological, Obama appeared to have taken to heart H. L. Mencken's injunction that for every complex problem there is an answer that is clear, simple, and wrong. Instead, the Obama Doctrine appeared to consist in a steadfast rejection of doctrine or visionary thinking as inappropriate and ineffective for today's especially complex world. In its place was a style of international leadership that resembled the one Obama had previously employed as a community organizer on Chicago's South Side – assiduously seeking broad consensus, working closely with allies, and assembling or enabling coalitions to achieve shared collective goals. In eschewing traditional foreign policy divisions, following a relentlessly cost-benefit logic, and seeking a pragmatic balance in US foreign policy, Obama's approach alternately frustrated realists and idealists alike. Increasingly, as his term progressed, Obama offered what one of his White House advisors infelicitously termed a "different definition of leadership than America is known for": "leading from behind."[14]

Obama's grand strategy: engagement

As his 2008 election campaign had made clear, Barack Obama's election as forty-fourth president promised major change in US foreign policy and a new phase in America's international relations; one calibrated to the arrival of a "post-American world."[15] Although relatively short on detailed policy specifics, the public record of Obama's many statements and speeches – from *The Audacity of Hope* through the long 2008 election campaign to his inaugural address – repeatedly emphasized several distinct but interrelated themes that implied a decisive break with the divisive George W. Bush years: America's growing interdependence with the world; the persistence and centrality – for good and ill – of globalization; the need to strengthen alliances and international institutions to tackle shared global challenges, from terrorism and failed states to climate change, nuclear proliferation and pandemics; reinvigorating multilateral action and institutions like the UN, NATO and G20 that conferred legitimacy upon collective action; engaging US adversaries in a spirit of mutual respect; and restoring the vital ethical link – widely viewed as having been fatally compromised under Bush – between America's internal values and external policies. Such clear commitments to renewing US foreign policy on a platform of strategic restraint served as an emphatic repudiation of his predecessor, and signalled a keen willingness to adapt the US to the emergence of a more multi-polar, interconnected and interdependent world.

Simultaneously, though, for all the obvious historic contrasts with its forty-three predecessors, Obama's administration also appeared as only the latest in the modern era to be committed to preserving and – if possible – enhancing and extending US primacy. In her US Senate confirmation hearings to become Secretary of State, in January 2009, Hillary Clinton declared that "we must strengthen America's position of global leadership" in order to ensure that America remained "a positive force in the world."[16] Similarly, although expressly recognizing the emergence of a "changed world" in his relatively subdued inaugural address of January 20, 2009, Obama also stated explicitly that "we are ready to lead once more."[17] The Obama administration thus commenced office in January 2009 apparently conscious of a changing world but at the same time committed to renewing US leadership in ways that – both directly and indirectly – implied that the international order had perhaps not altered so dramatically after all. This inherent and abiding tension, and the difficult accompanying adjustment to an era of limits on US international leadership, influence and global reach, emerged as constant features of the administration's first term and its various attempts at strategic retrenchment and restraint.

That was hardly surprising, given the unpropitious circumstances of Obama's arrival in the White House. From the outset, Obama's foreign policy "in-tray" was at least as problematic as his domestic inheritance. US forces were deployed in two major interventions of uncertain course and Obama was the first American president since Richard M. Nixon to enter the White House with a shooting war in progress. The threat of mass fatality attacks from al Qaeda, its affiliates and "home-grown" Islamist terrorists remained serious, even if the Bush-era rhetoric of the war on terror had been abandoned as counter-productive. Rising autocratic powers and petrodollar states were increasingly assertive from Latin America to Central Asia. Iran and North Korea's ambitions for nuclear weapons threatened regional destabilization in the Middle East and Northeast Asia. The unending Israel-Palestine conflict fueled Muslim extremism and threatened further wrenching Middle East wars. Failed, failing and weak states from Somalia and Yemen through Mexico and Haiti to Pakistan and Afghanistan continued both to experience terror at home and to export lethal violence to their neighbors (and further afield). International cooperation to advance free trade, combat climate change and prevent pandemics remained fitful at best.

The international challenges facing Obama on his entering the White House were therefore multiple, grave and urgent. But Washington's leverage in the international order appeared substantially diminished after the Bush era. American power was widely resented and US judgment questioned. The financial crisis and Great Recession compounded the spiraling budget deficits and national debt from 2001–09, raising serious questions regarding the material foundations of American power and the reality of "imperial overstretch." Attempts at increased burden-sharing with NATO and other allies remained only episodically successful.

The US public, moreover, was now disinclined to endorse major foreign commitments after the Afghan and Iraqi wars had cost so much in American blood and treasure, with so little to show for the profligate expenditure. A 2009 Pew Research Center/Council on Foreign Relations poll, for example, found that 49 percent of Americans believed that the US should "mind its own business internationally" – the largest-ever plurality recorded favoring such an "isolationist" stance. 44 percent of Americans also inclined towards unilateralism, agreeing with the statement that "we should go our own way in international matters, not worrying about whether other countries agree with us or not" – the highest proportion since Gallup first asked the question in 1964.[18] Although the US has military defense treaties with more than fifty allies, by 2010, majorities of Americans endorsed US military assistance to another nation-state that was under external attack in only five instances: Canada, the United Kingdom, Israel, Germany and Mexico.[19] A mere 11 percent of Americans believed that the US should continue to act as the "world's policeman."[20]

Upon becoming president, Obama therefore confronted some pressing political dilemmas that had major influences on shaping his presidency. First, as the *New York Times* foreign correspondent, David Sanger, presciently observed prior to Obama's entering the White House:

> The world he is inheriting from Bush will constrain his choices more than he has acknowledged, and certainly more than the throngs of supporters believed as they waved their signs proclaiming CHANGE. His biggest risk is that he will take the anti-Bush turn too far – that his cool, analytic approach will be seen, in times of crisis, as a lack of resolve; that his control and calmness might be viewed, over time, as a mask for an absence of conviction.[21]

Compounding that first challenge was a second major problem: the febrile pressures, poisonous partisan divisions and intense ideological conflicts of contemporary Beltway life. Obama had been elected to the US Senate in 2004, and had effectively served only three years in the chamber (since all of 2008, his fourth year – and a good proportion of 2007, too – had been given over to the heavy demands of the constant presidential campaign). Obama's exposure to Washington politics, while intense, was therefore decidedly brief. As Richard Wolffe, one of Obama's favorite American journalists, noted, a key dilemma for a president committed to a transformative agenda was whether he could "change the nation before the nation's capital changed him."[22] Equally, in terms of a phrase of which Obama was fond, would the president be able to exert a serious influence on the "arc of history" in the wider world, encouraging its incline towards justice, despite prioritizing domestic policy and having to overcome the extraordinarily polarized nature of partisan politics on Capitol Hill?

But the third, and arguably most difficult, dilemma that shaped his administration's course was that the urgency of the geo-political problems confronting Washington in the world at large sat uneasily with the need for sufficient strategic patience to bring about concerted international action to resolve them. Precisely because US hard and soft power resources alike were severely strained – not only by economic malaise and the military interventions of George W. Bush, but also because of the diplomatic confrontations, alliance fissures and public opposition that accompanied them in many nations – the policy instruments which the Obama administration could employ to effect decisive and rapid global change were relatively few and weak.

Undoubtedly, the US was still the strongest single power in the world and still constituted, as Madeleine Albright had (in)famously termed it, the "indispensable nation" – as an (even "the") essential component of any global system of collective security. But, whether or not one termed it a post-American era, it was increasingly manifest that the US would now have to share more fully the responsibility of maintaining global order with other rising powers and emerging power centers. While the US could not easily be excluded from regions such as East Asia and the Middle East, nor could rising powers such as China and India, the European Union (EU) or Brazil. Similarly, prominent international challenges, such as those related not just to the economy, environment and energy but also to broader questions of poverty and injustice, could not be regionally delimited. As two former US national security advisors argued, Washington's great task after the Bush years would be to align America with a "global political awakening" in which, for the first time in human history, "all of humanity is politically active"[23] – a reality brought vividly to life in 2011 with popular protests erupting around the world in a "year of global indignation."[24]

The cumulative result of the shifting international order meant that renewing US leadership in an increasingly multi-polar – or even, as Richard Haass termed it, non-polar[25] – international order required an intelligent and imaginative approach by the incoming administration. Obama's response was to emphasize a pragmatic but nonetheless ambitious international strategy that attended carefully to a new era of limits on unilateral US power while simultaneously devoting substantial resources to rebuilding America's faltering domestic base. The term most commonly invoked over 2009–12 to define Obama's foreign policy was strategic "engagement." The National Security Strategy (NSS) document of May 2010 defined engagement rather broadly as "the active participation of the United States in relationships beyond our borders."[26] A more precise definition might be "persuasion": employing positive and negative inducements to convince or cajole others to change their behavior, as their most rewarding or least harmful course of action. (Although, technically, a "pure" policy of engagement would abandon negative inducements or threats altogether,[27] the terms "engagement" or "strategic engagement" will be used here to cover both variants.)

As Thomas Wright argues, strategic engagement under Obama comprised five sets of interlocutors whom the administration sought to address: civilizations, allies, new partners, adversaries and institutions.[28] The underlying logic of such a strategy for the post-American world was reasonably clear and for many of Obama's admirers, compelling, in representing an important shift from the approach adopted by George W. Bush that targeted multiple audiences. Four elements combined here to endorse a new emphasis on a more engaged and less combative approach to international affairs.

First, as Obama pointedly declared in the NSS, "Our national security begins at home."[29] As Miles Taylor noted, unusually for a document typically focused on Washington's international challenges and grand strategic designs, fully one-quarter of the NSS was instead devoted to domestic policies and goals, such as rebuilding the nation's crumbling infrastructure and strengthening the American economy.[30] Second, the Bush administration's organizing US foreign policy primarily around national security threats such as al Qaeda and an "axis of evil" (comprising the "rogue states" of Iraq, Iran and North Korea) had simultaneously militarized American diplomacy while mistakenly marginalizing globalization as – for good and for ill – the primary driving force in twenty-first century geo-politics. Third, framing a threat-based global war on terror was dysfunctional diplomatically and invited "blowback," at once elevating terrorism to an unwarranted pre-eminence among America's multiple foreign policy challenges and placing unacceptable burdens on the US military, while at the same time alienating and radicalizing the world's 1.5 billion Muslims. Fourth, in a post-American international environment of rising powers, transnational challenges, and widespread anti-Americanism, overemphasizing American exceptionalism and the singularity of US leadership weakened Washington's capacity to persuade other states to responsibly burden-share in policing the fissiparous international order. As such, Bush had been persistently preaching to an American choir when he needed the global congregation.

In place of such a failed grand strategy, the Obama administration would substitute a new and distinctive approach. As Secretary Clinton declared on the publication and launch of the NSS:

> We are looking to turn a multi-polar world into a multi-partner world. I know there is a critique among some that somehow talking this way undercuts American strength, power, leadership. I could not disagree more. I think that we are seeking to gain partners in pursuing American interests. We happen to think a lot of those interests coincide with universal interests.[31]

Amplifying this, James B. Steinberg, US Deputy Secretary of State, later explained – on the ninth anniversary of 9/11 – the two central strategic premises that underpinned the Obama administration's foreign policy.[32] First was the conviction that the changes in the international order that had occurred since the end of the Cold War now placed a premium upon mobilizing international cooperation to deal with opportunities and threats that were manifestly shared, not isolated. But, second was the unchanged centrality of the US to enabling and coordinating such cooperation, in the absence of which shared threats were simply likely to grow or go unaddressed. The overarching problem for the Obama administration was how to facilitate strong US leadership in an era of imposing constraints, when US leadership capacities were constrained and its legitimacy doubted post-Bush, and when the shared interests that states identified did not automatically or easily translate into a commonality of purposeful action among them.

The administration's response was to place continuing importance on US strategic partnerships and alliances and to encourage their durability, but also to stress their adaptation to new circumstances quite different from those that originally inspired them. The latter aspect required the careful building – or rebuilding – of cooperative relationships with key players in the international system such as China, Russia and India, as well as with rising powers such as Brazil, Turkey and Indonesia. Moreover, these bilateral relationships would need to be embedded within a set of revived international institutions and stronger regional multilateral architectures, some of which needed to be more efficient and some more representative of changing power balances. As Steinberg described it, Washington's commitment to the "twin pillars" of global cooperation and US leadership could together advance important international efforts to deal with challenges as diverse as opening up the Arctic's resources, combating climate change and ending nuclear proliferation: "ultimately, the decision to reinvigorate global cooperation is not ours alone. But America's actions can powerfully shape the choices that others face."[33] In effect, it fell to Washington to "nudge" others in the international system in the appropriate directions.

Under Obama, then, as Wright observed, strategic engagement effectively "redefines international politics as a complex problem-solving exercise."[34] By emphasizing shared interests that necessitate every stakeholder in the international order exercising responsibilities in addition to rights, engagement attempted to reframe the parameters of international action, incentivizing others to a greater role in establishing and enforcing norms of international conduct and, thereby, sending unmistakeable signals to those entities – terrorist networks, failed states, crime syndicates, outlaw regimes and others – who refused to follow the order's agreed rules. In the latter case, the unambiguous character of their failure should smooth the road to effective sanction and isolation by the broader international community. As the NSS expressly stated, "Rules of the road must be followed, and there must be consequences for those nations that break the rules – whether they are non-proliferation obligations, trade agreements, or human rights commitments."[35]

Strategic engagement therefore not only recognized but also embraced the international order's shifting tectonics at a time of American economic stringency, military overstretch and public insularity. Faced with the need to exercise damage-control post-Iraq with a limited range of policy options, a more modest and humble US foreign policy appeared not only desirable but, in a sense, unavoidable in a post-American era. By "resetting" relations afresh with Russia and China, abandoning the war on terror's militaristic and supposedly anti-Islamic frame, pledging the US to adhere once again to common norms and shared international conventions, and addressing not only traditional allies but also long-established adversaries – and, moreover, by appealing to individuals and civil societies as well as governments among friends and foes alike – the Obama administration sought to convey the most potent symbolic and substantive contrast with its ill-loved predecessor. While no American administration, Democrat or Republican, would completely disavow the promotion of certain cherished ideals and values, democracy promotion and the "freedom agenda" were now clearly secondary to security concerns. Force, by necessity and choice, took a back seat to vigorous diplomacy. Open markets, in the aftermath of the Great Recession, required new global coordination and enhanced regulation. National sovereignty – whether that of the US or of China – needed to recognize and incorporate shared responsibilities.[36] Seeking greater balance and reciprocity in US foreign policy, Obama repeatedly stressed its essence as forging new global relationships "on the basis of mutual interests and mutual respect."[37]

It remains debatable whether these various assumptions and tenets really amounted to the oft-attributed return to "realism" that Obama was widely celebrated for overseeing after Bush. As the next section notes, in terms of his foreign policy personnel, realists – many of whom had previously served in the Clinton Administration (1993–2001) – certainly tended to occupy the key administration positions and to shape policies over 2009–12. But few American administrations can completely or consistently reject idealist strains in foreign policy, especially when – as occurred under Bush's tenure – international events can conspire to frustrate a purely *realpolitik* approach. Equally, a strong case can be made that Obama's case-by-case approach was not so much realism in action as simple pragmatism. Indeed, as Colin Dueck compellingly argues, in keeping with the Democratic Party's general direction since the Vietnam War, American power itself appears to be part of the problem on this interpretation:

> Obama's most fundamental instincts seem to be not so much realist as accommodationist ... Obama and his supporters appear to view the president as someone uniquely qualified to bridge divides over cultural, economic and political lines, an approach he first developed during his days as a community organizer in Chicago. This bridge-building approach is applied abroad as well as domestically. Tremendous emphasis is laid on the importance of conciliatory language, style, and personality. The president's instinct, in many cases, internationally, is not so much to think in geopolitical terms as to try to lay out multifaceted understanding of points of view on every side, recognizing some validity in each perspective ...[38]

Moreover, for some critics on the left, even the design of the supposedly "new" US approach to foreign affairs under Obama was highly questionable. Far from vindicating the campaign slogans of "Yes We Can" and "Change We Can Believe In" that together had heavily implied an urgent and major break with the Bush administration, the parallels and continuities between the two administrations were instead at least as striking. As Inderjeet Parmar argued:

> President Obama's 2010 National Security Strategy ... strongly echoes that of his predecessor, George W. Bush, and is also almost identical to that suggested by a large group of elite academics, military officials, businessmen and former Clinton administration insiders brought together as the Princeton Project on National Security (PPNS) back in 2004–2006. The Princeton Project was led by Princeton academics Anne-Marie Slaughter and G. John Ikenberry, featured Reagan's secretary of state, George Schultz and Clinton's national security adviser, Anthony Lake, as co-chairs. Francis Fukuyama, erstwhile neo-con, sat on the steering committee and was co- author of the Project's working paper on grand strategy. Henry Kissinger acted as adviser, as did Harvard's Joseph Nye, author of the concept of "Soft Power", morphing more recently into "Smart Power." PPNS represented a new cross-party consensus on how to "correct" the excesses and reckless enthusiasm for American power of the Bush administration.[39]

But whether the theoretical underpinnings of strategic engagement amounted to a decisive break from Bush and an internally coherent "Obama Doctrine" – the search for which, among the commentariat, proved decidedly more elusive than under prior presidents – was, for the administration, mostly secondary to their translation into effective practice and concrete international results. As Benjamin Rhodes, Deputy National Security Advisor for Strategic Communications, put it, in terms of foreign policy:

> The project of the first two years has been to effectively deal with the legacy issues that we inherited, particularly the Iraq war, the Afghan war, and the war against Al Qaeda, while rebalancing our resources and our posture in the world ... If you were to boil it all down to a bumper sticker, it's "Wind down these two wars, re-establish American standing and leadership in the world, and focus on a broader set of priorities, from Asia and the global economy to a nuclear non-proliferation regime."[40]

Implementing strategic engagement (2009–12)

The vast academic literature on the making and implementation of US foreign policy emphasizes that its relative success depends critically on a combination of presidential priorities and attention; the principals appointed by the president to relevant departments and agencies; his management of their inevitable personal, political and bureaucratic tensions, conflicts and rivalries; and the collective execution of optimal strategic and tactical prescriptions through effectively employed policy instruments. Obama's avowed intention during his presidential transition was to ensure that his foreign policy principals and advisors operated as a "team of rivals"[41] rather than rival teams, as had too often characterized US foreign policy under previous administrations (Democratic and Republican alike).

If an implicit model existed for both the content and structure of foreign policy-making, it was that of George H. W. Bush, whose foreign policy team from 1989 to 1993 was one of the most experienced, cooperative and effective in modern American history, and one unashamedly pragmatic rather than doctrinaire in its approach to world affairs. As Thomas Donilon, Deputy and subsequently National Security Advisor under Obama observed, his National Security Council (NSC) was "... essentially based on the process that was put in place by Brent Scowcroft and Bob Gates in the late nineteen-eighties," to ensure that the NSC – based at the White House – was "the sole process through which policy would be developed."[42] Although controversies were to surround the operations of the White House, the control of the foreign policy-making process was one of the most highly centralized and heavily politicized of any modern American administration, with Obama effectively serving as his own National Security Advisor and Secretary of State.

Obama's foreign policy nominees were widely approved within the Beltway, representing a blend of experience and freshness, policy expertise and political nous, drawing on experts from the academy and think-tanks such as the Brookings Institution and the Center for American Progress, and bridging the distinct realist and liberal internationalist foreign policy strands within the Democratic Party's coalition. (With the exception of "global rejectionists," Obama's team of rivals included all of the tendencies identified by Kurt Campbell and Michael O'Hanlon within the Democratic foreign policy coalition: "hard power advocates," "globalists," and "modest-power Democrats."[43]) With a strong – and, briefly, filibuster-proof – Democratic Party majority in the Senate during 2009–10, few nominees encountered confirmation problems.

Hillary Clinton's selection as Secretary of State was especially bold, imaginative and unifying – the third woman to hold the post being widely respected and, politically, tied closely to Obama's success as his principal diplomat. Retaining the Bush holdover, Robert Gates as Secretary of Defense made both political and policy sense, as a bipartisan pick and in ensuring continuity of control in the Pentagon during wartime (Gates and Clinton proved, with the exception of the Libyan issue in 2011, reliably united on foreign policy, a stark contrast to prior relationships between the Pentagon and State, such as Rumsfeld and Powell's repeated clashes in the Bush administration). The choice of James Jones as National Security Advisor consolidated the bipartisan and, as a military man and former John McCain advisor, centrist cast of the team (although he was increasingly marginalized and questioned as the first two years of the administration wore on, before resigning). Vice President Biden, a former chair of the Senate Foreign Relations Committee with extensive experience and contacts, promised to play an important role as well (albeit not the highly activist one of Dick Cheney). With Rahm Emanuel as Chief of Staff and David Axelrod contributing the more overtly political calculations, Obama's selections suggested a Chief Executive comfortable with a broad array of views and advice, albeit from a relatively narrow, centrist (and, prior to William Daley's replacement of Emanuel as Chief of Staff in late 2010, non-business) spectrum of opinion.

At the same time, those principals – along with key officials such as Donilon, Rhodes and Denis McDonough, another Deputy National Security Advisor – tended to err on the realist side of the realism/idealism divide. In line with the deliberate stepping-away from the idealism of the post-9/11 Bush years, those foreign policy officials whose pedigree tended to be on issues of humanitarian intervention, human rights and democracy promotion received less senior posts: Samantha Power was appointed Senior Director of Multilateral Affairs at the NSC; Anne-Marie Slaughter, a proponent of a "concert of democracies," was made Director of Policy Planning at the State Department; and Michael McFaul, another advocate of democracy promotion, was awarded a mid-level job at the White House. With the exception of Obama confidant Susan Rice, who was named US Ambassador to the United Nations, the ranks of the major Cabinet and NSC positions were held by realists rather than idealists (raising implicit issues about a gender divide at the heart of the Obama administration's foreign – as well as domestic – policy-making).

The implementation of strategic engagement rapidly became a dominant imperative for the members of the new administration, from the top down. As Stephen Wayne argues, Obama is not short of self-confidence and believes powerfully in the efficacy of his "going public," the value of the bully pulpit and his own ability to educate elites and mass publics in a series of "teachable moments":

> Obama has used the bully pulpit more than any recent president. During his first year alone, he gave two addresses before joint sessions of Congress; held six press conferences; gave 152 one-on-one interviews; made 554 public remarks, statements, and comments to assembled individuals and groups inside and outside the White House – and this was all in addition to his weekly radio addresses ... By the end of 2010, he had given 428 speeches and remarks, issued 245 statements, many of them hortatory, in addition to his weekly radio broadcasts, nomination announcements, disaster declarations, bill signings, and letters and messages to Congress.[44]

Initially, Obama appeared to take the high-profile positive outreach agenda as his own, while dispatching Clinton to do more of the "bad cop" diplomacy with America's more ambiguous and adversarial interlocutors.

That partly reflected the president's confident belief in his own ability to shape and sway opinion at home and abroad – not dissimilar to the prior self-regard of British Prime Minister, Tony Blair. From the outset of the Obama administration, its foreign policy principals engaged in one of the most concerted efforts at strategic engagement and renewed diplomacy seen by a new US administration, the symbolism of which was especially forceful after the polarizing Bush era. Hillary Clinton's first overseas visit was to China and Southeast Asia, while specially appointed envoys such as George Mitchell and (the late) Richard Holbrooke made several missions to their respective regions of Israel-Palestine and South Asia. In an important symbolic act, Obama gave his first media interview as president to *Al-Arabiya*, an Arab television satellite station. In a passage clearly intended to mark a decisive break with his predecessor, Obama also highlighted that a major part of his new job was to "communicate the fact that the United States has a stake in the well-being of the Muslim world, that the language we use has to be a language of respect."

In his landmark Cairo speech of June 2009, the president reiterated this message with even greater emphasis, repeatedly quoting the Koran and heralding a "new beginning between the United States and Muslims." In calling for an end to the mutually damaging cycle of acute distrust that had arisen between America and Islam since 9/11, the president declared:

> I have come here to seek a new beginning between the United States and Muslims around the world; one based on mutual interest and mutual respect; and one based on the truth that America and Islam are not exclusive; and need not be in competition.[45]

Stressing the need to confront "violent extremism" in all its myriad forms, Obama defended the US mission in Afghanistan while simultaneously emphasizing that US actions in America's self-defense should nonetheless be "respectful of the sovereignty of nations and the rule of law." While calling for a settlement of the Israeli-Palestinian conflict, the president also signalled his readiness to engage in negotiations with Iran "without preconditions and on the basis of mutual respect."

In addition to the potent symbolism, the ambitious pace and impressive scope of Obama's global ambitions also quickly became apparent. In only his first year as president, Obama: announced the intention to close the Guantanamo Bay detention facility in Cuba, end torture and approve the US rejoining the UN Human Rights Council and paying its UN dues; initiated a major campaign on nuclear non-proliferation that resulted in his chairing a UN Security Council session in September 2009 – the first time that a US president had done so – and convening thirty-eight heads of government in a Washington, D.C. security summit in April 2010; traveled to Ankara and Cairo to open a new dialogue with the Muslim world, to Accra to reach out to Africa, and to Prague and Oslo to advance the cause of a non-nuclear world (even if not achieved in his lifetime) and accept the Nobel Peace Prize, respectively; opened a bilateral diplomatic initiative to Tehran and spoke directly to the Iranian people; announced a firm date of August 2010 for the withdrawal of all US combat forces from Iraq and a comprehensive revised strategy for Afghanistan; and pledged to "reset" relations with Russia and advance strategic arms reductions while repairing US relations with Europe, Latin America and Asia. In terms of global perceptions, the dedicated effort to establish a new beginning after Bush could hardly have been clearer, better delivered or more pointed.

To this end, too, Obama visited more countries in his first year of office than any other American president in history, making ten trips in 2009 to twenty-one nations; his closest competitor was George H. W. Bush, who visited fourteen countries in 1989. The speeches the president made were undeniably crucial in transforming the tone of US foreign policy, especially those in Prague, Cairo and Oslo. The award of the Nobel Prize, while politically problematic for Obama at home and decidedly premature in terms of actual achievements, nonetheless testified to the overwhelmingly positive attitudes outside America towards the president. Indeed, the attention devoted by the president to foreign policy abroad contrasted markedly with Obama's domestic preoccupations and politics within Washington; the president did not even address international affairs in a direct televised White House broadcast to the nation until August 31, 2010.

Obama's dedicated efforts at renewing America's image paid off in terms of a decisive increase in pro-US attitudes, especially in Europe. But, as Table 3.1 shows, his restoration of US favorability ratings was not universal. Obama's immense popularity in Western Europe – confirmed in the "Obama Bounce" detailed in Table 3.2 – was somewhat less the case in central and eastern Europe, India and Israel. But the most conspicuous and consequential exceptions were those where the president expended the greatest effort to project an empathetic image: countries with predominantly Muslim populations. From his explicit and direct inaugural declaration that America was not at war with Islam, through his inaugural offer of an "outstretched hand" to Iran and repeated speeches emphasizing America's eagerness for a new relationship based on mutual interest and respect, Obama prioritized changing Muslim attitudes towards the US. His success, however, was slight. While polls during his first three years mostly documented a higher level of approval than had been obtained under Bush, this increase occurred from a very low base and still registered strong animus in many Muslim states, not least those formally classified as US "allies" (such as Egypt, Turkey, Jordan and Pakistan.) In the cases of Turkey and Pakistan, even fewer respondents approved of Obama's foreign policy than had that of George W. Bush, an "achievement" of some note.

Table 3.1 US favorability rating 1999–2011 (in percentages)

	1999/ 2000	2002	2003	2005	2006	2007	2008	2009	2010	2011
US	–	–	–	83	76	80	84	88	85	–
Britain	83	75	70	55	56	51	53	69	65	61
France	62	62	42	43	39	39	42	75	73	75
Germany	78	60	45	42	37	30	31	64	63	62
Spain	50	–	38	41	23	34	33	58	61	64
Poland	86	79	–	62	–	61	68	67	74	70
Russia	37	61	37	52	43	41	46	44	57	56
Turkey	52	30	15	23	12	9	12	14	17	10
Egypt	–	–	–	–	30	21	22	27	17	20
Jordan	–	25	1	21	15	20	19	25	21	13
Lebanon	–	36	27	42	–	47	51	55	52	49
China	–	–	–	42	47	34	41	47	58	44
India	–	66	–	71	56	59	66	76	66	41
Indonesia	75	61	15	38	30	29	37	63	59	54
Japan	77	72	–	–	63	61	50	59	66	85
Pakistan	23	10	13	23	27	15	19	16	17	12
South Korea	58	52	46	–	–	58	70	78	79	–
Argentina	50	34	–	–	–	16	22	38	42	–
Brazil	–	–	–	–	–	–	–	–	62	62
Mexico	68	64	–	–	–	56	47	69	56	52
Kenya	94	80	–	–	–	87	–	90	94	83
Nigeria	46	76	61	–	62	70	64	79	81	–

Source: Pew Research Center, Pew Global Attitudes Survey of 22 Nations, Q7a; 1999/2000 survey trends provided by the Office of Research, US Department of State; figures for 2011 from: http://pewglobal.org/2011/07/13/china-seen-overtaking-us-as-global-superpower/3/#chapter-2-views-of-the-u-s-and-american-foreign-policy.

The difficulty here, however, was that while Obama earned some significant political capital with his new tone and transparently sincere desire to establish a new beginning with the Muslim world, the raised expectations of his first-year efforts – culminating in the Cairo address – could potentially be squandered in the absence of actual progress on the ground across the Middle East and South Asia (and, to a lesser extent, in terms of intra-American and intra-European relations) in terms of results. Much as he had done with his

Table 3.2 The Obama bounce

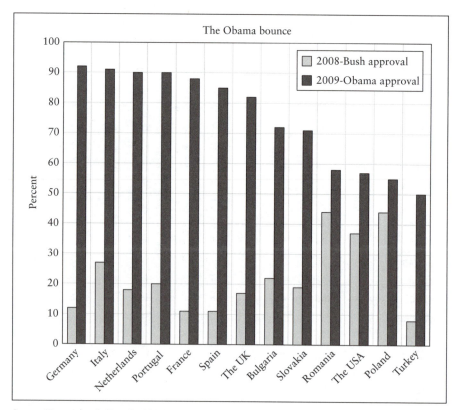

Source: Transatlantic Trends, 2009.

American supporters, by raising exaggerated expectations that this US leader was not simply another "more of the same" figure but rather a transformational and visionary president, the more prosaic realities of national and international politics were obscured. The overlapping tensions between the "all-American" and the "post-American" Obama, the conflict between American nationalism and a rooted cosmopolitanism, and the problems of strategic coherence inherent in a posture of "leading from behind" were nowhere more vivid than in this aspect of his engagement strategy. As one sceptical account argued, Obama's combined attempts to re-boot US soft power and restore American legitimacy could go only so far to rebuild US credibility and legitimacy among the world's Muslims:

The Muslim world continues to scrutinize the President's actions as much as his speeches. 24-news channels broadcasting images of US troops still fighting in Afghanistan and Iraq, not to mention Israelis in the West Bank and Gaza, serve to undermine any message of reconciliation. Obama's quiet abandonment of democracy advocacy, highlighted by recent congressional cuts in democracy and governance aid for Middle Eastern states, similarly risks increasing cynicism towards the new administration's approach. Whilst Bush's democracy promotion at gunpoint was detested, the Obama administration's continued support for unpopular dictators such as Egypt's Hosni Mubarak, its propping up of Mahmoud Abbas' legally questionable presidential mandate extension, and the near-farcical acceptance of Hamid Karzai's fraudulent re-election in Afghanistan have dampened any Muslim optimism Obama may have earned in Cairo.[46]

Moreover, despite Obama's best intentions and his efforts at outreach, important developments during his presidency implied a dangerous downward spiral in US efforts to combat Islamist terrorism. One, as detailed in a report by the National Security Preparedness Group (co-chaired by Tom Kean and Lee Hamilton), was the increasing efforts of groups such as al Qaeda to radicalize and recruit American Muslims. The success of such efforts, according to one senior US national security official, rested on disaffected American Muslims who had "internalized the idea that the United States is at war with Islam."[47] With the non-Muslim US population's concerns about domestic terrorism indicating an increasing popular suspicion of all American Muslims, the possibility gained ground that the two disturbing trends could reinforce each other – making the warnings of Bernard Lewis and Samuel Huntington about a "clash of civilizations" a reality – with Muslims convinced of a US at war with Islam and non-Muslim Americans convinced of an Islamic world at war with America. Should it materialize, such a development posed a significant threat for future US and Western national security.

Much as his broader foreign policy had sought not to impose results but to create and cajole choices for other states and institutions, so Obama had clearly wished to create the conditions for a new beginning with civilizations (most notably, Islam), old allies, new partners, adversaries, and institutions alike. But while his mix of symbolic and substantive departures from the Bush years was not lost either on Americans or peoples outside the US, its desired effects remained muted and unfulfilled. In the key case of the Muslim world, the raised expectations of Obama's first year became mostly dashed in the realities of the Hindu Kush, Gaza, the West Bank, Yemen and, latterly, in the Arab Spring of 2011. The rhetoric of mutual respect and mutual interest foundered on the increased US troops and drone strikes, the incursions of special forces and the CIA into Pakistan and elsewhere, alongside the lack of progress on a rapid and just settlement to the Israeli-Palestinian conflict. For all his efforts, global Muslim opinion barely shifted in attitudes to the US under Obama.

At the same time, the "teachable moment" that his presidency sought to employ to deepen and broaden American understanding of Islam and the US role in the world also foundered. Far from assuaging popular American concerns about the homeland's vulnerability to terror attacks, those that were attempted on Obama's watch deepened them. Nativist attempts to besmirch Obama's own credentials as an "authentic" American saw the proportion of

Americans who believed their president was a Muslim rather than a Christian actually increase rather than decrease over his first two years, to one in five (encompassing over one-third of conservative Republicans).[48] Although he retained the support of most Muslim Americans and had pledged early in his presidency to combat negative stereotypes of Islam "wherever they appear," Obama's outreach to the community was largely invisible: by the autumn of 2011, the president – in marked contrast to his predecessor – had neither visited a mosque in the US nor held a single event with Muslim Americans outside the White House.[49]

More ominously, amid periodic American moral panics over the "Ground Zero mosque" in Manhattan, threatened burnings of the Koran and attempted terrorist attacks, polls demonstrated that a large plurality of Americans continued to hold unfavorable views of Muslims. According to the biennial Chicago Council on Foreign Relations 2010 survey of national US opinion, Americans' attitudes towards relations with the Muslim world had deteriorated, with a growing overall pessimism gaining hold. Only a bare majority of Americans (51 percent) concurred that "because Muslims are like people everywhere, we can find common ground and violent conflict between the civilizations is not inevitable" (that compares with 66 percent who agreed with the statement in 2002). Instead, a substantial proportion of Americans (45 percent) agreed with the statement that "because Muslim religious, social, and political traditions are incompatible with Western ways, violent conflict between the two civilizations is inevitable" (an increase of 18 points from just 27 percent in 2002.)[50]

Reflecting, responding to, and in part reinforcing such sentiments, the president's own approach to counter-terrorism necessarily evolved over his first term. After the attempted Christmas Day Detroit bombing by the "underpants bomber" Umar Farouk Abdulmutallab in 2009, when Obama's initial (mistaken) response that he had acted alone had come under intense Republican criticism, the president vowed – in language reminiscent of the Bush era – to "…use every element of our national power to disrupt, to dismantle and to defeat the violent extremists who threaten us, whether they are from Afghanistan or Pakistan, Yemen or Somalia; or anywhere …"[51] In seeking a pragmatic middle ground that vindicated his aspirations for a new beginning with the Islamic world while reassuring Americans of his dedication to preserving US national security, the authenticity of Obama's voice became increasingly questioned by Muslims, progressives and – especially – conservative Americans in turn.

The conservative critique: Obama and the end of American exceptionalism

The flipside of Obama's impressive, if not wholly successful, international outreach efforts was how these comparatively unusual initiatives by a US president would be received within the US, where his controversial domestic agenda had rapidly ignited intense opposition from Republicans and conservatives, alienated Independents and spurred the Tea Party movement into mobilizing nationwide by the spring of 2009. Although censure of the quantity of his foreign trips was relatively muted, the content of the president's international travels quickly earned him trenchant criticism, typically of two forms.

The most common conservative tactic was to portray Obama as simultaneously weak, naive, narcissistic and arrogant. Obama's apparently sincere belief that his mere appearance and well crafted set-piece speeches via the ubiquitous teleprompter could change the deep-seated attitudes and beliefs of tens of millions of peoples towards the US and also alter substantive international policies was at once excessively self-confident and naive about the way the world works. Critics on the right charged Obama with conducting an abject and nationally embarrassing "apology tour," in which the president failed to sufficiently venerate the US, and not only conceded America's historic wrongs and missteps but also denied the reality of American exceptionalism – the notion that America had a distinctive, and even unique, God-given destiny.

Although Obama often referenced his own meteoric rise as ample proof of America's distinctive merits – the implicit message being, what chance a black British prime minister or French president? – his occasional downplaying of America's virtue, especially when abroad, offered at best an indistinctly American internationalism and an inviting target to his many critics. His reply to a question on his first tour of Europe as president, in April 2009, aptly illustrated this. When asked by the *Financial Times* journalist, Edward Luce, whether he subscribed – like his predecessors – to a view of America "as uniquely qualified to lead the world," Obama's response appeared to encapsulate a cultural relativism that rendered the US just one ordinary nation among others: "I believe in American exceptionalism, just as I suspect that the Brits believe in British exceptionalism and the Greeks believe in Greek exceptionalism."[52] The implication appeared to be that if everyone is exceptional in their own eyes, then no-one is truly exceptional, our differences trumped by our common humanity.

The result was that, for the first time in modern American history, according to Shelby Steele, "in Mr. Obama, America gained a president with ambivalence, if not some antipathy, toward the singular greatness of the nation he had been elected to lead":

Mr. Obama came of age in a bubble of post-'60s liberalism that conditioned him to be an adversary of American exceptionalism. In this liberalism America's exceptional status in the world follows from a bargain with the devil – an indulgence in militarism, racism, sexism, corporate greed, and environmental disregard as the means to a broad economic, military, and even cultural supremacy in the world. And therefore America's greatness is as much the fruit of evil as of a devotion to freedom.

Mr. Obama did not explicitly run on an anti-exceptionalism platform. Yet once he was elected it became clear that his idea of how and where to apply presidential power was shaped precisely by this brand of liberalism. There was his devotion to big government, his passion for redistribution, and his scolding and scapegoating of Wall Street – as if his mandate was somehow to overcome, or at least subdue, American capitalism itself.

Anti-exceptionalism has clearly shaped his "leading from behind" profile abroad – an offer of self-effacement to offset the presumed American evil of swaggering cowboyism. Once in office his "hope and change" campaign slogan came to look like the "hope" of overcoming American exceptionalism and "change" away from it.[53]

A second variant of this type of criticism of the president's de-emphasizing American virtue was to acknowledge that Obama had indeed restored US prestige in much of the world post-Bush, but to question its efficacy in terms of substantive international achievements. As James Ceaser put it, the president was behaving in an "un-presidential" manner:

> Obama still retains an aura of charisma abroad, though to date it has yet to bring any of the benefits that were promised. But this kind of soft-power realism hardly bespeaks a foreign policy conducted on the basis of "a decent respect to the opinions of mankind," where principles are set down as markers designed to help open eyes to the rights of man. It represents instead a foreign policy based on promoting an indecent pandering to an evanescent infatuation with a single personality.[54]

The award of the Nobel Prize for Peace was merely another such illustration, with Obama's good intentions being rewarded long before they had been translated into good results.

Given the hyper-partisan and sharply polarized nature of contemporary US politics, it was unsurprising, and arguably inevitable, that a sharp conservative critique should rapidly emerge of Obama's foreign policies. Although Obama attempted a brief *rapprochement* with some nationally influential conservative commentators at the outset of his presidency – sitting down to dinner with, among others, William Kristol and Charles Krauthammer, at George Will's house before his inauguration in January 2009[55] – the deep-seated divisions between the American left and right were never going to be transcended by a president who, in his own way, mirrored for the right the bogey-man that Bush had previously represented to the left. As Richard Skinner argues, the presidency since Ronald Reagan has become an increasingly partisan institution, one where partisans approve strongly of their president's job performance while overwhelmingly disapproving of the performance of a president from the other party.[56] Obama was only the latest Oval Office occupant to experience this bifurcated response where a substantial share of Americans perceive an enemy in the White House.

Moreover, strategic engagement, smart power and American renewal, however artfully constructed, effectively amounted to the Obama administration pursuing a goal of calibrated strategic retrenchment: scaling back commitments, reducing costs, minimizing unilateralism, encouraging multilateralism, cutting defense, and espousing less rather than more US assertiveness abroad. The central charge of the conservative critique of Obama foreign policy was that, rather than gracefully managing the inevitable decrease in US power that was the prevailing scholarly consensus about a post-American world, as Charles Krauthammer put it: "decline is a choice."[57] To many on the right, that purported choice was a deliberate decision by an ambitious president who, as Fouad Ajami had predicted, and as was noted in Chapter 2, was not a conventional centrist Democratic liberal but rather a genuine leftist and avowed cosmopolitan. Just as some conservatives had been insouciant about spiraling budget deficits and debt in the 1980s, on the basis that these would "starve the beast" of increased domestic spending, so Obama's combination of fiscal stimulus and spiralling deficits and debt at home seemed calculated to rein-in US adventurism overseas. As one former Bush official described it, Obama's choices were far from accidental or forced upon the president. Instead, Obama possessed a "grand strategic vision" that envisaged the president as an historic figure in the mould of Ataturk or Sadat in re-orienting his nation's foreign policy, and that encompassed – as part of that turnaround – a major downgrading in the US global role.[58]

In turn, the central conservative charge of ending American exceptionalism through choosing decline rested on three subsidiary claims about Obama's uniqueness as president.

First, Obama's evident desire to "normalize" America in the community of nations was both unprecedented and fatally misjudged. As the outspoken former Ambassador to the UN in the George W. Bush Administration, John Bolton, put it with typical acerbity:

> Obama is the first post-American President. Central to his worldview is rejecting American exceptionalism and the consequences that flow therefrom. Since an overwhelming majority of the world's population would welcome the demise of American exceptionalism, they are delighted with Obama. One student interviewed after an Obama town hall meeting during his first presidential trip to Europe said ecstatically, "He sounds like a European." Indeed he does.[59]

In place of a confident articulation and celebration of American values and virtues, Obama's carefully qualified speeches offered a lesson in humility rarely to be found in American Commanders-in-Chief. Following Obama's speech to the United Nations of September 2009, in which the president called for "a new era of engagement based on mutual interest and mutual respect" and "new coalitions that bridge old divides," the conservative commentator Michelle Malkin even declared that the president had "solidified his place in the international view as the great appeaser and the groveler in chief."[60] Speaking to the annual convention of Veterans of Foreign Wars in San Antonio, Texas, in August 2011, former Massachussetts governor, and past and future

Republican presidential aspirant, Mitt Romney, asked rhetorically, "Have we ever had a president who was so eager to address the world with an apology on his lips and doubt in his heart? ... He seems truly confused not only about America's past but also about its future."[61] At the same event, echoing the theme of a "weak" America under Obama, Texas governor Rick Perry and one-time Republican presidential frontrunner declared that, "We cannot concede the moral authority of our nation to multilateral debating societies, and when our interests are threatened, American soldiers should be led by American commanders."[62]

The second claim in the conservative charge sheet was that backtracking from the aggressively militaristic approach of the Bush administration was ill-conceived and counter-productive, simultaneously damaging traditional allies' confidence in US commitments while unduly weakening key elements of homeland security. The very idea that the Justice Department of the Obama administration could even entertain the idea of filing lawsuits against former federal employees – CIA operatives and the Office of Legal Counsel officials who drew up the standard operating procedures governing interrogation practices after 9/11 – was indicative of a worrying lack of firmness on counter-terrorism and homeland security. Similarly, the linguistic convolutions that sought to allay popular Muslim sensibilities and abandoned Bush-era terms such as "terrorist," "Islamist," "Islamo-fascist" and "jihadist" in favor of "militants" and "extremists" did a drastic disservice to the American public's wartime mentality and the reality of the global Islamist threat.

Third, but related, Obama's instrumentalist view of alliances – in terms of their contingent relevance to current US strategic challenges rather than by historical bonds of common experiences or shared values – neglected crucial relationships and allowed traditional ties to fray.[63] The decidedly cool reception given in Washington to Prime Ministers Gordon Brown of the United Kingdom in 2009–10 and Binyamin Netanyahu of Israel throughout Obama's term suggested to conservatives an unprecedented and worrying disdain for two of Washington's most reliable international allies, not least with British troops losing their lives alongside Americans in war-torn Afghanistan. The fact that Obama was at the same time making such a concerted effort to reach out to repressive regimes as brutal as Iran, Syria and Venezuela compounded the grievous insult to America's closest friends. America under Obama appeared to be retreating from its role as an active player on the world stage, taking sides and making clear preferences, into that of a more neutral "umpire." Romney, summarizing the contrasting approaches, claimed that Obama:

> ... envisions America as a nation whose purpose is to arbitrate disputes rather than to advocate ideals, a country consciously seeking equidistance between allies and adversaries. We have never seen anything quite like it, really. And in positioning the United States in the way he has, President Obama has positioned himself as a figure transcending America instead of defending America.[64]

Echoing the Ajami critique, Romney argued that the result of Obama's engagement was "much more than a departure from his predecessor, George W. Bush; it is a rupture with some of the key assumptions that have undergirded more than six decades of American foreign policy."[65]

How far such pointed criticisms from the right had analytic accuracy rather than merely ideological bluster and partisan purchase was a matter for debate. Certainly, elements of the American public were unimpressed by the president's performance. Obama's job approval ratings inevitably fell from the heights of his initial honeymoon period in January 2009, as the American public grew increasingly unhappy about his handling of the economy, his health care policy, and the increasing size of the federal budget deficit and national debt. But from the public's perspective, the president had actually done a better job on foreign than domestic policy although, as Stephen Wayne observed, prior to Osama Bin Laden's targeted killing in May 2011, Obama's "approval ratings have been modest even within this policy sphere."[66] As Table 3.3 illustrates, even the "bounce" gained by the president from the al Qaeda leader's elimination was brief, with – for the first time in his presidency – a majority disapproving of Obama's handling of foreign affairs by August 2011.

Table 3.3 Public views on Obama's foreign policy

Date	Approve %	Disapprove %	No opinion %
2009 Feb 9–12	54	22	24
2009 Jul 17–19	57	38	6
2009 Aug 6–9	53	40	8
2010 Jan 8–10	47	47	6
2010 Feb 1–3	51	44	5
2010 Mar 26–28	48	46	6
2010 Aug 5–8	44	48	8
2010 Nov 19–21	45	49	6
2011 Feb 2–5	48	45	7
2011 Mar 25–27	46	47	6
2011 May 12–15	51	43	7
2011 Aug 11–14	42	51	6
2011 Nov 3–6	49	44	7
2012 Feb 2–5	48	46	6

Source: "Presidential Ratings – Issue Approval," *Gallup Poll*, February 2009–February 2012, www.gallup.com/poll/1726/Presidential-Ratings-Issue-Approval.aspx.

Moreover, not all conservatives or partisans shared the conventional critique of Obama. As former National Security Advisor, Condoleeza Rice, argued after an extensive discussion of foreign policy with President Obama on October 15, 2010 that "covered the waterfront":

> Despite the fact there are changes and tussles, there is still a foreign policy community that believes that foreign policy ought to be bipartisan ... It was really great that he reached out in that way ... Nothing in this president's methods suggests this president is other than a defender of America's interests.[67]

Indeed, a closer examination of Obama's beliefs about the US and American exceptionalism suggested not a president lacking patriotism, but a leader capable of considerable complexity; a "fox" rather than a "hedgehog" in Isaiah Berlin's dichotomy. Obama's full reply to the Luce question about his belief in America's unique ability to lead the world illustrated this well:

> I believe in American exceptionalism, just as I suspect that the Brits believe in British exceptionalism and the Greeks believe in Greek exceptionalism. I'm enormously proud of my country and its role and history in the world. If you think about the site of this summit and what it means, I don't think America should be embarrassed to see evidence of the sacrifices of our troops, the enormous amount of resources that were put into Europe post-war, and our leadership in crafting an Alliance that ultimately led to the unification of Europe. We should take great pride in that.

> And if you think of our current situation, the United States remains the largest economy in the world. We have unmatched military capability. And I think that we have a core set of values that are enshrined in our Constitution, in our body of law, in our democratic practices, in our belief in free speech and equality, that, though imperfect, are exceptional.

> Now, the fact that I am very proud of my country and I think that we've got a whole lot to offer the world does not lessen my interest in recognizing the value and wonderful qualities of other countries, or recognizing that we're not always going to be right, or that other people may have good ideas, or that in order for us to work collectively, all parties have to compromise and that includes us.

> And so I see no contradiction between believing that America has a continued extraordinary role in leading the world towards peace and prosperity and recognizing that that leadership is incumbent, depends on, our ability to create partnerships because we can't solve these problems alone.[68]

By 2011, Obama's speeches regularly invoked America's virtue, his address to the joint session of Congress on September 8 of that year a typical example, ending with a rousing call to the assembled lawmakers to "... show the world once again why the United States of America remains the greatest nation on Earth."[69]

Contrary to some right-wing claims, Obama was never so naive as to believe that mere speeches could leverage US power anew; nor did he refrain from stating his belief in the distinctiveness of America. Nonetheless,

Table 3.4 Democratic and Republican support for Barack Obama's foreign policies, 2009

	Stabilize Afghanistan		Cut defense		Support diplomacy	
	Party Support	Party cohesion	Party support	Party cohesion	Party support	Party cohesion
Democrats	90%	80%	91%	83%	94%	89%
Republicans	2%	96%	25%	89%	15%	85%

Note: Roll call voting in the US House of Representatives from the first session of the 11th Congress. Number of roll call votes: stabilize Afghanistan (9); cut defense (19); support diplomacy (13).
Source: Peter Trubowitz, Politics and Strategy: Partisan Ambition and American Statecraft (Princeton, NJ: Princeton University Press, 2011), p. 147.

as Chapter 2 argued, the lack of clarity coming out of the 2008 election abetted what limited force the conservative critique held, especially among those sections of the American public that soured on Obama's presidency as America's economic conditions remained stubbornly problematic; as the persistence of attempted terror attacks on US soil became apparent; and as Washington's traction on multiple foreign policy fronts refused to yield tangible gains, visible results or major policy advances. While, as Table 3.4 confirms, the president retained the solid support of his own party on scaling-back defense spending and relying more heavily on diplomacy and foreign aid, according to Peter Trubowitz, "The differences between Democrats and Republicans in each of these areas could not be starker."[70] Moreover, Obama's domestic preoccupations clearly outweighed his foreign agenda for most Americans.

Conclusion

As a candidate, George W. Bush had promised in the 2000 presidential election campaign to end the divisiveness of the Bill Clinton years, to change Washington, and be a "uniter, not a divider" – promises that, as Gary Jacobson documented, went exactly unfulfilled as president.[71] Although Barack Obama avoided the Bush language, as was his wont, his 2008 campaign had also promised to transcend long-established lines of partisan division. As he had declared in his inaugural address of January 2009, "The time has come to set aside childish things ... On this day, we proclaim an end to the petty grievances and false promises, the recriminations and worn-out dogmas that for far too long have strangled our politics."[72] Moreover, his campaign relied heavily on the notion that Obama was, Mr Spock-like, the quintessential "un-Bush": cerebral, cool, cosmopolitan, analytic, detached, and un-emotive. Despite his impeccably progressive record as a state and national legislator, his calm demeanor and carefully reasoned speeches promised a centrist, pragmatic leadership style that eschewed partisan rhetoric or doctrinaire approaches and placed reasoned analysis over ideological dogmatism.

To the extent that, in renewing US foreign policy, the president delivered on that leadership promise, the more forceful conservative criticisms of Obama's foreign policies have had rather limited purchase. Inasmuch as Obama was never so naive as to believe that speeches alone could secure substantive policy changes, his efforts at outreach underscored those other acts of his administration that suggested a concrete break with his predecessor in the White House. The State Department assumed a greater prominence, given the emphasis on diplomacy, and the Pentagon was – at least by comparison with 2001–08 – somewhat marginalized under both Gates and, from the fall of 2011, Leon Panetta. A new emphasis was accorded process over decisive or crisp decision-making. And, in a highly politicized environment in which domestic politics and the electoral timetable loomed large, the process was very centralized and driven by an activist White House.

As Peter Trubowitz argues, "At a time when Obama and the Democrats have strong incentives to prioritize domestic needs, a grand strategy aimed at scaling back commitments and reducing costs is what we would expect of this president ..."[73] In pursuing a grand strategy of engagement designed to co-opt others into an American-led order just as a fading US power faced major challenges at home, Obama's conviction was that by demonstrating outreach, humility and appreciation of other cultures and peoples, the necessary, and possibly sufficient, geo-political space could be established to restore US standing and credibility at a time of chronic fiscal strife. In moving from organizing a South Side community in Chicago to organizing the international community from Washington, stealth, modesty and an "enabling" back-seat, reactive role had to supplement traditional "forward-leaning" forms of US hard military and economic power. The world's policeman had to be increasingly preoccupied with the desk job rather than the beat. As Dr McCoy of *Star Trek* might have referred to "leading from behind": "This is American leadership, Jim, but not as we know it."

Such an un-heroic style was always destined to prove difficult to prosecute successfully, clearly or consistently when commentators frequently expect and demand delivery of what George H. W. Bush famously termed "the vision thing." As the distinguished historian of US foreign policy, Walter Russell Mead, argued early in the president's term, Obama's strategic tightrope walk required him to judge carefully how to blend his Jeffersonian instincts – to limit commitments abroad, strengthen the US economy and renew the example of American democracy at home – with his Wilsonian idealism in support of universal values of human rights, the rule of law and constitutional liberal democracy.[74] But the irony – and, perhaps, the Shakespearian-style tragedy – of Obama's presidency was that a candidate who campaigned as a centrist, transformational, and even transcendent historical figure has proven to be anything but such a leader to large sections of an American public seemingly not reconciled – and apparently, in some cases, irreconcilable – to his presence in the White House.

Equally, as the Pew Global Attitudes Project reported, the professorial Obama's teachable moments all too often resembled more the proverbial "blonde" ones instead, delivering little in the way of genuine rather than superficial instruction: in all of the Muslim countries surveyed, majorities refused to believe that the 9/11 attacks were carried out by Arabs; the Muslim world and the West still regard each other as fanatical and violent; and Muslims view Westerners as immoral, greedy and responsible for Muslim disadvantage.[75] Remarkably, by the summer of 2011, America's standing among the Arab world under Obama – after Abu Ghraib, Iraq, Afghanistan, extraordinary rendition, indefinite detention *et al* – was *lower* than at the end of the Bush presidency.[76] As one editorial regretfully concluded, "... for all his fine speeches, Mr Obama's inept diplomacy ended in humiliation."[77]

If, then, elements of the strong conservative critique of Obama's foreign policy were excessive, inaccurate and unfair, the concrete results of Obama's quietly dogged pursuit of strategic engagement were decidedly mixed. On a number of critical foreign policy challenges, the Obama administration found itself frustrated, reversing course, and pursuing divergent paths that satisfied neither realists nor idealists, conservatives nor liberals, Westerners nor 'Resterners.' By examining a series of these key international challenges in the following chapters, the extent to which the attempt to craft a more humble and nimble post-American foreign policy achieved its intended objectives can be assessed – and, ultimately, challenged.

4

Afghanistan, Pakistan and the War on Terror

Our overarching goal remains the same: to disrupt, dismantle, and defeat al Qaeda in Afghanistan and Pakistan, and to prevent its capacity to threaten America and our allies in the future.
—President Barack Obama, West Point speech, December 1, 2009[1]

The US can no longer tolerate Pakistan's a la carte approach to going after some terrorist groups and supporting, if not owning, others. You are playing Russian roulette. The chamber has turned out empty the past several times, but there will be a round in that chamber someday.
—US National Security Advisor Jim Jones to President Zardari of Pakistan, May 19, 2010[2]

We will have to see whether we are allies or enemies.
—Rehman Malik, Pakistani Interior Minister, September 2010[3]

Introduction

While it was far from Washington's only serious problem in international affairs, the most immediate foreign policy priority facing the Obama administration on entering office in 2009 was South Asia – specifically, the distinct but related national security challenges of Afghanistan and Pakistan. In June 2010, almost nine years after its launch, Afghanistan succeeded Vietnam as the longest war in American history. After the George W. Bush administration's initial success in 2001 at removing the Taliban government that had provided a safe haven to al Qaeda and a base of operation for anti-Western terrorist activities, including those resulting in the devastating 9/11 attacks, over time the insurgency became increasingly threatening as American attentions became focused on Iraq and the Taliban regained strength, arms and personnel. Candidate Obama had repeatedly labeled the Afghan war a necessary and a just one, in stark contrast to the "dumb" Iraqi "war of choice." As Commander-in-Chief, the task of winning – and/or ending – the "good" war therefore fell directly to him.

But Obama's presidency saw the situation in Afghanistan grow increasingly grim. Despite two "surges" in US troop levels over 2009–11, three changes of military leadership in theater, and a shift from a counter-terrorism to a hybrid counter-insurgency approach, the war remained unresolved and deeply unpopular at home and abroad by 2012. American combat fatalities increased from 155 in 2008 to 317 in 2009 and 499 in 2010. Moreover, fighting became more intense and the Taliban grew increasingly confident of ultimately prevailing in its struggle to oust coalition forces and regain control of Kabul. At least 711 members of the NATO-led force were killed in 2010, the year of the US "surge" and the deadliest year of the war both for foreign troops and for Afghan civilians. An insurgent attack on a US helicopter in August 2011 caused America's worst single-day loss, killing thirty special operations troops and taking to 374 the number of foreign troops killed in Afghanistan in 2011.[4] Compared to the 2,976 killed in the 9/11 attacks, the US military had suffered 6,234 fatalities in Afghanistan and Iraq since 2001.[5] Against the preferences of the Pentagon civil and military leadership, Obama announced on June 21, 2011 that 33,000 US troops would be withdrawn by September 2012, 10,000 of whom would leave before the end of 2011. The expectation was that a more or less complete US and NATO withdrawal and transition of responsibility for national security to Afghan security forces would be complete, for better or worse, by the end of 2014.

As president, Obama confronted the profound dilemma of waging a difficult, unpopular military campaign that he had inherited and that – especially after December 2009 – he owned in full. Compounding the problem was a paranoid and corrupt Pakistani state, one dominated by the military rather than the elected government. Islamabad remained only notionally an "ally" of the US and the West, selectively cooperative under extraordinary American pressure but enduringly obdurate in its India-centric focus and unwilling to fully abandon the various terrorist proxies that served useful strategic purposes for Pakistan in the region. The killing of Osama Bin Laden by Navy SEALS in an audacious raid on his compound in a military town, Abbottabad, on May 2, 2011 appeared only to confirm the Faustian nature of America's post-9/11 pact with Pakistan. The symbolism of Bin Laden's demise, and the treasure-trove of information accompanying it, were powerful boosts for Obama's standing as Commander-in-Chief.[6] Simultaneously, however, they served only to humiliate Islamabad, to deepen the gulf between US and Pakistani interests in fighting the war on terror, and to strengthen the fears of some observers that America's "frenemy," Pakistan, could yet become the world's second nuclear-armed failed state (after North Korea). Moreover, Bin Laden's passing did nothing to dampen Pakistan's Frankenstein nurturing of terrorist groups such as the Haqqani network and Lashkar-e-Tayiba, or US concerns about nuclear proliferation, the security of Pakistan's nuclear weapons or the country's command-and-control arrangements.[7]

As a presidential candidate, Obama had caused considerable international controversy when he suggested that he might, as Commander-in-Chief, contemplate bombing Pakistan, seeming to concur with his predecessor in the White House that Islamabad's cooperation with Washington was more extensive when threatened with "stone-age" status than when induced by offers of financial assistance.[8] But, as president, the limited options Obama faced in resolving this excruciating strategic problem became ever more stark and frustrating. Despite extensive internal administration deliberations, forward-leaning diplomatic efforts, and occasional threats, Obama's "Af-Pak" predicament remained a serious and unresolved problem with deeply worrying international implications by the latter stages of his first term in office. Some 3,519 days after the 9/11 attacks, Bin Laden's long overdue demise was welcome, allowing Americans some "closure" and the potential finally to reconsider the threat of terrorism as no longer existential. But it did not represent the death of al Qaeda, as an organization, brand or ideology. Moreover, the nature of the covert operation – undertaken without notifying, much less attempting to cooperate with, Pakistan's government, military and Inter-Services Intelligence (ISI) spy agency – graphically exposed the long-standing duplicity of a supposed US ally. While, for some critics, Bin Laden's death represented a form of finality for the 9/11 attacks, and eased the administration's opportunity for drawing down from the theater, the strategic dilemma of how to deal with Pakistan remained acute. Moreover, the prospect of the US effectively having to accept a *de facto* partition of Afghanistan as the price of its exit – with Russia and India reconstituting the Northern Alliance while Pakistan invested its strategic reserve, the Taliban, to prevent their own encirclement – threatened not to end, but rather to extend, a deeply troubling geo-political sore.

Un-declaring the war on terror

One of the most conspicuous, consequential and problematic changes from the Bush administration's approach to counter-terrorism initiated by Obama was the effective abandonment of the term "war on terror" and its various associated formulations (the "global war on terror," the "war against Islamo-fascism," the "long war," "World War IV"). As noted in Chapter 3, a key aspect of Obama's strategy of engagement for the post-American world was predicated on minimizing the focus on terrorism that had been such a prominent – indeed, defining – feature of the Bush era. Not only did such a focus elevate terrorism to an unduly high and all-defining perch among the plethora of foreign policy problems facing Washington, but the widespread perception among Muslims that the US was waging a war on multiple fronts not against terror, but against their religion, deeply compromised US efforts, in Obama's view. Moreover, the panoply of associated controversies surrounding the war's prosecution and implementation – from Guantanamo Bay and enemy detainees held without trial to military tribunals, extraordinary renditions, Abu Ghraib, CIA "black site" prisons, and enhanced interrogation techniques – strongly undermined America's claims to adhere to its own ideals in terms of respect for human rights and the rule of law, opening it once again to accusations of double standards and hypocrisy when it came to foreign policy.

A key theme of Obama's presidential campaign in 2008 was that the very real threat posed by al Qaeda and its affiliates did not necessitate or justify the Bush administration's departure from US commitment to uphold basic international norms on torture and the humane treatment of prisoners, which he emphasized directly in his inaugural address when rejecting "as false the choice between our safety and our ideals." On his first full day in office, Obama issued four executive orders intended to convey a clear symbolic and substantive break from the Bush policies: suspending the operations of military tribunals at Guantanamo; undertaking to close the facility within one year; outlawing torture and requiring the closure of secret prisons operated by the CIA; and setting up an internal administration review of US detention policies. To underscore this new approach, the administration ceased reference to a war on terror. A memorandum circulated within the administration in March 2009 recommended, in place of "Global War on Terror," the use of the term "global contingency operations." In systematically avoiding military frames and language, the Obama administration viewed the *de facto* "un-declaration" of the war on terror as part of its multi-pronged effort at outreach to the world's 1.5 billion Muslims and a new beginning centered on mutual interests and mutual respect.

At an abstract level, such an approach no doubt had much to commend it. The failure to locate an appropriate terminology that adequately and precisely captured what the US was seeking to achieve in its efforts to defeat al Qaeda had been a running theme of the Bush years, attracting extensive academic and popular criticism, even derision. In seeking more precision and giving up on the global breadth that the term "war on terror" had implied, the administration could credibly claim to be focusing on the core substantive threat to US national security while assuaging wider Muslim fears of malign American motivations. In conjunction with Obama's outreach efforts to Islam as a civilization and to individual Muslim states and peoples, the more toxic elements of the Bush era could plausibly be mitigated, if neither forgiven nor forgotten. In addition, such an approach seemed well geared to domestic American opinion, since it expressly conceded that at a moment of national economic limits, an expansive US foreign policy dedicated to an unending war simply represented too expensive and excessive an undertaking. Most estimates placed the cost of the war on terror anywhere from $3–5 trillion.

But for all its virtues, the Obama administration's engagement approach had some highly problematic features of its own. Abroad, as the next sections

Table 4.1 International support for US-led efforts to fight terrorism

Country	Favor	Oppose	Don't Know
Indonesia	55	33	12
Lebanon	35	61	5
Egypt	21	68	11
Turkey	14	67	19
Pakistan	14	65	21
Jordan	9	80	11

Source: Pew Global Attitudes Survey, "Arab Spring fails to improve US image," May 17, 2011, Q52.

detail at length, it failed convincingly to account for US actions in Afghanistan and Pakistan, the "epicenter" of the Islamist terror threat (as Obama described it, in "rhetoric scarcely less reductionist than that of his predecessor"[9]). Not only was the continuation of the US presence a conspicuous exception to the more soft-toned and conciliatory engagement strategy elsewhere in the world, but the substantial increase in US troops in theater, the expansion of Unmanned Aerial Vehicle (UAV) Predator and Reaper drone attacks, and the greater use of CIA and special forces within Pakistan as well as Afghanistan belied – to many Muslims both within and outside those nations – the notion that US policy had become even marginally more benign, narrowly focused and carefully targeted. As Table 4.1 indicates, opposition to US counter-terrorism among Arabs and Muslims remained broad-based under Obama, as previously under Bush.

At the same time – at least until the killing of Bin Laden – Obama left himself open to charges within the US that he was not taking the military dimensions of counter-terrorism sufficiently seriously. Some of his administration officials' convoluted formulations seemed to be euphemisms culled straight from satirical shows such as *The Daily Show* or *The Colbert Report* ("global contingency operations against man-caused disasters" being perhaps the most notable), combined with occasional errors of fact and interpretation (such as Homeland Security Secretary, Janet Napolitano, insisting after the foiled attack of the Christmas Day, 2009 "underwear bomber" that the system had worked, and the president claiming that the bomber was an isolated individual, when in fact he had enjoyed extensive contacts with al Qaeda in the Arabian Peninsula in Yemen), suggested that the downplaying of the Bush-era language was now substantively in error. The shooting by Major Nidal Malik Hasan of thirteen Americans and wounding of thirty others on November 5, 2009 at the Fort Hood army base in Texas and the attempted bombing of the Detroit-bound flight both caused the administration serious political problems. Both had been linked to al Qaeda and radical Islamist preachers abroad, despite initial attempts to depict them as "lone wolves." For conservatives, who mostly supported the Obama administration's increase of military presence and counter-terrorist activity, its linguistic emphasis on avoiding offense to Muslims at all costs was at once misguided and ineffective, while these attempted killings (and the attempted Times Square bombing in New York of May 1, 2010) illustrated precisely why the Bush administration had been so aggressive in its relentless assertion that America was "at war." As Victor Davis Hanson argued:

> As president, Obama has now grasped that at least some of these once constitutionally suspect policies were, in fact, essential tools in ensuring the ongoing absence of terrorist attacks on the American homeland since September 11, 2001, and therefore must be continued. He likewise assumes that most of his supporters will be content with the symbolism of soaring civil libertarian rhetoric and forget the demand for changes in the Bush antiterrorism protocols that has kept them safe – especially given the multiple terrorist plots foiled by existing Patriot Act protocols in his first year administration. Thus, the war on terrorism has undergone a cosmetic surgery of euphemism ("overseas contingency operations" aimed at "man-caused disasters") that will end "the politics of fear" without fundamentally altering existing antiterrorism methods.[10]

Nor did the shifts in language win substantial approbation from the activist base of the Democratic Party, whose hopes and expectations for a complete reversal of Bush-era policies were only partially realized under Obama. On key aspects of counter-terrorism policy and homeland security, the denunciations of Bush's alleged constitutional illiteracy and the ringing and lofty declaration of Obama's inaugural address that the choice between Americans' safety and their ideals was a "false" one[11] met with a much harsher reality. As president, Obama made precisely those necessary choices and inevitable tradeoffs. In addition, although his administration abandoned the assertive language of the war on terror as counter-productive, its reversal of the policies that many of its members had decried as constitutionally suspect when they were out of office was decidedly partial.

Thus – ironically – while former Vice-President Dick Cheney, other members of the Bush administration, and many conservatives castigated the president's alleged "softness" on national security, many on the left instead condemned Obama's "neo-imperialist presidency"[12] for continuing Bush policies and, in the words of the American Civil Liberties Union, "establishing a new normal": escalating the Afghan war; vastly expanding the use of Predator and Reaper UAV drones there and in Pakistan, Yemen and Somalia; continuing indefinite detention, military commissions, and the Bagram Air Base prison; citing "state secrets" privileges to block judicial review of counter-terrorism policies; continuing intrusive domestic surveillance programs; and authorizing the CIA and US military to execute extra-judicial targeted assassinations.[13] Even on rendition, one of the more controversial aspects of Bush's war on terror, as

James Boys argues, "... the policy has not ended with Obama's election, but has been scaled back to a level at which it was believed to have been initiated prior to the Bush presidency."[14]

For many on the left, the stark continuity of policy under Obama demonstrated just how far the war on terror had not only become institutionalized; more subtly, according to some academics, it had also become normalized and embedded in American popular culture, linked by the national narratives surrounding 9/11 and the negative ideograph of "terrorism" to American identity. Given the degree to which counter-terrorism policy accords with the "deep cultural grammar of American identity," its institutionalization in American political practice and culture, and the ways in which it is rooted in the political-economic interests of the American polity and liberal empire, the extent to which Obama could have altered counter-terrorism policy was strictly circumscribed.[15]

Echoing the continuity theme (albeit without the arcane social science jargon), former Office of Legal Counsel official Jack Goldsmith trenchantly dismissed the "Cheney fallacy" that Obama had reversed Bush precedents when:

> The truth is closer to the opposite: The new administration has copied most of the Bush program, has expanded some of it, and has narrowed only a bit. Almost all of the Obama changes have been at the level of packaging, argumentation, symbol, and rhetoric ... The main difference between the Obama and Bush administrations concerns not the substance of terrorism policy, but rather its packaging.[16]

None of this is to deny the important changes that the Obama administration undertook, which resulted in some consequential policy shifts. But, even in symbolic terms, the distance between Bush and Obama can easily be exaggerated. Where Bush spoke of a single "axis of evil, arming to threaten the world,"[17] Obama described a "far-reaching network of violence and hatred."[18] Where Bush described terrorists as "the heirs of all the murderous ideologies of the twentieth century," destined to inexorably follow a similar path to "history's unmarked grave of discarded lies,"[19] Obama steadfastly declared on succeeding him that:

> We will not apologize for our way of life nor will we waver in its defense. And for those who seek to advance their aims by inducing terror and slaughtering innocents, we say to you now that "our spirit is stronger and cannot be broken. You cannot outlast us, and we will defeat you."[20]

The key failure of Bush was not to identify a serious terrorist threat of global reach to the US, in Obama's view, but rather to fail to deal with it effectively where it was most manifest and ominous: in Afghanistan and Pakistan. Obama would, then, remedy that critical deficiency by directing a new urgency against the central production lines of jihadist terror, located along Pakistan's lawless frontier provinces – "the most dangerous place" in the world.[21]

From the team of rivals to rival teams

Anticipating that the Afghanistan conflict he inherited would inevitably be portrayed as "Obama's war," the president approved the sending of 17,000 additional US troops in March 2009. That represented the largest increase of troops since the war had begun in 2001. In May 2009, Secretary Gates dismissed General David McKiernan, the top US and NATO commander in Afghanistan, after less than a year in post (an extremely rare occurrence in the US military during wartime). McKiernan's replacement was a man Obama barely knew, General Stanley McChrystal, the former head of special operations forces in Iraq. The same month, Obama hosted a trilateral meeting with Presidents Asif Ali Zardari of Pakistan and Hamid Karzai of Afghanistan where they agreed a common trilateral objective: "to disrupt, dismantle and defeat al Qaeda." After General McChrystal conducted an extensive strategy review – deliberately leaked to the media to pressure the White House – that requested some 40,000–80,000 additional troops, in August 2009 Obama launched the most detailed three-month presidential review of a national security decision since the 1962 Cuban Missile Crisis, with no fewer than twenty-five meetings to reappraise strategy.

Derided by former Bush officials as another instance of unnecessary and dangerous "dithering,"[22] the protracted deliberations reflected the acute difficulties posed by the war and profound divisions within Obama's foreign policy team. The more hawkish principals supporting a counter-insurgency strategy (especially Clinton, Gates and Admiral Mike Mullen, Chairman of the Joint Chiefs of Staff) were opposed by several officials favoring a narrower and more limited counter-terrorism approach (most notably, Biden, Jones, Emanuel, Holbrooke and US Ambassador to Afghanistan, Karl Eikenberry). Advocates of a population-based counter-insurgency strategy cited the success of the Iraqi "surge" of 2007–09 and the logic of building a credible government in Kabul as necessary (albeit insufficient) to deter al Qaeda's return and prevent the restoration of Afghanistan as a terrorist training base. Proponents of a more limited strategy recommended concentrating on targeting al Qaeda operatives via special operations units and UAVs – "Counter-Terrorism-plus" – as well as the difficulties plaguing a counter-insurgency approach: the partial reach of the Kabul government in Afghanistan; Karzai's rigged re-election in August 2009; endemic corruption; and insufficient Afghan army and police forces to assure order in a notoriously ungovernable, tribal nation. Since it was estimated that only some 150–400 of "core" al Qaeda remained in Afghanistan, a narrowly framed counter-terrorism strategy could plausibly ensure the exit of most US forces within a limited time-frame.

Obama's political pressures, the major divisions among administration principals, and the risk that a weak Karzai government could succumb to a resurgent Taliban without external support ultimately resulted in a political compromise, announced at the US Military Academy at West Point on December 9, 2009. In line with his commitment to remedying America's strategic over-extension, the president noted that some critics had called "for a more dramatic and open-ended escalation of our war effort – one that would commit us to a nation building project of up to a decade." But Obama emphatically rejected such a "win at any cost" mentality, since:

> It sets goals that are beyond what can be achieved at a reasonable cost, and what we need to achieve to secure our interests. As President, I refuse to set goals that go beyond our responsibility, our means, or our interests. And I must weigh all the challenges that our nation faces.[23]

While signaling to Kabul that America's patience was not unlimited, and that a long and costly project of nation-building was off-limits, the president nonetheless recommitted the US and its allies in ISAF to an expanded military presence with a more reduced goal and limited time-frame:

> We must deny al Qaeda a safe haven. We must reverse the Taliban's momentum and deny it the ability to overthrow the government. And we must strengthen the capacity of Afghanistan's security forces and government so that they can take lead responsibility for Afghanistan's future.[24]

The additional increase of 30,000 troops was – in a rare outbreak of bipartisanship on Capitol Hill – strongly endorsed by congressional Republicans, for whom "victory" in Afghanistan remained an urgent, if not clearly defined, strategic necessity. But the Democratic Party base, and important elements of the congressional party, remained unconvinced. By offering a strategy review in December 2010 to determine its efficacy and the subsequent beginning of a troop drawdown from July 2011, Obama sought to reassure his supporters and set a favorable political framework for his 2012 re-election campaign.

The Obama compromise was, at one level, eminently rational. McChrystal had been granted more troops, but Obama and Biden had narrowed the mission from defeating al Qaeda to denying al Qaeda a safe haven and "degrading" the Taliban, effectively mandating both a rapid escalation and prompt withdrawal. But the distinctly un-Churchillian West Point presidential speech – explicit about the financial as well as the human costs entailed, deliberately echoing President Dwight D. Eisenhower's 1961 farewell calls for budgetary prudence and balance among competing national priorities, and directly contesting popular parallels with Vietnam – made one deliberate but telling omission: "any definition of victory."[25]

Moreover, the Obama compromise was not entirely coherent. As one commentary scathingly observed, "Dispatching 150,000 troops to build new schools, roads, mosques, and water-treatment facilities around Kandahar is like trying to stop the drug war in Mexico by occupying Arkansas and building Baptist churches in Little Rock."[26] Symbolically, the "surge" raised the US military presence in Afghanistan over 100,000 forces, the same threshold that Lyndon B. Johnson had reached in Vietnam one year after his election as president in 1964. Such considerations inevitably weighed heavily on the president. But, as one Obama advisor explained, "Our Afghan policy was focused as much as anything on domestic politics. He would not risk losing the moderate to centrist Democrats in the middle of health care reform and he viewed that legislation as the make-or-break legislation for his administration."[27]

As Michael O'Hanlon observed, the message that Obama most wanted to emphasize to the US Congress and the American public was a fairly rapid end to a war that both were fatigued by, through trying simultaneously to "be muscular enough to create a chance to win the war while at the same time keeping the war's critics acquiescent."[28] But the geo-political price of preserving political capital for domestic ends was substantial and dangerous, in signaling to key regional players (the remnants of al Qaeda, the waiting Taliban, the dysfunctional Afghan government, the Pakistanis eagerly anticipating America's strategic departure, and an Iran as eager to inflict fatalities on the US in Afghanistan as in Iraq) that a US exit was now on the horizon. As one US Marine recalled, the most popular saying among Afghan tribesmen was "The Americans have the watches, but we have the time."[29]

Obama's new "surge and drawdown" strategy effectively echoed Richard Nixon's "Vietnamization" approach from 1969–74. "Afghanization" of the conflict was designed to allow US forces to ultimately exit completely by 2014, job done. But, while pointedly abandoning the language of a global war on terror, Obama proved no more able than his predecessor at resolving the central strategic problem that al Qaeda was no longer a major force in Afghanistan, but was increasingly active in Pakistan, Yemen and Somalia. As Gideon Rachman put it, "The west is fighting a war on terrorism in Afghanistan. But the terrorists are somewhere else. Meanwhile, our ability to combat threats around the world is sapped by the huge drain on resources caused by the Afghan war."[30] Expending hundreds of billions of dollars on the fifth-poorest nation on earth had not won over civilian Afghan hearts and minds. Attitudes to US forces ranged from wary to hostile inside Afghanistan, while al Qaeda's ultimate target – nuclear armed Pakistan – remained anything but a stable and reliable US ally.

Nor were hearts and minds in America convinced, 57 percent disapproving of Obama's handling of Afghanistan by August 2010.[31] Perhaps reflective of the relative lack of direct presidential attention accorded the war in public, and the competing views of the foreign policy principals, most Americans simply did not regard Afghanistan as "very important" to the US. In the Chicago Council on Global Affairs national survey of public opinion,[32] released in September 2010, only 21 percent of Americans thought it so, while 39 percent viewed it as "somewhat important." Nonetheless, 55 percent of Americans considered violent Islamist groups in Pakistan and Afghanistan a "critical" threat to US vital interests, and a fairly large majority (59 percent) held the

Table 4.2 Battlefield Trends in Afghanistan, 2005–10

	2005	2009	2010
US troops	18,000	57,000	95,000
US civilian officials	200	415	1,050
Other foreign troops	8,000	32,300	41,000
Afghan security forces	50,000*	170,000	230,000
Estimated size of insurgency	5,000	25,000	30,000
Reported weekly insurgent attacks	60	80	120
US troop fatalities#	58	86	202
Other foreign troop fatalities#	5	70	121
Afghan security forces fatalities#	200*	485*	500*
Afghan civilian fatalities#	300	580	700

*Approximate
#January-June of year
Source: Brookings Institution, Afghanistan Index, Michael O'Hanlon, "Staying Power: The US Mission in Afghanistan Beyond 2011," Foreign Affairs 89 (5) 2010, pp. 63–79, at 69.
Note: Data are for June of each year, unless otherwise indicated.

threat a worthwhile goal for American troops to fight and die for. Despite that, 53 percent believed the war was either going not too well (43 percent) or not well at all (10 percent). A large majority (75 percent) supported withdrawing forces within two years (44 percent) or an even longer commitment – "as long as it takes to build a stable and secure state" (31 percent). A non-binding resolution to end the war, sponsored by Dennis Kucinich (D-OH), was easily defeated in the House of Representatives on March 17, 2011. Nonetheless, despite the lopsided margin of 321–93, while only eight Republicans voted for the resolution (222 opposing it), almost half the congressional Democratic Party voted in favor of withdrawal. How far the Obama administration could sustain public support in the face of increasing battlefield fatalities and casualties (see Table 4.2) and an apparent lack of progress either militarily or in achieving better governance was increasingly unclear.

According to the US Army Counterinsurgency Manual, the US should have roughly one trained counterinsurgent for every fifty members of the population. That equates, in Afghanistan, to approximately 600,000 troops in order to provide security across the country. Even with the more optimistic recruitment estimates of Afghan National Army and police – which, given problems in training, corruption, and retention, remained deeply problematic – considered during the 2009 strategy review, the completed surge of US troops in 2010 would reach nowhere near these numbers. Even with General

David Petraeus in charge from the summer of 2010 through to the fall of 2011, Afghanistan was not Iraq: the former is 647,500 square kilometres in size with a population of 33 million; the latter an area two-thirds as large with 28 million. With Pakistan, a nation of 796,000 square kilometres and a population of 176 million, sharing a disputed 2,430 km border, the prospects of successfully stabilizing Afghanistan were never bright. Even with the extra 30,000 troops, the president gained force strength – albeit insufficient force strength – but lost vital time.

The beginning of a drawdown therefore made good sense primarily in terms of Obama's domestic political calculations. But, as Henry Kissinger cautioned in reference to the beginning of a similar drawdown in Vietnam:

> ... once you start a drawdown, the road from there is inexorable. I never found an answer when Le Duc Tho was taunting me in the negotiations that if you could not handle Vietnam with half-a-million people, what makes you think you can end it with progressively fewer? We found ourselves in a position where ... to maintain a free choice for the population in South Vietnam ... we had to keep withdrawing troops, thereby reducing the incentive for the very negotiations in which I was engaged. We will find the same challenge in Afghanistan. I wrote a memorandum to Nixon which said that in the beginning of the withdrawal it will be like salted peanuts; the more you eat, the more you want.[33]

Such a calculation was made even more pressing because of Washington's parlous relationship with Afghanistan's duplicitous and dysfunctional neighboring state: Pakistan.

Pakistan: failing state of terror

As Ahmed Rashid observes of central and south Asia, "The key to peace for the entire region lies with Pakistan. Pakistan's strategic goals in Afghanistan place it at odds not just with Afghanistan, India, and the United States, but with the entire international community."[34]

Because of the potentially terrifying prospect represented by the nexus of nuclear weapons and the export of radical Islamist terror, Pakistan rapidly became central to the Obama grand strategy. As the president – not entirely accurately, as we now know – described it in his March 27, 2009 speech:

> In the nearly eight years since 9/11, al Qaeda and its extremist allies have moved across the border to the remote areas of the Pakistani frontier. This almost certainly includes al Qaeda's leadership: Osama Bin Laden and Ayman al-Zawahiri. They have used this mountainous terrain as a safe haven to hide, train terrorists, communicate with followers, plot attacks, and send fighters to support the insurgency in Afghanistan. For the American people, this border region has become the most dangerous place in the world.[35]

Possessing an offensive nuclear capacity from 1998, in part due to prior US administrations' strategic and tactical errors in dealing with Islamabad, the possible collapse of the state or its capture by insurgent Islamist forces represents a potential horror story to dwarf the 9/11 attacks. As Obama described it to his former Senate colleague and friend, fellow Illinois senator Dick Durbin (D-Ill), while his plate as president was full of pressing issues, "there's only one that keeps me awake at night. That's Pakistan."[36]

Recognizing that the $10 billion provided Pakistan in military assistance under Bush from 2001 had not produced the desired results, the Obama administration rightly refocused US strategy to embrace Pakistan as the key to stabilizing Afghanistan. The Kerry-Lugar-Berman Enhanced Partnership with Pakistan Act of 2009 provided $7.5 billion in aid over five years, tripling economic aid and rebalancing military and civil-society contributions. The aid package was designed to signal a new era in the US relationship. In itself, though, this increased priority did little to extend US leverage or accelerate a definitive and lasting resolution. Not only was Washington spending only one dollar in Pakistan for every thirty in Afghanistan, but Islamabad resented being lumped together with Afghanistan as "Af-Pak" (relegating the importance of Pakistan as well as tying it to a culturally quite distinct entity) and resented suggestions from the Obama administration that it reformulate the designation as "Pak-Af" (implying, not unreasonably, that Pakistan was the actual threat, not Afghanistan).

Continued military aid had also been initially tied to a yearly certification by the US Secretary of State that the Pakistani military had refrained from interfering in politics and was subject to civilian control over budgetary allocations, office promotions and strategic planning. In response to opposition from the Pakistani military and opposition political parties, the bill's sponsors "defanged the conditionality" measures, the US reassuring the generals that it would not interfere in their affairs, leaving most contact between the two countries "behind closed doors between the two militaries or between the CIA and the ISI."[37] Moreover, with the rampant corruption of Pakistani civil and military structures siphoning-off large amounts of money intended for discrete purposes, in a nation in which only 9 percent of GDP is derived from tax receipts, the US taxpayer was in the invidious position of effectively subsidizing forces that were targeting US and coalition personnel while harboring al Qaeda leaders, other terror networks and Afghan Taliban operatives.

The internal pressures that the US campaign fueled caused consternation within Pakistani society and the military. When asked in a July 2009 *Al Jazeera*-Gallup poll, "Some people believe that the (Pakistan) Taliban are the greatest threat to the country, some believe India is the greatest threat, whereas some believe US is the greatest threat. Who do you think is the greatest threat for Pakistan?," only 11 percent cited the Pakistan Taliban. 18 percent suggested India but 59 percent identified the US.[38] Although such attitudes reflected longer-term trends, Obama's increased assertiveness was responsible for much of the adverse reaction. Conscious of the need to establish his national security credentials, Obama had authorized his first drone strike attacks just two days after his inauguration. In a dedicated attempt to decapitate the al Qaeda leadership, a senior US official claimed in June 2010 that some 650 extremists had been killed by drone strikes in the Federally Administered Tribal Areas since Obama took office. In the FATA, according to one account:

> ... strikes have intensified sharply since the December 2009 suicide attack on the CIA station in Khost, Afghanistan, in which seven CIA personnel were killed. There were 53 strikes in 2009, and 85 have taken place so far in 2010. A measure of the increased intensity is that as of 6 October 2010 there had been 27 attacks in the FATA since early September, most in North Waziristan, the one part of the FATA the Pakistani army has not attempted to enter. Strikes are targeted at specific individuals in line with well-honed targeting procedures and authorities delegated by the White House. Sometimes the CIA launches multiple or successive strikes, adopting an al Qaeda tactic of targeting associates coming to assist victims of the first strike. Generally, the program is directed at leadership, training and planning elements, not foot soldiers, unless they are in training for overseas terrorist operations.[39]

But US drone strikes on border areas, CIA and special operations incursions within Pakistani sovereign territory, and the relocation of al Qaeda leaders to Pakistani cities and towns abetted the rise of a radicalized Pakistani Taliban and associate groups that, while prioritizing national and regional goals, increasingly harbored international ambitions to attack the West.

Certainly, the Obama administration's cajoling and persuading realized some important steps from Islamabad. Towards the outset of the administration, Secretary Clinton had declared there to be an "existential threat" to Pakistan when the Taliban occupied the Swat valley and imposed sharia law just one hundred miles from Islamabad. The Pakistani army killed several hundred militants in Swat, resulting in the biggest internal displacement of refugees – some two million persons – since the 1994 Rwandan genocide. Subsequently, the army focused on South Waziristan and the tribal areas bordering Afghanistan, a major step given the links between the ISI and tribal militants. In virtue of such cooperation, not only has the Pakistani military suffered far greater casualties and fatalities than ISAF, but Pakistani civilians have died in their thousands thanks to the wave of attacks unleashed by the Pakistani Taliban and other Islamist groups: on mosques, hotels, police stations and even – in October 2009 – the headquarters of the 500,000-strong army. Some 34,000 Pakistanis are estimated to have lost their lives to terrorism since 2001.

But while elements of the state, especially within the military and the ISI, were willing – albeit under heavy US pressure – to deal coercively with insurgent forces in the FATA and some border provinces, along with the Pakistani Taliban and those al Qaeda forces targeting the Pakistani government, they were markedly less so in relation to the Afghan Taliban. Arguably, part of the problem with Obama's public diplomacy was an unwillingness or inability to explain to the American public the complex dimensions of the Pakistani challenge: the exact groups caught in the overlapping spirals of terror within Pakistan and Afghanistan. Faisal Shahzad, a thirty-year-old US citizen born in Pakistan, whose attempt to blow up a car bomb in Times Square in New York City failed on May 1, 2010 (and who was sentenced to life imprisonment in the US on October 5, 2010, for the attempt), had been trained by the Tehrik-e-Taliban (TTP), the Taliban branch fighting against the Pakistani government. Shahzad had only become a naturalized US citizen one year prior to the attack, a disturbing indication of the ability not just of al Qaeda but also of previously localized terror groups to recruit "clean skin" indigenous Westerners who could operate more easily in the US and Europe to execute mass fatality acts of terror.

Yet while Islamabad had claimed that it had prioritized the fight against the TTP, evidence suggested that it was simultaneously assisting the two Taliban groups killing US and coalition soldiers in Afghanistan: Mullah Omar's Quetta Shura, based in the south-western province of Baluchistan, and the Haqqani network. Moreover, there was also convincing evidence that the ISI, in particular, was continuing to help Lashka-e-Taiba, the group which carried out the brutal attacks that killed more than 190 in Mumbai, India in November 2008, and which both US and Indian intelligence firmly believed was directly assisted by Pakistan's ISI.

While collaborating with terrorists amounted to "a policy of almost lunatic recklessness," as one account noted, "high-risk duplicity has long been the hallmark of Pakistani foreign policy."[40] With the sixty-year-long conflict with its existential enemy, India, still Islamabad's most urgent geo-political priority, and the perceived security need to maintain "strategic depth" in Afghanistan as and when the US withdrew to prevent either chaos or enhanced Indian influence, Pakistan continued to play a decades-long double game with Washington, regardless of the party or individual occupying the White House.[41] Lacking incentives to induce Pakistan's compliance, and unwilling to use sufficiently coercive sanctions that might conceivably force cooperation, Washington under Obama has remained effectively in a state of strategic and tactical limbo – exasperated but unwilling to abandon a state "too nuclear to fail."

Whatever temporary successes democratic politics have known from time to time there, Pakistan's security policy remains firmly the domain of the army; indeed, it has often been said of Pakistan that while most states own an army, in Pakistan's case, an army owns a state. As the state's strongest and best-run institution, that – along with a sizeable middle class – provides at least some comfort to those fearing a collapse of the state. But, as with prior administrations, it has also left Washington's strategic default position as – in effect – bribing the Pakistani army leadership to commit sufficient resources to staving-off either an internal coup or an insurgent capture of the state. Admittedly, that is far better than the alternative but, as David Pilling observed of the peculiar case of the "state that has refused to fail" thus far:

> A partial explanation for Pakistan's staying power is that it has become an extortionary state that thrives on crisis. Islamabad is well versed in the art of prising cash out of panicked donors by sliding ever-more convincingly towards the abyss ... the state has long maintained a deeply ambiguous relationship with the very elements threatening to tear it apart.[42]

Nor, even prior to the Bin Laden assassination, was the deeply problematic status of Pakistan lost on the American public. Despite the substantial military and economic aid Islamabad received from the US after 2001 to assist in the war on terror, the nation's fragile economy, double digit inflation, dwindling energy supplies, febrile political situation and widespread corruption undermined what efforts existed within the state to crack down on terror groups. The unprecedented monsoon floods of the summer of 2010 – encompassing one-fifth of the entire country, with crops failing, disease spreading and millions rendered homeless – exacerbated the Pakistani socio-economic crisis still further. Moreover, while the US public responded with remarkable generosity to the floods, making the States the leading foreign donor within days, the international response more generally was notably lax compared to that for the Haiti earthquake of January 2010.[43]

Whatever "sticks" the US possessed to prod Pakistani officials into concerted action with Washington remained limited. While administration officials made clear that, should a terror attack in the US be traced to Pakistan, domestic political pressures would mandate a response, what this meant in practice was unclear. The most obvious response was to take action against the 150 or so safe havens that US intelligence held to be operative in Pakistan for al Qaeda and other terror groups. Yet such a response begged the question of how the tenuous "strategic partnership" between Washington and Islamabad could survive in such circumstances, not least since Pakistani opinion – already deeply hostile to the US – would harden ever more irrevocably.

To understate the matter, this series of dilemmas seriously complicated relations with Washington. Among Americans as a whole, feelings toward Pakistan were decidedly cool, at 35 on a scale of 0 to 100, placing it near the bottom of countries surveyed, alongside Iraq and the Palestinian Authority (and this prior to Bin Laden's demise). While only 19 percent of Americans rate Pakistan as "very important" to the US, with 40 percent considering it "somewhat important," Americans are very aware of the threat emanating from Pakistan. Not only do 55 percent consider Islamist groups a critical threat, but when asked if the US should take military action to capture or kill terrorists if it locates them operating in Pakistan, even if the government in Islamabad does not give the US permission to do so, 71 percent agreed that it should.[44]

By 2012, Obama's evolving South Asia strategy was therefore mired in a triple bind. First, Obama's engagement strategy was premised on the notion that terrorism had been wrongly elevated by the Bush administration to a defining and existential threat, when it was merely one of several pressing global challenges for America. But:

> Obama was acutely conscious that protecting the country was his first responsibility, and he devoted more time to confronting al Qaeda and other terrorist groups than to any other challenge of his presidency. That was the main focus of his daily National Security Sessions, his deliberations on Afghanistan and Pakistan, and, in a longer time frame, his attention to nuclear non-proliferation and public diplomacy.[45]

At the same time, Obama was also an obviously reluctant warrior, unwilling to be defined as a war president, experiencing "troubled" civil-military relations, and regarding military conflicts as "problems that need managing."[46] Psychologically, moreover, Obama was anything but invested in either Afghanistan or Pakistan, his rhetoric about long-term commitments notwithstanding: as he noted during his West Point speech of 2009, the nation he was truly focused on building was at home, not in South Asia. On the tenth anniversary commemorations of 9/11 in New York City, Obama barely mentioned Afghanistan.

The second problem was the continuing and deep divisions within the administration over Afghanistan. As Bob Woodward's *Obama's Wars* clearly demonstrated, far from his supposed team of rivals creatively debating and re-crafting foreign policies, on Afghanistan and Pakistan, his foreign policy principals more resembled the feuding rival camps that had historically ill-served US presidents at times of crisis. In July 2010, *Rolling Stone*'s expose of General McChrystal's team and their contempt for the administration's leadership posed a crucial test for civil-military relations.[47] With no real choice, Obama exercised the most direct assertion of presidential authority over the military since Harry Truman had sacked General Douglas MacArthur in 1951, firing McChrystal and replacing him with the only credible alternative, General Petraeus, then head of CENTCOM and architect of the turnaround in Iraq after 2007 that Obama had opposed as a US senator. The president thereby effectively tied his most pressing security concern to the assessments of Petraeus, the most outstanding soldier-scholar of his generation, a registered Republican and someone often mentioned – despite his repeated denials of interest – as a potential Republican presidential candidate in 2016. As David Ignatius noted of Petraeus:

> His discomfort with Obama's July 2011 timetable for the beginning of the withdrawal of US troops was obvious from the start. It wasn't the planned drawdown that seemed to worry Petraeus so much as the signal it would send to the Taliban – and the way it might undercut his political-military strategy. What tribal enemy would bargain with a superpower that advertized its departure?[48]

Petraeus's appointment as CIA Director from September 1, 2011, replacing Leon Panetta as he in turn moved to the Pentagon, partly resolved this dilemma and aimed to limit the potential damage that such a prestigious figure could cause Obama. But it made little difference to the broader dilemma of whether, when, and how to depart the Afghan nation.

If the fact that the general clearly did not support the speedy departure that Obama sought was bad enough, such disarray became even more vividly apparent when Ryan Crocker, who took over as US Ambassador in June 2011, also argued that the conflict should continue until more Taliban were killed: "The Taliban need to feel more pain before you get to a real readiness to reconcile them ..."[49] To issue such a statement – even though it accorded with other senior diplomats' and Pentagon officials' views – when the US, Afghan government and Taliban were in the midst of peace talks that Taliban insurgents were seeking to sabotage illustrated the deep divisions within the administration. According to Ahmed Rashid, the failure of either the president or Secretary Clinton to discipline their officials left Europeans fulminating "at what they see as chaos in Washington where foreign policy appears to be set by an ambassador – while a president cannot decide which side to back."[50]

Superficially, Obama had appeared in his December 2009 West Point speech to promise an early end to the war but, given subsequent qualifications about "conditions on the ground" and the acute problems in building Afghan forces, some knowledgable observers estimated that at least 50,000 troops would still be in Afghanistan through 2012.[51] By July 2011, it became clear that the administration was focused on transitioning to Afghan-led security forces, with most US troops coming home by 2014. But even were this to be successfully implemented, as Major General Bill Mayville, McChrystal's Chief of Operations, observed, the eventual outcome is more likely to resemble Vietnam than Desert Storm: "It's not going to look like a win, smell like a win or taste like a win ... This is going to end in an argument."[52]

Third, and far worse than an abstract argument about "who lost Afghanistan," was the continuing, deeply dangerous double game authored by Pakistan. Obama had made non-proliferation of nuclear weapons a cornerstone of his foreign policy and taken some major steps towards advancing that agenda. Yet, as Adrian Levy and Catherine Scott-Clark put it in their devastating exposé of the questionable deals and short-termism informing Washington's long-term tolerance of Pakistan's progression towards the bomb and its role in proliferating nuclear know-how, all of the world's nuclear-tinged crises from Iran through North Korea to global terrorism:

> ... emanated from the mismanagement of one wellspring: Pakistan ... The gravest consequence of the Pakistan deception was that in the name of political pragmatism the whole architecture of non-proliferation, the robust scaffolding that was erected in the 1950s by President Dwight D. Eisenhower to prevent nuclear secrets from getting into the wrong hands, has been brought crashing down.[53]

The killing of Bin Laden represented only the latest, albeit the starkest, exposure of the Pakistani complicity in terror. That Bin Laden was located in a compound in a prosperous and prestigious military district, Abbottabad, a mere 75 miles (120 km) from Islamabad, strained credulity. As one prominent Pakistani journalist, Cyril Almeida, pointedly observed: "If we didn't know [Bin Laden was in Abbottabad], we are a failed state. If we did know, we are a rogue state."[54] Responding to questions about the role of Pakistani authorities in Bin Laden's tenure in Abbottabad, President Obama noted, "What we know is that for him to have been there for five or six years probably required some sort of support external to the compound. Whether that was non-governmental, governmental, a broad network, or a handful of individuals, those are all things that we are investigating ..."[55] Reaffirming the commitment he first made publicly during the Democratic Party primary debates in 2007, the president restated his pledge to act if necessary to eliminate terrorist threats within Pakistan: "We are very respectful of the sovereignty of Pakistan. But we cannot allow someone who is actively planning to kill our people or our allies' people, we can't allow those kind of active plans to come to fruition without us taking some action."[56]

By the fall of 2011, bilateral relations had reached a new nadir. Following the controversy over Raymond Davis – a CIA contractor arrested for the murder of two Pakistanis in Lahore in January 2011, and released only after alleged Saudi government "blood money" payments to the victims' families – the ISI became determined to identify the rest of the CIA's "shadow network." After Bin Laden's killing, authorities expelled approximately 200 US trainers and withdrew permission for the US to use the Shamsi air base. The US responded by withholding some $800 million in military aid. Later in 2011 Islamabad sought a "memorandum of understanding" with Washington, limiting CIA operations in Pakistan, identifying all CIA agents and declaring what would occur if Ayman al-Zawahiri, Bin Laden's successor as al Qaeda leader, were discovered in Pakistan.[57] The death of twenty-four Pakistani border guards at NATO hands in November 2011 was merely the latest incident in a relationship headed at speed for the rails.

In such a deteriorating context, quite how long the fiction of Pakistan's "alliance" with the US can be maintained in the face of the voluminous evidence of its double-dealing, intimate complicity in terrorism and long-established abetting of proliferation is anybody's guess. But the moment is surely long overdue for Washington to drastically reconsider its strategic approach, much as it had in prior relationships that were clearly not working out as intended. As Seth Jones argued in relation to Pakistan's "dangerous game":

> When US and Egyptian interests began to diverge in the 1950s as Gamel Abdel Nasser gravitated toward the Soviet Union, President Dwight D Eisenhower cut ties and moved on. NATO is at an important crossroads with Pakistan today.[58]

Although mainstream commentators invariably caution against either abandoning or seeking to contain Pakistan,[59] in the absence of such a reconsideration, the options confronting policy-makers in this and successor American administrations will be few and unappealing. As former US Ambassador to Afghanistan and Iraq, Zalmay Khalilzad, rightly noted:

> We have to escalate the pressure on Pakistan in order to finally force it to choose whether to be truly a friend or an enemy of the United States, because the Pakistani generals think they've outsmarted us for a decade by taking our money and at the same time working for our defeat in Afghanistan ... It has sent the message that you can ignore US entreaties and pressure and not take us seriously, and there is no price to be paid. We can't ever forget that it has also led to quite a lot of American troops being killed and maimed by extremists who enjoy Pakistani support.[60]

If and when a withdrawal of US troops begins, Washington's leverage over Kabul and Islamabad will contract, which no amount of further subsidies is likely to compensate for (not least given the corrupt practices permeating both nations). A standing presence in Afghanistan will perhaps deter al Qaeda forces from re-entering the country, but in the absence of removing their safe havens in Pakistan, al Qaeda will remain degraded but not fully defeated. An attack on the US originating in Pakistan would also then compel a response that would likely render the "partnership" inoperable, at least in the eyes of mass publics in the two nations. Should the growing and highly vulnerable Pakistani nuclear arsenal become breached – whether via jihadist infiltration of the military, insurgent attacks, or an Islamist coup – the deeply unpopular prospect of US intervention is likely to become a necessity. As Jack Caravelli, a member of the Clinton National Security Council in the late 1990s, affirmed, "Both in the Bush Administration and certainly in the current Obama Administration the plans exist ... in the most dire of circumstances, that the United States would at least have the option to undertake operations to try and secure those weapons and materials, if necessary."[61]

The more deep-seated and abiding problem is one that is even less amenable to easy or rapid resolution. While Obama's efforts at public diplomacy with the Muslim world were sincere and heartfelt, they did not sufficiently address the basic reality that – as former British Prime Minister, Tony Blair, observed – the domestic and international threat from Muslim extremism "doesn't begin on the battlefield, it begins in the school"[62]:

> President Obama's speech in Cairo in June 2009, which was a brilliant exposition of the case for peaceful coexistence, marked a new approach, and if he is given the support and partnership he needs, it is an approach that can combine hard and soft power effectively ... It was in part an apology, and taken as such. The implicit message was: We have been disrespectful and arrogant; we will now be, if not humble, deeply respectful. But join us, if you will. The trouble is: respectful of what, exactly? Respectful of the religion of Islam, President Obama would say, and that is obviously right; but that should not mean respectful of the underlying narrative which many within Islam articulate in its politics today.[63]

Conclusion: the limits of strategic engagement in South Asia

President Obama inherited an Afghan situation that was in dire straits. Politically, pulling out completely in 2009 would not have been remotely realistic, given the domestic pressures on his presidency and the ambitious agendas he pursued at home and abroad. With national security a traditionally Republican electoral advantage, even in 2008, and having emphatically identified it as the necessary war, ownership meant Obama achieving some kind of credible "victory" as president. But as the important policy divisions among his team graphically demonstrated, devising a plan to do this without creating an open-ended occupation, the expenditure of trillions more dollars, and the loss of support of his own party – all in the face of a sceptical American public – was close to impossible. When asked about the July 2011 date for transferring responsibility to the Afghans for their own security and drawing down US troops, Vice President Biden replied, "In July 2011 you're going to see a whole lot of people moving out. Bet on it."[64] Yet Bob Gates, at a dinner with President Karzai in Washington on May 10, 2010, had stated bluntly, "We're not leaving Afghanistan prematurely ... In fact, we're not ever leaving at all."[65]

By the fall of 2010, respected foreign policy thinktanks such as the International Institute for Strategic Studies were commending a dramatic shift in military policy, abandoning counter-insurgency entirely in favor of the narrower objective of containing al Qaeda, to reduce forces in Afghanistan, deny the insurgents the claim of victory when US forces inevitably withdraw, and free up resources to confront other sources of global instability:

> War aims traditionally expand, but in Afghanistan they ballooned into a comprehensive strategy to develop and modernise the country and its government ... The Afghan campaign has involved not just mission creep but mission multiplication; narrowing the political-military engagement will allow for proper attention to be paid to other areas posing international terrorist risks.[66]

Moreover, while Obama correctly analysed the real source of the terror "cancer" as Pakistan, he proved no more successful than his predecessors at surgical operations to remove it, either by persuading or compelling Islamabad to seriously steer away from – much less abandon – its lethal double game. By increasing US forces and, against his wishes, abetting the Americanization rather than the internationalization of the war, Obama's substantive policies contradicted his stated downsizing of the global war on terror; most Muslim opinion – unsurprisingly – took the former more seriously than the latter in their evaluations of the US. Yet, simultaneously, by de-emphasizing the war on terror and seeking to abandon the overt and consistent securitization frame of his predecessor, Obama gained little credit inside the US for the sharply increased military and covert efforts against al Qaeda, at least until the revelation of Bin Laden's targeted assassination. But while this powerful symbolic act, and the substantive further leads it produced, cannot be gainsaid, in the wider picture the more acute problem remained a state in which democratic forces are entirely secondary to the overwhelming power of the India-obsessed military and terror-sponsoring ISI.

With popular sentiment against America at "shocking" levels, and over 60 percent of Pakistanis regarding the US as an "enemy," a former UK High Commissioner to Pakistan was surely correct to pen the still-born obituary of a dubious "alliance" and argue that, despite American governmental and civil generosity to the Islamic Republic, "rising American aspirations that this will turn the current animosity around seem bound to be disappointed"[67]:

> By 2010 it had become clear that the American efforts since October 2001 to forge a transactional partnership with Pakistan had failed. Pakistan's army had suffered more losses than the whole of ISAF; it felt no gratitude for America's attempted inducements; it declined to do American bidding over the Afghan Taliban, still less in relation to "freedom fighters" such as the Lashkar-e-Tayiba, which was implicated in the outrages in Mumbai; and the opening of US military markets allowed the army to purchase big-ticket weaponry to feed its fixation on India, at the expense of the nation's social welfare. The Pakistani population had further cause to resent the United States: for what they saw as attempted bribery; for diminishing their security and well-being; for increased violations of the sovereignty of a declared ally; and, in anticipation, for the "fourth betrayal" when, as they fully expected, the United States started to pull out of Afghanistan in mid-2011.[68]

The response of Pakistani authorities to the humiliation of Bin Laden's killing was also instructive. Prime Minister Yusuf Raza Gilani made a trip to Beijing within days, returning with a commitment from the Chinese to take over the operation of the port of Gwadar and upgrade it to a naval base. Charges that the Chinese had been allowed to examine the downed US stealth helicopter in the Abbottabad raid compounded the mistrust. The implicit warning to Washington that the US was not the only game in town was abundantly clear (even if such an approach was not entirely welcome in a Beijing rightly wary of its erstwhile ally).

Obama thus entered the 2012 presidential election race with a major symbolic triumph of understandably powerful emotive resonance to the American people: the death of Osama Bin Laden; a scalp that – much to his predecessor's frustration – had eluded George W. Bush. Vindicating the Obama strategy, Leon Panetta claimed in July 2011 that, "We're within reach of strategically defeating al-Qaeda," while General Petraeus had similarly predicted the "strategic dismantling" of the organization.[69] Only time will tell whether or not that broader obituary was premature. But the basic strategic dilemmas facing Obama's administration, much like Bush's before him, remain mostly unaltered by Bin Laden's individual passing and the losses that al Qaeda has suffered in South Asia: a heavy Afghan albatross; a war against an Afghan Taliban coalition that must be a part of an ultimately political solution to the troubled nation's ills; a transfer of control to Afghan military and police forces that remain barely credible as security guarantors for the nation; negotiations between the Karzai government and groups such as Mullah Omar's Quetta Shura, mediated by the Saudis, that are themselves tightly controlled by an Islamabad wary of an unfriendly government emerging in Kabul; a Pakistani state not simply unwilling to stamp out terrorism, but keen to use as proxies terrorist groups such as the Haqqani network and Lashkar-e-Tayiba; a set of al Qaeda safe havens in Pakistan that, despite the administration's best efforts, remain untouched and continue to recruit, equip and train *jihadists* intent on attacking the West; a set of al Qaeda groups outside Pakistan, such as al Qaeda in the Arabian Peninsula and al-Shabaab in Somalia ('the "youth," in Arabic) and Nigerian Islamists that posed ongoing threats; and a US presence that, while beginning to scale down, appears set to remain in the South Asian and Gulf theaters for several years to come. The gravest threat – of the unanticipated consequences of a Pakistan-sourced terror strike, the collapse of the Pakistani state, a war with India that sooner or later is surely probable, or an internal coup resulting in radical Islamists with access to nuclear weaponry – remained all too serious.[70] Exacerbated by the monsoon floods of 2010 that affected some 20 million Pakistanis, the failings of the state threatened still further ruptures.

Remarkably, Pakistan did not merit even a single index entry in *The Audacity of Hope*, perhaps because – as a US senator sitting on the Foreign Relations Committee and a potential presidential candidate – Barack Obama was all too aware of just how vexing a problem it would pose; less something emblematic of hope than of despair. Or perhaps, more worryingly, the absence of Pakistan from Obama's survey of the world signified a lack of awareness of its centrality to American, and Western, national security and counter-terrorism efforts. Whatever is the case, its place in his future presidential memoirs, for better and worse, is assured, as Islamabad's status as either a genuine US ally or a failing pariah state of the first order – alternating between extortion, alibi and virtual collapse – becomes a matter upon which Washington can no longer equivocate and extemporize without severe geo-political consequences and Pakistan's emergence as a new, and unequivocal, enemy state.

5

Iran

*To those who cling to power through corruption and
deceit and the silencing of dissent, know that you are on
the wrong side of history, but that we will extend
a hand if you are willing to unclench your fist.*
—President Barack Obama, Inaugural Address,
January 20, 2009[1]

*When the Israelis begin to bomb the uranium-enrichment
facility at Natanz, the formerly secret enrichment
site at Qom, the nuclear-research centre at Esfahan,
and possibly even the Bushehr reactor, along with the
other main sites of the Iranian nuclear program, a short
while after they depart en masse from their bases across
Israel – regardless of whether they succeed in destroying
Iran's centrifuges and warhead and missile plants, or whether
they fail miserably even to make a dent in Iran's nuclear
program – they stand a good chance of changing the Middle
East forever; of sparking lethal reprisals, and even full-blown
regional war that could lead to the deaths of thousands of
Israelis and Iranians, and possibly Arabs and Americans as well;
of creating a crisis for Barack Obama that will dwarf Afghanistan
in significance and complexity; of rupturing relations between
Jerusalem and Washington, which is Israel's only meaningful
ally; of inadvertently solidifying the somewhat tenuous rule
of the mullahs on Tehran; of causing the price of oil to spike to
cataclysmic highs, launching the world economy into a period
of turbulence not experienced since the autumn of 2008, or
possibly since the oil shock of 1973; of placing communities
across the Jewish diaspora in mortal danger, by making them
the targets of Iranian-sponsored terror attacks, as they have been
in the past, in a limited though already lethal way; and of
accelerating Israel's conversion from a once-admired refuge
for a persecuted people into a leper among nations.*
—Jeffrey Goldberg, September 2010[2]

Introduction

If the notion of a post-American world held forth the promise of transformative change, one important feature of the international landscape appeared mired in geo-political inertia. Barack Obama became the sixth US president since 1979 to be confronted by the vexing dilemma of how to productively shape American relations with the Islamic Republic of Iran. Iran represented "Exhibit A" in the readjustment of US foreign policy from the Bush era, and the marquee test case for the administration's strategic engagement approach, which saw several public and private overtures – some unprecedented – to the Iranian leadership and people during 2009–10. The Obama administration's overt emphasis on multilateralism, diplomacy and engagement received crucial tests in several bilateral relationships, but none so explicitly as Iran.

Iran also posed a fundamental test to the logic underlying the Bush Doctrine and, hence, the extent to which Obama could successfully depart from that logic: no rogue state can be permitted to develop a militarized nuclear weapons capacity that can be made available to anti-American terrorists, not least those for whom martyrdom counted as a divine blessing. While engaging with Iran to find a diplomatic solution to the nuclear impasse, the Obama administration also sought to revive the stalled international momentum against nuclear proliferation in general and to build strong multilateral support against Iran's nuclear ambitions in forums such as the UN and the International Atomic Energy Agency (IAEA).

The notoriously opaque features of Tehran's governing regime make it very difficult to assess how far internal Iranian deliberations seriously entertained any concessions on its nuclear program, still less a broader "grand bargain" with Obama's Washington that might normalize bilateral relations. As Karim Sadjadpour rightly observes, "If 20th-century Russia was to Winston Churchill a riddle wrapped in a mystery inside an enigma, for observers of contemporary Iran, the Islamic Republic often resembles a villain inside a victim behind a veil."[3]

What is reasonably clear is that the ultimate outcome of such discussions in Tehran was a decisive rejection of Obama's outstretched hand. US policy options therefore became focused on four possible approaches (engagement, sanctions, military strikes, and containment/deterrence) and bounded by five possible outcomes on Iran policy: an Iranian retreat; an effective set of unilateral and international diplomatic and economic sanctions; regime change in Iran; containment and deterrence; and military action, on a continuum from covert attacks to a full-scale air assault. With the costs of strong military action widely seen as prohibitively high, and the open endorsement of containment and deterrence a concession of effective defeat, administration policy shifted from an initial emphasis on engagement to one that oscillated between a sanctions approach that sought to alter regime behavior and a more open effort – abetted by covert action – to encourage regime change, albeit from within rather than through direct US intervention.

Ultimately Obama's administration appeared to settle on a policy of extended "wait and see and delay," seemingly more in hope than expectation that either an Iranian back-down, the success of sanctions or domestic regime change might materialize. The administration appeared to reach a consensus of sorts to put off the crisis point of decision – the supremely difficult moment when Washington has to choose between taking military action against another Muslim nation, sanctioning a surrogate Israeli attack, or accepting a nuclear-capable Iran as a *fait accompli* – until a later date, either for a second term or a new administration after 2013. But in some key respects this ultimate outcome appeared to resemble less a coherent policy – never mind a deliberately calibrated strategy – than an aspiration. In this instance, Obama's appeals to "hope" seemed to rely on the notion that a combination of the Green Movement, acute internal divisions within the Tehran governing authorities, the contagion of the Arab uprisings and covert action against the program would together propel the regime uneasily into "the dustbin of history."[4]

But, although the eruption of the Arab Spring threatened a region-wide democratic contagion that could potentially encompass Iran as well, nervous Iranian authorities nonetheless relished its adverse consequences for the "Great Satan." As Robert Satloff of the Washington Institute for Near East policy testified to the House Foreign Relations Committee in June 2011:

> Over just the past six months, Iranian leaders revelled in the demise of US allies in Egypt and Tunisia, the departure of the pro-American ruler of Yemen, violent clashes in Bahrain, and the deep tensions that have emerged between Washington and its two most significant strategic pillars in the region – Saudi Arabia and Israel.[5]

As both domestic divisions and international concerns on Iran mounted during his presidency, Obama's outstretched hand itself appeared to be steadily but inexorably closing in the face of implacable Iranian intransigence on its nuclear program and a carefully calculated pragmatic fanaticism by Ayatollah Khamenei – waging an intense internal battle against the more accommodationist President Ahmedinajad – on increasing its malign regional influence.

Extending a hand, unclenching a fist: towards a "grand bargain"

During his campaign for the Democratic Party nomination and subsequently the presidency, Obama's stated position towards Iran encompassed two key elements. First, he made it clear that he was willing to reach out to US adversaries and seek a dialogue to end long-held enmities and make progress towards new relationships based on mutual interests and mutual respect.

On several occasions, Obama cited the example of Ronald Reagan negotiating with the Soviets as proof that, no matter how difficult and ideologically distant the parties, dialogue was invariably preferable to isolation. In one Democratic Party debate, his willingness to do so "without preconditions" was even pounced-on by his primary opponents – not least Hillary Clinton – as a sign of his alleged lack of international experience and policy expertise, and his more general political naivety.

At the same, time, however, Obama made it clear that the US would defend Israel's security and that, like his predecessor in the White House, no option – including military action – would be prematurely ruled off-the-table regarding Iran's nuclear ambitions. As early as 2007, Obama had asserted that "Iran and North Korea could trigger regional arms races, creating dangerous nuclear flashpoints in the Middle East and East Asia. In confronting these threats, I will not take the military option off the table."[6] Obama also reassured an influential domestic lobby, the American Israel Public Affairs Committee (AIPAC), that he would "do everything in my power to prevent Iran from obtaining a nuclear weapon."[7] A nuclear Iran was "unacceptable."

In terms of his strategic engagement approach, an obvious logic informed a change in how the US dealt with Iran. Bush's "Global War on Terror," Obama reasoned, was a classic example of overreach. Bush had defined the strategic threat as the convergence of state sponsors of terrorism, terrorist groups, and weapons of mass destruction. That definition placed the United States in conflict with al Qaeda, obviously, but also with Iran, among other states. From Obama's perspective, lumping all terror sponsors together was an excessively crude, un-nuanced and expensive strategy: it forced a number of potentially helpful states, including Iran, solidly into the enemy camp. The Iranian regime might be deeply unsavory, Obama reasoned, but it shares with the United States a strong hostility to the Sunni al Qaeda – albeit that it approached the group pragmatically – and a desire for stability in Iraq. While Obama did not appear to share the provocative analysis of former CIA operative Robert Baer[8] – that Iran could potentially prove a far more reliable and effective ally for the US than Sunni Saudi Arabia – a less Manichean approach could nonetheless allow Washington to exploit the overlap in national interests and, perhaps, move towards some kind of more ambitious "grand bargain."

Consequently, Obama defined the strategic threat facing America much more narrowly: as the previous chapter detailed, he declared war to be waged narrowly rather than expansively, with a specific focus on al Qaeda and its affiliates. Iran, though certainly not a friend of the US, was no longer clearly defined as an implacable adversary. On balance, Obama's initial approach leant heavily towards reconciliation, renewal and accommodation, more so – in both public and private – than any American president since Jimmy Carter. In March 2009 Obama recorded a *YouTube* address targeted directly at the Iranian people. The president also sent private letters to Ayatollah Ali Khamenei, the Supreme Leader of the Islamic Republic.

The calculus informing the outreach effort was readily understandable. But the difficulties of engaging the Iranians were threefold. First, the approach relied on minimizing the salience of the form of regime that Washington was dealing with, along classical realist prescriptions. While historic examples here pointed in different directions, the evidence overall seemed to weigh more heavily in the direction of "ideology" broadly conceived as a factor, even if not the dominant one. As with the Soviet Union in the 1970s, ideology did play a role in Iran's strategic calculations, alongside geo-politics. Second, as Colin Dueck notes, diplomacy may be desirable or undesirable, bur rather than being an end in itself it constitutes but one important tool among several in a nation's foreign policy toolkit:

> The notion that diplomatic contact or unilateral concessions on their own can transform hostile regimes is not well supported by historical experience, to say the least. Diplomatic promises and warnings must be supported by other forms of power, including military power, or else they are meaningless in practical terms.[9]

Third, for those other forms of power to be meaningful – whether sanctions, blockades, or the threat or use of military force – the administration (and, ideally, its allies and "partners") needed to be unified in its public face. One of the problems of the Obama administration was that, like its immediate predecessors, the internal stresses and differences among its members occasionally found public expression. In particular, the obvious doubts expressed by figures such as Clinton, Gates and Mullen about the use of military force against Iran substantially undercut the credibility of invocations by others of that particular dimension of US power. Moreover, the Obama administration proved only marginally more successful than its predecessor in assembling a united international front against the Tehran regime.

The Iranian presidential election crisis of 2009

Iran's domestic political crisis profoundly complicated the Obama outreach effort, notably with the popular demonstrations that erupted after the June 12, 2009 presidential election was widely seen as having been stolen by incumbent President Mahmoud Ahmadinejad. While most outside observers conceded the possibility that the president might indeed have won re-election legitimately, the claimed landslide of almost twice as many votes as his nearest competitor was simply not credible. Some three million Iranians took to the streets, claiming the vote had been rigged. Ayatollah Khamenei's intervention, describing the result as a "divine assessment," increased the sense of injustice while undermining his own legitimacy as Supreme Leader. Determined to prevent an Iranian "velvet revolution," the violently repressive reaction to the protests reflected longer-term trends in which the theocratic regime was increasingly morphing into a security state or quasi-military dictatorship, with the Iranian Revolutionary Guards Corps (IRGC) assuming ever greater influence in economic policy, politics and foreign policy-making.[10] The government arrested hundreds of protestors, employed the plainclothes *Basij* paramilitary militia to use brutal deadly force, and detained many young men and women in prison, among reports of widespread torture and rape.

Obama's policy towards Tehran had been one of strategic patience from the outset, in part to afford the Iranian regime time to reach a unified reaction to his overtures, but also because with the June 12 elections no rapid response was likely to be forthcoming. When Israeli Prime Minister Binyamin Netanyahu urged Obama to speed up the outreach efforts with a clear three-month deadline, Obama replied that he expected to know by the end of the year whether Iran was making "a good faith effort to resolve differences." The post-election turmoil both implicitly endorsed but also complicated Washington's new efforts at engagement. In one respect, Obama's open-hand policy in some ways assisted the protests, since the Iranian regime could not credibly accuse a US transparently seeking *rapprochement* with Tehran either of malign intent or pursuing regime change. Indeed, many Iranian protestors were deeply disappointed with Obama's initially muted response, with "Obama, Obama, either you are with them or us" a popular chant. But the popular protests also ensured that Obama faced a difficult tactical decision. Overt public support from Washington could taint the opposition cause, leading to charges of the protestors as foreign puppets and facilitating even greater repression. Yet the size and vehemence of the crowds, and the existing fissures within the Tehran regime, together held out the enticing potential for an internal struggle that could result in an opposition victory. While not a panacea for the US, a less hard-line government might at minimum prove a more willing negotiating partner for Washington; conversely, the popular opposition made the existing hard-line government even less likely to abandon its nuclear aspirations, one of the few remaining sources of its dwindling popular legitimacy.

Many reform-minded Iranians and American proponents of regime change therefore supported a greater emphasis on enriching human rights than opposing uranium enrichment, arguing for ceasing US engagement in order to deepen the legitimacy crisis and hoping that a successful Green Movement would at least prove more willing to negotiate on the nuclear issue. Even prior to Obama's election, even erstwhile "hard-line" neo-conservatives such as Robert Kagan had urged an opening to Iran.[11] With the turmoil in the nation of the summer, though, influential commentators such as Kagan and Richard Haass concurred that the moment had passed and that embracing regime change now made optimal sense for Washington.

Obama's evolving response anticipated that of the Arab Spring in 2011. His relative silence after the elections suggested that his realist inclinations were triumphing over his Wilsonian idealism, preferring a quiet subsidence in the protests so that diplomatic engagement with Tehran could continue apace. But the increasingly repressive regime response caused a steady shift in the Obama administration's approach. In his December 10, 2009 Nobel Peace Prize acceptance speech, the president called forcefully for the respect of human rights and liberties, condemning the "violent and unjust suppression of innocent Iranian citizens," and the White House also that month accorded moral support to the popular opposition by joining the public mourning of the funeral of Grand Ayatollah Hossein Ali Montazeri, an outspoken opposition cleric. But the waning, after several months, of opposition protests encouraged the administration to quietly abandon a human rights focus and instead concentrate increasingly on how best to employ targeted sanctions against Iran.

From engagement to sanctions to regime change

Obama's outstretched hand had yielded some modest movement in Tehran. In June 2009, Iran had requested help from the International Atomic Energy Agency (IAEA) in obtaining replacement fuel for its Tehran Research Reactor (TRR). By October 2009, an offer was placed on the table: if Iran would export the bulk of its low-enriched uranium (LEU) to Russia, Russia would enrich it to 19.75 percent and ship it to France for processing into fuel assemblies for the TRR – sufficient to produce fuel for the reactor. But because the French would take a year to reprocess, Iran would have to part with its LEU before receiving the TRR fuel. Surprisingly, President Ahmadinejad's representatives accepted the principles of an exchange in an October 1 meeting in Geneva (one that featured a rare bilateral meeting with US officials), only for domestic opposition to cause him to reverse course.[12] No further discussions with the P5+1 (the permanent UN Security Council members plus Germany) were to occur, due to Iranian refusals.

By early 2010, US policy shifted further with a renewed emphasis on economic sanctions and diplomatic attempts to increase Iran's international isolation. In May, Iran suddenly agreed to a deal brokered by Turkey and Brazil, incorporating elements of the October 2009 fuel swap. But due to its more lax provisions, the major powers declared it too little, too late. UN Security Council Resolution 1929 was adopted on June 9, 2010 by a 12-2-1 vote, over the objections of erstwhile US allies Turkey (a NATO member) and Brazil, who both voted "no," and Lebanon, which abstained. While far less than the crippling sanctions sought by the US, UK and France, 1929 imposed new targeted sanctions on Iran. China and Russia ensured that there were no measures targeting Iran's oil and natural gas sectors and few mandatory restrictions of any type. The US went along with that on the basis that Security Council unity was more valuable than tough content, of which there nonetheless were some examples: specified categories of arms sales to Iran were banned; Moscow agreed to interpret the ban as including S-300 ground-to-air missile systems Iran had been keen to import; and ballistic missile development activity by Iran was prohibited.

Most significant, 1929 called on countries to restrict a number of financial activities, including transactions involving the IRGC that could contribute to sensitive nuclear and missile programs. EU heads of government agreed on June 17, 2010 to go beyond the UN measures by prohibiting new investment and technology transfers in key parts of the gas and oil industries, and to focus additional sanctions on trade, insurance, banking and transport sectors. On July 1, 2010, Obama also signed legislation – the Comprehensive Iran Sanctions, Accountability, and Divestment Act of 2010 – imposing new extraterritorial sanctions on foreign entities doing business with key Iranian banks or the IRGC and involved in refined petroleum sales. (Most congressionally imposed sanctions on Iran would be terminated if the president certified that Iran has "ceased the pursuit, acquisition, and development of nuclear, biological, and chemical weapons and ballistic missiles and ballistic missile launch technology" and is no longer a state sponsor of terrorism.[13])

In essence, UNSC 1929 reiterated demands made in resolutions 1737 (2006), 1747 (2007), and 1803 (2008) and required Iran to "cooperate fully with the IAEA on all outstanding issues ... without delay comply fully and without qualification with its IAEA Safeguard Agreement ... ratify promptly the Additional Protocol, and ... suspend all reprocessing, heavy water-related and enrichment-related activities." Beyond this, 1929 also: embargoed eight categories of heavy military equipment; expanded penalties against Iranian companies, including those associated with the Iranian Revolutionary Guards Corps; restricted the sale and transfer of missile technologies; prohibited Iranian investment in nuclear industries, including uranium mining; and called for more stringent measures on Iranian shipping, financial, commercial and banking activities.

UN sanctions and penalties against Iran would be lifted if the IAEA Board of Governors confirmed that "Iran has fully complied with its obligations under the relevant resolutions of the Security Council and met the requirements" of the Board.[14]

By tightening the economic pressure on Tehran, and especially through exerting pressure on foreign firms to limit or abandon economic activities with Iranian entities directly or indirectly supporting the nuclear program, the administration sought both to bring Tehran back to the negotiating table and to further hamper the program's advance. But implementing sanctions is typically

an imprecise and unreliable science. Even if effectively adhered to, monitored and enforced, the impact of tightening a sanctions regime is normally unclear. One possibility is that, much like Saddam Hussein's tyranny through the 1990s, sanctions simply serve to entrench the Tehran regime in power. Alternatively, sanctions could – as in South Africa in the 1980s – embolden the opposition forces amid an economy in turmoil or, equally, encourage the regime to enact even more repressive measures to crush dissent. Or, possibly, the economic, political and social impact could be such that they alter the calculus of key elements within the regime to either halt or delay the nuclear program's progress.

The evidence of Obama's efforts here was inconclusive. On the one hand, the various new sanctions agreed to in 2010–11 did appear to be having a serious effect on aspects of the Iranian political economy. The factional conflict and rifts within the regime that had been growing for decades also seemed to be exacerbated by the new sanctions and the willingness of key non-US players, such as all twenty-seven EU member states, to go along with them. After mobs stormed the British Embassy in Tehran in November 2011, the EU also moved to impose an embargo on oil imports from Iran to cripple its economy. As the former parliamentary speaker of the Majlis and a leading opposition figure, Mehdi Karoubi, wrote in an open letter to Akbar Hashemi Rafsanjani, the former president, the consolidation of power by the IRGC that had previously been prevented by the leader of the Iranian revolution, Ayatollah Khomeini, now "threatens the nation": "Chaos is evident in all of the Government's decisions ... The sanctions against us ... are due to the lack of wisdom, lack of expertise and continuous bragging by the Government, especially by the President."[15]

Tighter international sanctions appeared to be biting deep into the national economy, reinforcing Iran's domestic economic problems and fuelling political unrest and dissent. In a nation possessing the third-largest oil reserves in the world, and the second-largest natural gas reserves, the population had long been shielded from the full costs of consumer goods by government subsidies on basic foodstuffs and other essentials such as petrol, gas and electricity. The unsustainability of these subsidies was expected to see their controversial termination in 2011 or 2012.[16]

On the other hand, three weaknesses hampered the extent to which the sanctions could bite sufficiently to induce a genuine shift in the decision calculus in Tehran.

First, the evidence that key states were complying with sanctions packages was not fully compelling. States as varied as China (the only major foreign nation still active in Iran's oil exploration, and for whom Iran represents the third-largest supplier of crude oil and a key guarantor of price stability), Austria and Switzerland have either refused to authorize sanctions or tried to undermine and circumvent those that were agreed. Moreover, Iran was actively responding to the tightening knot by seeking either to subvert or circumvent the sanctions. For example, after the US Treasury Department blacklisted sixteen Iranian banks for allegedly supporting Iran's nuclear program and terrorist activities, other countries responded with their own measures against Iran's banking sector. Iran in turn attempted to secretly establish banks in Muslim countries around the world – including Iraq and Malaysia – using dummy names and opaque ownership structures in order to skirt sanctions that have increasingly curtailed the Islamic republic's global banking activities. Although US officials suggested that Tehran's search for new banking avenues was a clear sign of the growing effectiveness of the sanctions, others interpreted Iran's response as an indication of their limited impact.[17]

Second, while the Iranian economy was adversely affected, this has rarely been a dominant factor in the regime's assessments on the nuclear program's relative costs and benefits. As in the Arab states across the region, the welfare of the people has rarely been a motivating factor in authoritarian regimes' strategic calculations. Moreover, while US, EU and UN sanctions appear to be having an effect to some degree, sanctions have often not generated the sought-after results, even when imposed on nations that are more vulnerable than Iran, such as Syria and Cuba. Strategic patience is also an important issue, since tough sanctions entail political costs and can also erode over time, as was memorably the case with Iraq under Saddam Hussein.

Third, in geo-political terms, the Iranians believed themselves to be in a strong regional position. While, in virtue of this, some analysts recommended either a conventional Cold War-style containment and deterrence posture, others still favored a new detente in which the US would "publicly recognise Iran's legitimate security requirements and offer credible security guarantees to Iran, in terms that relate to objective but not fanciful Iranian requirements, provided, of course, that Iran meets key US requirements, as well as those of regional countries."[18] But as the twin sets of "requirements" in Table 5.1 suggest, the prospects of reconciling such stark differences and basic conflicts of interest remain slight. Iran's shadow wars with the US in Iraq and Afghanistan reflected the core conviction of its leaders that while it cannot properly compete with the US, "it does believe it can exhaust it,"[19] a strategy reliant on the inherent anarchy of the ever-volatile Middle East. By the end of Obama's term, visible symptoms of that growing US exhaustion were increasingly clear as the Arab Spring convulsed the region.

Evaluating Obama's Iran strategy

Like the Bill Clinton administration (1993–2001) previously, which had pursued a policy of "dual containment" of Iran and Iraq that then latterly sought tentative outreach to Tehran under the reformist Khatami presidency, the well-intentioned efforts by Obama to engage Iran were ultimately unproductive, a case less of "hope" than of "giving futility its chance."

Table 5.1 US-Iran security requirements and guarantees

Key US requirements

i. An adequate resolution of issues regarding Iran's nuclear-development program, in particular relating to concrete steps for determining (absolutely verifying) that Iran is not seeking to develop nuclear weapons or even, for purposes of confidence, nearing a break-out capacity.

ii. Iranian abstention from efforts to make more difficult resolution of key issues, both security and political, in Iraq's immediate future.

iii. Iranian willingness to support efforts to stabilize Afghanistan or at least not to make matters worse for the US and NATO.

iv. Iranian willingness to seek positive, constructive relations with its Persian Gulf neighbors, assuming that they would be willing to reciprocate on the basis of common-sense standards.

v. Iranian willingness to abandon support for any organization or persons (including Hezbollah and Hamas) who could be considered to be terrorists or either to practice or support terrorism.

vi. A halt to commentary by Iranian leaders regarding the Holocaust and Israel's right to exist.

vii. Iranian willingness, if not to support the Arab-Israeli peace process, at least not to interfere actively to oppose diplomatic efforts to resolve it in any of its key particulars, including Israeli-Palestinian relations.

Likely Iranian requirements

i. Security guarantees to Iran, underwritten by the United States and others and with a high degree of credibility, provided that Iran met security and other reasonable requirements propounded by the United States and others (especially regarding the Iranian nuclear program but also regarding terrorism, Israel, and subversion of regional states or governments).

ii. An end to economic sanctions, both unilateral and multilateral, and a full reintegration in the global economy and commerce.

iii. An end to efforts to destabilize the Iranian regime/government that can reasonably be seen as illegitimate, especially those that entail violence, subversion or active support for dissident elements.

iv. An end to efforts to split up Iran, including promoting subversion among Iranian minority populations.

v. Recognition of Iran's right to a peaceful nuclear-energy program (this has already happened).

vi. Recognition of Iran's major-country status in the Persian Gulf, within the limits of others' own legitimate interests (Iran would like to be the dominant country in the Gulf).

vii. A role in the future of Iraq sufficient to reduce to an adequate degree risks of spill-over of any continuing conflict to Iran (Iran would like to dominate Iraq if it could).

viii. A role in the future of Afghanistan to reduce the risks of insecurity stemming from the Taliban, al Qaeda or the trade in drugs (Iran would want to have major, continuing influence in Afghanistan).

ix. Respect as a country, society and people, with both equal rights and obligations within the region and in the international community.

Source: Adapted from Robert E. Hunter, "Rethinking Iran," *Survival* 52 (5) 2010, 148–149.

But the Obama administration's approach nonetheless entertained from the outset the prospect of Tehran refusing to unclench its fist and soften its hard-line approach. As Colin Dueck observed:

> The irony of Obama's diplomatic overtures toward Iran is that they may well reveal, more fully than Bush's approach ever could, the underlying intransigence of Iranian policy. Whether or not this result is intentional, it will have the effect of hardening opinion against Tehran inside the United States and perhaps even among America's leading allies.[20]

That was precisely the intention underlying the engagement strategy. The fourth round of UN sanctions, the very pointed Iranian exception to the new Nuclear Posture Review (NPR) of 2010 that made it US policy not to employ nuclear weapons against states that were not nuclear-armed,[21] and the subsequent revival of speculation about possible military action – whether genuine or merely a tactical bluff – occurred after a number of transparent American tests of Iranian intent had conspicuously failed. By September 2010, the effective abandonment of strategic engagement in favor of a type of hybrid policy of tightening sanctions while promoting regime change from within was complete, with Hillary Clinton publicly calling for "some effort inside Iran, by responsible civil and religious leaders, to take hold of the apparatus of the state."[22] 2011 also saw an increase in malware computer attacks on the nuclear program, targeted assassinations of nuclear scientists, and covert attacks on missile and uranium processing plants in Iran – widely attributed to Israel but with the possible assistance of the US and others.

The downside of the Obama administration's much vaunted patience, however, was four-fold.

First, Arab alarm at Iran's growing power grew substantially over 2009–12.[23] Arab concern about Iran has a very long pedigree. In recent years, for example, after the revolution of 1979, Arab states assisted in arming Saddam Hussein's Iraq for its invasion and war with Iran during 1980–88. While unsuccessful in toppling Khomeini's regime, the effort nonetheless halted the spread of Khomeinist revolutionary fervor to Iraq and the Gulf. But the prospect of Iran marrying its arsenal of long-range ballistic missiles with unconventional warheads – including, over time, nuclear warheads – represents the greatest threat facing Gulf Arab states. In the case of Saudi Arabia, in particular, the traditional rivalry between Riyadh and Tehran has been exacerbated in recent years by perceptions of a steadily shifting balance of power towards Iran: the unchecked nuclear program; greater influence in the region's conflict zones, from Iraq and Lebanon to the Palestinian territories, and the construction of a Shia crescent menacing Sunni Muslims across the region; the removal of the *Baathist* check in Iraq and the imminent US withdrawal of all its military forces; and the possibility of Iranian retaliation against Saudi territory in the event of an Israeli, or American, strike against its nuclear and military facilities.

In the fall of 2010, the Saudis requested eighty-five new F-15 fighter jets and the upgrading of seventy existing F-15s from Washington; the UAE submitted requests for Patriot and THAAD missile defense systems along with assorted helicopters, transport aircraft and UAVs; Oman requested eighteen new F-16 jets and upgrades to twelve existing ones; while Kuwait asked for thirty-nine F-18 jets to be replaced, to upgrade Patriot missile defenses and command-and-control computer systems. The Saudi deal alone, at $67 billion, represented the largest order in US arms history.[24]

Beyond the conventional weapons and defense deals, though, the Iranian program also encouraged other states in the region to pursue their own nuclear programs – assisted by the renewed political and economic viability of nuclear power in the face of rising oil prices and concerns about the environmental impact of fossil fuels. Some estimates suggested that by 2025 at least fifteen new nuclear reactors would be built in the Middle East, including sites in Jordan, Egypt, Turkey, Kuwait, Saud Arabia and the UAE. While some states, such as the UAE, had ruled out the uranium enrichment or reprocessing required to make weapons-grade material, the danger remained that other states would be less scrupulous if their security or regional status became under threat.

Notwithstanding such commitments to the IAEA, the dangers of a volatile region in which several aspirant nuclear states exhibited high corruption levels, low political stability and limited regulatory capacity are strikingly acute. The resumption of the Iranian uranium enrichment program after 2005 was married to a fast-track plan to construct a nuclear power plant on the Gulf, just over sixty miles from several major Arab cities, including the Kuwaiti capital. Not only is the plant located in an earthquake zone, but its waste will likely be washed into the shallow Gulf waters, threatening an ecological disaster.[25] It was hardly surprising, in this context, when the Wikileaks disclosure in late 2010 of thousands of US State Department cables featured as a lead item several pleas from Arab leaders to the US to take decisive military action against Iran – most notably, Saudi King Abdullah's request to the Bush administration in 2008 to "cut off the head of the snake."[26]

The second problem with Obama's patient engagement approach was that, while intelligence assessments admittedly varied, further advancement in the Iranian nuclear program had clearly occurred since 2009, as even the ever-cautious IAEA confirmed in November 2011. The revelation by President Obama and the leaders of the UK and France at the UN in September 2009 that intelligence had uncovered a secret nuclear facility at the Iranian holy city of Qom had added to international concern about Iran's intentions and Iranian duplicity. Iran's consistent games of cat-and-mouse and bait-and-switch echoed those of Saddam during the 1990s and early 2000s – a disquieting example, especially in the context of intelligence services' historic failures to estimate accurately the extent of the adversarial regime's WMD stocks. While the Stuxnet computer virus attack in the fall of 2010 and a "decapitation" strategy involving assassinations of Iranian nuclear scientists in 2010–11 – widely attributed, without clear or conclusive evidence, to Israeli saboteurs – undoubtedly created serious problems in the uranium enrichment program, this appeared at best a temporary, albeit important, palliative by Iran's international enemies.

Third, even greater repressive control exerted by the regime on the most pro-American population in the region (outside Israel) occurred throughout 2009–12. Obama's studied silence in the immediate aftermath of the popular protests in the summer of 2009 reflected the delicate balancing act between offering steadfast support to a people whose grief after 9/11 for America's pain was spontaneous and heartfelt – unlike the gleeful street demonstrations of some Palestinians and the obvious relish of Saddam Hussein – and worsening their plight still further by inadvertently discrediting their independence. As a succession of horrific instances of regime brutality revealed, however, such reticence in support of human rights and democratic values did nothing to alter the thuggish mindset of an embattled and divided regime increasingly fighting for sovereign control between the military and the mosque, with elements of the Revolutionary Guard alleged to be complicit in exporting drugs to the West and the mullahs increasingly resistant to the attempts of Ahmedinajad to end Iran's international isolation.

Finally, a reassertion of Iranian influence across the Gulf, the Levant and Gaza was apparent as Tehran sought determinedly to bog the US down in the region and advance an ignominious American retreat. As Frederick Kagan observed, "Iran sees both a threat and an opportunity in the Arab Spring, and it's trying to take advantage and extend its reach by engaging in proxy conflicts all around its periphery, to include in Afghanistan, Yemen, Bahrain, and especially Iraq ..."[27] Despite the inherent contradictions in its approach – hailing the Arab Spring as a popular "Islamic Awakening" inspired by its own revolution in 1979, yet at the same time backing Damascus in its repression of a supposedly foreign-inspired revolt akin to its own in 2009 – Iran's proclivity for pragmatism over doctrinaire religious or ethnic positioning once more prevailed. Even if this appeared to be taking international *chutzpah* to a breathtaking new level, such a choice was especially important in the context of Iran's popularity declining among the Arab masses while that of a growing regional rival, Turkey, soared over 2009–12.

In the Syrian case, for instance, Tehran felt it necessary to balance its interest in preserving a friendly regime in Damascus with its unwillingness to stand squarely against popular Arab opinion. While assisting Assad's brutal repression, some Iranian officials hedged on the ultimate outcome by making contact with opposition groups in Syria and commending reform by the autumn of 2011. Iran's approach to Iraq and Afghanistan, too, amounted to a pragmatic policy of systematically promoting "managed chaos": assisting indigenous insurgents to cause sufficient problems to US and allied forces to hasten their withdrawal, but without hastening a total state collapse that could threaten Iran's vital interests.

Iran thus declined to participate in a January 2010 conference in London on Afghanistan's future, but while Ahmadinejad condemned the US presence there in a visit to Kabul in March 2010, he simultaneously called for ISAF to do more to tackle Afghanistan's narcotics trade, a major problem for Iranian youth. In Iraq, Tehran concluded six agreements deepening economic, technological, health and cultural cooperation between it and Baghdad in 2011, causing alarm among American and Saudi officials that a US abandonment of Iraq could prompt its re-emergence as a proxy battlefield between Sunni groups supported by the Saudi and Persian Gulf monarchies and Shiite militias supported by Iran.

The fundamental dilemma for US policy-makers was therefore no closer to resolution towards the twilight than at the dawn of the Obama administration. If an Iranian nuclear capability, or actual weapon(s), represented a strategic "red-line" for Washington, what coercive measures would the White House realistically contemplate to prevent it, given both the inevitable Iranian military response across the region to American or Israeli strikes and – as Table 5.2 documents – the limited international support for yet another US use of military force against a Muslim state? Well prior to the Obama

Table 5.2 International support for preventing Iran from developing nuclear weapons (2010)

	Percentage willing to consider:		
	Tougher sanctions	Military action	Difference
US	85	66	−19
Britain	78	48	−30
Spain	79	50	−29
Germany	77	51	−26
France	76	59	−17
Russia	67	32	−35
Poland	72	54	−18
Turkey	44	29	−15
Lebanon	72	44	−28
Egypt	72	55	−17
Jordan	66	53	−13
Japan	66	34	−32
China	58	35	−23
India	46	52	+6
Pakistan	19	21	+2

Source: Pew Research Center, *Pew Global Attitudes Project 2010*, Q84 and Q85. (Questions asked only of those who oppose Iran acquiring nuclear weapons.)

administration, a fairly broad (though by no means universal) consensus had developed among the majority of Iran observers that a military strike was, on balance, not the optimal solution to the threat of the Iranian nuclear program. Reflecting the general parameters of that consensus, then Defense Secretary Robert Gates stated on April 13, 2009 that, "Militarily, in my view, it [a bombing of Iran's nuclear facilities] would delay the Iranian program for some period of time, but only delay it, probably only one to three years."[28]

Not only was international support for military action against Iran limited, but the post-Bush American public too was deeply sceptical about US options. While opinion surveys confirmed that most Americans supported actions to try to stop Iran enriching uranium and developing a weapons program, they were hesitant about resorting to military action because of the perceived dangers and presumed limits of such a response. Even though 54 percent opposed restoring diplomatic relations with Iran, for example, 62 percent favored US leaders meeting and talking with Iran's leaders. Only 18 percent agreed that the US should carry out a military strike against Iran's energy facilities, with 41 percent preferring economic sanctions and 33 percent wanting to continue diplomatic efforts to encourage Iran to cease enriching uranium. 77 percent nonetheless opposed engaging in trade activities with Iran.[29]

Having said that, while Americans were pessimistic about the prospects of a strike causing Iran to give up its nuclear program, or even slowing it down, and believed that an attack would increase Muslim hostility to the US and prompt retaliatory action against US targets in the region and even America itself, almost as many supported a military strike (47 percent) as opposed it (49 percent) in the event that diplomacy and economic sanctions ultimately failed.[30] It is worth noting in this context that, far more so than Iraq, Afghanistan or Pakistan, the place of Iran in American history has a very powerful resonance, given the chequered post-1979 history: the fall of the Shah, the American Embassy hostages held by the regime, the abortive rescue attempt in 1980, and the Iran-Contra affair. There are, after all, few other nations in which a presidential candidate could happily recite in public a popular song calling for another nation's bombing (and relatively few where such a popular song would be made [and reissued seven years later]).[31] Moreover, among the commentariat, the options for military intervention were not universally held to be prohibitively costly. As Amitai Etzioni argued, it may be that a successful military strike need not – and perhaps should not – target the nuclear facilities in whole or even part in order to induce the required effect on the existing, or an alternative, Iranian governing regime.[32]

As the Arab Spring erupted, ebbed and flowed through 2011, and the Obama administration became increasingly erratic in dealing with the unanticipated popular challenges to entrenched (and, mostly, pro-US) Arab autocrats, it became increasingly apparent that the prospect – if it ever had existed – of large-scale US military action against Iran was now minimal under Obama's leadership. Admittedly, the president still sought to provide reassurance about the steadfastness of the US position. In his May 22, 2011 speech to AIPAC, Obama stated:

> You also see our commitment to our shared security in our determination to prevent Iran from acquiring nuclear weapons ... Its illicit nuclear program is just one challenge that Iran poses. As I said on Thursday, the Iranian government has shown its hypocrisy by claiming to support the rights of protesters while treating its own people with brutality. Moreover, Iran continues to support terrorism across the region, including providing weapons and funds to terrorist organizations. So we will continue to work to prevent these actions, and will stand up to groups like Hezbollah who exercise political assassination, and seek to impose their will through rockets and car bombs.

But the uprisings across North Africa, the Gulf and the Levant distracted both American and international attentions from Iran's nuclear program. Moreover, as Jennifer Rubin observed, Obama no longer even offered the standard mention of "all options being on the table." As she ruefully concluded, "The threat of military action is now clearly not credible."[33]

Iraq

One final factor in the Obama administration's strategic calculus was bringing to a ultimate end the expensive and unpopular eight-year war with Iraq. The Bush administration had negotiated the Strategic Framework Agreement and the Status of Forces Agreement towards the end of 2008; the former laid out a framework for future US-Iraqi cooperation on matters such as diplomacy, trade, education, science and technology, while the latter committed all US forces to be removed from Iraq by December 31, 2011. Obama increased the momentum by withdrawing all US combat forces by August 2010, leaving a remaining presence of 50,000 troops for training, counter-terrorism and selective combat operations with Iraqi forces.

But with 46,000 US troops still in the country in the summer of 2011, and despite the looming urgency of the end-of-year deadline, American and Iraqi forces found it difficult to agree what a follow-on US presence – and the broader bilateral relationship – might look like. Despite his pledge for a complete withdrawal, the Obama administration had made it clear to Iraqis that they would provide a stay-on presence if so requested. The benefits of such a force appeared clear: helping to defend Iraq's porous borders, preventing Iranian weapons smuggling and insurgent meddling, providing counter-terrorism support against al Qaeda in Mesopotamia, and reassuring Iraqi

Kurdistan. Above all, for US strategic interests, an American presence could help to maintain Iraqi independence from Tehran's malign orbit.

American officials were insistent that the Iraqi government had to come forward with a request, placing the responsibility for a long-term US presence on the fragile coalition of Prime Minister Nouri al-Maliki. But, while al-Maliki was granted the authority to engage in negotiations in August 2011, he did not make a public request for the US to stay. al-Maliki feared the political costs such an extension of the "occupation" would imply, and depended for support on the Shiite party of Moqtada al-Sadr – an Iranian client who threatened that his militia would wage war against US troops if they remained in Iraq. The protracted process of internal bargaining in the Iraqi government compounded the problem of being seen to concede the desirability of US forces staying put.

At the same time, the Obama administration was once again wrestling with its own internal rifts and rivalries. Eager to depart in a responsible manner that safeguarded the post-invasion political settlement, the Pentagon – including the US Commander in Iraq, General Lloyd Austin – had lobbied for follow-on forces ranging from 14,000 to 18,000 troops. But senior Pentagon officials let it be known in early September 2011 that a much lower number, reputed to be in the range of 3,000, had been imposed by the White House as adequate, if not optimal, for US interests.[34] Much as had occurred previously over the surge and drawdown in Afghanistan, strategic considerations were trumped by domestic ones for Obama. Ensuring the withdrawal of almost all US forces and underscoring the end of the Iraq war would represent a timely asset to his re-election ambitions and "nation-building" at home. But in strategic terms, a US force of fewer than 10,000 would encounter serious problems in defending itself against Iranian-sponsored militants and al Qaeda, much less carrying out effective training or counter-terrorism missions. It also would necessitate abandoning any effort to prevent violence in Kurdistan. In the context of an already deteriorating security situation – with attacks by Sunni *jihadists* on the increase and the Sadrists threatening to mobilize – a premature US withdrawal could threaten to unravel the fragile gains of the 2007–11 years, imperilling Iraqi sovereignty and stability and empowering Iranian ambitions still further. As even the normally pro-Obama *Washington Post* argued, "Any continuing military mission in Iraq should be founded on clear goals and a calculation of the troops needed to accomplish them – not an estimate of what troop number will acceptable to Congress or the president's base of supporters."[35] Ultimately, the failure of the Obama administration to secure a deal that provided US forces with immunity from Iraqi lawsuits resulted in, once more, an outcome more congenial to the president's domestic electoral interest than necessarily America's strategic one: the withdrawal of all US troops from Iraq by the end of 2011.

Conclusion: the limits of strategic engagement with Iran

Despite the unmistakeable symbolic contrast with its immediate predecessor, the Obama administration encountered very similar challenges in seeking even a mild *rapprochement* with Tehran, much less the "grand bargain" often touted by "realist" foreign policy commentators: a fractious Iranian regime mired in intra-conservative and theocratic convulsions, corrupt and despised by the Iranian people; a growing crisis of state legitimacy, founded on a set of chronically dysfunctional economic and social problems and exacerbated by the fraudulent presidential election of 2009 and subsequent repression; an appalling tolerance for human rights abuses, torture and terrorism; an abiding desire to project regional influence by stoking anti-Sunni, anti-Jewish and anti-Western sentiments, harboring and supplying terrorists (not just from Hezbollah and Hamas but also al Qaeda and other groups) and targeting US forces in Iraq and Afghanistan; and a dogged pursuit of an Iranian nuclear capacity that serves as the only moderately unifying force in an otherwise deeply divided and fissiparous society, one characterized by pervasive ethnic, religious and socio-economic divisions.

Faced by such intractable and unpropitious forces, the Obama administration's attempts to effect a post-American foreign policy through moves towards normalizing bilateral relations were always likely to encounter close to insurmountable obstacles. However commendable and sincere the effort, by the fall of 2009 the weight of opinion within the administration was shifting to a harder-line position, one remarkably reminiscent of the Bush administration post-2004 but strengthened politically by the consistent Iranian rejection of Washington's transparently clear wish for improved bilateral relations.

Predictably enough, Obama's evolving positions – from outreach to sanctions to a *sotto voce* endorsement of regime change from within married to covert operations – encountered caustic opposition from both ends of the political spectrum. On the left, in a typically sober and balanced castigation, veteran Marxist agitator Tariq Ali lamented that "From Palestine through Iraq to Iran, Obama has acted as just another steward of the American empire, pursuing the same aims as his predecessors, with the same means but with a more emollient rhetoric."[36] In similarly judicious and restrained commentary, the Iranian scholar Elaheh Rostami-Povey asserted that "the US policy of asserting global control over strategic resources – especially oil – and expanding its power militarily, economically and politically is continuing under Barack Obama," as clearly demonstrated in the president's continuing support for Israel and the lack of "substance" to his supposed outreach to Muslims worldwide:

> The Obama administration has seemingly not learned the lessons of the failure of these policies and of the death and destruction they have brought to the people of the

Middle East as well as to the US military. Therefore, sanctions, "regime change" and democratization Iraq- and Afghanistan-style are on the agenda, and the threat of war with Iran persists. Although unilateralism is unlikely under Obama's administration, multilateralism is just a tactical adjustment, reflecting an accommodation to the limits of American power rather than a strategic reorientation.[37]

On the right, Tehran remained an outpost of extremism that the US should altogether shun, recognizing that as far as engagement was concerned, that dog was never going to hunt. Obama's outreach efforts represented yet another instance of a naive and weak post-American foreign policy – one which imagined that apologizing for American arrogance and errors could somehow magically yield a "forgive-and-forget" reciprocal gesture from a tyrannically thuggish theocratic regime intent on stoking regional fires rather than putting them out. Reflecting on the Undersecretary (and latterly, Deputy Secretary) of State, William Burns's, testimony on Iran to the House Foreign Affairs Committee on December 1, 2010 – in which Burns noted US concerns about Iran before observing that there was "still room for a renewed effort to break down mistrust, and begin a careful, phased process of building confidence between Iran and the international community" and declaring that "The door is still open to serious negotiation, if Iran is prepared to walk through it" – Stephen Hayes and Thomas Joscelyn argued:

> Yet Burns said nothing about Iran's efforts to fund, train, and equip jihadists in Afghanistan. He said nothing about the extensive Iranian backing of radical Shiite groups in Iraq over the past seven years. He said nothing of Iran's ongoing support for al Qaeda – support that might have been particularly interesting to his audience of American lawmakers. In his remarks on Capitol Hill, Burns simply chose not to mention that the leaders of Iran have been fighting a stealth war against the United States, its soldiers, and its citizens. It is this fact that complicates the Obama administration's efforts to engage Iran. So it is simply set aside.[38]

Certainly, the Obama administration's approach reflected an important underlying difference with his predecessor. Unlike the Bush administration, which took seriously the proposition that regime type had an important effect on external behavior (at least until 2006[39]), the Obama administration viewed Tehran through a classical realist lens, as simply one among many states with whom it could – potentially – do constructive business, despite its more disagreeable practices, internal repression and destabilizing regional policies. But the central and inescapable feature of Iran's strategic personality in the Middle East is that it views itself as the pre-eminent geo-strategic rival to Washington – not to mention Saudi Arabia and Israel – rather than as a potential partner. Moreover, while the priority for the Obama administration was the Iranian nuclear program, too myopic a focus on cutting a deal on that alone – while a very desirable outcome, without doubt – would neglect the multiple ways in which Iranian interests and ambitions pervade the region and run directly against those of the US. As the leading British scholar of Iran, Ali Ansari, wrote:

> ... the nuclear impasse is a consequence of a far wider problem between Iran and the United States, not its cause. A solution to the nuclear issue will only defer and not solve the Iranian question. That question, which has been inherited by the United States, can trace its roots further back than 1979 or 1953, to the humiliation of Turkmenchai in 1828 and the gradual realization that Iran has suffered an imperial fall from grace. Our current preoccupation with the nuclear issue should not deflect us from the fundamentals of this historic situation and the political myths it provides.[40]

Or, to put it another way, as one former Iranian president explained, Ayatollah Khamenei's position is, *"Ma doshmani ba Amrika ra lazem dareem"*: "We need enmity with the United States."[41] By the latter stages of his first term, Obama appeared to finally be reconciled to the notion that no amount of bridge-building or strategic engagement could alter that fundamental feature of Iranian statecraft: in turn, isolating Iran as far as feasibly possible became the central goal of American statecraft.

Where to go from there, however, remained highly problematic. The *New York Times* reported in January 2010 that a memo from Bob Gates to the White House claimed the administration lacked an effective strategy to counter Iran in the event that existing policies failed. While the Secretary subsequently claimed the memo had been "mischaracterized," it was widely seen as a prelude for a resigned acceptance of a nuclear-capable Iran and a nascent shift to a Cold War-style strategy of containment and deterrence, rather than a military confrontation damaging to America's regional position. Although other members of the administration repeated the familiar mantra of "all options" still being on the table, Secretary Clinton had seemingly given the strategic game away when she stated in Thailand on July 22, 2009 that, "If the US extends a defensive umbrella over the region, it's unlikely that Iran will be any stronger or safer, because they won't be able to intimidate and dominate, as they apparently believe they can, once they have a nuclear weapon."[42] Gates, too, made clear on a number of occasions his strongly sceptical view of the utility or efficacy of military action. Such positions won modest international relief at the price of substantially undercutting the credibility of the military option within the overall US posture towards Iran, while simultaneously unnerving America's Arab allies in the region and Israel.

Moreover, the brute reality remains that Iran is already nuclear capable – it possesses the technology to produce fissile material. Its leaders must judge how close to crossing the red line to nuclear weapons production and how large a stockpile of LEU it can accumulate before it provokes a large-scale military response from – if not the US under Obama – Israel. Facing what Tel Aviv perceives as the genuine threat of another *Shoah*, how far Israeli tolerance of Iran's efforts would last remained to be seen, since the Israelis themselves are clearly divided on how much of a threat a nuclear Iran would pose and on the merits of a military attack to prevent such an outcome. Moreover, in terms of domestic American opinion, Iran is one of the relatively few global issues where bipartisanship still prevails, with Democrats and Republicans overwhelmingly agreed on a tough line – a position likely to intensify even further in the absence of an American diplomatic breakthrough or economic sanctions working (during the Republican Party presidential debate in Iowa of August 11, 2011, for example, only the neo-isolationist Ron Paul [R-TX] departed from a strongly anti-Iranian line). As Andrew Parasiliti presciently observed in October 2010:

> There seems to be only a fragile and largely unenthusiastic congressional constituency for engagement with Iran, and no constituency for living with an Iranian nuclear weapon. Congressional pressure on Iran will likely increase mid-2011 and into the 2012 US presidential campaign, especially if Republicans enjoy substantial gains in the November 2010 congressional elections. Republicans may seek to portray President Obama as naive or misguided for seeking to engage Iran.[43]

As the intended marquee example for strategic engagement, Iran proved the gravest disappointment. The upheavals across the Middle East, the feuding between Washington and its key allies in Tel Aviv and Riyadh, the internal fissures in the regime, and the advance of Tehran's nuclear program and regional ambitions together provided explosive potential. Dana Allin and Steve Simon ominously but accurately concluded in their review of the increasingly parlous predicament: "The compressed coil of disaster linking Iran, Israel and the United States is not the only problem facing the Obama administration, and it may not even be its worst problem. But Iran's defiance and Israel's panic are the fuses for a war that could destroy all of Obama's other ambitions."[44] Even if this now appears an unlikely outcome for Obama's presidency, it may yet prove prescient for whoever occupies the White House after January 2013.

6

Israel, Palestine and the Arab Spring

And so to all other peoples and governments who are watching today, from the grandest capitals to the small village where my father was born: Know that America is a friend of each nation and every man, woman and child who seeks a future of peace and dignity, and that we are ready to lead once more.
—President Barack Obama, Inaugural Address, 2009[1]

One benefit of the Obama Presidency is that it is validating much of George W. Bush's security agenda and foreign policy merely by dint of autobiographical rebranding. That was clear enough yesterday in Cairo, where President Obama advertised "a new beginning between the United States and Muslims around the world." But what he mostly offered were artfully repackaged versions of themes President Bush sounded with his freedom agenda.
—"Barack Hussein Bush," *Wall Street Journal* editorial, June 5, 2009[2]

... a voluntary agreement between the parties is unattainable. The only possible path forward is an externally imposed solution.
—Avi Shlaim, *Israel and Palestine*[3]

... an administration strongly committed to pursuing Arab-Israeli peace almost always trumps the opposition of domestic interest groups, but not without some messy fights ...
—Aaron David Miller, *The Much Too Promised Land*[4]

Introduction

Unlike both his immediate White House predecessors – Bill Clinton and George W. Bush – Barack Obama had publicly pledged to focus from day one of his presidency on advancing a lasting settlement of the Israel-Palestinian conflict, both for its intrinsic importance and because he viewed rapid progress on this festering strategic sore as being essential for securing wider US national interests in the Middle East and beyond. While Bush had waited several years before seriously confronting the problem, in part because of Clinton's frustrating experiences negotiating a peace settlement during his final year of office, Obama's engagement strategy was launched from his first day in the Oval Office. As an illustration of its priority status, the president's first international phone call from the White House was to Palestinian Authority president Mahmoud Abbas, followed by calls to then Israeli Prime Minister Ehud Olmert, President Hosni Mubarak of Egypt and King Abdullah II of Jordan. On his second day in office the president then named the well-respected former Democratic senator from Maine, George Mitchell – Clinton's successful envoy in the Northern Ireland Peace Process – as his Middle East special envoy.

But, much as for several of his predecessors, few issues proved as stubbornly intractable. Obama himself considered the Israel-Palestinian conflict his one area of foreign policy "failure" in 2009, conceding that the administration had "overestimated our ability to persuade" the two parties to take concrete steps to advance the peace process "when their (domestic) politics ran contrary to that."[5] Complicating the president's task was not only the missteps of his own administration on the issue and the intransigence of the Binyamin Netanyahu coalition government in Israel, but also the sweeping protests across the region that saw long-standing US allies overthrown or challenged in the so-called "Arab Spring" of 2011. In one of the many ironies of his administration, having repudiated his predecessor's ambitious reform agenda for the Middle East and seeking instead to re-orient the priority of US foreign policy to the Asia-Pacific, Obama found himself – reluctantly and after considerable internal deliberation and disagreement – supporting, albeit highly selectively, the very "freedom agenda" that he had previously shied away from; in turn prompting emotive accusations that the president "has no alternative strategic vision to replace the neo-conservative fantasies of his predecessor" and "that the United States has little to offer the region and its people."[6]

Obama found himself caught on the horns of the historic strategic dilemma of US foreign policy: between a realist policy focused on influencing the external behavior of states and their inter-relations, and an idealist one seeking to alter the internal nature of states. Much as the momentous events of September 11, 2001 had transformed George W. Bush's initially "humble" foreign policy into something much more ambitious, so Obama's early distancing himself from the region in pursuit of an Asian-Pacific priority was – at least for 2011 – temporarily confounded by the dramatic and destabilizing uprisings from Tunisia to Syria.

By the latter stages of his first term, the Middle East had assumed a prominent part of a post-American international landscape, but with Washington keener to lead from behind than from the front. American foreign policy towards the region remained in uncertain flux, traditional US allies having been displaced, Saudi Arabia and Iran having become engaged in a proxy war across the region, Israel and Iran effectively in the midst of a secret war, and conditions on the ground having made a genuine peace between Israelis and Palestinians even more dim and distant than in 2009.

Moreover, the impending transformation of the Arab states augured poorly for existing peace treaties between Israel and its neighbors, with the voice of Arab peoples no more favorable towards either the US or Israel at the end of Obama's first term than at its outset: an outcome given vivid expression by the Muslim Brotherhood in Egypt, and the more extreme Salafist parties, together winning some 60 percent of the vote in the nation's November 2011 parliamentary elections. As Robert Kaplan argues, "In truth, the Middle East is undergoing less a democratic revolution than a crisis in central authority,"[7] one with unstable and decidedly troubled futures. Far from the Arab Uprising having made what Netanyahu regularly referred to as a "tough neighborhood" more gentrified, the region threatened to get still tougher, not only for its long-suffering residents but also for the preservation of US national interests and influence. Moreover, in resisting Washington's waxing and waning pressures to compromise and conciliate, an Israel facing concerted attempts at "de-legitimation" delivered to President Obama what some regarded as "the most dramatic foreign-policy defeat of his first term in office."[8] By the latter part of his term, with Saudi Arabia threatening ominously to end its own "special relationship" with Washington, America's evaporating influence in the Middle East threatened to reach rock bottom amid a diplomatic tsunami of epic proportions.

Obama's strategic options

After the attacks of 9/11, the Middle East became the key theater of US foreign policy for the first time in American history. The controversial policies of the Bush administration, and in particular the 2003 invasion of Iraq and subsequent occupation, prompted widespread outrage within the region and polarized debate within the United States. In response, some scholars of US foreign policy effectively embraced a neo-isolationist position, arguing that the region's reliably dystopian features made it "the middle of nowhere" and calling for US withdrawal.[9] Others, however, insisted that its geo-political importance and centrality to the functioning of the global economy was such that the US needed to remain engaged, no matter how difficult, frustrating and costly the commitment.[10] For the Obama administration, although the inherited problem of Iraq, the festering wound of Israeli-Palestinian conflict and the rising challenge of Iran all demanded urgent attention, the increasing importance of the Asia-Pacific region to US geo-political interests recommended instead a decisive rebalancing of Washington's focus away from the Middle East.

In strategic terms, the fundamental national interests of the US in the Middle East are broadly agreed upon by most observers within the Beltway: ensuring the uninterrupted flow of oil at stable and reasonable prices (not so much for US consumption but rather to sustain the global economy); blocking the proliferation of weapons of mass destruction, and nuclear weapons in particular; protecting key US and Western allies, including Israel, Saudi Arabia and Egypt; countering terrorism, political violence and extremism; and promoting democratic and liberalizing reform in ways that bolster rather than undermine a US-led regional order. How best to accomplish these multiple goals invariably poses a major test for policy-makers in Washington of both parties.

As Michael Scott Doran argues,[11] three approaches offered distinct perspectives on which principles should best guide US strategy in navigating the region's internecine conflicts and multiple challenges on Obama's assuming office in 2009. First, reflecting traditional Wilsonian precepts and the long-standing repression of the Arab peoples under authoritarian or monarchical rule, one perspective emphasizes the enlargement of political participation as the key step towards a more stable and just region, stressing democracy promotion as the touchstone for the US's regional strategy. A second view rejects overarching principles such as democratization or liberalization entirely, instead highlighting the complexity of the region, the distinctive challenges of each state therein, and advocating an un-doctrinaire, pragmatic country-by-country approach. A third perspective views the achievement of an elusive Arab-Israeli peace, including the establishment of a functional Palestinian state, as the essential first step towards boosting US credibility and revitalizing the US-led regional order.

As elsewhere, Obama's strategic engagement ebbed and flowed between these approaches across time. Initially, as his early phone calls indicated, the administration made the Arab-Israeli peace process the organizing principle of its Middle East policy. Indeed, rarely had a US president so clearly and repeatedly focused on the cause of peace as a strategic priority for Washington. In his June 2009 Cairo speech pledging a "new beginning between the United States and Muslims around the world," for instance, Obama expressly identified "the situation between Israelis, Palestinians, and the Arab world" as a major cause of tension between America and Muslims.[12] Seeking to demonstrate American goodwill and casting the US as an honest broker under his leadership, the peace process thus became more than just a practical instrument for normalizing relations between Israel and its neighbors – it also emerged as, in effect, the defining litmus-test of American intentions towards Arabs and Muslims worldwide. As such, regardless of tangible outcomes, the peace process could not be abandoned under Obama as long as the US wished to continue to demonstrate goodwill towards the Muslim world.

Such an approach, even if it had been successful, was then seriously complicated by the Arab Spring of 2011. As the section below details, this in turn commended first a country-by-country approach to the administration and subsequently, after much internal deliberation, a return to an explicit embrace of democracy-promotion as dovetailing with both the national interests and the values of the United States. By the end of Obama's first term, the precise contours of his administration's Middle East strategy were in dramatic flux, with elements of all three approaches present but none seemingly dominant. George Mitchell had resigned on May 13, 2011 in frustration at the lack of progress on an Israeli-Palestinian settlement, with Hamas and Fatah having formed a nominal "unity government" on May 4. Facing the potential for mass revolts that had motivated other Arab populations to rise up against their rulers – protesting corruption, nepotism, cronyism, and incompetence – the Palestinians risked American and Israeli ire by seeking support for statehood at the United Nations in New York in late September 2011. At least as important to the Obama administration's fate, in terms of substantive results, was a region in which hardliners on all sides had, in effect, been inadvertently encouraged, emboldened and empowered, making the resolution of long-standing conflicts more rather than less straightforward. Democracy in the Middle East, one of the most fraught and problematic issues of the Bush era, re-emerged as the signature conflict of Obama's foreign policy presidency too. As with other aspects of Obama's post-American foreign policy, the limits of strategic engagement became starkly apparent in the febrile geo-politics of a Middle East in the twin throes of revolution and reaction.

Israel and the Palestinian territories

In their controversial book, *The Israel Lobby and US Foreign Policy*, John Mearsheimer and Stephen Walt began their analysis by reviewing the breadth of agreement on Israel among the leading Democratic and Republican candidates for the presidency in the 2008 election. Referring to a speech given by Barack Obama to an AIPAC audience in Chicago in 2007, Mearsheimer and Walt noted that – despite Obama having previously expressed sympathy for the Palestinians – the then junior US Senator for Illinois "made it manifestly clear that he would do nothing to change the US-Israeli relationship."[13]

But, as with much of their analysis, Mearsheimer and Walt were wrong. From the outset of his tenure as president, Obama struck a more realist, cool and at times even confrontational tone than prior US administrations in his dealings with the Israelis. The president appeared to agree unequivocally with the notion that more-or-less unconditional American support for Israel, and especially its continued occupation and settlement expansion in the West Bank since 1967, was manifestly not in the national interest of the US. This was in stark contrast not only to his Republican predecessor, George W. Bush, but also to Bill Clinton, two presidents whom most Israelis regarded as among the strongest of all White House advocates for Israeli interests.

As so often, Obama's seeking a middle way satisfied few of the more ideologically committed in the divisive debate over Israel. For some on the right, President Obama had betrayed a long pattern of bipartisan defense of a key ally and effectively "declared war" on Israel.[14] For many on the left, by contrast, any notion of Obama's minimal antipathy towards Israel was starkly belied by "his total silence on Israel's war on Gaza or its recent illegal attack on a ship carrying aid for Israel's million-and-a-half victims in Gaza, not to mention the billions of dollars of US military and other aid to Israel."[15] As with so much of his approach to a post-American world, Obama's Israel policy evidently stoked deeply divergent viewpoints both within and outside the US.

From the beginning of his presidency, and in contrast to the mostly incremental approach adopted towards Iran, the Obama administration favored the pursuit of a "comprehensive" peace settlement – a peace treaty involving not only the Palestinians and Israel but also the Arab states across the region and, especially, Syria and Lebanon (an added benefit of which might be, in the rather naive White House view, uncoupling Damascus from its Iranian ally, thereby also undermining Hezbollah and Hamas in the process).

The focal point for Obama's diplomatic efforts was Jewish settlements. In a White House keen on its theoretical sophistication, this represented a potentially shrewd choice to exert leverage on Tel Aviv – since most Israelis were not strongly supportive of further settlement expansion, especially in the West Bank (the bulk of which had occurred in 1992–96, when the number of settlers increased by 50 percent at the height of the peace process). Nor, additionally, was settlement expansion something with especially strong support in the reliably pro-Israel US Congress. But diplomatic execution of the strategy by the administration was notably poor – an inexperienced White House staff substantially overestimating the extent of presidential influence while seriously misjudging the internal dynamics of Israeli coalition politics – with the ultimate result that the precondition of a freeze politically hobbled both sides to deeply detrimental effect.

Obama's capacity for persuasion was fatally undercut almost from the outset by popular Israeli distrust of the president and declining Israeli confidence in the two-state solution and land-for-peace formula. Obama's Cairo speech inadvertently exacerbated this predicament, since it was not accompanied by a visit to Israel – an apparent indication of American indifference to Israeli interests – and since the president's public demand for an Israeli settlement freeze was not echoed by US calls on Arab states to take commensurate risks for peace. The president's otherwise courageous attempt to confront Arab and Muslim Holocaust denial also proved politically problematic, since his grounding of support for the state of Israel in the Nazis' World War Two genocide rather than in wider biblical and historical claims to Palestine, and his implicit comparison of Palestinian suffering since 1948 to the *Shoah*, together struck many indignant Israelis as deeply insensitive, ill-informed and gratuitously insulting.

Since domestic political pressure on Binyamin Netanyahu's governing coalition came most heavily from the right side of the spectrum, the focus on settlements also allowed the prime minister to stand firm on an issue of key importance to the right-wing, nationalist and ultra-religious elements in his fragile coalition government. Facing no pressure from the left, the political leverage that the settlers could therefore wield was formidable, the Jewish population on the Palestinian side of the Green Line having grown to half a million by 2009. In a comparatively rare example of Obama's allowing personal relations to impinge on foreign policy, the barely concealed personal animosity between Obama and Netanyahu powerfully exacerbated the strategic dilemma. As the former US State Department negotiator, Aaron David Miller, observed, "Prime Minister Netanyahu looks at President Obama as cold and unsympathetic to Israel's needs, and Obama sees Netanyahu as essentially a fast-talking con man."[16]

Such tensions were never fully appeased subsequently. An eventual compromise on settlement activity, reached in November 2009, for a ten-month freeze excluding Jerusalem, generated a new crisis when Secretary Clinton declared it "unprecedented" and a clear demonstration of Israeli "restraint," a statement that most Arabs found at once hilarious and ludicrous. At the same time, the embattled Palestinian Authority (PA) weakened further. Abbas, whose term had technically expired in January 2009, and who had already been undermined by his embarrassing reversal on the United Nations Goldstone report investigating the 2008 Gaza War, followed Obama's line on settlements as a condition to resuming peace talks, despite his awareness of the futility of the gambit. But, having taken a clear stand, the Palestinian leader was unable to climb down on the issue – yet until he did so, Israel in turn refused to resume negotiations, thereby effectively freezing the peace process for 2009–11. The Obama administration had been incensed when Vice-President Biden was humiliated on a visit to Jerusalem in March 2010 that saw the Israeli housing minister declare the construction of 1,600 new units in East Jerusalem, a public rebuke returned in kind when Obama abruptly left Netanyahu alone in the Oval Office on a subsequent meeting in Washington.

After months of frenetic diplomacy, the resumption of the first direct peace talks between Israeli and Palestinian leaders in twenty months occurred in Washington on September 2, 2010, with regular fortnightly efforts scheduled thereafter. The initiative had offered very tentative hopes of progress – Netanyahu having finally declared in public his acceptance of a demilitarized Palestinian state – subject to a formidable array of obstacles on all sides: for the Israelis, extremist religious and right-wing parties in the coalition; for Palestinians, the division and antipathy between Fatah and Hamas; and for Americans, the competing pressures on the administration from AIPAC, J-Street, Christians United for Israel and other lobby groups.

But the talks collapsed almost as soon as they had commenced, after Israel refused to extend its building freeze. Obama's unceasing pressure on Israel to halt its building of new settlements was again adopted by Palestinian leader Mahmoud Abbas in an unprecedented prerequisite position for entering negotiations. Abbas professed that he was unable to be "less Palestinian than the US President himself."[17] Despite Israel temporarily freezing its settlement-building, the United States undermined its credibility as an arbiter when it ultimately reversed its position on the requirement of a prohibition on settlement-construction, enabling Abbas to walk away from the negotiating table. Although the nation-building efforts of PA Prime Minister, Salam Fayyad – to weed out corruption and create the institutions of a nascent working state – continued apace, in diplomatic terms the entire year of 2011 was effectively wasted, with Palestinian attentions directed instead to its high-risk gambit of building support through the UN to become the world's 194th state.

Despite his obvious motivation to advance the peace, Obama encountered substantial problems that his predecessors had also confronted time and again in seeking to broker a deal between the rival parties. The underlying sources of conflict and distrust had long been based on the absence of a credible Palestinian interlocutor for the Israelis, one both representative of Palestinian opinion and capable of delivering genuine results on the ground. The Palestinians had been weak and divided since the passage of the Oslo Accords in 1993, unable to overcome their fractious divisions to secure tangible dividends. But the signing by Fatah and Hamas of an agreement in Cairo on May 4, 2011 brought to an end four years of especially intense hostilities. The agreement sought to lay the foundation for President Abbas to seek recognition of Palestine as a sovereign nation-state before the United Nations in September 2011. To become a full UN member state requires approval from the Security Council, not just the General Assembly. Such a strategy therefore had the attraction, to the Palestinians, of likely gaining majority support in the Assembly, highlighting and compounding Israel's increasing international isolation, and gaining access to the International Criminal Court. In the event of nine Security Council members supporting the bid, a reluctant US would be forced either to use its veto power to prevent its passage – thereby affronting Muslims across the Islamic world – or not vetoing the measure, which would leave Israel feeling betrayed. At minimum, Abbas might secure the smallest upgrade in the Palestinian status at the UN from an "observer entity" to an "observer state," like the Vatican.

On the Israeli side, the visit of Netanyahu to Washington on May 20, 2011 encapsulated in miniature the broader fissures and frustrations in the bilateral relationship. Rarely has the actual, as well as the body, language between an Israeli prime minister and American president been so obviously cold. In a speech to AIPAC on May 22, 2011, Obama sought to reassure the most ardent pro-Israeli supporters in the US that his commitment to Israel was "ironclad" while his interest in peace was driven by the fact that the existing situation was unsustainable. The president cautioned the Palestinians against going to the UN to secure independence and reiterated that:

> ... the recent agreement between Fatah and Hamas poses an enormous obstacle to peace. No country can be expected to negotiate with a terrorist organization sworn to its destruction. We will continue to demand that Hamas accept the basic responsibilities of peace: recognizing Israel's right to exist, rejecting violence, and adhering to all existing agreements.[18]

Obama then attempted to place his views squarely within mainstream US positions over decades and to clarify exactly what his administration's position was in regard to a future settlement fair to both sides:

> There was nothing particularly original in my proposal; this basic framework for negotiations has long been the basis for discussions among the parties, including previous US administrations. But since questions have been raised, let me repeat what I actually said on Thursday.

> I said that the United States believes that negotiations should result in two states, with permanent Palestinian borders with Israel, Jordan, and Egypt, and permanent Israeli borders with Palestine. The borders of Israel and Palestine should be based on the 1967 lines with mutually agreed swaps, so that secure and recognized borders are established for both states. The Palestinian people must have the right to govern themselves, and reach their potential, in a sovereign and contiguous state.

> As for security, every state has the right to self-defense, and Israel must be able to defend itself – by itself – against any threat. Provisions must also be robust enough to prevent a resurgence of terrorism; to stop the infiltration of weapons; and to provide effective border security. The full and phased withdrawal of Israeli military forces should be coordinated with the assumption of Palestinian security responsibility in a sovereign, non-militarized state. The duration of this transition period must be agreed, and the effectiveness of security arrangements must be demonstrated.

> That is what I said. Now, it was my reference to the 1967 lines with mutually agreed swaps that received the lion's share of the attention. And since my position has been misrepresented several times, let me reaffirm what "1967 lines with mutually agreed swaps" means.

> By definition, it means that the parties themselves – Israelis and Palestinians – will negotiate a border that is different than the one that existed on June 4, 1967. It is a well known formula to all who have worked on this issue for a generation. It allows the parties themselves to account for the changes that have taken place over the last 44 years, including the new demographic realities on the ground and the needs of both sides. The ultimate goal is two states for two peoples. Israel as a Jewish state and the homeland for the Jewish people, and the state of Palestine as the homeland for the Palestinian people; each state enjoying self-determination, mutual recognition, and peace.

> If there's a controversy, then, it's not based in substance. What I did on Thursday was to say publicly what has long been acknowledged privately. I have done so because we cannot afford to wait another decade, or another two decades, or another three decades, to achieve peace. The world is moving too fast. The extraordinary challenges facing Israel would only grow. Delay will undermine Israel's security and the peace that the Israeli people deserve.[19]

But to Israel's strongest supporters, the president's speech presented a number of serious problems. Obama gave no indication that he would cut off financial aid to the new Fatah-Hamas unity government and never even mentioned the issue of the historic right of return of Palestinians. Nor did the president reiterate specifically the necessity of an Israeli military presence in the Jordan Valley. In effect, and perhaps in intention too, Obama underscored rather than downplayed the obvious fact that the United States had major differences with Israel – albeit differences between erstwhile "friends." Two elements here were especially troubling to supporters of Israel.

First, absent in the president's address was an explanation for his prior statement in his May 19, 2011 address that it was now official US policy to press for a peace-deal based on 1967 lines, accompanied by land swaps. Obama's immediate predecessors in the White House, presidents Clinton and Bush, had deliberately and consistently refused to refer to the 1967 borders. The Clinton Parameters, which were withdrawn by the president before he left office, while referring to land "swaps and other territorial arrangement," did not expressly mention the 1967 borders. Bush's April 2004 letter to then Israeli Prime Minister Ariel Sharon – endorsed by both houses of Congress – referred to both parties having to agree to any swaps of territory, and had declared that "in light of new realities on the ground, including already existing major Israeli population centres, it is unrealistic to expect that the outcome of final status negotiations will be a full and complete return to the armistice lines of 1949, and all previous efforts to negotiate a two-state solution have reached the same conclusion." Bush also wrote that "an agreed, just, fair, and realistic framework for a solution to the Palestinian refugee issue as part of any final status agreement will need to be found through the establishment of a Palestinian state, and the settling of Palestinian refugees there, rather than in Israel." President Obama's failure to restate these positions inevitably struck many Israelis as a dangerous shift in the US approach.

But perhaps the central contradiction in the president's position was the claim that Israel could not be expected to negotiate with those who want to destroy it – but that, simultaneously, negotiations nonetheless needed to resume. In this, as in other aspects of its approach to the Middle East more generally, the Obama administration's efforts hardly amounted to a clear, well-conceived or coherent strategy. The release in January 2011 by *Al Jazeera* of records of prior negotiations between the two sides – the so-called "Palestine Papers" – showed that, in 2008, Palestinian negotiators had in fact been prepared to give up nearly all of East Jerusalem and to accept many Israeli settlements to be included within Israel's final borders, in exchange for land swaps with Palestinian majorities within the 1949 armistice lines. But even these offers were scorned by the Olmert government. Such revelations produced vituperative Arab reactions towards Abbas, severely undermining his credibility as a leader and indicating the resistance of many Palestinians to the compromises a two-state solution would require.

Moreover, Obama failed to reiterate the official position adopted by previous administrations that rejected the prospects of a right of return which would demographically overwhelm the state of Israel. In so doing, Obama effectively created a hardened prerequisite position on the part of the Palestinians before entering negotiations. As the former Palestinian negotiator, Saeb Erekat, responded after the speech, unless and until Israel's Prime Minister Netanyahu accepts the 1967 lines as a territorial basis for a Palestinian state, there would be no negotiations. The willingness of the Obama administration for Israel to withdraw to the 1967 borders in the absence of negotiations precluded the need for Fatah and Hamas to declare an end to the conflict. The effect of Obama's shifting away from the post-Oslo accords approach of Clinton and Bush, and for many Israelis the clear presidential intent as well, was actively to seek to isolate Israel at the same time that the Palestinians' own position was ever more emboldened. As Benny Morris, the Israeli historian, observed:

> Abbas is now pursuing a Palestinian state without having to pay the price of recognizing Israel or making peace. Once the Palestinians get their West Bank-Gaza state, they will use it as a springboard for their second-stage assault, political and military, on Israel and they will no doubt lodge claims "at the United Nations, human rights treaty bodies, and the International Court of Justice" as part of that assault. But the major basis of political and moral assault on Israel will be the Palestinian demand for a "Right of Return" and its international acceptance and implementation of the 1948 refugees, who now number, them and their descendants, 5–6 million souls ... the refugee problem will need to be resolved "justly" on the basis of UN General Assembly resolution 194, of December 1948, which, in the Palestinian interpretation, endorses the "Right of Return." If the world accepts this Palestinian demand and there is implementation, Israel will cease to exist (Israel's current population consists of close to 6 million Jews and 1.4 million Arabs: Add to it 5–6 million Palestinian refugees and the country will have an Arab, not a Jewish, majority. Ergo, no Jewish state.).[20]

In such light, it was hardly surprising that Netanyahu should exploit the situation to pressure Obama further. In his May 2011 speech to AIPAC, and again in an address to a joint session of Congress during the same D.C. visit – during which he received no fewer than twenty-nine standing ovations – the Israeli premier flatly rejected the 1967 parameters as "indefensible" and a non-starter. Such rejection suggested strongly to the White House that, contrary to his recent and grudging acceptance of the two-state concept, the prime minister was not remotely sincere in his commitment to such a solution: to Obama, Netanyahu was an ideologue rather than the pragmatist he claimed to be.

In retrospect, the Obama administration's approach promised little in terms of convincing a distrustful, and an increasingly wary, Israeli mass public that it would genuinely deliver permanent peace and enduring security for the Jewish state. For foreign policy "realists" and his critics on the left alike, Obama's cardinal error was to maintain a fundamental continuity with his predecessors: not exerting sufficient pressure on Tel Aviv; adhering stubbornly to the maxim of not negotiating with Hamas and other militant groups; continuing to wield US power in the United Nations – as he did in February 2011 to veto a Security Council resolution condemning Israeli settlements – to thwart efforts to censure Israel and assist the Palestinians to statehood; cutting off US funding to UNESCO once it recognized the Palestinian Authority as a member of the body in October 2011; and failing to propose a comprehensive peace settlement of his own to cut through the Israeli and Palestinian feuding and posturing. As the settlements grew and the prospect of a Palestinian state receded square mile by square mile, Washington's posture as an honest broker appeared increasingly hollow.

Castigating Obama for backtracking on foreign affairs generally, former president Jimmy Carter argued that, "When he said no more settlements, that was a major step forward. But then he backed away from that, as he's backed away from all of his other demands."[21] The inability of the administration to either persuade or cajole Netanyahu into serious concessions generated intense and widespread frustration. As Jeffrey Goldberg recalled, to senior figures in the Obama administration – including the president – the Israeli PM's self-destructive behavior during his Washington visit (arranged by the Speaker of the House of Representatives, John Boehner) in May 2011 was "something to behold":

> In a meeting of the National Security Council Principals Committee held not long before his retirement this summer, Gates coldly laid out the many steps the administration has taken to guarantee Israel's security – access to top-quality weapons, assistance developing missile-defense systems, high-level intelligence sharing – and then stated bluntly that the US has received nothing in return, particularly with regard to the peace process. Senior administration officials told me that Gates argued to the president directly that Netanyahu is not only ungrateful, but also endangering his country by refusing to grapple with Israel's growing isolation and with the demographic challenges it faces if it keeps control of the West Bank. According to these sources, Gates's analysis met with no resistance from other members of the committee.[22]

For others, though, Obama's central failing was to push the Israelis too far and too fast towards profoundly risky deals that ultimately promised more, not less, conflict: insisting for the first time in public by any US president that Israel retreat to its pre-1967 borders; refusing to note that existing settlements had to be acknowledged by Palestinian interlocutors; demanding the withdrawal of Israeli security forces from the Jordan River; and rejecting a unilateral Palestinian approach to the UN while effectively encouraging rather than hindering such efforts by enabling the Palestinians to invoke the authority of the US president to reject even entering negotiations. As Khaled Elgindy observed:

> Having identified Palestinian statehood as a vital national security interest, Washington would again be in the awkward position of voting down its own

stated policy if it actively worked to prevent or defeat the UN vote, particularly at such a sensitive moment in this history of the Middle East.[23]

Ironically, an administration that attempted to demonstrate its even-handedness and honest broker role ultimately encouraged both sides in the conflict to harden rather than soften their positions. With the Palestinian bid for statehood at the UN threatening to internationalize the conflict and galvanize Palestinian anger further, while pushing the US Congress to cut off aid and Israel to abrogate previous agreements with the Palestinians in reprisal, the prospects for conflict were on the rise, while those for peace appeared minimal: a fig-leaf rather than an olive branch. Such an unfortunate development was exacerbated by the popular uprisings that convulsed the Arab world through 2011, the strategic implications of which placed important new pressures on both the US and Israel, making the latter's occupation even less tenable in the longer term in the face of newly unstable and antipathetic neighbors.

The Arab spring: the inevitable surprise

Although Obama's Cairo address of June 2009 had walked a difficult tightrope between reaffirming American ideals and sustaining a hard-headed *realpolitik* calculation of US interests in the region, the events of 2011 posed a fundamental challenge to Washington's traditional approach to the Middle East. Part of Obama's efforts to repair relations with the Muslim world required a deliberate and methodical distancing of Washington from the ambitious, idealistic and – for many in the region – quasi-imperial elements of George W. Bush's "freedom agenda." This was not only a matter of winding-down the US presence in Iraq and eschewing overt talk of military action against Iran, but also relegating the question of democracy promotion and human rights to, at best, a second order priority. Not only were references to democracy notably few in Obama's public diplomacy during 2009–10, but his administration moved early on to cut the foreign assistance budgets directed to promoting democratic reform. Diplomacy and development instead assumed a predominant role in the Obama administration's plans for the Middle East.

In many respects Obama's initial approach appeared, as in other regions, to represent something of a return to normalcy after the apparent aberration of the Bush years and, especially, the Bush first term that had so convulsed the region and generated such worldwide antipathy. In relation to the twenty-two states of the Arab League, this meant a pragmatic case-by-case approach: shoring-up relations with traditional US allies such as Hosni Mubarak and King Abdullah; forging tentative steps towards engaging oppositionist states such as Bashar al-Assad's Syria; developing closer ties with Yemen's President Saleh in order to contain the serious and growing threat of al Qaeda in the

Arabian Peninsula; and extending reassurance to Saudi Arabia and the Gulf Cooperation Council states in order to sustain an effective anti-Iranian coalition of Sunni-majority or Sunni-led states without formally framing an explicit strategy of containment against Tehran. In order to do this, Obama zealously avoided the kind of public and private emphasis devoted by the Bush administration to pressing for democratizing and liberalizing reforms, cutting the democracy promotion budget to Egypt by half in 2009–10, and instead repeatedly stressing a desire for a new beginning between the US and Muslims worldwide.

Even prior to 2011, the probable returns to such an approach appeared relatively modest. But the remarkable developments of late 2010–11 cast Obama's strategy strongly into question. Beginning with the self-immolation of a twenty-six-year old Tunisian fruit vendor, Mohamed Bouazizi, who set himself on fire on December 17, 2011 out of frustration and despair with the state's widespread corruption, a wave of mass protests erupted and swept spontaneously across several Arab states in North Africa and the Gulf. For optimists, the Arab Spring promised the greatest advance for human rights, freedom and democratic values since the fall of communism in Eastern Europe in 1989 and the end of the Cold War. Moreover, no more forceful and eloquent a rejection of al Qaeda's discredited "clash of civilizations" narrative could have been imagined than Arabs and Muslims in their tens of thousands peacefully protesting for universal rights, education and jobs.

For sceptics, however, the uprisings presaged a dangerous and unpredictable turn of events with potentially disastrous consequences for the region, US and Western interests, and the wider world. Lacking firm democratic foundations, elections in and of themselves did not promise to transform traditionally authoritarian Arab states into either genuine pluralist polities or peaceful neighbors. In addition, as Daniel Byman summarized US strategic calculations succinctly, "Arab tyranny has often served US purposes,"[24] from assisting military interventions, intelligence collection and covert operations to facilitating post-9/11 counter-terrorism policies. The vacuums left by the removal of corrupt but long-standing autocratic rulers such as Mubarak, Saleh, Qaddafi and, potentially, even Assad was ripe for exploitation by Islamist groups of various hues. While the demands for open government, action against corruption and nepotism, and greater political participation reflected genuine aspirations shared by peoples around the globe, the fragility of the fluid situation threatened a collapse into even more authoritarian regimes, increased violent conflict and a possible spread of terrorism. Finally, as the Saudis made vehemently clear to Washington, the abandonment of long-term US allies set a worrying precedent for other "pro-US" autocrats who might encounter a similar popular fate.

In the light of such competing strategic considerations, the Obama administration's response was somewhat uncertain, and not until his major

Middle East speech of May 19, 2011 did the president outline a clear set of strategic goals for the region as a whole, after a period of what Philip Stephens termed "sustained and intense dithering."[25] In part, this reflected the basic difficulty – faced by Bush previously – of how best to calibrate a comprehensive strategy when the priorities, preferences, and value to the US of the various actors in distinct national dramas differed so dramatically. Partly, as Shadi Hamid notes,[26] the uncertainty also stemmed from "the Islamist dilemma" that had effectively paralyzed US policy for decades: how can the US successfully promote democracy in the region without risking bringing Islamists to power? Partly, as the head of one influential Arab American organization put it, the dynamics within the administration also had an important role to play: "Obama 'gets it,' but some old hands such as Dennis Ross, along with Hillary Clinton, are hampering his finding a new way forward."[27]

But, in addition, the administration's calculations reflected a new and important dynamic that was especially volatile. As Michael Scott Doran observed, "After a long absence, a strategic player has returned to the Middle Eastern stage: the people."[28] Such a presence offered a positive strategic contribution inasmuch as the uprisings from Tunisia to Syria were – for once in the Middle East – manifestly not about America. Driven by grievances both economic (unemployment, poverty, corruption) and political (the absence of freedom, accountability and popular participation in government), the mass protests saw almost no burnings of the Stars and Stripes or even references to Obama or the US. But the widespread cries for justice and dignity by the Arab protestors also served as forceful reminders to Washington that America's interests in the region were not theirs. Characteristically hedging, as Ryan Lizza remarked, "Obama's instinct was to try to have it both ways," his ultimate position being "to talk like an idealist while acting like a realist."[29]

Egypt

The most important case, in terms of the region as a whole as well as US interests, was Egypt – home to half of the world's Arabs. For three decades after the assassination of Anwar Sadat in 1981, Egypt had represented a strategic pivot for the region. Mubarak had maintained a close and steadfast alliance with the US, assisted by approximately $1.5 billion in annual American aid. Assisting in the interrogation and elimination of Islamist terrorists, Mubarak had also presided over a cold-but-durable peace with Israel, honoring the 1979 peace treaty between the two states and closing the border with Gaza after Hamas gained power there in 2006. Triggered by the Jasmine Revolution in Tunisia, eighteen days of mass protests from January 25 to February 11, 2011 finally, and ignominiously, forced the country's president of thirty years from power. As Dina Shehata notes, it was a potent combination of increasing corruption and economic exclusion, an alienated and large youthful population, and the rigged 2010 parliamentary elections and divisions among the Egyptian elite over Mubarak's successor that underpinned the successful protests.[30] Ultimately, it was "the unity of the opposition and broad-based popular mobilization that forced the military to oust Mubarak"[31] from power.

What this meant for the long-term interests of the US – whose strong military-to-military contacts helped convince the Egyptian military to oust one of their own from power – remains unclear. While elite relationships between the two governments and militaries were close, Egyptian public opinion is overwhelmingly hostile to the US. In a 2010 Pew global survey, for example, only 17 percent of Egyptians expressed a favorable view of the US, which tied with Pakistan and Turkey for the lowest rating in any of twenty-one countries. Almost three-quarters of Egyptians opposed US anti-terrorism efforts and four-fifths wanted the US to withdraw from Afghanistan. Attitudes to Israel among Egyptians are even more vehement. In a 2007 Pew survey, for example, 80 percent of Egyptians agreed that the needs of the Palestinian people could never be met as long as Israel exists; only 18 percent said that the two societies could co-exist fairly. According to Edward Walker, US Ambassador to Egypt under President Bill Clinton, "Of all the countries in the Middle East the population of Egypt is the most hostile to Israel."[32] Egypt's decision to open the border with Gaza in June 2011 – which in turn resulted in attacks by Islamists on Israelis in August 2011 – represented, to Benny Morris, "a definite move away from the spirit of non-belligerency."[33] The ransacking of the Israeli Embassy in Cairo, on September 9, 2011, augured badly for the maintenance of the two countries' three-decade-old "cold peace," much as the attacks on Coptic Christians demonstrating in Cairo in November 2011 – resulting in twenty-five deaths – augured badly for religious tolerance.

Admittedly, some regional analysts remained sanguine about the impact of such popular attitudes on a democratically elected Egyptian government. Aaron David Miller, for example, notes that "It's not in Egypt's political, economic or security interest" to renounce the Israeli peace treaty and the $1 billion of annual US security assistance that comes with it.[34] Middle East expert Kenneth Pollack similarly argues that "a stable Egyptian democracy" would probably calculate that "its interests are best served by peace with Israel, being part of the global economy … and maintaining a good relationship with the United States."[35] But other observers, fearing either greater Islamist influence in government through the well-organized Muslim Brotherhood and fellow Islamists, a return to a military dictatorship, or some hybrid deal between the Islamists and the military, are less optimistic. Henry Kissinger, for example, was not only critical of the rapid abandonment of Mubarak by Washington ("When you are associated with an individual for 30 years, you do not just throw him over the side as if relationships have no meaning. Not that we owed him ten years in office, but that we owed him a graceful exit."[36]), but also rightly cautious about the consequences of a precipitate handover of power in Cairo for both the US and the protesters in Tahrir Square: with a more managed departure and a negotiated handover of power, "The Facebook and Google crowd would have been better off than now, where they are being marginalized by the Army and the Muslim Brotherhood."[37]

Libya

If Egypt was the most important, the starkest case of regime change involved Libya. Colonel Qaddafi had enjoyed a partial, albeit hesitant, return to the international community after his decision to abandon his support for international terrorism and his weapons of mass destruction programs in 2003. But an upsurge of popular protests at his autocratic forty-two years of eccentric rule, beginning in February 2011, threatened to end his regime. As Qaddafi's forces advanced on the rebel stronghold of Benghazi, the United Nations – for the first time in it sixty-six years – authorized military action to prevent an "imminent massacre." UN Security Council Resolution 1973, passed on 17 March by a vote of 10–0 (with abstentions by Brazil, China, Germany, India and Russia), authorized "all necessary measures" to protect civilians, excluding ground occupation, and established a no-fly zone over Libyan airspace as well as sanctions. After committing US forces to the operation on March 19, Obama emphasized that the US would play a supporting role once NATO took command, which it did on April 4. The US contribution to NATO operations included intelligence, jamming of communications, surveillance by unmanned aircraft, aerial refuelling, logistical support and search and rescue. But having used cruise missiles to destroy much of Qaddafi's anti-aircraft capability at the war's start, the Pentagon stunned allies by refusing to engage in direct combat and not deploying aircraft to attack the regime's military assets. Obama said Libya would be better off with Qaddafi out of power and that he "embraced that goal." But he added that "broadening our military mission to include regime change would be a mistake."

It was not a surprise that President Obama should expect Europe to take a leading role in dealing with a crisis such as Libya's, since he had argued during the 2008 campaign that Europe should assume greater responsibility for its own backyard. From the outset of his tenure, he insisted that a post-Bush United States would not rush to intervene unilaterally in crises, would seek to mobilize the international community, would partner with regional actors and would prioritize multilateralism. Theoretically, then, either the EU or NATO's European members should have been the appropriate leaders through which to tackle the Libyan crisis – perhaps in conjunction with bodies such as the African Union, the Arab League and the Organization of the Islamic Conference.

Once more the president found his cautious and carefully calibrated approach yielding the worst of all worlds. The extended discussions within the administration – with Gates strongly opposed to US participation and Clinton, Susan Rice and Samantha Power supportive – caused critics to charge Obama with "dithering" once again and failing to appreciate the urgency of the need for humanitarian intervention. The reluctance to intervene, and the emphasis upon the US role being modest, likewise attracted charges of a failure of US leadership. Simultaneously, however, the ultimate willingness to participate in the effort to protect Libyan civilians – particularly in the light of the fundamental logistical and political problems that plagued the European NATO members' ability to wage an effective campaign – raised criticisms that the US under Obama was leading (albeit, once more, "from behind") the third military intervention in a Muslim nation in ten years. Moreover, while the UN resolution was carefully worded to stress a carefully limited humanitarian role, its studied ambiguities implied that the ultimate goal of the coalition was regime change (a subtlety that was lent credence by NATO pursuing against Qaddafi, in effect, the second-longest targeted assassination campaign in history, after that of Cuba's Fidel Castro). Far from vindicating his status as the "un-Bush," the Arab Spring seemed instead to confirm Obama as, depending on the viewpoint, either a kinder, gentler version of his Texan predecessor, a more insidious version promising better relations in speeches but failing to deliver in substance (the true manifestation of the master seducer, the "Great Satan"), or a hopelessly ineffective leader – "inaction man" – unable to achieve the rather modest reforms he sought to achieve.

When the forces of the National Transitional Council – recognized as the legitimate authority by the UK, France and other states early in the conflict – finally took control of Tripoli in the last week of August 2011, Libya appeared another foreign policy success for the Obama administration. E. J. Dionne, noting that Obama "can't win for winning in Libya," claimed, "It's remarkable how reluctant Obama's opponents are to acknowledge that despite all the predictions that his policy of limited engagement could never work, it actually did."[38] One of the world's longest serving-dictators had been ousted after forty-two years in power, with not a single loss of American life, no US ground troops present in Libya, and a coalition operation led by NATO but with prior UN authorization and active Arab support (especially from Qatar and the UAE). Anne-Marie Slaughter, Director of Policy Planning in the Obama State Department from 2009–11, claimed Libya as vindication of Obama's approach and the West being able to make the "tough choices of foreign policy in the 21st century":

> ... the depiction of America "leading from behind" makes no sense. In a multi-power world with problems that are too great for any state to take on alone, effective leadership must come from the centre. Central players mobilise others and create the conditions and coalitions for action – just as President Barack Obama described America's role in this conflict. In truth, US diplomacy has been adroit in enabling action from other powers in the region, and then knowing when to step out of the way.[39]

But such an analysis – and the rather strained claim that US intervention stemmed from its "strategic interest to help social revolutions fighting for the values we espouse and proclaim"[40] – obscured two more salient aspects.

First, the Libyan campaign illustrated less the viability of "enabling" coalitions of the willing – a concept that Obama had previously repudiated in favor of renewing established alliances – than the graphic limits of such an approach. Only nine NATO nations deployed aircraft to attack ground targets. Turkey and Spain simply refused to attack ground targets, key NATO members such as Germany and Poland offered nothing at all to the operation, while at one stage France and the UK were perilously close to running out of munitions. American assistance remained crucial. As the European contribution to ISAF – one more symbolic of transatlantic comity than the outcome of a genuine sense of shared threat – became even more limited in the face of the US troop surge and the Afghan operation's increasing unpopularity, Secretary Gates had lamented Europe's "demilitarization" as "an impediment to achieving real security and lasting peace," in a speech at the National Defense University in February 2010.[41] In a valedictory address in June 2011, a clearly exasperated Gates made clear that a NATO "alliance" where the US contribution had actually increased from 50 percent of total defense spending in 2001 to 75 percent in 2011 was profoundly imbalanced.[42] While the assistance of Qatar and the UAE was crucial to preparing the rebels' armed forces, the mission represented not a coherent alliance operation but a quintessential "coalition of the willing." Far from confirming the "enabling" role of the US, it reconfirmed the operational and diplomatic strains in the transatlantic alliance – Europe lacking both the will and the means to carry out a limited mission, and American technical and logistical resources remaining central to NATO's success.

Second, as in the Clinton interventions of the 1990s – and unlike the Bush ones of the 2000s – US participation occurred without the authorization of the US Congress. In a series of votes, the administration failed to secure approval from Congress, with the opposition to the operation receiving bipartisan backing.[43] As such, Libya indicated less a model for Washington's post-American diplomatic and military blueprint than confirmation of a disturbingly inward-looking, uncertain and war-weary nation.

The administration's mixed messages and indecision about Libya's revolution in March confused allies as well as powers hostile to intervention, such as China and Russia. The legal mismatch between the goal of removing Qaddafi and the narrower mandate of United Nations Security Council Resolution 1973 led to bipartisan condemnation of the administration's actions by Congress. The administration decision to limit its involvement several weeks into the conflict caused cash-strapped European governments to run short on ammunition and scramble to effectively deploy their limited military resources. A more robust use of American force during this initial period, including greater use of ground-attack aircraft such as AC-130s and A-10s, could have crippled

Qaddafi's forces at the onset. The president's declaration that there would not be any American boots on the ground left allied special forces on their own to assist the untrained rebel forces and guide NATO air strikes. The participation of US special operators would have undoubtedly put the alliance in a stronger position to pressure Qaddafi. All of these actions allowed Qaddafi to stay in power for months longer than necessary, resulting in countless unnecessary deaths.

Moreover, while President Obama called for Qaddafi to go on March 3, it was not until July 15 that the United States officially recognized the Transitional National Council (TNC) as Libya's legitimate governing authority. Doing so earlier might have bolstered the TNC's international credibility and led to an earlier resolution of the effort to allow frozen Qaddafi assets to be handed over to them. Apart from his initial address to the nation on March 28, the president made very little effort to explain the strategic rationale of the Libyan operation to a doubtful Congress and American public. The standoff reached its nadir in late June when, in a bizarre echo of the congressional opposition to Bill Clinton's intervention in Kosovo in 1999, the House of Representatives voted not to authorize the operations in Libya but refused to cut off funding. While the actual impact of those votes was negligible, the dubious message being sent to friends and foes alike was one of waning American resolve. As one commentary concluded, "For the foreseeable future, political resistance will meet any suggestion of new foreign missions for the US military."[44] In sum, rather than offering emphatic support to a strategy of "leading from behind," Libya represented a mostly pyrrhic victory for the Obama administration.

Syria

The traditional charge against US foreign policy of American double standards also found powerful echoes in the contrasting US responses to Libya and other Middle Eastern states where authoritarian powers resorted to violent force to repress popular protests during the Arab Uprising. Aside from Saudi Arabia, whose ruling family managed to quell popular disturbances quickly through a combination of bribery and repression, the most notable instance in this regard was Syria. As part of its broader approach of strategic engagement, the Obama administration (like Bill Clinton previously in the 1990s) had attempted a *rapprochement* with Damascus, premised on the notion that Syria could be persuaded to assist in an Israeli-Palestinian peace process and be lured away from its ominous "resistance" alliance with Iran, Hezbollah and Hamas. This engagement included enlisting Senator John Kerry (D-MA), chairman of the Senate Foreign Relations Committee, to meet directly with Assad, and resuming full diplomatic relations with a US ambassador, Robert Ford, in place from January 2010, in an attempt to encourage the regime to develop a more constructive role in the region (especially in relation to Israel, Lebanon and Iraq).

The Assad regime's response to the outbreak of popular demonstrations in the summer of 2011 was brutal (and rumored to be orchestrated with Iranian assistance from the *Quds* force), with some 2,000 civilian deaths estimated by the fall of 2011, but the Obama administration's reaction was typically muted. As even the reliably liberal *Washington Post* noted, in an acerbic but penetrating editorial:

> Massacres on this scale usually prompt a strong response from Western democracies, as they should. Ambassadors are withdrawn; resolutions are introduced at the U.N. Security Council; international investigations are mounted and sanctions applied. In Syria's case, none of this has happened. The Obama administration has denounced the violence – a presidential statement called Friday's acts of repression "outrageous" – but otherwise remained passive. Even the ambassador it dispatched to Damascus during a congressional recess last year remains on post. The administration has sat on its hands despite the fact that the Assad regime is one of the most implacable US adversaries in the Middle East. It is Iran's closest ally; it supplies Iranian weapons to Hezbollah in Lebanon and Hamas in the Gaza Strip for use against Israel. Since 2003 it has helped thousands of jihadists from across the Arab world travel to Iraq to attack American soldiers. It sought to build a secret nuclear reactor with the help of North Korea and destabilized the pro-Western government of neighboring Lebanon by sponsoring a series of assassinations. Yet the Obama administration has effectively sided with the regime against the protesters. Rather than repudiate Mr. Assad and take tangible steps to weaken his regime, it has proposed, with increasing implausibility, that his government "implement meaningful reforms," as the president's latest statement put it ... the administration, which made the "engagement" of Syria a key part of its Middle East policy, still clings to the belief that Mr. Assad could be part of a Middle East peace process; and it would rather not trade "a known quantity in Assad for an unknown future." As a practical matter, these considerations are misguided. Even if his massacres allow him to survive in power, Mr. Assad will hardly be a credible partner for Israel. And no matter what happens, Syria will not return to the police-state stability it has known during the past several decades. As a moral matter, the stance of the United States is shameful. To stand by passively while hundreds of people seeking freedom are gunned down by their government makes a mockery of the US commitment to human rights. In recent months President Obama has pledged repeatedly that he would support the aspiration of Arabs for greater freedom. In Syria, he has not kept his word.[45]

That administration stance ultimately altered in tentative ways during the summer of 2011. In a curious echo of then Secretary of State, Condoleezza Rice's, 2005 Cairo speech that had insisted that the US would no longer accept autocracy as the price for stability, Obama's May 19, 2011 speech at the State Department finally declared democratic reform to be the formal US policy priority in the Middle East. Stating that "Strategies of repression and diversion won't work any more ... Change cannot be denied," and affirming that, "After decades of accepting the world as it is in the region, we have a chance to pursue the world as it should be," Obama publicly faulted Bahrain, Yemen and Syria for failing to respond adequately to the mass calls for change while expressing confidence that Qaddafi would step down or be forced from power. After imposing a new round of sanctions on Assad and other members of his Allawite regime the previous day, the president also declared that, "The Syrian people have shown their courage in demanding a transition to democracy. President Assad now has a choice: He can lead that transition, or get out of the way." Although confirming the US would pursue its interests in the region, such as energy security and nuclear non-proliferation, Obama noted that "failure to speak to the broader aspirations of ordinary people will only feed the suspicion that has festered for years that the US pursues our own interests at their expense." Referring to political and economic reform and human rights, the president declared that "Our support for these principles is not a secondary interest. Today I am making it clear that it is a top priority that must be translated into concrete actions, and supported by all of the diplomatic, economic and strategic tools at our disposal." Announcing plans to forgive up to $1 billion in Egyptian debt and extend loan guarantees of up to $1 billion to Cairo, the president sought to incentivize Arab reformers elsewhere for similar results. While one of the US's strongest "allies" in the region, Saudi Arabia, went entirely unmentioned in the address, Obama was emphatic that "A failure to change our approach threatens a deepening spiral of division between the US and the Arab world."[46]

Not until August 2011, however, did the Obama administration's softly-softly approach to Syria finally undergo a Damascene conversion and issue an unequivocal demand, coordinated with the UK, France and Germany, for Assad to step down – Obama declaring that "For the sake of the Syrian people, the time has come for President Assad to step aside." Announcing a new round of targeted sanctions, freezing all Syrian assets within US jurisdiction and barring Americans from business dealings with the government in Damascus (including prohibitions from exporting or importing oil), Obama nonetheless explicitly ruled out military intervention: "The United States cannot and will not impose this transition on Syria. We have heard their strong desire that there not be foreign intervention."[47] Although Syria represented more of a strategic interest for the US than Libya – and much more of a consistent threat to US interests over several decades – Washington's hopes for decisive pressure to work still rested on European governments, on whom 90–95 percent of Syria's oil exports relied, themselves taking decisive action to impose sanctions on the regime. On September 2, 2011, the EU adopted a ban on imports of Syrian crude oil, to take effect from November 15.[48] But the *volte face* of the Obama administration lent little in the way of coherence to its overall stance. As Hillary Clinton had declared, in the week prior to Obama's demand for regime change, "If the US called for Mr Assad's head, then what?"[49]

It remains to be seen whether in substantive terms this new commitment to reform and regime change represented a genuine refutation of the notion that "the United States remains a status quo power in a region undergoing

Table 6.1 Muslim views of Obama's handling of Middle East issues (percentages approving [A] and disapproving [D])

	Calls for political change							
	The Middle East		Israel-Palestine		Afghanistan		Iran	
	A	D	A	D	A	D	A	D
Turkey	8	65	6	68	5	70	5	68
Egypt	45	52	15	82	18	76	27	68
Jordan	31	65	17	82	12	87	21	77
Lebanon	41	52	12	85	23	71	40	55
Palestinian Territories	33	63	13	84	15	81	16	80
Indonesia	30	49	26	57	28	56	23	56
Pakistan	5	40	6	45	9	52	10	50

Source: Pew Research Center, Q79b-e, Pew Global Attitudes Project, *Obama's Challenge in the Muslim World: Arab Spring Fails to Improve US Image*, May 17, 2011, 11.

radical change."[50] From the American side, not only does Obama confront significant congressional opposition to his policies towards the region and a deep partisan divide, but in an environment of stringent economic constraints and deficient US demand, the prospects for extending serious economic and financial assistance to liberalizing Arab states appeared slim. Moreover, as Table 6.1 confirms, substantial scepticism born of a long history of US double standards still informs mass opinion towards Washington across the Middle East. As James Zogby observed, while Obama's Cairo speech of 2009 was very effective as a public address, "... Arab hopes were deflated by the lack of change" subsequently.[51] The possibility that successful uprisings conclude with a ransacking of government offices, only to discover the extent of US complicity with prior authoritarian rulers and their repressive methods, also stores up potentially explosive medium-term consequences for Washington's relations with states across the region.[52]

Much as with other aspects of his foreign and domestic policy, Obama's attempts to balance competing interests and attend to the complexities of the challenges posed by the Arab Spring ultimately satisfied few. Instinctively conservative and incremental in his approach, and predisposed to splitting the difference when confronted by tough choices, the administration's policy effectively emerged in bifurcated fashion, emphasizing democracy in North Africa but stability in the Gulf. But, as a Pew Research Center study documented – released in May 2011, in the same week that the president made his major Middle East strategy address – Obama's hesitant and selectively calibrated response had, in conjunction with other US foreign and national security policies, largely undone whatever limited goodwill and cautious optimism had been earned by his 2009 Cairo speech and other outreach efforts that had sought to restore America's abysmal moral authority among Muslims.[53] Significantly, this was not only a matter of US favorability ratings continuing to crater across the region, but also of declining Muslim confidence in Obama personally, dwindling support for US actions under his leadership, and increasing conviction across the Muslim world that their own governments cooperated too much with Washington. Together the findings starkly demonstrated continuing and marked hostility to the US, whose stock could barely fall lower in the region. For a post-American grand strategy, there appeared to be as much despair and misgivings as "hope" in Washington's complex relationship with the Middle East, from Tunis to Tehran.

Conclusion: the limits of strategic engagement in the Middle East

In contrast to those who worry that the ousting of Mubarak from Egypt may represent a blow to US interests as significant as the fall of the Shah of Iran in 1979, Marc Lynch argues that – while Obama's approach to the popular uprisings satisfied almost no-one – his cautious and Egypt-centric response "worked," at least within certain narrow parameters and in the short term.[54] But as the results of the November 2011 Egyptian parliamentary elections demonstrated, positive medium and long-term results for Washington remained highly doubtful. Whether, moreover, Obama's highly selective strategy of support for self-determination "worked" more broadly across the region remains even more questionable. Indeed, whether any conceivable comprehensive effort from Washington could do so is a question worth asking. Perhaps, as Adam Kushner suggested – reflecting on the failure of both realist and idealist approaches to the Middle East under successive US administrations – "... the true mistake in the Middle East has not been getting the policy (or the means) wrong: it has been assuming we could ever get it right." In the messy real world, especially today, there may be "no disgrace in muddling through when there is no alternative" since "the best that American policymakers can do is labor at the margins and react to unforeseen events"[55] – a singularly un-heroic but eminently sensible summary of the Obama record thus far.

In many respects, the destabilizing Arab Spring only served once more to underline the necessity for, but absence of, robust American leadership in world affairs and presidential leadership at home and abroad. Both were sorely lacking. For an administration so committed to engagement, its approach appeared quixotically disengaged and the Arab Awakening ultimately underscored the sharp limits to Washington's ability even to anticipate – much less to dictate or control – events of seismic strategic consequence; not, admittedly, for the first time. To the extent that popular sentiments are now more accurately represented and reflected in the corridors of Arab power, the US and its allies – in particular an increasingly isolated and threatened Israel – face a more conflictual, and even adversarial, set of relations with several key regional actors. Moreover, the very absence of clear and unequivocal public US support for popular change – at least until Obama's May 19, 2011 speech – that had helped to convince some Arab rulers not to quit threatened to exacerbate the longer-term legacy of popular antipathy towards Washington in newly empowered governments and among the 60 percent of Middle Eastern populations under thirty years of age.

The Obama administration will almost certainly be forced in future "to take more into account the views and interests of empowered Arab publics who have conclusively and profoundly rejected the status quo upon which American grand strategy has been based."[56] Although Israel and Palestine barely figured in the Arab revolts, much less constituting catalytic drivers of the uprisings, the sudden removal of "moderate" Sunni regimes and the burgeoning regional roles of Turkey and Egypt also make the prospect of a genuine and lasting resolution of an Israeli-Palestinian peace more rather than less distant. Such an "un-heroic" style of US leadership may have ultimately been the outcome of a series of unpalatable choices facing Washington but it also, as Lynch rightly observes, chimed well with the Obama administration's conservative – in the sense of prudently cautious – foreign policy DNA. Nonetheless, in making an already complex situation still more complicated, as Aaron David Miller argued:

> Thirty months in, a self-styled transformative president with big ideas and ambitions as a peacemaker finds himself with no negotiations, no peace process, no relationship with an Israeli prime minister, no traction with Palestinians, and no strategy to achieve a breakthrough.[57]

The marked irony was that America's value to Arabs stemmed in large part from its influence on Israel, and likewise its value to Israel relied in part on its salience to Arab governments. But by 2012, Washington's value to both parties was much reduced, with Obama's resistance to involving the UN centrally on the Israeli-Palestinian conflict running directly against his oft-touted claims that America could not solve international challenges alone.

As with other priorities in Obama's attempt to craft a post-American foreign policy, the president could not be faulted for making a sincere and serious effort to change the diplomatic landscape in order to reboot America's image and boost US geo-political interests in the Middle East. Long prior to the convulsions of the Arab world that erupted in 2011, though, Obama's well-intentioned efforts were constrained by a set of deeply unpropitious circumstances and unhelpful interlocutors: a set of actors in both Israel and Palestine who remained beset by mutual mistrust, deep internal divisions and adverse conditions on the ground; a set of rising powers newly willing and able to assert their own interests in the region, including even erstwhile US allies such as Turkey; a widespread perception of America as a distracted and weakening global Gulliver increasingly marginal to regional developments – a declining, unreliable and distracted regional power; an obdurate "resistance bloc" of Iran and its proxy allies Syria, Hezbollah and Hamas; and a set of apparently entrenched autocratic rulers whose inattention to the profound internal maladies of their nations increasingly threatened to dislodge even the most brutal of corrupt authoritarian regimes, even at the cost – as in Syria – of *de facto* civil war.

Faced by an unprecedented combination of total stasis in the peace process and unanticipated, startling and rapid change in the Arab world, Obama could perhaps be forgiven for a lack of clear and consistent policy responses. As Reuel Marc Gerecht and Mark Dubowitz put it, while on his first visit to the region in 2009 Obama's "narrower, humbler" conception of America's interests abroad had "confused the majesty of Islam with the dignity of Muslim potentates," the president's personal background – as the son of an African Muslim and an American woman who dedicated her life to the disadvantaged – made him "tailor-made to lead the United States in expanding democracy to the most unstable, autocratic and religiously militant part of the world."[58]

The Great Arab Revolt of 2011 did not fully convince Obama to embrace his "inner Bush" in public.[59] But his administration's strategy underwent sharp shifts from one premised on the understanding that anti-Americanism in the Middle East had its roots in Muslims' legitimate grievances with Washington's foreign policies, and above all the intimate US relationship with Israel, to one that instead stressed the need for Arab self-determination, regime change and much of the same contentious "freedom agenda" that Bush had previously articulated to an astonished and disbelieving Middle East. Ironically, as Walter Russell Mead provocatively noted, having initially distanced himself from his predecessor's foreign policies, "in general, President Obama succeeds where he adopts or modifies the policies of the Bush administration. Where (as on Israel) he has tried to deviate, his troubles begin":

> The most irritating argument anyone could make in American politics is that President Obama, precisely because he seems so liberal, so vacillating, so nice, is a more effective neo-conservative than President Bush. As is often the case, the argument is so irritating partly because it is so true … President Obama is pushing a democracy agenda in the Middle East that is as aggressive as President Bush's; he adopts regime change by violence if necessary as a core component of his regional approach and, to put it mildly, he is not afraid to bomb. But where President Bush's tough guy posture ("Bring 'Em On!") alienated opinion abroad and among liberals at home, President Obama's reluctant warrior stance makes it easier for others to work with him.[60]

By the latter stages of Obama's term, his administration's regional strategy appeared more a haphazard hybrid of the peace process, democracy promotion, and pragmatic nation-by-nation approaches than a clear or consistent endorsement of any one organizing frame. Unfortunately, whatever its purported centrality to the emergence of a more stable and prosperous region, the prospects for conflict resolution on Israel-Palestine remained demonstrably weak, not least since the breakdown in US-Israeli relations that developed over 2009–12 – while not historically unprecedented – was deeper and more alarming for supporters of close bilateral ties than in previous instances. While popular American warmth towards Israel remains steadfast, fewer than half of Americans now support the US defending Israel against an attack by its neighbors[61] and an increasing partisan polarization has arisen on the issue, with Republicans – driven in large part by Christian evangelicals, security hawks and neo-conservatives – far closer to near unconditional support than an increasingly sceptical cohort of disenchanted Democrats.[62] While Jewish Americans remain strongly Democratic, this is not set in stone. Whether Jewish American financial and electoral support stays solid for Obama – at 78 percent in 2008 – may also influence the 2012 result, not least in key Electoral College states such as Florida and Pennsylvania. Obama will no doubt be aware that, after winning 71 percent of Jewish American votes in 1976, Jimmy Carter captured only 45 percent in 1980.

For all of Obama's tenacious attempts at outreach to Muslims, the seemingly chaotic, unreliable and ineffective efforts of his administration to pressure Tel Aviv – along with the continued US military presence and activity in Muslim lands from Yemen to Indonesia – substantially undercut symbolic signs of reconciliation and the expression of renewed respect with Islam. Those outreach efforts, absent comparable concern for Israeli sentiments, in turn compounded the acute mistrust in Israel that its national interests were marginal to those of the US president. Obama appeared – amidst deliberate and concerted international efforts to de-legitimize Israel and increase its diplomatic isolation – to regard Israel with disdain as more an albatross than an ally; as, in the words of Turkish premier Recep Tayyip Erdogen in September 2011, "the West's spoilt child."[63]

Resolving this basic tension in Obama's approach constitutes a necessary – if difficult and insufficient – condition of ensuring regional progress. But, given the feuding and the diplomatic paralysis of the past three years, together with the worsening relations between Israel and its Arab and Turkish neighbors, this seems highly unlikely. The growing American debate as to whether Israel is more a liability than an asset to US national security is increasingly echoed in Israel about America under Obama. Most clearly, if – despite Obama's repeated assertions that the US-Israel bond is "unshakeable" and a nuclear-armed Iran is "unacceptable" – Israel's closest ally is unable or unwilling to defend its security and disarm its one existential threat, the broader relationship faces serious challenges with profound regional consequences. Not least, Israel appears increasingly unable to sustain the notions that it is both uniquely vulnerable but irresistibly powerful; what former Israeli Prime Minister Levi Eshkol once termed the "poor little Samson."

Far from mitigating regional animosities and tensions, US policy over 2009–12 left Israel even more internationally isolated, and hence more indisposed to offering comprehensive concessions for peace, than at the outset of Obama's term – without significantly improving conditions on the ground on the West Bank or Gaza. With the Arab revolutions leaving Israel facing growing regional hostility, traditionally good Israeli relations with Turkey turning icily cold – after the deaths of nine pro-Palestinian activists when the Israeli navy intercepted a Turkish aid flotilla to Gaza, the *Mavi Marmara*, on May 31, 2010 – and the Saudis exasperated by American policies toward the region, the US appeared increasingly adrift and ineffectual to Israelis and Arabs alike. The once unthinkable – a strategic rupture not only between Washington and Tel Aviv but also between Washington and Riyadh – no longer appeared impossible.

Transformative change in the Middle East had indeed occurred on President Obama's watch, but not of his own design. Anything but triumphalism therefore appeared appropriate in relation to Obama's Middle East policy. As Boris Pasternak once wrote, "It is often difficult to distinguish victories from defeats." The revolts across the Middle East over 2011, for once, were mercifully free of angry mobs engaging in ritualized burnings of American and Israeli flags, still less carrying revolutionary placards bearing Osama Bin Laden's visage or vision. But while al Qaeda and its allies and affiliates cannot possibly seize power anywhere in the Muslim world, such groups typically thrive on state failure, societal chaos, and civil war. Only the most confident of observers could guarantee the outcomes of all the uprisings in the region avoiding such fates. Not only did the Arab Spring threaten to deteriorate into an Arab Winter of indeterminate duration, but the prospects for peace in the Middle East appeared at least as dim and distant by the latter part of Obama's first term as at its beginning. And, as Zbigniew Brzezinski questioned, "Our exit from the region – which is not an exit willed by us but rather forced by circumstances – will continue and perhaps become more marked ... What happens in the region as we exit, and who on the outside will begin to capitalize on it?"[64]

7

China

It is not an issue of integrating a European-style nation-state, but a full-fledged continental power. The DNA of both (America and China) could generate a growing adversarial relationship, much as Germany and Britain drifted from friendship to confrontation ... Neither Washington nor Beijing has much practice in cooperative relations with equals. Yet their leaders have no more important task than to implement the truths that neither country will ever be able to dominate the other, and that conflict between them would exhaust their societies and undermine the prospects for world peace.
—Henry Kissinger, speech to the International
Institute for Strategic Studies, Geneva,
September 2010[1]

We are a resident power in Asia – not only a diplomatic or military power, but a resident economic power, and we are here to stay.
—Secretary of State Hillary Clinton, "Principles for
Prosperity for the Asia-Pacific" speech in Hong Kong,
July 2011[2]

With the American economy hanging over Obama's re-election, the signs are that many [of the Chinese] view his presidency as the inflection point in American decline.
—Michael Sheridan[3]

The days when the debt-ridden Uncle Sam could leisurely squander unlimited overseas borrowing appear to be numbered. To cure its addiction to debts, the United States has to re-establish the common sense principle that one should live within one's means ... (China) has every right now to demand the United States to address its structural debt problems and ensure the safety of China's dollar assets ...
—Xinhua statement (China's official news agency),
August 2011[4]

Introduction

According to the prevailing conventional wisdom, if any one change in the international order has underpinned the arrival of a post-American world, it is the remarkable rise of the People's Republic of China (PRC). For the United States and the West more broadly, as Michael Schiffer and Gary Schmitt argue, the rise of China represents the "principal strategic fact of the 21st century."[5] In economic terms, as a profligate America's banker and foremost creditor – possessing the largest foreign reserves in the world, with an estimated two-thirds of the $3,200 billion denominated in US dollars in 2011 – American economic prospects relied heavily on China continuing to purchase US debt: a "red menace" quite different from that of the Cold War era but, potentially, of equally devastating long-term danger. In 2010, China overtook Germany to become the world's largest exporter, eclipsed the US to become the world's largest market for cars, and edged out the US as Brazil's largest trading partner. China now leads the world in consumption, from cement to eggs, while Chinese banks now rank among the largest in the world by market capitalization. If China were to use the same amount of oil per capita as America currently does, it would require more barrels per day than the world's total output combined.

In strategic terms, the Pentagon's Quadrennial Defense Review of 2006 concluded that China also had the greatest potential to compete militarily with the United States of any potential rival power. The 2008 US National Intelligence Council report, *Global Trends 2025: A Transformed World*, emphasized that China's growing role in the global economy – from purchasing two-thirds of Sudan's oil to transferring technology and military hardware to Zimbabwe and Nigeria – will propel it into direct competition with Washington, in other nations, particularly given its major foreign investments and intensive search for mineral and energy resources in Africa, Latin America and the Middle East.[6] Under Leon Panetta, the Pentagon's annual assessment of Chinese military might, issued on August 24, 2011,[7] concluded that China's sustained military modernization program was "paying visible dividends": "During 2010, China made strides towards fielding an operational anti-ship ballistic missile, continued work on its aircraft carrier program and finalized the prototype of its first stealth aircraft." The US remained "unclear" about how China would ultimately employ its growing military capabilities.[8]

As Schiffer (Deputy Assistant Secretary of State for East Asia in the Obama administration) and Schmitt contend, "managing" China's rise is largely out of US hands. While US policy may be reliably "pragmatic," the "right mix of engagement and hedging in practice is no easy thing" for Washington to judge.[9] The dangers of misjudging that mix are formidable for the simple reason that, as Michael Mandelbaum notes, China "is the obvious candidate to disrupt the twenty-first-century international order."[10] It is therefore not surprising that China, America's most important bilateral relationship, has remained one of Washington's most testy, complex and fragile, from the administration of George H.W. Bush to that of Barack Obama.

Cooperative, competitive and at times openly conflictual relations co-exist between the world's most dominant power and its principal challenger, the world's second-most powerful country. Even absent the historical legacies and ideological differences that still haunt US-China relations today, such a mix of cooperative and competitive market and military pressures could hardly be otherwise. Despite voices variously urging the US either to develop a strategic partnership with China or to recognize that strategic competition with the Chinese was inevitable, President Obama's experience continued to demonstrate the impossibility of Washington adopting anything but a strategy of "modified hedging" towards Beijing. As several incidents demonstrated during Obama's presidency, despite US efforts to engage Beijing constructively, there continues to exist a fundamental vacuum at the center of the United States' relations with China: the absence of strategic trust. Although President Obama has repeatedly stated that the United States welcomes China's rise, significant parts of the US government view China as a serious and growing threat to America's national security, on dimensions that range from economics, finance and trade through intellectual property rights and cyber-war to the militarization of space. Moreover, the trust gap not only encompasses relations with its regional neighbors – India, Japan, Taiwan, South Korea, Vietnam and the Philippines – but also represents a major obstacle for China and its companies as they seek to enter more sensitive parts of the global economy.

Where the George W. Bush administration had aspired to China becoming, in the famous formulation of former US deputy secretary of state Robert Zoellick, a "responsible stakeholder" in the international order, the Obama administration's initial platform of "strategic reassurance" in effect behaved as if that had already transpired. While zealously avoiding the terminology, Obama's highly empathetic approach to Beijing implicitly suggested that a *de facto* G2 was emerging, with China being actively encouraged to assume a greater international leadership role and global responsibilities through the UN Security Council, World Trade Organization and other multilateral forums. Washington initially sought significantly to deepen cooperation with China in 2009 on multiple fronts: multilaterally through the G20, building on the initial invitation from Bush to attend the first meeting of the G20 in 2008; bilaterally through a revamped annual Strategic and Economic Dialogue; symbolically, via a presidential visit in November 2009 (making Obama the first US president to visit China during his first year of office, a testament to China's paramount importance to America); through careful diplomacy, deferring the traditional meeting between the US president and Tibet's Dalai Lama in the fall of that year; and examining revisions of Washington's increasingly close relations with India in order to accommodate Chinese concerns about a nascent American-Indian geo-political partnership unsubtly aimed at "containing" Beijing's ascent in Asia.

But almost as rapidly as it was crafted, this policy of strategic reassurance effectively collapsed by early 2010. Several setbacks illustrated the seemingly intractable limits of American engagement with Beijing. Despite warnings and implicit threats from Washington, China was perceived to bluntly resist pressure to cease manipulating its currency, one cause of the major financial imbalances with the US. Obama's historic visit to China was more tightly controlled by Beijing than prior presidential ones, ending with few tangible accomplishments and the palpable impression among China's politburo that Obama was weak. China's hard-line at the Copenhagen climate-change summit in December 2009 not only snubbed Obama in a remarkable act of diplomatic humiliation – the president having physically to muscle into a room where China's premier was stitching-up a deal without the US – but also conspired to leave Washington with the lion's share of the blame for the negotiations' failure. In January 2010 Google declared its intention to withdraw from China amid allegations of cyber attacks from Chinese nationals. By early 2010 the Obama administration had concluded that the financial crisis and subsequent Great Recession had convinced Beijing of America's accelerating decline and the cost-free option of greater assertiveness.

The administration thus shifted tack, effectively abandoning the very premise of the strategic engagement approach that underpinned Obama's post-American foreign policy: that China had the same interest as America in addressing shared challenges to the global order. In January 2010 Clinton made a major speech defending Internet freedom. In February, Obama met the Dalai Lama. The US also agreed to imposing punitive tariffs on all Chinese car and light-truck tyre imports and to sell defensive weapons to Taiwan. Ironically, these less emollient approaches induced some shifts in Beijing, with President Hu Jintao attending the Washington nuclear security summit in April 2010 and the Chinese agreeing to the new round of UN sanctions on Iran in June 2010. But the bilateral relationship remained beset by mutual mistrust, suspicion of the other's motives, and a competitive dynamic to assert long-term primacy in the Asia-Pacific region.

Tellingly, Obama's speeches increasingly used the China card not to emphasize mutual respect and mutual interests, but instead as a call to arms to Americans to support his domestic agenda. Thomas Friedman and Michael Mandelbaum deployed one such reference as the title of their detailed 2011 prescription for reviving America:

> It makes no sense for China to have better rail systems than us, and Singapore having better airports than us. And we just learned that China now has the fastest supercomputer on Earth – that used to be us.[11]

In his 2011 State of the Union speech to Congress, the president explained:

> Meanwhile, nations like China and India realized that with some changes of their own, they could compete in this new world. And so they started educating their children earlier and longer, with greater emphasis on math and science. They're investing in research and new technologies. Just recently, China became the home to the world's largest private solar research facility, and the world's fastest computer.[12]

During his address to a joint session of Congress on September 8, 2011, Obama once again invoked the China challenge to pressure lawmakers to support his American Jobs Act and a new stimulus package of $447 billion:

> Building a world-class transportation system is part of what made us an economic superpower. And now we're going to sit back and watch China build newer airports and faster railroads? At a time when millions of unemployed construction workers could build them right here in America?[13]

In short, just as the Obama administration's foreign and national security policies towards Pakistan, Iran, Israel, and the Arab Spring ebbed and flowed with no clear, consistent and at times credible design, so Washington's China policy remained mired in the competing interpretations of how best to simultaneously hedge and engage an increasingly influential but unbiddable great power competitor.

US China strategy for the 2010s: peaceful rise, post-ascent aggression or unpeaceful collapse?

The strategic dilemma posed by China's rise has prompted major divisions among foreign policy commentators as to how best the US should respond to its most serious competitor and greatest international challenge.[14] As Peter Dombrowski puts it, "Two-plus decades into the most recent re-emergence of China on the world stage, the United States does not have a coherent policy for adjusting its regional and global strategies to accommodate a new great power."[15] Vindicating Deng Xiaoping's famous declaration that "To get rich is glorious," by 2005 China had overtaken the US as the preferred destination for Foreign Direct Investment. By 2006, China and India together accounted for 47 percent of global economic growth. China surpassed the US as the largest automobile market (comprising some 14 million sales) and accounted for 46 percent of global coal consumption in 2009, with Beijing predicted to consume one-fifth of all global energy supplies by 2035.

Whether or not Gerard Lyons – chief economist of Standard Charter Bank – is correct to argue that the three most important words over the past decade have been "made in China" rather than "war on terror," there can be no doubt that the world's largest economy (the US) and its fastest-growing one (China) appeared ever more tied together. With Beijing buying-up US debt with its accumulation of surplus dollars (approximately $1.3 trillion by 2007), China kept US inflation down while providing another motor for the global economy. But that predicament raised the specter of the economic clout of China as a serious national security threat to the US. Periodic outbreaks of China-bashing in Congress – featuring charges of China as a currency manipulator, an illegal export subsidizer, a violator of rights to intellectual property and trade law, and maintaining a lopsided trade surplus with the US ($233 billion in 2006) – echoed prior fears about the rise of Japan during the 1980s. For some, US power thus appeared to be in critical decline in South-east Asia, a region with three of the world's eleven largest economies (China, Japan and South Korea) and three of its four largest standing armies (China, North Korea, and South Korea). That perception fed into American fears that China was, variously, coming to join us, to get us or to buy us. Central to the question of US policy was whether Washington could, and should, seek to contain, to accommodate (or appease), or to "partner" China?

For some observers, the optimal response from the Obama administration was one centered on a sanguine, or even optimistic, outlook that viewed Beijing as a likely strategic partner for the US and a responsible stakeholder in a post-American, but not necessarily post-Western, international order. Given the material dynamism of China, accounting for some 30 percent of global economic production by 2008, and with security on the cheap from America's global role and an open US market for Chinese goods, Beijing had little obvious incentive to challenge the status quo. With the interdependence of the Chinese and American economies a brute fact of geo-economics and geo-politics, neither partner had an interest in initiating a cycle of mutually assured financial destruction. At the same time, the self-interest of the Chinese in regionalism rather than globalism tempered past rivalries. With an essentially benign set of neighbors in South Korea, Taiwan and Japan, a ruling communist party whose primary focus was inward looking, and an apparently clear allergy among the Beijing leadership to protracted international conflict, China represented a status quo power, not a revolutionary one. As Peter Trubowitz assessed the situation, "... Obama has geopolitical slack. The threat of terrorism remains, but today the United States does not face a geopolitical challenger, and the risk of a sudden shift in the distribution of international power is low."[16]

Echoing such an assessment, one of the most prominent proponents of this interpretation, G. John Ikenberry, concluded that, "Today's Western order, in short, is hard to overturn and easy to join."[17] But "The United States 'unipolar moment' will inevitably end. If the defining struggle of the twenty-first century is between China and the US, China will have the advantage. If the defining struggle is between China and a revived Western system, the West will triumph."[18] Although China constituted both a military and an economic rival to the US (unlike both the USSR and Japan previously), history demonstrated that there

Table 7.1 China versus the US and the West (OECD)

	Projections of GDP, 2005–30 at Purchasing Power Parity (US dollars [trillions])				Projections of Defense Expenditures, 2003–30 in US dollars (billions)*		
	China	US	OECD		China	US	OECD
2005	9	12	34	2003	60	417	740
2010	14	17	44	2010	88	482	843
2015	21	22	55	2015	121	554	962
2020	30	28	73	2020	152	628	1089
2025	44	37	88	2025	190	711	1233
2030	63	49	105	2030	238	808	1398

Source: Ikenberry, OECD, Economist Intelligence Unit.
*Calculated as a constant percentage of GDP (2003 as the baseline), OECD/EIU.

exist different types of power transitions. In this regard, the contemporary international order itself is historically distinctive – and arguably unique – because the US-led order is far more liberal than it is imperial, being "dense with multilateral rules and institutions – global and regional, economic, political, and security-related."[19] When combined with the existence of nuclear weapons among the major powers, which effectively abolished war-driven change as a historical process, the incentive structure confronting China compelled Beijing increasingly to work within, rather than outside, the established Western order, through institutions such as the UN Security Council, the World Trade Organization, and the G20. Since the road to global power, in effect, runs through the Western order and its multilateral economic institutions, Ikenberry argued, the key thing for US leaders to appreciate is that although it may be possible for China to overtake the US alone, it is much less likely that China will ever manage to overtake the Western order (as Table 7.1 illustrates). On that basis, the possibility of a genuine strategic partnership is in fact only risked by alarmists on the American side: Republican defense hawks fearful of Chinese militarism and Democratic trade protectionists (echoed to some extent by Tea Party Republicans) hostile to the results of free trade and the "outsourcing" of American jobs.

In stark contrast to Ikenberry, several influential analysts take a more pessimistic view, seeing China as a strategic rival to the US. Viewing the South-east Asia region as one "primed for rivalry," competition and conflict, perhaps leading to war, becomes increasingly likely. The model here is less the peaceful transition of power from the United Kingdom to the US of the mid-twentieth century, but rather the challenge posed to the UK and France by a rising Germany during the late nineteenth century. Whereas optimists held the prospect of South-east Asia resembling the post-1945 liberal security community in Europe, pessimists instead speculated that Europe's 1914–45 bloody past could yet be South-east Asia's future.

For some writers, the primary catalyst here stemmed from the external motives informing Chinese expansionism. A number of realist scholars, for instance, contended that China is using, and will continue to use, its growing influence to reshape international rules and institutions to serve its particular interests, and other states will view it as a growing security threat – a familiar feature of power transition politics. The offensive realist theorist, John Mearsheimer, warned starkly that China's impressive economic growth would mean that over coming decades a "policy of engagement is doomed to fail," and that China and the US are "destined to be adversaries."[20] The US and China are likely to engage in an intense security competition with considerable potential for war. Policy-makers in Washington should therefore ensure that the US did everything it actively could to slow the PRC's rise – a prescription that ran directly into the dilemma that Washington cannot halt or even greatly slow down China's rise without seriously damaging its own economic well-being.

Nor were such warnings about the ascent of China confined to realists. In heralding the "return of history," the influential neo-conservative commentator, Robert Kagan, argued that Chinese foreign policy thinkers envisage two worlds: either a Euro-Atlantic area pitted against Asia, or three contending forces based, respectively, on the dollar, the euro and the yuan. But whatever their differences, all Chinese foreign policy specialists consider "the trend toward Chinese regional hegemony unstoppable by any external force." On that basis, South-east Asia is emphatically not a zone of great power competition. The Chinese 2006 Defense White Paper noted that "Never before has China been so closely bound up with the rest of the world as it is today" and hence China needs a modern, capable military – not just national interests but national pride are at stake. As Kagan argues:

> This equation of military strength with international standing and respectability may be troubling to postmodern sensibilities … Lying behind this global complaint about China's military program is the postmodern assumption that an increasingly rich and secure nation like China doesn't need to build up its military capacity or seek self-reliance in preserving access to resources and markets … Chinese leaders don't believe any of this, and with reason.[21]

While the Chinese leadership deem it prudent not to claim interest in traditional forms of power, their actual policy is to accumulate more of it. Kagan concluded ominously that "If East Asia today resembles late-nineteenth century and early-twentieth century Europe, then Taiwan could be the Sarajevo of the Sino-American confrontation."[22]

For others, however, it is less the external ambitions of Beijing that raise the prospect of trouble ahead than the internal dynamics of China that appear worrisome. On this interpretation, the legacy of a tormented history across the centuries has meant that China remains caught between the Scylla of xenophobia and the Charybdis of hungering after modernization and innovation: "between global responsibilities and internal transitions."[23] As Chinese Premier Wen Jiabao stressed in both public and private, China's greatest challenges, along with the most serious threats to its stability, come from within rather outside. This view was echoed by Stefan Halper, who claimed in *The Beijing Consensus* that:

> ... two Chinas co-exist in the international system: the good neighbor and the rogue state ... this duality in China's global posture cannot be gradually transformed by the will of Western engagement or the leverage of Western coercion. This is because China's growing presence in the world at large is a function of the ruling party's drive to maintain control at home – and its immovable, historical fear of chaos.'[24]

Susan Shirk similarly argues in *China: Fragile Superpower* that "It is China's internal fragility, not its growing strength that presents the greatest danger."[25] The danger is that China's leadership employs a "wag the dog" strategy to mobilize domestic support by creating an international crisis, or responds with threats to a crisis that it cannot back down from fear of looking weak or "losing face." Leadership competition at home reveals the two faces of Chinese foreign policy: the responsible one that seeks to act cautiously in order to preclude international balancing against China; and the emotive or impetuous one that seeks to appeal to various domestic constituencies – the Chinese public, military, and Communist Party – through belligerently demonstrating their nationalist credentials. As Shirk notes, "Historically, rising powers cause war not necessarily because they are innately belligerent, but because the reigning powers mishandle those who challenge the status quo in one way or another."[26] For Washington, "Preventing war with a rising China is one of the most difficult foreign policy challenges our country faces."[27]

The historian Niall Ferguson also outlined four quite distinct future paths for China in his *Civilization: The West and the Rest*.[28] First, China could follow a path analogous to Japan. Second, it could witness extensive social unrest, with China only eighty-sixth in the world in per capita income, 150 million citizens living on $1.50 a day or less (1 in 10 of the population), and 0.4 percent of Chinese households owning 70 percent of the nation's wealth. When combined with high rates of pollution, an aging profile, and an acute gender imbalance, either revolution or radical nationalism could be the outcome. Third, a rising middle class could act as a break on imperialist adventurism. Fourth, Chinese missteps might antagonize its neighbors into forming an anti-Beijing balancing coalition led by a reinvigorated US.

Ironically, given the quite distinct analytic lenses on China, relatively little prescriptive difference exists among leading China scholars. At a basic level, most concur that some form of increasing, if inexact, parity between the powers is developing, requiring an adaptation on both parties' sides. The difficulty, however, resides in delineating just how far and fast such co-evolution should occur. For some Chinese observers, emboldened by China's ascent and America's seeming political and economic disarray, the US appears – even, or perhaps especially, under Obama – congenitally indisposed to gracefully acknowledging and accepting a reduced power status, role and responsibilities. As one critic put it, the Obama "... administration's penchant for self-righteous universalism, often revealed in coded phrases such as 'defending the global commons'," demonstrates that "the United States remains preoccupied with defending its 'second to none' position (in President Barack Obama's words)."[29] For the US, equally, the "declared goals of American policy have not changed since 1989":

> The United States wants to steer China in what Americans regard as a beneficial direction, smoothing and hastening its integration into the existing international order both economically and politically, enmeshing it in international economic agreements, taking advantage of the fact that economic development has been China's overriding priority to nudge China in a more liberal direction politically. In the meantime it strengthens American alliances, reassures China's democratic neighbours, and creates sufficient American military, economic and political strength in East Asia to prevent China from achieving its regional ambitions. Contain and transform, or, in the more polite phrases of diplomacy, "hedge" and engage. Given its beliefs and its history, it is hard to imagine the United States pursuing any other kind of policy toward China.[30]

Obama and China: from engagement to hedging

Upon assuming office, the Obama administration faced both positive and negative influences in renewing Washington's bilateral relations with Beijing. In terms of the former, Chinese leaders clearly perceived the US to be the key power with whom to do business over the medium term. While the European Union loomed as a trading partner of consequence – albeit mired in its own economic crisis – and while the US appeared stuck in relative decline, American economic, military, diplomatic and political weight meant that China's relationship with Washington would be the key global relationship for decades to come. That opportunity was nonetheless balanced, partially at least, by the historic tensions between the two states, the dangers inherent in great power transitions, and the historic unease felt towards Democratic rather than Republican administrations among China's leaders (stretching back to Mao).

Hillary Clinton's first high-profile visit to Beijing as Secretary of State, in March 2009, initially set a positive tone for the administration, stressing the importance of China for the region and the world, emphasizing China's role in the global economic recovery and, critically, framing the relationship in broad terms rather than – as China had feared – on narrower questions of human rights, democracy and civil liberties. The administration's creation of an enhanced "Strategic and Economic Dialogue" to supersede the Bush administration's more narrowly focused Special Economic Dialogue set up in 2006 – the first meeting of which was convened in Washington in July 2009 – offered an institutional means to implement a broader and enhanced interchange, and was welcomed by Beijing in indicating that Washington was animated by more than a purely economic relationship. The positive initiatives were also consolidated when presidents Obama and Hu met at the London G20 in April 2009, reaching broad agreement on how to combat the global recession. Although both rejected the notion of a *de facto* G2, the meeting confirmed that the quality of the US-China relationship would be critical to the resolution of almost all global economic, political and environmental challenges.

The latter stages of 2009 and 2010–12, however, witnessed a more difficult pattern of relations emerge, with a discernible shift in the administration's approach, from seeking a path of "strategic reassurance" to a less ambitious language about "building strategic mutual trust."[31] In part, this was unsurprising, given the mixture of cooperative and competitive relations inherent in the emerging relationship. With China having the most to lose from any fall in the value of the dollar, given its disproportionate dollar holdings, America's 2011 debt and default crisis proved an especially difficult moment for bilateral ties – China expressly calling on the US to implement substantial cuts in its "gigantic military expenditure and bloated social welfare costs" while warning that "a new, stable and secured global reserve currency may also be an option to avert a catastrophe caused by any single country."[32] Partly, though, the more conflictual elements that punctuated the dynamic reflected and reinforced some of the deep structural problems facing both the US and China in adapting to the relative power shifts of the other. Although President Hu's state visit to the US in January 2011 represented the eighth face-to-face meeting between the Chinese and US presidents in just two years, three areas especially stood out as reliably problematic strains in the bilateral relationship: the recovery from the Great Recession; Chinese military developments; and the perennial issue of Taiwan.

Economic relations

Although China's remarkable economic growth has fueled its increasing political clout, the US economy continues to dwarf that of China. While the latter is now the second-largest economy in the world in terms of purchasing power parity, China's gross domestic product – measured in the same terms – was barely half that of the US in 2008. Commonly referred to as *fu guo going min*, or "rich country, poor people," Chinese per capita income was some one-eighth of the US. The state and its branches may be rich and strong, but the average citizen remains relatively poor, often lacking access to rudimentary social services. But with the International Monetary Fund estimating that China would surpass the US as the world's largest economy by 2016, it was perhaps unsurprising that three-quarters of Americans (76 percent) in 2011 viewed China as more an economic than a military threat to the United States.[33]

The US remains China's largest export market, a key source of technological expertise and the principal pillar of the global economic stability that Beijing prizes. As the July-August 2011 controversy over a potential US default on its debt obligations also demonstrated, China has a large financial stake in the US. The leading foreign owner of US dollars (estimated in 2010 as some 70 percent of its total foreign exchange reserves worth US$2,000 billion) and the largest holder of US government debt, Beijing has a vital national interest in American economic solvency. Since, at the same time, the US relies heavily on credit from China to help finance persistent fiscal and current account deficits and to support the dollar – reliance that only deepened with the post-financial-crisis bank bail-outs and economic stimulus packages – the two nations' fates were inextricably linked together. While the US remains China's main national export market, fueling Chinese economic growth, cheap Chinese imports have facilitated US prosperity by enabling its economy (at least until 2008–09) to grow at a rapid pace without accompanying high inflation.

That linkage proved difficult for the Obama administration to leverage. At his confirmation hearings as US Treasury Secretary in February 2009, Timothy Geithner was quoted as accusing the Chinese of currency manipulation that underpinned China's lopsided surplus in bilateral trade (although the undervaluation of the renminbi contributed to this, the more influential factor was the glaring gulf between China's high savings rates, which generated persistent trade and current account surpluses and swelled its foreign exchange reserves, and the propensity of both spendthrift American government and households to favor debt-financed consumption, leading to large external deficits). During Obama's November 2009 visit to China, Beijing showed little flexibility in relation to the exchange rate of the yuan, the trade deficit or specific trade disputes with Washington.

Some Chinese (and Russian) officials exacerbated tensions by periodically floating the idea of the dollar being replaced as the global currency with an alternative, but the unconvertibility of the renminbi precludes such a course thus far. Despite much speculation about the end of the dollar's status as the reserve currency, no credible challenger has arisen to seriously displace the supremacy of the greenback. Despite recent developments, the Chinese renminbi is far from being a currency that non-residents want to hold as a store of value. Nor is it entirely clear whether China has the ambition, expertise or nerve to become the issuer of the key reserve currency. With the euro in deep difficulty amid sovereign debt crises and social and political unrest across Europe in 2010–11 – and a currency always intended for regional rather than international ambitions – there exists little incentive for the US to change the course of its dollar policy. That, in turn, presents a more serious problem for China and other dollar-holding nations than for the US, since the former are essentially stuck in the dollar-trap with limited scope for manoeuvre, aside from some minor diversification on the margins.

Although the US remains a huge military, diplomatic and economic presence in the Asia-Pacific, Washington cannot assert its interests as forthrightly as it once could. Obama's strategy relied on renewing US primacy in the region without antagonizing China, a difficult balancing act. Building on the Zoellick approach, economics and trade policy was "a priority of our foreign policy," according to Clinton in July 2011, with the US seeking to bind Asia in general – and China in particular – into a rules-based trading system: "We must reach agreement on the rules and principles that will anchor our economic relationships in the coming decades."[34]

But three substantial problems limit the potential of such an approach to succeed.

First, the network of trade pacts that has developed in the Asia-Pacific – with over 100 bilateral trade deals concluded in the past decade – does not resemble the type of consistent, transparent rules-based system advocated by Washington. The ten-member Association of South East Asian Nations represents the most coherent trade bloc in the region, and ASEAN concluded an important free trade agreement with Beijing in January 2011, allowing Chinese companies preferential access to a 600 million-plus market. But Washington was not a party to this compact.

Second, under Obama, Washington's own approach to trade policy – and regional trade policy especially – was, as David Pilling termed it, "something of a shambles."[35] Substantial elements of the congressional Democratic Party, along with labor unions and others active in the party base, were heavily opposed to expanding free trade agreements that, they alleged, outsourced US jobs overseas. Although, under George W. Bush, the US had signed a free trade agreement with South Korea in 2007, it still remained for the US Senate to ratify in 2011 – despite President Obama calling for action on the measure in his 2011 State of the Union speech and repeating this in his address to a joint session of Congress on September 8, 2011. With the twenty-one-member Asia-Pacific Economic Cooperation Group (APEC), of which the US is a member, many years from concluding a free trade deal, the Obama administration instead invested political capital in promoting a Trans-Pacific Partnership agreement among a sub-group of nine APEC members, including Australia, Chile and Singapore. But a TPP – even with the unlikely participation of Japan – would remain a very limited anchor for a genuine regional compact. While the US remained at the margins of some of the key economic relationships

Table 7.2 China's rank as a trading partner for selected Latin American Countries, 2000 and 2008

Country	Exports		Imports	
	2000	2008	2000	2008
Argentina	6	2	4	3
Bolivia	12	10	8	6
Brazil	12	1	11	2
Chile	5	1	4	2
Colombia	35	4	15	2
Costa Rica	26	2	16	3
Ecuador	13	9	10	2
El Salvador	35	16	18	5
Guatemala	30	18	15	4
Honduras	35	11	18	7
Mexico	25	5	6	3
Nicaragua	19	14	18	4
Panama	22	4	17	4
Paraguay	11	9	4	1
Peru	4	2	13	2
Uruguay	5	8	6	3
Venezuela	37	3	18	3

Source: Economic Commission for Latin America and the Caribbean; International Institute for Strategic Affairs, *Strategic Survey 2011: The Annual Review of World Affairs* (Abingdon: Routledge, 2011), 161.
Note: Data for Honduras and Nicaragua are for 2007 rather than 2008.

in the region, China was an increasingly prominent player in America's "backyard" of Latin America (see Table 7.2).

Third, as with other elements of the Obama advocacy of strategic engagement, the abstract theory of shared interests ran against the practical realities of power politics. While Washington necessarily had to be engaged in the Asia-Pacific in order to advance its strategic goals, persuading China to abide by its vision of a rules-based trading order was a difficult task. Although the Obama administration continued, both privately and (less directly) in public, to cajole Beijing into altering what it deemed to be unfair trade practices – from the abuse of intellectual property through closed procurement policies to preferential treatment (including subsidies and cheap funding) for state-owned enterprises – China's ascent allowed it to mostly ignore such pressures. Given the state of the bilateral relationship, Washington possessed very few incentives or sanctions either to persuade or to coerce China into preventing practices it considered unfair. Moreover, while Obama's marginalization of democracy and human rights was welcomed in Beijing, as Aaron Friedberg argues, showing softness on core values tends to reinforce Chinese views that the US is in terminal decline – potentially encouraging Beijing to miscalculate American resolve.[36]

American and Chinese economic interests are now so closely connected that provocative measures on trade by either side would likely backfire quickly. Whether the effect of the Great Recession mitigates the dangers inherent in such close interdependence remains to be seen. Until the Great Crash of 2008, China – thanks to cheap labor costs – exported deflation to the rest of the world, financing the US current account deficit by recycling its own surplus into US Treasury bonds. Now, deleveraging in the US, with reduced consumption and higher savings rates in the face of the credit crisis, could reduce the current account deficit and result in weaker demand for imports from China (and elsewhere). But the paralysis of the American political system that was displayed during 2011 counts against serious reductions in the deficit and debt of the "US of AA+" over the medium term.

At the same time, China's own problems are increasingly widely recognized. The nation's growth over the past decade has been fueled by an ever-growing trade surplus that has reached unsustainable levels. The Chinese leadership must refocus its economy away from export-oriented manufacturing and towards domestic sources of demand, all the while managing the job losses and social unrest that such restructuring will generate (this in the context of an estimated 180,000 riots, strikes and protests annually). Beijing's concerns about an American economic system once widely admired but now viewed with profound scepticism may yet see less willingness on the part of China to finance US debt. As the Obama administration discovered, the room for innovative policy-making – and for pressuring China to adjust its own economic approach – is strictly circumscribed. With China on course to overtake the US as the largest economy, global economic activity would nonetheless be more widely distributed than when, for example, the US accounted for more than half the world's wealth during the late 1940s. The US, Europe and Japan would likely balance China's growth and, as Malaysia's Prime Minister, Dato' Sri Mohd Najib bin Tun Abdul Razak, optimistically put it, "Our economies are so integrated and interdependent, and production processes are so dispersed across borders, that it no longer makes sense for global powers to go to war; they simply have too much to lose."[37]

To sceptics, the evolution of China's military hardware, grand strategy and personnel suggested otherwise. Whatever the priority attached to economics in Obama's foreign policy, more strategic themes were inextricably linked.

Chinese military developments: enter the dragon

Much as the economic ascent of China has altered the dynamics of trade relations and global economic governance, so its military modernization, expansion and occasional sabre-rattling has generated new concerns in Washington about regional stability in East Asia (and more widely afield), resource competition in the South China Sea, and the plight of the strait of Malacca (the corridor between Malaysia and Sumatra, through which one-quarter of the world's seaborne oil, two-thirds of its shipped gas, and half of world trade passes). Although the Chinese economy has been estimated to overtake that of the US by 2020 (among other speculative dates), some Sinologists have argued that China still falls far behind its superpower rival in terms of military might and readiness (China not having fought an actual war since it was defeated by Vietnam in 1979) – a situation that is unlikely to change for decades and should hence reassure US policy-makers of the benign nature of China's rise. But while Chinese officials consistently sought to portray military modernization as a natural outgrowth of the nation's economic rise and path of peaceful development, others were less convinced that China's military posture was the purely defensive matter that Beijing insisted upon, rather than the basis for a "force projection" capacity of substantial proportions.

Moreover, this was not merely a matter of Chinese modernization developments, since budgetary pressures on defense in the US threatened serious cuts in the Pentagon, with the Obama administration seeking defense reductions of $487 billion over ten years (with possibly double that figure, after the congressional deficit-cutting "super-committee" failed to reach agreement, in November 2011 – thereby mandating automatic additional cuts of approximately £500 billion from January 2013). Major cuts would leave the smallest US Army, Marines and tactical Air Force since 1947. With the navy at its smallest fleet-size since 1915, and budgetary pressures to cut the stealth Joint Strike F-35 fighter – the key for the continued salience of aircraft carriers, the basis of the US strategic presence in the Western Pacific – the Pentagon's ability to meet multiple national security challenges threatened to rapidly erode and degrade America's global power.

As with its economic policy, the Obama administration's defense policy towards China was a constant work in progress. Under Bob Gates, the Pentagon experienced periodic tensions with Beijing. During 2009, occasional spats occurred between rival submarines in the South China Sea, in what the US claimed were international waters but China argued were within its territory. Throughout Obama's term as president, evidence emerged of increasingly aggressive cyber-attacks against US public and private entities (including the Pentagon), originating in China and prompting the administration to establish a special office to coordinate the US response to cyber-war. Washington repeatedly called for more transparency in China's military modernization, to no effect. At one stage, US plans for arms sales to Taiwan resulted in a temporary suspension of military-to-military contacts. A number of incidents in the resource-rich South China Sea – which China claims in its entirety, rejecting partial claims by Vietnam, Brunei, Malaysia, the Philippines and Taiwan – involving China, Vietnam, the Philippines and India also excited concerns about China's growing maritime ambitions. When Gates visited China in January 2011, the authorities revealed the existence of a Chinese J-20 stealth fighter aircraft – a deliberate attempt to humiliate the Pentagon's boss – and shortly thereafter launched the maiden voyage of its first aircraft carrier, a refurbished Soviet-era vessel, the *Varyag*.

These specific tensions occurred against the broader backdrop of whether, and how, the US would seek to remain the key regional player in East Asia, given the ascent of China and the changing relationships with its neighbors that this appeared to imply. Led by Gates, the Obama administration consistently made clear its commitment to remaining an Asia-Pacific power, including the maintenance of a robust military presence in the region. Indeed, attempts to heighten and institutionalize military-to-military links with China were themselves emblematic of increasing US engagement with the region. Under Gates's leadership, Washington had deepened bilateral ties with India, Vietnam and South Korea, and expanded relations with Australia (including an agreement to place 2,500 Marines in the Northern Territories) and Singapore; in addition, Gates personally had attended the new ASEAN Defense Ministers Meeting Plus grouping. Moreover, despite tensions in the relationship, the rapid response of the US military to the earthquake and tsunami in Japan of March 2011 – involving 24,000 US personnel, 190 aircraft, and twenty-four ships working closely with Japan's Self-Defense Forces – testified to the continued US engagement in the region. In reply to a question from Singapore's Kishore Muahbubani at the IISS Shangri-La Dialogue of 3-5 June 2011, Gates even ventured that, "I will bet you $100 that five years from now, United States influence in this region is as strong if not stronger than it is today."[38]

Against this, however, was the widespread acceptance of China's developing "anti-access/access denial" capabilities to potentially deny the US a presence in the Western Pacific, the build-up of Chinese missiles targeted at Taiwan and a variety of other activities – from targeting space stations with missiles to developing a blue-water navy with aircraft carriers and underground ports – that clearly suggested a forward-leaning and offensive approach that could not possibly be purely defensive in nature. The sensitivity of these issues became especially apparent when the Pentagon issued its annual report to Congress on Chinese military developments in 2011. Reviewing the previous year, the Department of Defense concluded that by 2020 China would be able to project maritime power well beyond its shores. China was planning to build "multiple" aircraft carriers, with its first indigenous carrier due to operate by 2015.

Despite some signs of improved US-China military relations and a positive Chinese contribution to counter-piracy, disaster relief and peacekeeping operations, Beijing's growing military capabilities – including anti-ship ballistic missiles, new submarines and warships, enhanced cyber-warfare technologies, and a planned road-mobile intercontinental ballistic missile – posed an increasing level of concern for the Asia-Pacific region, not least in the context of competing territorial disputes and resource claims in the South China Sea, with its untold quantities of crude oil and natural gas.[39] The official Chinese response, through the Xinhua state news agency, was to echo its earlier vehement condemnation of American "addiction" to debt, this time accusing Pentagon analysts of inventing an "utterly cock and bull story" based on "a wild guess and illogical reasoning" that massively exaggerated the threat posed by Chinese military expenditure.[40]

Such strategic ambiguity on defense was not mitigated by Beijing's assisting Washington in other areas of geo-political concern to the US. Although, admittedly, China acquiesced in the 2010 round of new sanctions on Iran, not wishing to unnecessarily antagonize an America for which this was a top priority, this was in large part for fear of looking isolated in the face of UN Security Council agreement among the permanent powers (facilitated by Russian cooperation). Moreover, it came at the practical cost – along with Russian insistence – on weakening the package of measures implemented. At least as significant for the East Asian region, China's lack of effective pressure on North Korea, in relation to Pyongyang's nuclear and missile-development programs, its sale of these technologies to other countries, and its conventional and cyber weapons attacks on South Korea offered another example of a rather meagre return on Obama's investment in strategic engagement. With the development of long-range missiles, especially, North Korea was morphing from a regional gadfly whose provocations could lead to unpredictable, but containable, escalation on the peninsula into a direct threat to the United States. While Washington remained committed to the notion that the 2005 agreement on denuclearization reached at the Six-Party talks must be implemented, it remained determined to break the past pattern of providing concessions to persuade Pyongyang to join negotiations only to see it renege on past promises. Although Gates publicly affirmed that the Obama administration had "no interest in regime change" or in destabilizing North Korea, he was also adamant that the administration was "tired of buying the same horse twice."[41]

But while China worked behind the scenes to restart the Six-Party negotiations, it did not agree with the need for an improvement in North-South relations as a prerequisite to these recommencing. China steadfastly refused to condemn North Korea for its various provocations towards South Korea. For example, the UN Security Council issued a presidential statement condemning the sinking of the South Korean ship, the *Cheonan*, in July 2010, but without assigning blame to the perpetrator, North Korea (thanks to Chinese and Russian opposition). When the North bombed the South Korean island of Yeonpyeong, in November 2010, China avoided blaming either side and instead called for "maximum restraint," while Washington, Moscow and Tokyo all issued immediate condemnations of the North.

One final element also complicated the strategic calculus in the Asia-Pacific; namely, China's increasingly blatant employment of water as a political weapon. At the hub of Asia, China provides the source of cross-border river flows to the largest number of countries in the world, including Russia, India and the Indochina peninsula. But, in water disputes with almost all of its neighbors, not only does China steadfastly reject the concept of a water-sharing arrangement – as one of only three countries to vote against the 1997 UN convention on rules governing the shared resourcing of international watercourses – but it is also acquiring substantial leverage over neighboring states' behavior through its construction of major dams in disputed or insurgent territories (such as Kashmir and Burma) and on international rivers (such as the Mekong, Brahmaputra and Amur). With water becoming an increasingly scarce resource and an important cause of competition and conflict in Asia, as Brahma Chellaney notes, "That the country controlling the headwaters of major Asian rivers is also a rising superpower, with a muscular confidence increasingly on open display, only compounds the need for international pressure on Beijing to halt its appropriation of shared waters and accept some form of institutionalised cooperation."[42]

The 1982 UN Convention on the Law of the Sea, to which China is a party, provides an obvious basis for an agreement in the case of the South China Sea. But progress thus far has been stymied by China's insatiable quest for resources and its unwillingness to submit its extensive claims to arbitration by third parties. Once more, despite the obvious benefits that Beijing would gain from a stable system of accepted rules and norms, there appeared little sign that Washington's desire to establish a rules-based order was one that China was eager to join. Indeed, Hillary Clinton's well-intentioned offer during 2010 to mediate between the several disputatious parties, in the context of an insistence that the South China Sea was of strategic importance to the US as well, served only to antagonize Beijing even further.[43] Despite the overlapping claims of Malaysia, Vietnam and others, in 2010 China planted a flag at the deepest part of the South China Sea to mark its "undisputed sovereignty" over the territory. In 2011, Beijing sent warships there to patrol the waters. The implications for regional peace, and further escalation, are potentially disturbing in the extreme.

Taiwan

The third flashpoint in US-China relations is a more familiar one than the evolving economic and military challenges posed by Beijing: a leaf-shaped island some hundred miles off the coast of south-eastern China, over which it continues to claim sovereignty. As Richard Bush and Michael O'Hanlon remark, "War between China and Taiwan is a distinct possibility. Such a war could easily drag in the United States, pitting the world's only superpower against its main rising power and thus leading to the first serious conflict in history between nuclear weapons states."[44]

Alongside fear of US capacities stemming from the Gulf War of 1991, the growth of China's military power from the 1990s was initially driven by a desire to protect its particular interests in Taiwan, before this became more about fielding a military commensurate with its great power status during the 2000s. Amidst its carefully calibrated diplomacy stressing its "peaceful rise" and "harmonious world" vision, Taiwan has proven the one issue where China has repeatedly made clear its willingness to go to war. As Michael Mandelbaum notes:

> Taiwan has a particular resonance among Chinese because, having been seized by Japan in 1895 and protected from the mainland by the United States after 1950, it symbolizes the long decades of Chinese submission to the will of foreigners. By all accounts, the commitment to the eventual "reunification" of the island and the mainland pervades every stratum of Chinese society. Taiwan is one issue over which China does seem prepared to challenge the status quo in East Asia by force.[45]

The Obama administration largely maintained the long-term American position on strengthening its strategic position with Taiwan. While professing its willingness to defend its ally, Washington also pursued the logic of a using economic and military aid to support internal reform and a liberalizing economic order, encouraging Taipei to develop its multiplying economic ties with China on the basis that closer economic integration would provide additional incentives to both parties to avoid armed conflict in the Taiwan Strait.

Unfortunately, two problems undermined such logic. One was that an increasingly self-confident China concentrated ever greater military forces at the Taiwan Strait, about which the Chinese leadership remains neuralgic. The Obama administration's decision to sell Taiwan a weapons package worth $6.4 billion prompted a ten-month freeze in China-US military-to-military exchanges in 2011. When the administration announced another arms package in September 2011, it was careful to minimize the damage to relations with Beijing, offering to refurbish F-16 jets sold to Taiwan in 1992 but not to sell more sophisticated F-35s to the island. Such actions dismayed Taipei as yielding to Chinese pressure. Even so, the People's Daily – the Chinese Communist Party's organ – responded by decrying the Taiwan Relations Act requiring Washington to help the island defend itself as a "cancer."[46]

The second problem was that the Obama administration's pursuit of strategic engagement, combined with its downplaying of democracy promotion and a values-oriented agenda, failed to reverse Taiwan's uneasy slide into relative international isolation. As Gary Schmitt observed, "Making Taipei more confident about its place in the world is a necessary step in preventing it from taking sudden initiatives to reassert itself in the face of what it sees as affronts to its existing sovereignty."[47] But it remained the case that US Secretaries of State and Defense avoided visiting Taiwan while the visits of senior Taiwanese officials to the US remain tightly circumscribed. The strategic ambiguity of the US over Taiwan and the "one China" policy appears not only increasingly anachronistic, but also untenable, as the costs – and, increasingly, the very feasibility – of US military intervention in the Taiwan Straits in the mould of Bill Clinton's 1996 dispatch of two US aircraft carriers becomes ever more diminished.

Conclusion: the limits of strategic engagement with China

The relative decline and rise of America and China, respectively, can sometimes be viewed as a return to the US-Soviet pattern of bipolar competition of the Cold War. But the transition to a post-American world that China's rise denotes is not directly analogous to the Cold War. Rather, the growing influence of Beijing, and Asia more generally, signifies nothing less than the creeping end of 500 years of Western global predominance. Although no other country, China included, can yet replace the US as the center of the global financial system, the downgrading of its triple-A credit status in the fall of 2011 – once a core assumption, not a variable, of the system – is likely over time to erode the standing of the global public goods it supplies, from the dollar as the world's reserve currency to its financial markets as the best destination for other countries to deposit savings. This in turn will weaken America's effectiveness as the global anchor, accelerating an unsteady migration to a more multi-polar order. For Chinese communists to lecture the US on sound fiscal policy represented – to put it mildly – a telling indicator of the depths of America's contemporary fiscal disorder.

Whether the Chinese are genuinely committed to a "peaceful rise" or instead seek some kind of global "hegemony with Chinese characteristics" cannot reliably be ventured. Although one American strategist conceded that, in his interactions with Chinese officials, "the Chinese are very happy to see the world divided up between them and the US,"[48] it is important to emphasize that there exists not one single view in China but a plurality – some holding to a view that hegemony is the only way to secure China's future, others happy with the idea of a G2 dominating the global order, and still others viewing Beijing's global aspirations as the road to Chinese ruin.[49] Whether, equally, as some suggest, the US-China relationship conceals or obscures the real conflict in international politics – a clash of ideas between the "western" and the market authoritarian models – and whether a clash of Orientalist and Occidentalist civilizations is more likely than a crash on the part of one or other protagonist remains to be seen. Fear of China is palpable from India through Japan and the Philippines to Vietnam, and has partly pushed these nations into closer relations with the US. But, thus far, whatever the more opaque aspects of their statecraft, neither party seems to have yet made a colossal misreading of the other's strategic calculus (unlike the case of Anglo-German misunderstanding prior to the First World War). What does appear to be the case is that there exists, for Washington, no serious alternative to a strategy of "modified hedging" – absent a decisive or abrupt shift in China's strategic approach – since neither engagement nor containment can adequately address the duality of the PRC's "strategic personality." As one account persuasively put it:

> It will take time to reach the point where no major international question can be resolved without China, but that will be the aim. While avoiding confrontations, even over Taiwan, she will be a prickly and wilful power. As her strength and influence grow she will promote them with increasing finesse but also determination, by means short of war. And however much we might disapprove, with the sinews of the Chinese economy reaching into all major countries, what will we do to stop her? When American presidential candidates threatened to impose tariffs on Chinese imports if she refused to revalue her currency Beijing's response was to hint that she might off-load US dollars and bonds in retaliation. The lesson – never try to blackmail your communist banker – is an example of the unchartered waters the world is in where China is concerned.[50]

US-China relations under Barack Obama therefore continued a broad pattern set since at least 1989; one where the benefits of strategic engagement to the US were matched – and, arguably, exceeded – by its costs. While Washington and Beijing may "objectively" share certain interests in common, neither party shares the same priorities, values or long-term geo-political calculus. Sino-US relations remain in a state of uneasy accommodation, with Beijing viewing Washington as – at best – "neither friend nor enemy." As Andrew Nathan notes:

> It is no wonder that Chinese statecraft aims to establish the cultural relativity of human rights and to pose talk of human rights as the enemy of friendship. After all, the failure to respect human rights is a glaring weakness of Chinese power both at home and abroad, whereas promoting human rights has been among the United States' most successful manoeuvres on the wei qi board of world politics ... Emphasizing the principled centrality of the human rights idea to American ideology and keeping the issue active in bilateral relations even though it cannot be solved would seem to be – along with exercising the United States' strengths in other fields – a good way to set the boundaries within which a rising Chinese power can operate without threatening US interests.[51]

Selective cooperation is possible where some convergence can be created, but increased cooperation in some areas co-exists with a basic competitive dynamic and instances of increased competition and outright conflict in others.

Most obviously, Washington's attempts to remain a regional powerhouse in the Asia-Pacific region confront China's ascendant power. Although the leadership in Beijing fears its internal problems and the constant need for foreign trade to sustain a growing economy, the leverage possessed by the US to craft a rules-based trading order and to convince China to join that order is minimal. Moreover, while Washington fails to set its own economic house on a sound and sustainable course, Beijing's concerns about the safety of its assets raises major questions about the medium-term willingness of lenders to fund the US public debt. The military modernization that China's remarkable economic growth since 1978 has funded likewise raises fears in Washington of an inevitable conflict, while China's failure to exert pressure on North Korea to return to the Six-Party talks reflects its concern about state collapse, a secondary issue for Washington to its nuclear arsenal, long-range missile capacities and complicity in proliferation.

As Richard Haass, President of the Council on Foreign Relations, noted of the Obama administration, "If your goal is to reorient or refocus or rebalance US policy, the Administration's commitment to so doing is at the moment more rhetorical than actual."[52] Despite his quest to forge renewed relationships under the mantle of a post-American foreign policy, Barack Obama's policy towards Asia-Pacific has been "fundamentally similar" to that of George W. Bush inasmuch as it is intended to consolidate US strategic primacy in the Asia-Pacific, to maintain a robust presence to hedge Chinese military power and reassure Japan, Taiwan, South Korea, Australia and India while at the same time seeking greater cooperation on global concerns – especially in global economic management.[53] While the term has a somewhat hackneyed ring to it, little alternative presented itself to Washington to encouraging China to become a responsible stakeholder in world affairs. Some of the explanation for the lack of innovation under Obama can be laid at the door of the continuing focus of US energy on the Middle East, partly out of choice (the wars in Afghanistan and Iraq) and partly because of the unexpected impact of the Arab Spring. But US-China relations also continue to exhibit deep structural features that limit their straightforward renewal or improvement. Increasing mutual dependence and economic integration co-exist with serious ideological differences, a substantial trust deficit, and military budgets headed in contrasting directions. That effectively mandates a continued US policy of modified hedging to encourage China to be a strategic partner and to develop a shared strategy to that end, but also to respond – if necessary – in a timely and judicious manner to an increasingly pro-active China that challenges US influence not only in the Asia-Pacific, but also in key parts of the wider world.

8

Russia

*Russia has the potential to be richer, more powerful,
and more self-assured in 2025 if it invests in human capital,
expands and diversifies its economy, and integrates with
global markets.*
—Global Trends 2025: A Transformed World[1]

*They [Americans] are living beyond their means and shifting
a part of the weight of their problems to the world economy ...
They are living like parasites off the global economy and
their monopoly of the dollar ... If over there [in America]
there is a systemic malfunction, this will affect everyone.
Countries like Russia and China hold a significant part
of their reserves in American securities ... There should
be other reserve currencies.*
—Russian Prime Minister Vladimir Putin,
August 1, 2011[2]

*The basic fact of the current relationship is that many
Russians think, with good reason, that the United States
has essentially reneged on key parts of its settlement
with post-Soviet Russia. As a result, what most marks
Russia's orientation to the world, and to the United States
in particular, is a thick and toxic narrative of grievance.
The key to a successful reset policy is for the United States
to address these grievances, which are intelligible only
in terms of the Cold War settlement.*
—Daniel Deudney and G. John Ikenberry,
"The Unravelling of the Cold War Settlement"[3]

*Russia is claiming openly that all these countries
belong to the Russian zone. But the west should remember
something ... In old Soviet slang, "zone" meant
prison.*
—Vytautus Landsbergis, Lithuanian MEP
(and former leader of Lithuania)[4]

Introduction

Few capitals around the globe could rival Moscow's enthusiasm to welcome the departure of George W. Bush from the White House, herald the end of US hegemony and heartily toast the arrival of a post-American world. Ever since, in 1835, Alexis De Tocqueville famously predicted the eventual global dominance of the two continental powers of the US and Russia, bilateral relations between the two nations have been tense, suspicious and characterized by an abiding absence of mutual trust and confidence. The end of the Cold War, the wrenching collapse of the Soviet Union, and subsequent triumphalist "end of history" spread of the US-led West – and NATO, in particular – into the "post-Soviet space" has simply exacerbated long-standing historic rivalries and an acute Russian sense of national humiliation. While some Russians may disagree with Vladimir Putin's lamenting that the implosion of the Soviet Union represented "the greatest geo-strategic catastrophe of the twentieth century," relatively few viewed the subsequent aftershocks and the political, economic and social dislocation uncritically.

Whatever the impact on American power of major events from 9/11 and the Iraq War to the Great Recession, the US remains the leading nation-state in the world. By contrast, Russia has been a European outlier: oppressive, impoverished and resentful. Russia possesses just 2 percent of the world's population and a mere 2 percent of the world's gross domestic product, its economy on a par with that of the Netherlands. Its demographic crisis – combining low fertility rates with diminishing life expectancy, rampant alcoholism, high rates of HIV/AIDS and a collapsing health care system – means that its population is declining rapidly, especially in the eastern part of the state. With the average Russian of fifteen years old now having a shorter life expectancy than a Somali teenager of the same age, depopulation threatens steadily to erode the material base of Russian resources, economic growth and geo-political influence.

Partly as a consequence, a growing gap characterizes Russia's self-perception as a major power in a multi-polar world and the reality of the actual – attenuated – role that it plays in global and regional affairs. Less a neo-imperial power than a post-imperial one where the necessary will to expand and dominate is mostly exhausted, Moscow's occasional bouts of grandstanding – from the invasion of Georgia in 2008 to cyber attacks on Baltic states and energy blackmail threats against former Soviet republics and Europe – excite intermittent international concern. But, unlike China, Russia's future prospects as a world power appear singularly unpromising, as a declining power rather than an "energy superpower." Reliant on its nuclear deterrence to counter-balance other powers, Russia's conventional military forces pose a limited threat to former Soviet republics such as Georgia and Ukraine but represent an increasing global irrelevance.

Given that profoundly unpropitious context, the US could perhaps be forgiven for permanently relegating US-Russian relations to a secondary status in its statecraft. But after a turbulent eight years under George W. Bush that saw bilateral relations with Moscow descend into mutual acrimony and recrimination, Barack Obama made the renewal and improvement of bilateral relations with Russia a key objective of his post-American foreign policy. Aside from its intrinsic benefits and practical achievability, the prospect of better US relations with Moscow offered a number of potential strategic and tactical gains for Washington, from non-proliferation and arms control to Iran and Afghanistan. Moreover, a renaissance in relations with Russia appeared timely.

Perhaps more than in most US bilateral relations under his presidency, Obama's declared policy to "reset" relations with Russia enjoyed some success during his term as president, partly facilitated by a Moscow that – owing to the deep impact of the Great Recession in 2009, which saw Russian GDP decrease by 10 percent that year, and the partial eclipse of the ex-KGB chief and ultra-nationalist Vladimir Putin by the younger and more pragmatic Dimitri Medvedev as president – was less implacably activist, assertive and obstructive during 2009–12. Yet even here, the tangible results of a more empathetic US approach proved limited in number, decidedly ambiguous in quality, and of uncertain duration. Moreover, while selective aspects of the bilateral relationship showed demonstrable improvement over the course of Obama's term, the future of Russo-American relations remained largely in flux by its latter days. A new model of US-Russian cooperation premised on addressing the realities of the twenty-first century, rather than echoing the Cold War, had yet to be constructed by Obama.

For some critics of the Obama administration, on the left and the right, the Russian case provides another unfortunate example where traditional US values have been egregiously compromised for the sake of transient short-term interests. In particular, in the headlong pursuit of improved relations with Russia, Obama is castigated as having betrayed Eastern Europe and ex-Soviet republics by abandoning a promised missile defense system, freezing the Bill Clinton-initiated policy of NATO enlargement (extending to those states that could meet the necessary terms of a "double security" within both NATO and the European Union) and leaving Moscow effectively free to aggressively dominate its "Near Abroad." Administration silence on Russia's internal corruption – the state falling in 2011 to its lowest rating on Transparency International's corruption index, at 154 out of 178 nations – and repression was almost as deafening as that towards Saudi Arabia. Moreover, that silence was – not unlike that towards Saudi Arabia – also revealed to be hypocritical. While the public face of the Obama administration sought zealously to treat Moscow with exaggerated respect, the disclosure by Wikileaks of internal State Department cables in the winter of 2010 suggested a much less sanguine and positive private view, in which Medvedev was derisively depicted as "Robin" to Putin's "Batman," the Russian prime minister was described as an "Alpha-dog," and a definitive verdict was offered that:

> Russia is a corrupt, autocratic kleptocracy centered on the leadership of Vladimir Putin, in which officials, oligarchs and organized crime are bound together to create a "virtual mafia state," according to leaked secret diplomatic cables that provide a damning American assessment of its erstwhile rival superpower. Arms trafficking, money laundering, personal enrichment, protection for gangsters, extortion and kickbacks, suitcases full of money and secret offshore bank accounts in Cyprus: the cables paint a bleak picture of a political system in which bribery alone totals an estimated $300bn a year, and in which it is often hard to distinguish between the activities of the government and organized crime.[5]

Among the Wikileaks claims were allegations that: Russian spies used senior mafia bosses to carry out criminal operations, such as arms trafficking; law enforcement agencies such as the police, spy agencies and the prosecutor's office operated a *de facto* protection racket for criminal networks; rampant bribery served as a parallel tax system for the personal enrichment of police, officials and the KGB's successor, the Federal Security Service (FSB); investigators looking into Russian mafia links to Spain compiled a list of Russian prosecutors, military officers and politicians who had dealings with organized crime networks; and Prime Minister Putin had amassed "illicit proceeds" from his time in office, which various sources claimed are hidden overseas.

Such unedifying features of contemporary Russia hardly made for an easy partner for Obama's Washington, with the opaque nature of the Putin-Medvedev relationship complicating assessments of both power politics and policy. Nonetheless, a pragmatic and transactional relationship – encompassing diplomatic, military and economic aspects – developed under the guise of a genuine personal rapport between Obama and Medvedev. With only mild objection from the US administration, Russian reassertion of its military, diplomatic and economic weight in the post-Soviet space advanced from the Kremlin's recognition of the independence of Georgia's separatist regions of Abkhazia and South Ossetia after the 2008 Georgian war to the seemingly more benign project of a "common economic area" involving the free movement of goods, services and capital in Russia, Belarus and Kazakhstan in 2011–12. Whether the trade-off reached by Obama between promoting American values and securing US interests was on balance reasonable remains to be seen, not least since the future of the "reset" appeared highly uncertain by 2012. But the Russian example, while still illustrative of the limits of strategic engagement for a post-American foreign policy, proved to be a relatively rare and clear – if qualified and contingent – success story of sorts for President Obama's grand strategy.

Resetting Russian-American relations

Despite its neuralgic nationalism and chronic internal problems, Russia's manifest salience to a post-American foreign policy cannot be denied. As Michael Mandelbaum notes:

> Russia's importance comes from its size – it is geographically the world's largest country – its substantial stockpile of nuclear weapons, which rivals that of the United States, its considerable reserves of minerals, especially oil and natural gas, and its location. It is part of the world's three most strategically important regions: the Middle East – the Persian Gulf with its even greater energy reserves lies to Russia's southeast; East Asia, via the country's long Pacific coastline and border with China; and Europe, where Russia has functioned as a great power since the time of the tsar Peter the Great in the seventeenth century.[6]

Since the end of the Cold War and the collapse of the Soviet Union in 1991, relatively little in the way of elite consensus has emerged over how US foreign policy should approach post-Soviet Russia. The influential book by Edward Lucas, *The New Cold War*, aptly summarized one school of pessimistic thought. Highlighting Moscow's often bellicose pronouncements, suppression of free expression and civil rights, its looming menace to the Baltic states and Georgia, and its habitually zero-sum approach to international relations, Lucas framed Russia as an adamant Western rejectionist in which "bribery and corruption are not part of the system, they are the system."[7] A corrupt and kleptocratic regime resistant to Western interests and rejecting Western values such as political freedom, the rule of law, the separation of powers, a free press and individual rights, the ruling monopoly of the United Russia party was, according to former Soviet premier Mikhail Gorbachev, a "worse version of the Soviet Communist party."[8]

The Lucas school was framed by the Putin era from 1999–2008, in which Russian recovery from Boris Yeltsin's desultory presidency and the oligarch-dominated 1990s was driven by a petro-boom that allowed the president to deliver economic prosperity – with economic growth at 7 percent or more annually from 2000–07 – while simultaneously rigging the political system, dismembering the independent mass media and taking on the oligarchs that dominated Russia's business world. Through the zealous recruitment of former security and military officials, many with personal ties to him from his years in the KGB at St Petersburg, President Putin's deployment of the *siloviki* assisted his administrating the national economy through a newly centralized system of "managed" or "sovereign democracy." More interested in extracting rents from their economic holdings than engaging in productive investment or portfolio diversification, the *siloviki* presided over an era of rampant crony capitalism that, while not necessarily in the best interests of the nation, nonetheless produced substantial popularity for Putin as president – assisted by a combination of economic nationalism, post-imperial nostalgia for the

Soviet era, and Putin's "cult of personality" aggressively heralding the overdue return of Russia to great power status.

At the same time, a more tempered interpretation instead stresses not the robustness but the fragility of Russian recovery. Two aspects in particular stand out here. First, as a controversial article by Jeffrey Tayler in *The Atlantic* put it in 2001, whatever the Putin bluster, the reality remains that Moscow's days as a great power are effectively "finished":

> Russia's thousand-year history has destined it to shrink demographically, weaken economically, and, possibly, disintegrate territorially. The drama is coming to a close, and within a few decades Russia will concern the rest of the world no more than any Third World country with abundant resources, an impoverished people, and a corrupt government. In short, as a Great Power, Russia is finished.[9]

Second, with the Cold War's demise and the implosion of the USSR, Russia has experienced a national trauma and a transition from imperialism that it has, arguably, handled relatively well. The vast Soviet military industrial complex proved a massive burden for the economy and, as Dmitri Trenin – director of the Carnegie Moscow Centre – documents, by any reasonable standard, Russia achieved one of the most stunning demilitarizations in modern history after 1991.[10] Compared in particular to the protracted and violent post-World War Two transitions from empire of France, the United Kingdom and Portugal, Russia measured up comparatively well. Indeed, as Stephen Kotkin argues, given the scale of the social, economic and political turmoil that transpired after 1991, in retrospect it appears staggering that the mayhem of 1990s Russia – tumultuous as it then seemed – was not infinitely worse.[11]

Whatever interpretation best persuades, however, one undeniable feature of Russia's international standing was clear as Obama assumed office. By the end of the George W. Bush presidency, Russian-American bilateral relations were in as poor a shape as they had ever been in the post-1991 era. Although the 2000s had begun well enough, with Bush initially keen to re-emphasize great power relations (prior to 9/11 and, subsequently, through the lens of the global war on terror), seeing Vladimir Putin's soul by looking at his eyes, and having an opportunity to share interests in countering Islamist terrorist threats across Central Asia, most of the decade saw periodic bilateral tensions flare over key flashpoints: the legacy of the 1999 Kosovo war and NATO expansion; the Anti-Ballistic Missile (ABM) Treaty and missile defense; the Iraq war; the Rose revolution in Georgia and the Orange revolution in Ukraine; and Iran's nuclear program. While there was occasional cooperation on some issues of mutual concern, such as North Korea, disagreements between Washington and Moscow remained marked throughout the decade. Although Moscow ultimately accepted the US unilateral withdrawal from the ABM Treaty of 1972, it refused to countenance Bush administration plans for a defensive anti-Iranian ballistic missile defense shield in Poland and the Czech Republic.

The fallout over the August 2008 war in Georgia capped a steady deterioration in bilateral relations that appeared set on an inexorable path towards an adversarial Cold War-style relationship.

Obama's capturing the presidency offered a new opportunity for a relaxing of the US-Russian relationship. First, the two themes that had largely defined the parameters of bilateral relations previously – nuclear parity and ideological confrontation – had lost much of their impetus by 2008. Obama's campaign, which had emphatically rejected "forward-leaning" ideological assertion by the US and embraced arms reduction and non-proliferation as key strategic priorities, offered a serious opportunity to move beyond past patterns of pathological behavior. Second, by rejecting the emphasis on democracy promotion and human rights of the Bush years (at least during the Bush administration's first term), an Obama administration promised a more pragmatic interlocutor for Moscow, one willing and able to abandon patronizing lectures on Russia's democratic deficit and dysfunctional internal arrangements. Third, although US relations with Russia were at their lowest point for some twenty-five years when Obama assumed office, that very trough offered opportunities for tangible gains for both parties out of their own self-interest. Establishing improved relations with Moscow was not a utopian but an achievable foreign policy goal – one more so, arguably, than reaching a genuine strategic partnership with China or making substantial progress in the Israel-Palestinian conflict and the broader Middle East – that could also potentially provide a useful demonstration effect to other states wavering in their attitude to Washington. Fourth, although Russia did not figure prominently in Obama's foreign policy statements in his election campaign, it did represent a prominent part of the new administration's emphasis on strategic engagement, fresh beginnings and American renewal. As Obama had written in 2007:

> Although we must not shy away from pushing for more democracy and accountability in Russia, we must work with the country in areas of common interest – above all, in making sure that nuclear weapons and material are secured. We must also work with Russia to update and scale back our dangerously outdated Cold War nuclear postures and de-emphasize the role of nuclear weapons. America must not rush to produce a new generation of nuclear warheads. And we should take advantage of recent technological advances to build bipartisan consensus behind ratification of the Comprehensive Test Ban Treaty.[12]

In sum, improved relations with Russia fitted easily and well with a host of other Obama administration concerns, from non-proliferation to counter-terrorism, and offered several prospects for real gains without inflicting major costs or climb-downs on either party. Not least, Russian assistance could potentially prove crucial in key areas of US interest, especially in Afghanistan (where Moscow could offer valuable logistical support and diplomatic pressure on Central Asian republics) and Iran (where Russian decisions would exert a major influence on diplomacy, possible sanctions and even the prospect of US military action).

Perhaps more so than in most of Washington's bilateral relations – and certainly more so than in his relations with traditional US allies such as France and the UK – Obama (and Hillary Clinton, in particular) therefore assiduously cultivated a very public "reset" of relations with Moscow from his administration's earliest days. Meeting in London during the G20 in April 2009, Obama and Medvedev issued an important joint statement declaring that the two states were both "ready to move beyond Cold War mentalities and chart a fresh start in relations between our two countries."[13] In a speech during a summit in Moscow on July 7, 2009, addressing the future direction of US foreign policy under his leadership, Obama reiterated his call for a "reset" in US-Russia relations that would move both parties away from a zero-sum outlook on world affairs that viewed other countries largely as pawns to be moved around on a global chessboard. Underpinning that new relationship between the two great powers, Obama identified five key areas that could form the base for a new foreign policy framework between Washington and Moscow: reversing the spread of nuclear weapons; isolating and defeating violent extremism; increasing global prosperity; protecting human rights; and advancing international cooperation while respecting the sovereignty of states.[14]

Missile defense, New START, and Afghanistan

Translating those commitments into tangible policy achievements focused on three areas in particular: ballistic missile defense, arms control and non-proliferation, and Afghanistan.

Missile defense

An initial focus for prompt action by the Obama administration concerned ballistic missile defense, a bone of great contention in bilateral relations during the George W. Bush era. Bush had shown little interest in arms control or disarmament. Not only did the US unilaterally abrogate the ABM Treaty with Russia in 2001, but the Bush administration worked with the nuclear-industrial complex, sympathetic Pentagon officials and security hawks in Congress to develop a new class of "bunker-busting" nuclear weapons designed to destroy hardened or buried weapons-of-mass-destruction facilities (aimed at Iran in particular). The Bush administration had also supported Pentagon efforts to maintain "replacement" nuclear warheads in addition to those officially included in the inventory of the active US nuclear arsenal.

Such an approach worsened relations with Russia, but Moscow was especially troubled by the Bush administration's stance on missile defense.

Bush's 2007 decision to deploy missile defense systems in Central Europe was intended to defend the US against an Intercontinental Ballistic Missile (ICBM) attack from Iran, which analysts believed could occur by 2015. Bush proposed a "Third Site" system – to complement the two existing missile defense sites in California and Alaska – comprising ten silo-based interceptors in Poland and an X-band tracking-radar base in the Czech Republic. Critics of the system charged it with being too partial, since the ICBM threat from Iran to Western Europe and America was less credible than the short and medium-range Iranian threat to south-eastern Europe and Turkey, which were not covered by Bush's system of layered defense.

Consistent with his 2008 campaign commitments, Obama changed course within his first hundred days as president, making a new commitment to arms control and non-proliferation. This was most clearly outlined in his first major speech on arms control and non-proliferation, delivered in Prague, the Czech Republic capital, in April 2009, where the president set out an unequivocal American commitment to seek the peace and security of a world without nuclear weapons.[15]

Obama also moved quickly to reverse the Bush administration's decision to construct the anti-Iranian missile defense system in Poland and the Czech Republic, an initiative that had provoked Moscow into threatening Poland with severe military consequences for its acquiescence in the plan. In its place, Obama proposed a new architecture. A "European Phased Adaptive Approach" (EPAA) substituted the Bush silo-based system with a mobile, adaptable missile shield. Focused on medium-range threats to Europe from the Middle East, this involved fielding sea-based interceptors deployed on Aegis cruisers and versions of the Navy's Standard Missile (SM)-3 to protect US allies in the whole of Europe, as well as Turkey. Only in the longer run would the EPAA focus on intercontinental missiles threatening the United States.

Russia responded favorably to the Obama reversal, both in terms of its substance and also, simply, because Obama implemented what he had previously pledged to do (something that Moscow had not reliably experienced under Bush). In return for Obama's reconfiguring the proposed missile shield, Moscow felt obliged to respond in kind and abandoned its threat to station Iskander missiles in Kaliningrad (a warning provocatively issued by President Medvedev the day after Obama's election, on November 5, 2009), an ominous threat to Eastern Europeans. The revised missile defense plans also increased hopes for the new strategic arms control agreement to replace the START I treaty, which was due to expire on December 5, 2009. Initially, Russia had balked at a new agreement, in the hope of extracting a commitment from the Obama administration to forego entirely any future construction of an anti-ballistic missile system in Europe. But Obama refused to accede to the Russian demand, to the point of threatening to end the talks, leading to the dropping of Moscow's demands and the eventual conclusion of a new treaty.

Once Moscow abandoned the ambitious idea of a European security treaty, a series of NATO-Russia summits and meetings attempted to reach a consensus on missile defense. Having proposed a "sectoral approach," in which Russia would assume responsibility for protecting north-eastern Europe, by March 2011 Moscow instead insisted that NATO – by which it meant the US – should provide legally binding guarantees that future land-based interceptors aimed at intercontinental ballistic missiles would not be targeted to intercept Russian missiles. The US instead proposed to begin practical cooperation on earlier, shorter-range phases of the missile defense system and to build trust in that fashion. Conscious that strong opposition from Republicans in Congress would preclude the US offering legally binding guarantees, the Obama administration made important progress on a previously divisive issue for Moscow – but the matter of missile defense remained a key, and problematic, issue in bilateral and NATO relations with Russia. Three aspects of the revised system also raised problems.

First, the initial announcement of the realigned system was very poorly timed. Rather than following consultations with key allies such as Poland and the Czech Republic – which one might reasonably have anticipated, given Obama's unrelenting criticism of the Bush administration's "unilateralism" – the announcement was made without coordination. Moreover, the fact that it coincided with the seventieth anniversary of the Russian invasion of Poland was, to understate the matter, hardly a triumph of diplomacy.

Second, while its supporters viewed favorably a less American-centric system that covered south-eastern Europe and Turkey, this ignored some of the key reasoning behind the previous administration's approach. According to a former senior official in the Pentagon under Bush, part of the rationale for the silo-based system was to try to encourage European members of NATO to contribute more to their own collective self-defense.[16] Although NATO's European members could supply additional components such as radars or interceptors to complete or strengthen the system, the Obama version essentially exempted them from such pressures. The US-supplied EPAA instead provided Europe with a missile defense system for free, an outcome that Secretary Gates would subsequently come to rue in regard to other aspects of Europe's diminishing defense capacities within NATO.

Third, the dynamics of the negotiations over missile defense captured in miniature some of the broader tensions in Washington-Moscow relations and the reset. Mark Fitzpatrick asserted that:

> Although Obama's decision to realign the defense shield was not made as a concession to Russia, many Russians believe otherwise, not least because Obama's opponents in the United States have said so. The danger is that Russia will believe this rhetoric and take to heart the lesson that belligerence pays.[17]

While Fitzpatrick was arguably wrong on the first aspect – the revised system was, at least in part, a "goodwill" concession to Russia – Moscow's analysis did seem to embrace the notion that belligerence could yield positive results.

New START

Securing an arms control replacement to START I offered the second, and major, symbolic achievement, offering a win-win prospect for both parties. Beginning in May 2009, several rounds of talks followed to agree a new treaty. Ironically, while Russia had more to gain from this, Washington acted in a way that suggested it needed the agreement more urgently. By resuming the path of reducing their warheads and calling on other powers to follow suit, Moscow and Washington could rapidly create a symbolic statement of intent to advance Obama's non-nuclear agenda. In substance, as with many prior arms reductions agreements, the extent to which the cuts were substantive rather than cosmetic could legitimately be questioned. Moreover, Moscow evidently had more to gain from the compact than Washington, but the Obama administration viewed passage of the treaty as key for the reset, its non-proliferation agenda and increasing pressure on Iran and North Korea.

The New START treaty replaced the Moscow Treaty of 2002 (SORT), which had been scheduled to run until the end of 2012. Under the New START terms, a limit of 1,550 was placed on the number of offensively deployed warheads, a 30 percent reduction from SORT's maximum allowable: 2,200. New START also placed a limit of 800 deployed and non-deployed strategic nuclear-delivery vehicles (intercontinental ballistic missiles, submarine-launched ballistic missiles and nuclear-capable heavy bombers), 700 of which can be deployed. The treaty also allowed for satellite and remote monitoring, as well as eighteen on-site inspections per year for verification purposes.

Such headline figures were somewhat misleading, though, with the genuine reductions more modest in scope. Existing deployments were already less than under START I and SORT, thanks to the growing obsolescence of the nuclear arsenals developed during the Cold War. The US reduction would amount to 10 percent over seven years. An additional aspect of the more ambiguous nature of the arms control initiative was that New START placed no constraints on non-deployed nuclear weapons, including those removed from deployed systems under the terms of the treaty. Such weapons – in storage or awaiting dismantlement – amounted to several thousand on both sides. By reducing deployed-launcher levels to 700 while keeping warhead levels high and discounting bomber loads, New START also created an even greater incentive for Russia to field land-based missiles with multiple warheads. Nor did New START address "sub-strategic" weapons, such as Russia's estimated 2,000 deployed tactical nuclear weapons or some 200 gravity bombs at US bases in Europe. The agreement's silence on "tactical" nuclear weapons – as though any nuclear weapon can be purely tactical or "sub-/non-strategic" – was especially welcome to Moscow, allowing Russia to preserve its estimated 10-to-1 advantage in this category of weapons. If anything, the Russian advantage was even greater, since the Obama administration's Nuclear Posture Review (NPR) of 2010 eliminated the US sea-based nuclear-cruise-missile force without getting anything from Moscow in return.

Even this relatively modest proposal generated significant political opposition in Washington.[18] Strongly backed by Senator John Kerry (D-MA) and Richard Lugar (R-IND), chair and ranking member of the Senate Foreign Relations Committee respectively, the Committee voted 14–4 in favor of ratifying New START on September 16, 2010. The measure had support from three Senate Republicans: Lugar, Bob Corker (R-TN), and Johnny Isakson (R-GA). Despite pressures from some Republicans and Democrats such as Ben Nelson (D-NEB) not to do so, Obama made passage of New START a priority for the lame-duck session of Congress after the midterm elections of 2010, knowing that a delay until January 2011 – with the entry of a new cohort of conservative Republican senators and an even more conservative GOP caucus – would almost certainly jeopardize the treaty's ratification. Republican opposition, led by Senator Jon Kyl (R-AZ) centered on three areas: verification, missile defense, and modernization of America's nuclear arsenal.

Undercutting the famous Reagan adage of "trust but verify," while New START allowed for on-site visits and data exchanges, it abandoned on-the-ground monitoring of Russia's missile-manufacturing facilities and allowed Russia to withhold telemetry of some of its missile tests, undermining Washington's ability to know what nuclear materials were being produced and developed.

The most pressing question related to New START and the Nuclear Posture Review is whether or not they helped the US to meet its most important security challenges, which the NPR – in a striking continuity with the Bush administration – correctly identified as nuclear terrorism and the emerging nuclear powers of Iran and North Korea. The NPR recommended building on efforts like the Proliferation Security Initiative, the Global Nuclear Energy Partnership, the Global Initiative to Reduce Nuclear Terrorism, and the Department of Energy's non-proliferation activities. It also called for hardening US Command, Control, and Communications networks for nuclear weapons and studying the requirements for maintaining the necessary industrial base for follow-on systems to the Minuteman ICBM and Trident SLBM.

To its critics, New START appeared in direct tension, if not contradiction, to the NPR of 2010. First, the NPR had stated that the US could reduce its reliance on nuclear weapons because of new developments in missile defense and conventional military capabilities.[19] But, despite repeated assurances from the administration that the treaty would not limit either category, New START contained both explicit and implicit limitations on both. Regarding missile defense, Article 5 of the treaty expressly precluded any further conversion of ICBM silos for use by defensive interceptors. Although the

Obama administration had developed no plans to convert additional ICBM silos for that purpose, it had been considered by prior administrations and, given the additional limitation on using submarines to launch missile-defense interceptors, the limitation could prove problematic in the future if it is determined that more interceptors are needed to defend the United States. It may also become problematic if the administration's Phased Adaptive Approach – which had encountered non-trivial technical and cost problems by 2010–11 – is eventually abandoned in favor of the "hedge" announced by Secretary of Defense Robert Gates in September 2009, the two-stage version of the Ground Based Interceptor. Such an eventuality would incense Moscow, which has already threatened to leave the New START treaty if the US increases its missile-defense capabilities. New START also counts conventional Global Precision Strike weapons – supposed, under the NPR, to relieve the US of some its nuclear weapons arsenal – in the same column as nuclear ones.

Second, while the NPR called for maintaining a safe and secure nuclear force capable of performing the national security tasks of deterring attack on the United States and reassuring friends and allies about America's extended deterrent, it also announced a new declaratory policy that undercut US capacities to deter biological attacks that could prove as lethal as and more probable than nuclear attack. As the Graham-Talent Commission on the Prevention of Weapons of Mass Destruction Proliferation and Terrorism noted, while Obama had prioritized arms control and nuclear non-proliferation, the administration displayed "no equal sense of urgency" regarding the most probable source of WMD attack on America: biological weapons.[20] More directly, and despite welcome commitments of resources to the nation's nuclear infrastructure, the NPR imposed severe constraints on the modernization and maintenance of the US nuclear stockpile. Unlike all other nuclear states, there can be no new weapons, missions or designs for America's stockpile, only the refurbishment and reuse of existing weapons and components.

Although some on the right – such as Robert Kagan – saw New START as too insignificant to merit partisan rancor,[21] other hawkish critics viewed the treaty as seriously flawed.[22] Not only did New START impose more obvious costs and limits on the US than Russia, it also incentivized China to increase its missile stock to reach, or exceed, parity with the two other powers. Since Russia had no interest in reducing its stock of tactical nuclear weapons, New START arguably represented not the beginning of an ongoing process of arms reduction that Obama had promised, but its outer limit.

Despite the problems and criticisms of New START, the US Senate gave its "advice and consent" to the ratification of the treaty on 22 December 2010, by a vote of 71 to 26. Thirteen Republican senators crossed party lines to vote in favor of the resolution, along with all fifty-six Democratic senators and both Independent senators. Obama signed documents completing the US ratification process on February 2, 2011, the treaty entering into force three days later. It was expected to remain in force until 2021.

Afghanistan, Central Asia and the "post-Soviet space"

A third area of productive agreement was Afghanistan. Although their interests did not coincide exactly, neither Washington nor Moscow wished to see a return of the Taliban to Kabul. Russian agreement to provide transport routes for NATO supplies and transit routes for the US air-force offered an important alternative to the increasingly dangerous routes through Pakistan, which had been subject to sudden closures by Islamabad and intermittent attacks by Taliban and other Islamist forces. While Russia was hardly invested in NATO's ultimate success in Afghanistan, it nonetheless had a clear interest in regional stability and sought both to assist NATO while simultaneously preparing for what appeared to be an inevitable NATO withdrawal by 2014.

To some extent, then, the Obama administration's emphasis on a "reset" won some important gains from Russia.

Nor, contrary to some of Obama's critics, should this be interpreted as some kind of abject betrayal or "sell-out" of eastern European interests and security. Arguably, the main security problem in the post-Soviet region was never adequately addressed by the Bush administration: the near defenseless state of the Baltic states of Estonia, Latvia and Lithuania. Their security rested on the treaty pledge of NATO Article V that provides for collective self-defense, but most practical measures to ensure this (such as planning and joint exercises) were not undertaken. The Baltic states were thought to have sought specific military guarantees from NATO under Article V of its charter ever since joining the alliance in 2004 – requests that intensified after Estonia came under cyber attack (widely thought to be at Moscow's direction) in 2007 and, especially, after the Russian invasion of Georgia in 2008. The Obama administration instead prompted NATO to do so, with the result that several major military exercises occurred in 2010 in the Baltic, with more scheduled for 2011 and 2012. While the Russians had carried out military exercises in 2009, including ones that practiced invading and occupying the Baltic states, the US response passed without diplomatic incident. Moreover, the December 2010 Wikileaks revelations exposed NATO's plans – "Operation Eagle Guardian" – to send nine ground divisions, British warships and squadrons of US fighters to the defense of Poland and the Baltic states in the event of Russian aggression.[23]

Moreover, while the bids of Georgia and Ukraine for NATO membership had effectively been postponed indefinitely after Russia's 2008 war with Georgia – for the most part to the relief of Washington – this owed as much to internal divisions within NATO and the two post-Soviet republics as to Obama administration entreaties. Instead, Western attentions focused on ways to integrate the two nations more closely with the European Union, a less provocative and destabilizing route to bringing Georgia and Ukraine further into the European orbit.

Compared to the Bush era, Russian-American relations thus went some way to being repaired, and appeared in fairly good shape under Obama during his first two years as president. While the US interest in improving relations is easily enough explained, the shifting Russian approach can largely be accounted for by four factors. First, the 2008 Georgia war had exposed both the limits of Russian bellicosity and the extent to which relations with the US could deteriorate spectacularly and rapidly. Second, sharp shifts in the energy market accompanying the Great Recession revealed just how fragile and exposed the Russian economy was to the price of oil and natural gas. In the oil and gas sectors, it is Western (especially American and British) companies, not Russian ones, which have the technology necessary to reach Russia's increasingly remote reserves. In addition, should Moscow seek to diversify her economy away from oil and gas, Russia will require Western capital and technology even more intensively. As James Sherr aptly put it, "One year before Barack Obama took office, Russia's policy towards the West was based on three foundations: nationalism, resentment and self-confidence. Today, it based on nationalism, resentment, and disorientation."[24] Third, the "Obama factor" clearly altered the decision-making calculus for some in the Russian regime. Precisely how far this encompassed Putin was unclear. Nonetheless, Obama's public commitments, evident sincerity, and his administration's delivering on promised changes emboldened a notoriously suspicious governing class to take limited risks for an improved bilateral relationship. Fourth, the seemingly inexorable rise of China posed major challenges to Russian national interests. A position of relative international isolation appeared decreasingly attractive when, for a relatively modest price, better relations with Washington appeared genuinely feasible.

Resetting the reset?

As Eugene Rumer and Angela Stent had anticipated at the outset of the Obama presidency, "The task of pressing the reset button in East-West relations promises to be arduous."[25] Russia remains, as ever, a truculent, difficult and frequently reluctant partner for the US. Like other post-Soviet states that enjoyed large hydrocarbon reserves, Russia has both benefited and suffered from the "resource curse." When oil prices were low during the 1990s, Russia's imperfect democracy pursued liberalizing reforms, extending even into the first three years of the 2000s under Putin. As oil and gas prices rose subsequently, the need for reform stalled in the face of huge revenues. Not only did these embolden Russia's cronyist leadership to maintain a firm authoritarian rule while buying-off opposition through raising wages and pensions, but it also permitted it increased leverage over neighboring states that lacked similar resources.

Ukraine, for example – the biggest ex-Soviet republic in population terms, after Russia – relied on cheap Russian natural gas to fuel its heavy industry. Twice after 2006 Moscow cut supplies during the winter amid pricing disputes. Energy subsidies from Russia also sustained the autocratic Alexander Lukashenko in power in Belarus, making the state essentially a vassal of Russia despite Lukashenko's poor relations with Putin and Medvedev. While the "common economic area" with Belarus and Kazakhstan announced in 2011, and building on 2010's customs union, promised a single market of 165 million people (about 60 percent of the former Soviet Union), stimulating foreign direct investment and revitalized industrial links, its economic benefits also appeared likely to combine with political pressures from Moscow to compromise the states' independence. (Putin also tried to entice Ukraine to join the common market with the offer of cheap gas.) Under Obama, no less than previously under Clinton or Bush, post-communist Russia did little to hide or compromise its view that the vast lands of the former tsarist and Soviet empires remain of vital strategic interest and Moscow will not abandon attempts to keep the other republics under its sway.

Moreover, despite Obama's regular assertion of the US and other great powers sharing key interests, the more prosaic and uncomfortable reality remained that – as with China – Russian interests are multiple and only selectively overlapping with Washington's. Moscow's attitude to Tehran is probably the clearest example. In return for Obama's scrapping the Bush missile defense plan, a grateful Moscow adopted a somewhat stronger position on the Iranian issue. Russia was content to participate in the deal, mentioned in Chapter 5, in which Moscow would purchase spent nuclear fuel from Iran and return it at a later date in a processed form unusable for weapons. But its willingness to tighten the economic sanctions regime in principle was not synonymous with endorsing a particular package of enhanced sanctions, which was invariably much less strong.

As with innumerable international challenges, the lenses by which Moscow and Washington view Iran remained quite distinct, the former viewing Iran through a regional prism, the latter through a global one. While the prospect of Iranian nuclear capacity to its south is not welcome to Moscow, nor is it of the core interest that it is to America. A nuclear Iran would represent a major blow to America's global prestige and position, its prohibition being at the heart of American regional and non-proliferation strategies. For Russia, Iran has maintained the potential to create major headaches in its sphere of influence but has thus far eschewed them. Despite being a southern neighbor and a revolutionary Islamic power, Tehran has resisted exploiting Russia's problems with its Muslim regions, such as Chechnya, or in former Soviet republics such as Tajikistan (where the population shares cultural and linguistic ties with Iran), or in disputing the still unresolved status of the Caspian Sea. Equally, trading interests are substantial between the two nations, with Russian exports to

Iran amounting to $3.3 billion in 2008. Moreover, more cynically, improved Iranian relations with the US and EU would not serve Russian energy interests, potentially undercutting its near monopoly of supply of natural gas to several EU states. As such, partial isolation but limited rather than comprehensive sanctions represents a reasonable outcome for Moscow: while Russia voted with the US for new sanctions on June 9, 2010, its price was to substantially narrow their scope and impact.

Similarly, on North Korea, while China is the key interlocutor, Russia too has a potentially major and constructive role to play in relation to Pyongyang. But, as with Iran, Russian and US priorities do not exactly converge, much less coincide. In the autumn of 2011, for example, Kim Jong-Il met Russian president Medvedev in Siberia, who hailed the North Korean as one of Russia's "partners." Russian trade interests were apparent as Moscow announced that it would work with Pyongyang on a potential 1,100 km pipeline that could ship natural gas from Russia to South Korea, 700 km of this via North Korea. Discussions were also underway about rail links with South Korea to access its burgeoning market. But no progress was made on the resumption of the Six-Party talks, the suspended process in which Russia, China, Japan, the US and the Koreas have discussed Pyongyang's denuclearization. Kim repeated his call for the resumption of talks "without preconditions," a position unacceptable to Washington, Seoul and Tokyo, for whom concrete signs of a willingness to dismantle its nuclear program are requisite prior to resuming talks.[26]

Even on Afghanistan, where Moscow's cooperation was highly valued by Washington, the outcome arguably reflected more a convergence of interest than a soft power triumph for newly effective US diplomacy. Russia requires stability at least as much as the US in Central Asia. Like Iran, Moscow is deeply concerned by the narcotics traffic from Afghanistan, with heroin a particularly virulent scourge of young Russian lives and increasing drug addiction across Central Asia. Instability in Afghanistan would also destabilize Moscow's authoritarian allies in Central Asia and, indirectly, Russia itself. An Iranian nuclear capability is, marginally, tolerable for Moscow; a Talibanized Afghanistan or Pakistan with nuclear weapons would be far less so. In a move that drew condemnation from Afghan authorities, Russian and US forces conducted their first joint operation to raid an opium factory in northern Afghanistan in 2010. In 2010, the US also lifted a 2005 ban on arms trading with *Rosoboronexport*, Russia's state arms exporter, which had been imposed on the company for alleged dealings with Iran. In May 2011, *Rosoboronexport* agreed to supply military helicopters to the US for use in Afghanistan, signing a contract worth approximately $375 million with the US army to supply 21 Mi-17 helicopters to boost the capacity of the Afghan air force.[27]

As these examples suggest, the list of foreign policy concerns for the US and Russia are quite similar in geography and structure but differ considerably in content. At the center of attention for both powers are regional conflicts that have the potential to spill over into global ones. But their respective priorities are quite different. For Washington, the list of concerns comprises Iran, Afghanistan and Pakistan (implicating India), Middle East peace, and North Korea. For Moscow, by contrast, Ukraine, Central Asia and the Caucasus occupy central national concerns. American priorities do figure on the Russian list but appear much further down the hierarchy. The same applies to Russian priorities on America's list of concerns. This asymmetry allows for some cooperation between Moscow and Washington on a selective basis but is poorly suited to a comprehensive agreement on regional policy between the two powers.

By the latter part of 2011, the future of the "reset" appeared uncertain after a series of difficult negative encounters. First, at the end of July, the US Senate passed a resolution reaffirming US support for Georgia's territorial integrity and demanding the withdrawal of Russian troops from South Ossetia and Abkhazia. The Russian Foreign Ministry criticized such action as encouraging a "revanchist" mood in Tblisi, while Putin's comment that, "The future will depend on the people of South Ossetia themselves," appeared to hold out the possibility of Russia annexing South Ossetia after a possible referendum in the territory.[28] US intelligence agencies had also concluded that a Russian military intelligence officer was probably involved with the explosion of a bomb near the US Embassy in Tblisi in September 2010.

Second, the US State Department imposed travel bans on sixty-four unnamed Russian officials. The officials were suspected of being involved in the murky prison death of a lawyer, Sergei Magnitsky, who had worked on one of Russia's highest-profile corruption cases. Magnitsky was said to have exposed a fraud scheme by Russian tax administrators that siphoned roughly $230 million from state coffers. Russia's Foreign Ministry stated that "unfriendly steps" such as the travel restrictions would be met with "adequate measures," while Russian officials threatened to cease cooperating with Washington over Afghanistan, Iran, Libya and North Korea if Congress passed the Sergei Magnitsky sanctions legislation.

Third, Russian leaders continued to challenge the US on the Phased Adaptive Approach missile defense plans. Dmitry Rogozin, the Russian president's Special Representative for Missile Defense Cooperation with NATO, met with Senators Jon Kyl (R-AZ) and Mark Kirk (R-ILL) in July 2011 but the two sides disagreed sharply on what had occurred. Rogozin claimed that the senators had admitted that missile defense was targeted at Russia, not Iran, vividly recalling how:

> ... I had the impression that I was transported in a time machine back several decades, and in front of me sat two monsters of the Cold War, who looked at me not through pupils, but targeting sights.[29]

This was denied by the senators, who instead insisted that the problem was an inability of the two sides to come a common definition of the threat from Iran.

It would be naive to imagine that the US and Russia could overcome decades of zero-sum logic about international relations, bipolar competition, nuclear parity and ideological rivalry in a matter of four years. With the Russian economic growth model broken after the Great Recession, with anaemic investment and sluggish growth, a more aggressive and adventurist foreign policy was a probability. Nonetheless, the very fact of engaging in discussions with Moscow enabled the Obama administration to make important – if limited – progress on some key fronts. Both parties remain, understandably, committed to a partial hedging strategy. Despite the presence of numerous weaknesses that threaten the future development of the state, Russia remains one of the few powers left in the world that is capable of both strategic thinking and the use of force. Its seat on the UN Security Council continues to lend it a symbolic power of note, one that Moscow regularly leverages to extract maximum political capital. With Europe possessing neither a coherent strategic vision nor force projection potential (despite defense spending levels second only to the US and some two million Europeans serving in the armed forces), and China still mostly focused on internal development questions, Russia offers Obama's Washington both a potentially valuable partner and – if antagonized – a formidable opponent: less a "super-" than a "spoiler" or "sniper-power."

Moreover, although Russia has benefited in economic and diplomatic terms from arms sales to China, Venezuela, Syria and other states with either adversarial or ambiguous relations with the US, and engages in periodic sniping with Beijing at Washington's expense – over Iraq, Iran, the debt crisis and the dollar's status as the international reserve currency – there exists little evidence of a "soft balancing" against America.[30] Russian apprehension about the growth of Chinese economic, military and political power is extensive (not least among the generally xenophobic *siloviki* populating the Russian regime's higher echelons) and, whatever the periodic populist bluster – such as Putin's remarks about America's parasitical impact on the global economy – Russian elites mostly appreciate that China constitutes a greater potential threat to Mother Russia than does the US.

Conclusion: the limits of strategic engagement with Russia

As John Thornhill notes, "Russians sometimes say it is impossible to predict anything in their country – even the past."[31] Evaluating Obama's Russia policy after three years is equally problematic, since the suspicion and mistrust that Moscow still harbors towards Washington has such deep historic roots and contemporary resonance. Even if a post-American world is emerging, the US remains Moscow's foremost foreign policy preoccupation, and prioritizing relations with America and Europe – especially in the face of the threat of

Chinese expansionism, not least in its under-populated eastern region – underscored Russia's reformed foreign policy after 2008.

The divisions and conflicts that occurred under George W. Bush reflected and reinforced a more profound reassessment of the post-Cold War relationship with the US. Where US officials in the 1990s and 2000s had seen themselves – through a combination of self-interested, instrumental and altruistic motives – assisting an historic post-communist transition to liberal democracy, the rule of law and market capitalism, Russian perceptions that the period was one in which American statecraft deliberately weakened a once great power economically while exploiting that weakness to aggrandize its unipolar dominance around the world have only intensified. NATO's expansion was perceived, not unreasonably, as a betrayal of US and European promises made at the Cold War's end, while US support of the "color" revolutions in Georgia, Ukraine and Kyrgyzstan over 2003–05 represented unacceptable outside interference in Russia's traditional sphere of influence. Anti-American and anti-Western appeals remain reliable populist staples of Russian politics and culture in a febrile environment where nationalism, chauvinism and xenophobia constitute potent social and political forces.[32]

Overcoming this legacy and ending the Cold War for good was never destined to be the work of a single presidential term, but Obama's reset has gone further than any prior post-Cold War US administration to creating the foundations for a constructive partnership between Washington and Moscow. Although a duumvirate leadership, Putin's marginally less direct, though still extensive, foreign policy role as Prime Minister assisted this. Relations between Obama and Medvedev (separated by only five years in age, with Obama turning fifty in 2011 and Medvedev forty-five) were good from the outset, the two establishing a real rapport. Obama's visit to Moscow in July 2009 assisted a warmer bilateral atmosphere, and – ironically, given the professional expertise of Condi Rice on the Soviet Union and Russia – Obama was perceived to be both more genuine and more open to thawing bilateral relations than his predecessor in the White House.

Washington also deftly removed serious irritants in the relationship by reconfiguring prior commitments to install a missile defense shield in Poland and the Czech Republic, more or less putting an end to public hectoring of Russian deficiencies on human rights and democracy, and generally downgrading – without totally abandoning – its engagement in post-Soviet nations. Washington and Moscow cooperated effectively in encouraging the normalization of Turkish-Armenian relations in 2009 and managing the Kyrgyztan crisis of spring 2010. Most notably, although they missed the December 5, 2009 deadline for replacing the START I treaty, and while ambiguities and tensions remained over the status of European security and missile defense, Obama and Medvedev signed the New START agreement on April 8, 2010. Although this required some fractious bargaining before gaining confirmation by the US Senate in the lame-duck congressional session following the 2010 midterm elections, the progress was notable for the two presidents' personal involvement, the agreement's rapid completion (in only forty-five weeks, compared to the nine years of START I), and its bolstering Obama's broader non-proliferation efforts. Although twenty-six US senators voted against ratification, making the measure one of the least well-supported or bipartisan in the history of US arms control agreements, the treaty's passage in the context of a corrosively poisonous partisan atmosphere on Capitol Hill represented an important foreign policy achievement for the Obama administration. Moreover US-Russian military cooperation, suspended under George W. Bush, resumed in 2011.

Although Moscow proudly boasts the largest number of billionaires of any city in the world, the reset has done little to encourage the emergence of the cleaner and more transparent business and legal environment that Russia urgently requires if the nation is genuinely to prosper economically. Corruption plagues the state capitalism that, despite Medvedev's attempts at modernization, remains dominant, with the government owning more than half of all shares listed on the Moscow stock exchange and the state-owned Rosneft and Gazprom two of the largest energy companies in the world. Nonetheless, to encourage Russian economic interest in the reset of bilateral relations, the US under Obama pressed hard for Russian membership of the World Trade Organization (now some eighteen years in the negotiating), a necessary prelude ultimately to establishing normal trade relations with the US on the Chinese model. Such positive intentions, even absent complete success, also assisted the broader cooperative environment between the two nations, exemplified by the $3.2 billion agreement between ExxonMobil with the Russian state oil group, Rosneft, to form an Arctic exploration partnership in August 2011. As Cliff Kupchan, a Russian specialist at the Eurasia Group consultancy in Washington, noted, such a partnership represented nothing less than a "sea-change": "US oil companies were hardly welcome partners for Russian firms during the [George W.] Bush administration."[33]

Moreover, while the US approach to Moscow has eschewed assertive rhetoric or – in the eyes of its critics – a sufficient emphasis on human rights, constitutional democracy and the rule of law, Obama's tilt towards Jeffersonian restraint over Wilsonian idealism in this instance has been mostly prudent and paid off politically. Admittedly, the cost of Washington's more pliant diplomacy has been anxieties among Russian democracy activists, and several East European and post-Soviet states (unused to being referred to as "partners" rather than "allies"). At the end of November 2011, the dissident Russian, Boris Nemtsov, called on Obama to publicly label Putin a dictator. Several ex-Soviet capitals are wary that the Obama "reset," especially in conjunction with American and European preoccupation with the effects of the Great Recession, essentially means that the West has *de facto* granted the

Kremlin the regional "zone of privileged interest" it has long demanded, hindering the future for democracy within Russia and other states in the region for years to come. Nonetheless, the diplomatic, military and economic involvement of the US in the region has remained active and, in some respects – such as military planning, joint exercises, and European energy security – been more engaged and committed than that of its Republican predecessor.

In sum, in the context of a constrained internationalism and the limits of engagement, Russia has proven a limited success story of sorts for Obama's post-American foreign policy. The "reset" with not so much a one-party as a one-clique, corrupt and autocratic Russia has yielded some low-hanging fruit, halting the slide to a fully adversarial resurgence of "Cold War" rivalries and substantially reducing – without fully eliminating – the mutual suspicion, toxic Russian nationalism and extensive distrust of the later Bush years. In some important respects, bilateral relations are in better shape than at any time since the end of the Cold War. But the extent to which such beginnings can be solidified into a genuine strategic partnership remains to be seen. Russian and American interests diverge as much as they converge in critical areas, the reset remains a work in progress, and the temptation to resort to a deep-seated anti-American populism for the Russian political class is ever present (as it is also in nations from China through Turkey to France).

Obama's embrace of strategic modesty has also consolidated the *de facto*, if not the *de jure*, conditionality of future US military interventions. Russian consent, along with that of China, now represents the key determinant of whether humanitarian interventions (such as that in Libya in 2011) can meet the important test of international legality – a rather dubious and unpromising situation for proponents of the "responsibility to protect," but one that chimes well with Obama's lack of enthusiasm for liberal interventionism and an American grand strategy of "leading from behind." Perhaps more than on most foreign policy challenges during his presidency, the nascent shift effected under Obama paved the way for a more constructive dialogue with a major player on the world stage. But, with Vladimir Putin's near inevitable victory in the Russian presidential election of March 2012 – with a new six-year term, and potentially extending his leadership to 2024, a longer period in unchallenged charge of Russia than even Josef Stalin's – Obama may yet encounter a much less cooperative and more truculent Moscow; one that has clearly gone as far it wishes to in terms of compromising either its vital or its more peripheral interests, or its use of the one potent card – nationalism – remaining in its diminished arsenal.

9

Keep the Change: Continuity
We Can Believe In

*No matter how dark the day may seem, transformative
change can be forged by those who choose to side with justice.
And I pledge that America will always stand with those who
stand up for their dignity and their rights ... the United States
of America will never waver in our efforts to stand up for the
right of people everywhere to determine their own destiny.*
—President Barack Obama, UN General Assembly,
September 23, 2010[1]

*We need the suasion in argument of an Obama (or Clinton)
and the simplicity in approach of a Bush (or Reagan).
We need an intellectual case, brilliantly marshalled,
combined with a hard-headed ability to confront.*
—Former United Kingdom Prime Minister,
Tony Blair[2]

*Since I entered government 45 years ago, I've shifted my views
and changed my mind on a good many things as circumstances,
new information, or logic dictated. But I have yet to see evidence
that would dissuade me from this fundamental belief: that America
does have a special position and set of responsibilities on this planet ...
More than any other secretary of defense, I have been a strong
advocate of "soft" power – of the critical importance of diplomacy
and development as fundamental components of our foreign policy
and national security. [But] Make no mistake: the ultimate guarantee
against the success of aggressors, dictators, and terrorists in the
21st century, as in the 20th, is "hard" power – the size, strength,
and global reach of the United States military.*
—Secretary of Defense, Robert Gates, May 2011[3]

*When I said, "Change we can believe in," I didn't say,
"Change we can believe in tomorrow."*
—President Barack Obama, Chicago, August 2011[4]

Introduction

Barack Obama's bold attempt to advance a "post-American" foreign policy represented a carefully crafted effort to adjust America to the combination of a rapidly changing world order, widespread doubts over US global leadership and his own domestic political ambitions for nation-building at home. Abroad as well as in America, President Obama employed his formidable charismatic authority to present himself as the cathartic "un-Bush": articulate, mild-mannered, methodical, cool, intellectual, urbane, sophisticated, cosmopolitan and – like Bush's father – un-doctrinaire, prudent, and pragmatic. Despite his inhospitable political inheritance, the poor economic fortunes of the US and limited foreign policy advances under his leadership, Obama continued to command widespread international admiration and respect, navigating a debt-ridden and war-weary United States through a tumultuous international environment at a time of profound and disconcerting global change. As Vice-President Joe Biden reflected, "No president has had so many disparate but consequential foreign policy dilemmas to deal with all at once."[5]

Moreover, Obama appeared to many outside the United States not only to represent the "better angels" of contemporary America, but also to offer symbolic expression of a nation simultaneously changing demographically and evolving positively in its relations with the wider world under his presidency – embracing a mosaic of ever greater ethnic diversity, cosmopolitanism and pluralist tolerance at home while forging a carefully calibrated "smart power" diplomacy abroad. As the American political scientist, John Mueller, put it, "Under Barack Obama, the country has become more inclined to seek international cooperation, sometimes even showing perceptible, if occasional, signs of humility."[6] To his many admirers within and outside the US, Obama – like Ronald Reagan previously – provided confirmation of the adage of the nineteenth-century German philosopher, Georg Hegel, that "The great man of the age is the one who can put into words the will of his age, tell his age what its will is, and accomplish it. What he does is the heart and essence of his age; he actualizes his age."[7]

But beyond the powerful symbolism, the stylistic departures and rhetorical "altitude" that he achieved, Obama's concerted attempts to adapt America to a new and uncertain international environment faced powerful limits that impeded the hoped-for achievements of strategic engagement. As a result, in many ways what Obama ultimately offered as forty-fourth US president was less a completely post-American approach embracing the wholesale rejection of the controversial Bush Doctrine than a promise of its more competent execution – a promise that has been delivered in several important instances, from the unrelenting prosecution of the war on terror and improved relations with Russia to the strategic hedging over China and the selective embrace of regime change in the Middle East. In this, as Mark Twain reputedly said, history may not quite repeat itself but it does sometimes rhyme. By 2012, Obama resembled less a transformative successor to his unloved predecessor, but was more analogous to Dwight Eisenhower following the equally unpopular Harry Truman in 1953: criticizing his foreign policy on the stump with impressive vigor, pledging wholesale changes, but then trimming rather than transforming it in office.

As Stanley Renshon correctly predicted at the outset of the new president's term, the pervasive national security tension within the Obama administration has been between Obama's instinctive liberal internationalism and his more pragmatic, if reluctant, embrace of some of Bush's more controversial policies.[8] Especially where vital US national interests exist, the much-anticipated transformative change has therefore been significantly more limited and sometimes merely cosmetic. Ryan Crocker, former US ambassador to Iraq, rightly observed of America that strategic "patience is not our strong suit ..." But Crocker also commended, in relation to both Afghanistan and Iraq, the "welcome and extremely important" continuity in policy from Bush to Obama;[9] a commendation "rewarded" by his taking over from Karl Eikenberry as US Ambassador to Afghanistan in June 2011.

Across the daunting gamut of foreign policy challenges, but especially on the now undeclared but still functioning war on terror, such continuity was in marked supply. While, in his inaugural address, Obama boldly asserted that "the choice between our safety and our ideals"[10] was "false," as America's forty-fourth president – like the forty-third – he made precisely those necessary and inevitable tradeoffs, from Guantanamo Bay and invocations of state secrets privileges through military commissions and renditions to special operations and drone strikes. And although the administration quickly abandoned the assertive language of the war on terror as overblown and counterproductive, Obama's reversal of supposedly constitutionally suspect counter-terrorism policies was at best partial and halting. The "rooted cosmopolitanism" that his most admiring supporters hoped would reframe and revitalize US foreign policy has had notably limited reach and impact – though the clamor among Democrats against the "shredding" of the US Constitution under Bush had become a deafening silence under the similar policies of his supposedly constitutionally literate successor. Constitutional vandalism, evidently, is in the eye of the beholder.

With the evolution of the major foreign policy problems facing Obama over 2009–12, it is therefore possible to discern an approach to international relations that – while seeking to adjust to a post-American era in which relative power is redistributed and the global order no longer belongs to the West – is ultimately not fundamentally at odds with that of his White House predecessors. At least, it has not been at odds in most substantive – as opposed to stylistic, declaratory, symbolic and rhetorical – terms. While Obama regularly appeared "fired up and ready to go" on the campaign trail to renew American leadership, in office – from Washington's relations with other great powers such as China and Russia, through the challenge of newly developing relations with rising powers such as Brazil and Turkey, to the hard cases of Afghanistan, Pakistan, Iran and Israel-Palestine – the extent and the pace of foreign policy shifts under Obama have been less all-encompassing and less fiercely urgent than his strongest supporters might legitimately have anticipated, and his adversaries certainly feared, back in 2008.

But a more sound and sober assessment of Obama's administration, taking into account both the international and the domestic pressures constantly at work on, and in, Washington, would likely have cautioned against too sweeping or ambitious expectations of transformative change. As Obama himself sometimes noted, changing US foreign policy is more akin to re-routing a super-tanker than deftly steering a speedboat. Whatever their merits, extensive turnover in administration personnel, seeming shifts in foreign policy emphasis, and newly evocative speeches and national security strategy documents can often obscure the more stark limitations on policy options and instruments available to US decision-makers – even (or especially) in times of national and international crisis. In this regard, the partial shaping of a post-American approach has been constructive and important without being transformative. While some observers prematurely identified Obama's remarkable personal ascent as bringing to a close the "Age of Reagan" in the US,[11] as the essays in one scholarly volume on American power and identities in the "Age of Obama" instead concluded:

> The Obama administration's change agenda ... falls foul of its deeper attachments to American preponderance and desire to perpetuate the "American century." The United States ... is neither post-racial nor post-imperial and post-religious/ evangelical in pursuit of its self-proclaimed historic mission. Even more, there are deep-seated and long-term processes that will, it is claimed, thwart an ambitious change agenda. The Obama administration ... is proving more continuous with the past than some of its supporters, and detractors, care to admit.[12]

In short, the desire to adapt the US to a changing international order while retaining the leading role in the world, combined with the many limits to strategic engagement, circumscribed how far Obama could achieve a genuinely post-American approach for the post-American world order. However much it was beset by its own tensions and contradictions, lacking both internal coherence and long-term viability, the Obama Doctrine of "leading from behind" was the end result.

In this context, it would be absurd to depict a uniform succession from George W. Bush to Barack Obama. To be clear, the changes that Obama initiated in US foreign policy were significant. In tone, emphasis and symbolism, the much ballyhooed re-embrace of multilateralism, diplomacy and consultation, and the relegation of aggressive confrontation, unilateral actions dismissive of other nations' reservations, and preventive war was arguably well attuned to a new era of constrained internationalism. Under Obama, the return of a restrained pragmatism – if not necessarily realism, *per se* – in place of the "Teddy Rooseveltism" of Bush's first term (2001–05) was much anticipated, unsurprising and widely welcomed.

But this shift had actually begun prior to Obama's arrival in the White House, back in 2005, when the soaring ambition to "end tyranny in the world" of Bush's second inaugural address appeared increasingly unfeasible in practice and the growing limits on American power became ever more forceful – with the result that Obama's foreign policy resembled more that of Bush's second term than the Bush second term had resembled its first. As one authoritative account argued, for example:

> ... both the Pentagon's Quadrennial Defense review (released in February 2010) and the White House's National Security Strategy (released in May 2010) were evolutionary rather than revolutionary. They continued to endorse, for example, US-led counter-insurgency and strike capabilities as major instruments of counter-terrorism.[13]

Even the tone of Obama's 2009 Nobel Peace Prize acceptance speech in Oslo, Norway, "which among other things underlined the sober necessity of war, sounded in some ways not unlike the philosophy of George W. Bush"[14] (perhaps constituting the resurrection of the satire that Tom Lehrer had famously claimed to have died when the Nobel Peace Prize was awarded to Henry Kissinger in 1973.) That Obama retained Bush-era personnel such as Bob Gates, John Brennan and David Petraeus added to an impression of marked familiarity rather than fundamental discontinuity in foreign affairs.

To the obvious disappointment and disdain of some on the left (within and outside America,) who had invested so heavily in his historic election, Obama's audacity instead appeared a pulp fiction sold to a gullible global audience. An apparent opportunity to effect a decisive break with modern American foreign policy was squandered, confirming the existence of deep structural forces shaping and reinforcing all-too-conventional patterns of traditional US engagement with the post-American world.

Michael Doyle, for example, sought to explain the supposed conundrum of why two successive US administrations – conservative Republican and liberal Democratic – both concluded that fighting terrorism must involve democracy promotion, on the basis of the combined effect of three factors: the framing of the September 11 attacks in a way that increased the receptivity of Americans to the conceptual opposition between freedom and fear; the pervasive ideological influence of the Wilsonian idealistic tradition, as manifested today in an unusual *de facto* consensus between neo-conservatives and liberal internationalists on the desirability of democratic reform as a means of changing the foreign policy behavior of other states; and a powerful bipartisan domestic constituency in favor of democracy promotion. As a result, the "contraposition" of democracy and terrorism in American political discourse is effectively over-determined because it strongly mirrors the dominant ideological and political preferences of American elites. This fixed preference for democracy promotion explained why – most notably during the convulsions of the Arab Spring – the Obama administration remained wedded to the binary distinction between freedom and fear in its public statements, despite its efforts to break in style and substance with the policies of its predecessor.[15]

Those hard security realities were informed, too, by the strictly limited room for manoeuvre that the severe economic constraints of the Great Recession imposed. At least for his first three years in office, Obama's 2008 campaign pledges to transform US foreign policy were largely overtaken by a flat-lining economy, the possibility of a "double-dip" recession and the prospect of, at best, a Japanese-style "lost decade" of anaemic or deflationary growth, with stagnation accompanied by chronically high unemployment. As Colin Dueck argues, despite evincing a genuine intellectual interest in foreign policy and international relations, Obama's core political priorities were always focused on enacting sweeping progressive reforms at home and (ironically, given the "shellacking" blowback of the 2010 congressional elections) consolidating a long-term center-left Democratic governing majority. These formidable domestic ambitions, as well as the unfavorable international conditions he inherited, together relegated foreign policy to little more than "an exercise in damage control" for Obama.[16] International retrenchment, peaceful diplomacy, and repeated exhortations to mutual respect and mutual interests were on this basis less principled strategic commitments than, as policy instruments, about all that there was left to resort to for his battered and bruised administration – one that became increasingly preoccupied with playing defense in foreign policy, trying above all to avoid making costly errors rather than advancing imaginative innovations or creative solutions.

If that still amounted to something more substantial than Clintonian "foreign policy as social work,"[17] the legacy of the deep recession that followed the 2008 financial crisis compounded the longer-term geo-politics that rendered cash-strapped America – the global borrower of first resort – a diminished and "frugal superpower,"[18] beset by multiple deficits: at once budgetary, sovereign, manpower, attention, credibility, legitimacy and strategic in nature. As such, Obama was left with only limited resources and incremental means to pursue transformational ends, although that represented a predicament that arguably suited quite well the president's prudential blend of Jeffersonian realism and Wilsonian idealism. While needing to demonstrate sufficient mettle on Afghanistan to avoid being tagged a dove, Obama's demotion of democracy promotion, inherent wariness about military threats and interventions by force, and more generally accommodationist approach accorded with the general turning-away of the Democratic Party from hard-line internationalism since the Vietnam War. However much it departed from a muscular foreign policy in the service of an unapologetic American nationalism – leaving Obama open to conservative charges of his being a Hamlet of a president presiding over "the Hamlet of nations, worrying endlessly over whether and how to respond"[19] – leading from behind seemingly fitted well with the downbeat mood of an insular, albeit still internationalist, American public and a world that had not, contrary to expectations in 2008, fundamentally altered its Janus-faced view of the United States.

The four limits of strategic engagement

To many observers of American foreign policy, Obama's engagement strategy therefore had much to commend it, especially in the context of the negative legacies of the Bush era abroad and the clear desire of Americans for nation-building, jobs and economic recovery at home. With the brief exception of the killing of Bin Laden, the American public – like mass publics in all countries, never overly interested in the minutiae of international politics – was far more preoccupied with the domestic woes of the United States than with foreign affairs during Obama's presidential term. Obama and the Democrats therefore faced powerful domestic, as well as global, incentives to pursue a course of international retrenchment and foreign policy restraint. As his presidency progressed fitfully and his grey hairs multiplied, Global Obama-mania receded somewhat in comparison with the heady days of late 2008 and early 2009. But thanks to Obama's dedicated efforts at American renewal, some global catharsis was achieved: the prestige of the US "brand" was substantially restored over 2009–12 and the lethal toxicity of the Bush years mitigated, if neither forgotten nor forgiven, in many parts of the world – with the notable, and crucial, exceptions of the Arab and Muslim worlds, where hearts and minds for the most part remained unmoved.

If enthusiasm for Obama's transformative promise was understandably curbed by the latter stages of his presidency, at least one cheer for Obama's foreign policy therefore seemed in order. But it was difficult to make a convincing argument that the global power and influence of the US were greater at the end than at the outset of Obama's term in the Oval Office. While his grand strategy had its obvious strengths for an increasingly insular America and a post-American era, strategic engagement suffered not so much from an Achilles' heel as from an entire leg. Although not an exhaustive list, as the administration's approach evolved, the key weaknesses of engagement emerged as four-fold: strategic naivety; lack of conditionality; inattentiveness to the domestic setting of foreign policy; and a failure consistently to prioritize. Though distinct, each of the four problematic aspects were related and mutually reinforcing in harmful ways – in combination projecting an image of overall American weakness, uncertainty and decline, and severely hampering the extent to which Obama could successfully execute transformative changes to achieve his desired policy objectives.

The first serious problem was the erroneous assumption that shared interests represented not only necessary, but also – with appropriately deft public diplomacy, carefully crafted incentives and serious sanctions – sufficient conditions of great power alignment and effective international cooperation on key global problems and threats. A cursory examination of diplomatic history (or even a basic international relations textbook) ought to have cautioned strongly against basing US foreign policy upon such a deeply flawed premise. However dedicated, engaged and well-informed – and, to his considerable credit, most of Obama's foreign policy appointees excelled on all three dimensions – US diplomats cannot simply convince other governments of the merits of policies, initiatives or actions that the latter do not regard, from their own self-interest, as either necessary, desirable or feasible. Invariably, in politics, as in sport, a good strategy is to do what one's opponents would least like. But, at times, rather like being shocked that gambling is going on in a casino, the Obama administration appeared uncomprehending of international realities. That other states did not share Washington's view of their own interests and resisted American blandishments to form a new concordat to police global peace and security appeared beyond the administration's intellectual grasp.

Quite why is a mystery. In marked contrast to much of the sometimes naive public diplomacy of the Obama administration, sovereign, as well as shared, interests matter greatly and, most of the time, predominate for all nation-states. Moreover, while not all foreign relations are zero-sum games, some certainly are, and most are relative-sum games. The Panglossian notion that initially underpinned Obama's post-American approach – that some type of new great power consortium could be corralled to stabilize an international order in flux – proved mostly mistaken. It fatally neglected the key role that values and regime-type play in shaping constructions of the national interest, definitions of key challenges and the evolution of threat perceptions, from Israel through Turkey to China. As an astute and otherwise sympathetic observer of US foreign policy under President Obama, James Lindsay, argues:

> What Obama stumbled over was not the diagnosis but the prescription: even if Washington led wisely and sympathetically, others might not follow. Consultations could not guarantee consensus. Governments could and did disagree over which issues constituted threats or opportunities, what priority they should be given, how they should be handled and who should bear the responsibility for addressing them. The result too often was inaction or gridlock.[20]

Such elemental features of international politics should perhaps have been better appreciated by the Obama administration earlier than they eventually were (to the limited extent that they ultimately were). After all, if politics in Washington is – notoriously – a "two-level game,"[21] so it is also in the capitals of America's allies and adversaries. A greater appreciation of the powerful domestic constraints facing US allies such as Israel, especially, appeared to have emerged by the latter part of 2010 and early 2011, one entirely consonant with the public message of mutual respect that Obama so often articulated. But, as the Libyan operation of 2011 illustrated, even NATO's very status an alliance rather than at best a *de facto* coalition of the willing (and at worst, as Gates alluded to in his final year as Defense Secretary, an irrelevance) is now highly questionable after the fraught experiences of Kosovo, Afghanistan and Libya. Even with France and Britain taking the lead role, the overthrow of Qaddafi required extensive US involvement, not Washington's distance, to be effective, with the malign consequences of decades of European under-investment in defense egregiously manifest. The overarching problem with the US "leading from behind" appeared not so much that this was an especially bad form of global leadership for Washington, but more that it was not a genuine form of international leadership at all.

Moreover, the administration's rather unsubtle de-emphasis of long-established American allies in favor of old and new "partners" compounded the disaffection in several traditional client states such as the UK and Israel, while gaining little buy-in from less familiar US targets of American affection such as Brazil. While, under Obama, America now proudly boasts a seemingly unending stream of international partners greater than the combined efforts of Mick Jagger, Charlie Sheen and Silvio Berlusconi, the appearance has something of the proverbial quality of an aging superpower lothario in the throes of a male menopause, seeking-out younger models after a seven-decades' itch. Nor, if Obama's experience is any guide, does quantity not necessarily trump quality. From Cairo to Tokyo, the quality of Washington's many relationships remains markedly varied and inconsistent. All too often, for erstwhile intimates, getting into bed with America is no longer any guarantee that the US will be worth respecting – let alone admiring or fearing – in the morning.

The second flaw in the Obama administration's embrace of strategic engagement was less one of theoretical design than practical execution. In implementing foreign policy changes, Obama could never be accused of making the perfect the enemy of the good. But, as the Iranian, Russian and Chinese examples attested, Obama's conservative (with a small "c") approach at times erred more towards a policy of pure and unconditional engagement, entirely absent negative inducements and effective penalties, than the more ambiguous "incentives and sanctions" framework more conventionally evoked by the term. Obama's strategic engagement frequently appeared well-intentioned and constructive, but rarely conditional. As a result, the perception that the president, and by extension his nation, were "weak" had gained increased credence in a number of capitals as his term progressed and, as Clive Crook observes, "People hate weakness in a leader, even when 'weakness' is rational."[22] While the US under Obama was regarded much more benignly in most foreign ministries than it had been under Bush (admittedly, not the most difficult of achievements), important and seemingly intractable policy differences remained with allies and antagonists alike, indicative of the profound limits of the much-touted "smart power" approach.

Furthermore, as the country-specific chapters in this book have illustrated, the precious commodity of American "credibility" – not unlike its triple-A credit rating – suffered something of a downgrade under Obama, as states from Pakistan and Turkey to Israel and China felt able to confidently ignore US entreaties and resist its diplomatic pressures more or less with impunity. Such a situation reflected poorly on the self-styled "realist" who expressed "enormous respect" for the notoriously vision-free foreign policy of George H. W. Bush. As Dueck aptly summed up Obama's "satisficing" approach:

> The president's instinct in many cases, internationally, is not so much to think in geopolitical terms as to try to lay out a multifaceted understanding of points of view on every side, recognizing some validity in each perspective. These efforts to split international differences are matched by an assumption of the powerful potentialities of unilateral diplomatic outreach. Obama has suggested repeatedly that if the United States takes the lead by making important concessions on global issues – for example, climate change or arms control – then other countries will follow. Open hands have been extended, diplomatically, to virtually every international competitor or adversary of the United States. These particular elements of Obama's foreign policy approach, which emphasize the transformative possibilities of conciliation, style, and international bridge building as an end in themselves, may be inspiring to many, but they do not exactly constitute realism.[23]

Implementing strategic engagement therefore proved much more problematic than had been initially anticipated. Even for someone as self-assured and rhetorically gifted as Obama, the belief in the transformative possibilities of working in the style of a back-seat international community organizer/enabler faced major impediments. As much recent presidential scholarship has demonstrated, presidents rarely command the persuasive powers commonly attributed them in relation to American public opinion, even at home, during "honeymoon" periods and in relation to domestic policies.[24] Domestically, too, partisan motives inevitably loom large for presidents, especially in their first terms – however much they portray themselves as non-partisan representatives of the national interest.[25] In terms of international relations, the practical utility of the US "bully pulpit" is typically even less pronounced.

Obama, as the world's most powerful leader and well-known celebrity, attracted widespread international admiration and even affection. But that did not automatically or easily translate into the necessary or sufficient political and diplomatic momentum for policy change. Not only, for example, did

Obama's manifest lack of suasion in regard to Iran, North Korea, Myanmar and Pakistan undercut his administration's broader nuclear non-proliferation effort, but the New START treaty achieved little beyond cosmetic measures to reduce US and Russian nuclear stockpiles – while at the same time placing new question marks over America's longer-term security interests. Moreover, Obama rarely sought to explain and justify foreign policies to the American people directly, leaving a sense of confusion as to whether and why Washington was involved – or not – in particular states, and why, for example, Libya was a strategic interest of the US meriting a "kinetic military" operation but Syria was not. In addition, far from assembling a constructive "team of rivals," Obama's decision-making process could be highly centralized, frequently relying on small, tightly knit groups; and contentious where it was not so, the Obama administration's internal divisions over foreign policy sometimes being at least as significant as those on domestic affairs.[26] When combined with the self-inflicted errors on Israel, hesitancy over the Arab Spring, and overtly political, electoral and partisan calculations on the Afghan surge and drawdown and withdrawal from Iraq, Obama's statecraft too often appeared overly invested in theoretical complexity and insufficiently blessed by long-term strategic clarity, tactical coherence and political assurance.

The third problem with strategic engagement was that, even if a dwindling number of other capitals are minded to respond positively to Washington's diplomacy, as a reflexively familiar diplomatic default option, such an approach to international affairs cannot be fully effective without also attending closely to American foreign policy's domestic foundations. Although domestic politics intruded on foreign policy in relation to Afghanistan, Iraq and Israel, rarely did Obama seek to shape domestic opinion towards a new grand vision for the US. But the need to articulate directly to Americans a compelling grand vision for America's world role is invariably integral to sustaining ongoing public support for internationalism. To the extent that Obama's hybrid "Commander/Cosmopolitan-in-Chief" role championed a contrite admission of historical US errors, a humbler Washington and a less uncritical take on American exceptionalism,[27] more Americans might have accepted the bargain had they observed a clearer or richer return on the risky investment. But, curiously for such a shrewd and perspicacious individual, Obama has not proven able easily to "connect" with the American people as president. Mr Spock-like rather than populist by natural inclination, his professorial, cerebral and detached approach has smitten the pundit class but not proven something to which most ordinary Americans can readily relate. Unlike his Democratic predecessor in the White House during the 1990s, Obama does not easily "feel your pain."

Moreover, Bin Laden's killing, the overthrow of Colonel Qaddafi and the partial (and fragile) Russian "reset" aside, the substantive results of Obama's approach have been relatively modest. An impression has been given, through a lack of clear or consistent articulation of foreign policy goals, that Obama is, as one – admittedly, partisan – former Pentagon official put it, "uncomfortable with US power and US leadership."[28] White House demands for steep reductions in the defense budget, persistent tensions with the uniformed military and a constant stress on what America cannot – rather than can – do together compound the sense of a nation in near-terminal decline and turning inwards to an inauspiciously bleak future, recalling *The Simpsons* episode in which a statue of a beaming Jimmy Carter stands insouciantly above the memorable injunction, "Malaise Forever."[29]

No matter how reasonable Obama's diagnoses of American ills, his "leading from behind" prescriptions also risk advancing a neo-isolationist turn just as his post-American foreign policy demands ever more creative and subtle forms of international engagement. As even a sympathetic Democratic realist, Zbigniew Brzezinski – an Obama campaign advisor – conceded of Obama's foreign policy, "So far, it has generated more expectations than strategic breakthroughs."[30] Reflecting on the disconnect between the high expectations raised in 2008, and the lack of follow-through on those campaign commitments, Brzezinski lamented that, "He makes dramatic presidential speeches ... but it's never translated into a process in which good ideas become strategies."[31]

Finally, the multiple ambitions of Obama's transformative foreign policy lacked clear and consistent priorities upon which to concentrate the president's finite political capital, focus administration energies and coalesce a fledgling international consensus. As Donald Rumsfeld once observed in one of his famous Rumsfeld Rules, "If everything is a priority, nothing is a priority."[32] Admittedly, some of the lack of clarity in this regard was the inevitable result of unforeseen events, such as the Arab Spring, that could not easily have been anticipated and profoundly complicated the administration's original efforts to rebalance its global priorities towards China and the Asia-Pacific. But others – such as his seeming disregard for Europe, distance from Latin America and lack of empathy for Israel – were more self-inflicted. Perhaps most seriously, at no stage during Obama's presidency was it truly clear where his central international focus resided. As such, not only did the administration arguably pursue an unmanageably large and overly ambitious global agenda with an excess of cooks – innumerable "czars" blurring clear lines of administration policy responsibility and political accountability – but it also missed opportunities to advance important US strategic goals and national interests.

Perhaps most notably, the major advances in bilateral relations with India that had occurred under Bill Clinton and, especially, George W. Bush, largely stalled under Obama. After fifty lost years of coolness between the world's most populous democracies, the signing of the "123" deal on civil nuclear cooperation in 2008 offered a robust new strategic partnership between Washington and New Delhi and a counterweight to the rise of China. Given the strategic importance of the world's largest democracy to the Afghanistan and Pakistan conundrum, New Delhi's fears of a "collusive threat" from its nuclear-armed neighbors in China and Pakistan, and its burgeoning economic influence, the underinvestment by Obama in strengthening Washington's deepening ties with India was a costly – if not quite inexplicable – failing on the part of the world's oldest democracy. Pakistan is most assuredly not a better long-term bet.

So, too, was a series of missed opportunities for Washington in South America, effectively the forgotten foreign policy of the US since 9/11. As Bronwen Maddox rightly notes, "In Europe, except in Spain, Latin America often feels a long way away. The odd thing is that in America it does too. It's long occupied a curious place in Washington: treated more as domestic policy – drugs and immigration – than foreign and, if the latter, then shadowed by the murk of the CIA."[33] Under Obama, despite optimistic beginnings, not much changed in this hemispheric regard during his presidency.[34] On the side of opportunity costs, China – in search of commodities and agricultural products – has overtaken Europe as a trading partner for South America, becoming the largest foreign investor in Brazil and concluding trade deals with Chile, Costa Rica and Peru. Beijing's trade with the continent as a whole – which emerged from the Great Crash of 2008 virtually unscathed – stood at $180 billion in 2010, fourteen times higher than it had been in 2000.

With the exit of most (though not all) of the continent's dictators, increasingly sound economic management, and mostly high rates of economic growth (between 4–6 percent over 2010–11), the case for US engagement with the continent is compelling. Politically, too, the emergence of states such as Brazil as influential actors on the global stage commends greater efforts by Washington to develop closer ties. From a more ominous viewpoint, in terms of potential threats, governments in Brazil and Chile have not invested sufficiently in education and infrastructure to increase productivity, and growth could yet stall. And, in the failing state of Mexico, the US confronts a genuine security threat that is already spilling over its southern borders. Despite stepped-up security cooperation, with drones and American agents deployed south of the border, and increased cooperation on trade, Obama has made no more of a coherent attempt to address the twin issues of drugs crime and illegal immigration – and the obviously failing "war on drugs" – than did his Republican predecessor. In particular, much to Mexican chagrin, Obama has displayed no willingness whatsoever to take on the American gun rights lobby to tighten firearm regulations on the US side of the border.

Ultimately, while Obama was well aware of Rahm Emanuel's notorious injunction not to let a crisis go to waste, all this need not matter politically for the president in terms of his own self-interest in 2012 and beyond. After all, just as his international agenda did not win Obama the 2008 presidential election, nor did foreign policy cause the extensive Democratic losses in the US House of Representatives and Senate at the 2010 midterm elections.

Admittedly, Obama came in for much criticism from Republicans on foreign affairs both before and after the midterms, and political skirmishes between the White House and Obama's outspoken conservative critics on Capitol Hill were a predictably reliable constant of his time in office. For some, such conflict suggested nothing less than the collapse of bipartisan endorsement of American internationalism and, W. B. Yeats-like,[35] a demise of the "center" on foreign affairs as consequential as that on domestic policy.[36]

That claim may be too strong to be totally convincing. But what is clear is that, although there is frequently less distance between the Democratic and Republican parties than the shrill tone of politics inside the Beltway typically suggests – especially on key concerns such as Afghanistan, Pakistan, Iran and Iraq – the current pattern of partisan and ideological polarization ensured that the president faced major opposition to many aspects of his foreign agenda. Institutionally, the attractions of developing serious foreign policy expertise in Congress have diminished, with the Foreign Relations Committee of the Senate – once a prestigious assignment – now increasingly occupied by freshmen. Even when, ironically, on Libya, there existed broad bipartisan agreement on foreign affairs, this was in opposition to US involvement in the intervention – bipartisan opposition that perhaps represented telling expression of an "Iraq Syndrome" limiting the American appetite for future US interventions abroad.

Republican electoral gains – in 2010, in special elections during 2011 and, as appears probable, in the congressional elections of 2012 – need not necessarily preclude further progress for the Obama administration on international affairs, especially on national security matters and trade issues (where the president mostly resisted protectionist pressures and where GOP hawkishness and support for the trade pacts with South Korea, Panama and Colombia were sufficiently solid finally to gain ratification in 2011). But the 2010 midterm results did raise serious obstacles to Senate ratification of the Comprehensive Test Ban Treaty – effectively abandoned by the administration – and renewed legislative efforts on climate change, immigration reform and energy independence, among many other matters. Moreover, although they had no prospect of passing the Democratic Senate or being signed into law by the president, the 112th Congress saw the House of Representatives "playing chicken with American leadership abroad."[37]

During 2011, as well as proposing sharp reductions in the budgets for the State Department and USAID operating budgets, House committees passed bills on party-line votes with strong ideological edges: to end funding for the Organization of American States; end the US contribution to the UN Human Rights Council and Population Fund; rescind $108 billion in funds previously appropriated to the International Monetary Fund (to stop its bailouts of indebted European governments); zero-out multilateral climate-change initiatives;

relocate the US Embassy in Israel from Tel Aviv to Jerusalem; establish a US consulate in Tibet; and reinstate the global "gag rule" prohibiting federal funding to any organization that discusses abortion.[38] Such partisan brinkmanship with American diplomacy, while not especially unusual historically, poses additional problems for an administration seeking a distinctive and new approach to a changing world. Furthermore, to the extent that the new lawmakers in the 112th and 113th Congresses remain preoccupied with America's fiscal and monetary maladies, debt and deficit – rather than the looming strategic deficit in US foreign policy – the domestic resources for a successful foreign policy may be further undermined.

Dynamics within the Republican Party – likely to control one or both houses of Congress after 2012 – will therefore have a powerful impact on the future of an American or post-American foreign policy, whether under Obama or a future Republican president. The GOP coalition remains one of great heterogeneity: social and moral traditionalists, economic and social libertarians, Christian evangelicals, Catholic communitarians, small government Tea Partiers and anti-tax Club for Growth-style populists, Hamiltonians, Jacksonian/Rooseveltian nationalists, Kissingerian/Continental realists, and neo-conservatives. For all of the recent attention devoted to the rise of the Tea Party, its influence on the Republican Party remains emblematic of a long-standing foreign policy divide on the conservative wing of American politics.[39] On the one hand are those conservative internationalists who strongly favor a "forward leaning" posture in the world. Some of these can be classified as traditional realists, most as American or conservative nationalists, others as neo-conservatives. While differing strongly on many foreign policy issues, from Iraq and Israel to non-proliferation and arms control, they share a deep suspicion of international organizations limiting American sovereignty and a strong commitment to an interventionist and assertive US foreign policy. On the other hand are those Tea-Partiers, neo-isolationists and paleo-conservatives who oppose nation-building, democracy promotion and too expansive or expensive a world role: a right-wing version, in its way, of a post-American foreign policy.

This abiding tension, sometimes breaking out into open schisms, dates at least back to the early years of the twentieth century. In this respect, the lack of a foreign policy focus on behalf of the Tea Party movement, and the divisions within its ranks on international affairs, reflects and reinforces wider differences within the conservative coalition. How this plays out remains to be seen. As Peter Baker observed, about the only thing that Tea Party activists could agree on in relation to foreign affairs was an "aversion to international organizations."[40] When the House of Representatives voted on March 17, 2011 to reject a non-binding resolution to withdraw all US forces from Afghanistan – introduced by Dennis Kucinich (D-OH) – by the lopsided margin of 321–93, only eight Republicans endorsed the effort. Of the eighty-seven new GOP freshmen, none voted in favor of the resolution. But GOP opposition to Libya was much more widespread in the House.

In discussing the future of the Republican Party, James Reichley persuasively observed that:

> The new Obama administration was warmly welcomed by millions all over the world who were disheartened and frightened by the frequent truculence and arrogance of the Bush administration. But America's national interest and international responsibilities will continue to require any conscientious administration to defend positions and take actions that will not be popular with many of the world's governments and peoples. If Obama's foreign policy initiatives are perceived to have failed or to have poorly served American interests, the usual tendency of American voters since the Second World War to put greater trust in Republicans than Democrats to deal with dangers from abroad may well be reasserted. If that happens, conservative foreign policy realists and neoconservative interventionists, both conceivably having learned from past mistakes, may achieve some kind of truce to work together constructing a coherent Republican foreign policy.[41]

The 2012 election will certainly test that proposition to breaking point, amid the rival tribal claims of Republicans charging Obama with weakness and the president responding with his international achievements, from Bin Laden's killing on. But even if a genuine truce can be concluded between the GOP's rival foreign policy tendencies, it remains to be seen whether the Republican primaries and caucuses will yield, as William Buckley always sagely recommended, "the most conservative candidate who can win" the presidential election – or will instead allow Obama successfully to make the charge that the Republicans today are intent on pursuing a faith-based foreign policy abroad and "repealing the twentieth century" at home.

Conclusion

With a view to his re-election in 2012, international affairs offers Obama – as it had done previously to many of his predecessors in the White House – a tempting arena in which to recover his standing as not just a politician but as a statesman of the first rank. As Lawrence Korb of the liberal Center for American Progress observed, "If he has success there, it will help him with his re-election bid. If he fails, I don't think the American people are going to say, 'We want to put someone else in there who could bring peace to the Middle East'."[42]

Given the overwhelming preoccupation of most voters with the shaky US economy, Obama's relatively modest achievements in foreign policy may ultimately matter little in the broader scheme of salient issues to the American electorate – although, significantly, they automatically translate into an experience surplus compared to any potential Republican Party presidential nominee and challenge him to outline a plausible alternative. Ironically, leading from behind may yet prove to be an optimal electoral strategy, even if it is not so clearly an effective international one. As David Ignatius, a firm Obama supporter, summarized the assessments of former national security advisors Brzezinski and Scowcroft:

> Obama's achievement is that he has reconnected America to the world. The United States was much too isolated and unpopular when he came into office. That isn't so true now. But even though the United States is less hated, it may also be taken less seriously by other nations. Obama has turned the page in American foreign policy, but he hasn't written enough yet on that fresh, blank space.[43]

The echoes of Niccolo Machiavelli's advice about the relative merits of leaders being feared or loved clearly remain powerful in 2012.

Whatever its international limitations, a post-American foreign policy has potential electoral benefits for Obama, even if he could not fully realize a complete break with the foreign policies of George W. Bush and his other presidential predecessors and has hence been forced to keep the change. Where some presidents are content to pursue a strategy of "winning ugly," Obama's preference has been contentment with polite decline and, on occasion, with losing gracefully. Managing American decline with subtly artful grace rather than directly or aggressively contesting the forces shaping that decline appeared a short-term advantage for a president deeply conscious of his symbolic importance, progressive electoral base and erstwhile historic legacy.

"Leading from behind" therefore became an attractive proposition, one well suited to Obama's unruffled temperament, domestic priorities and the constrained international position of the US entering the second decade of the twenty-first century. Moreover, for every American president, translating a coherent strategic vision from an abstract theoretical design into an effective operational reality is typically a difficult work-in-constant-progress. By comparison with most of his predecessors in the White House, Obama has not been obviously deficient or especially wanting in that regard. His statecraft has mostly been subtle, serious and ambitious in scope but modest in substantive accomplishments. By its nature, though, a policy of strategic engagement requires adequate time and diplomatic patience to ultimately bear fruit. Where this falters – as it has done with Israel, Pakistan, Iran, China and, to an extent, Russia – the diplomatic and political contexts allow for future policy corrections, to facilitate tactical revisions towards more coercive or confrontational approaches. Obama's case-by-case approach, willingness to embrace caution and extended deliberation, and aversion to a "forward leaning" US approach both reflected and reinforced America's shifting geo-political position in a world in substantial flux; one – as Philip Stephens characterizes it – "betwixt and between ... a brief period of unparalleled US might [and] a new, and chaotic, multi-polar world."[44]

In that context, it is perhaps worth reminding ourselves of the messy reality of political life. In the year of Obama's birth, when – by comparison to today – government was trusted to do the right thing and American politics was a relative paragon of partisan comity rather than fevered antagonism, President Kennedy cautioned in his 1961 inaugural address that, "All this will not be finished in the first 100 days. Nor will it be finished in the first 1,000 days." Overnight successes are rarities in foreign, as well as domestic, policy for good reason.

But the genuine statesman finds opportunity even in adversity. As such, America's grand strategy may yield successes sooner or later, through commission or omission, shrewd design or simple good fortune. It may yet be the case that what Daniel Drezner termed Obama's "counter-punching"[45] becomes more heavy- than light-weight, ensuring that Guantanamo Bay is finally closed, Afghanistan and Pakistan are stabilized, Iran is persuaded to abandon its military nuclear ambitions, Syria is induced to change its ways and cease its pariah status, China is locked into being a constructive and peaceful part of a stronger liberal international order, and the Israelis and Palestinians are coaxed and cajoled into a permanent peace respected by all the nations of the Arab League, democratic and authoritarian alike. But so far, the strategic punches that Obama has occasionally landed have had modest geo-political impact. Obama's diplomatic outreach, downsizing of militarism, and demotion of democracy promotion have yielded mostly tentative baby-steps and undeclared U-turns in pursuit of ambitious long-term objectives.

Should he secure a second term in the White House, like presidents before him, Obama may find that foreign policy assumes a more prominent and problematic place in coming years as congressional opposition to his domestic agenda proves difficult to overcome and gathering storms in Afghanistan, Pakistan, Syria, Yemen, North Korea, Iran, and Israel loom increasingly large and ominous after January 2013. But the danger also remains that, in crafting a post-American foreign policy while simultaneously seeking to preserve US primacy, "this president's pragmatic search for the middle way is in danger of satisfying nobody. It is turning into the recurring pattern, and may become the ultimate tragedy, of his presidency."[46]

As the influential American liberal internationalist, G. John Ikenberry, rightly argues, the shape of the new global order that is steadily and inexorably emerging from the legacies of the bipolar Cold War and unipolar post-Cold War eras is one where "... the United States will not be able to rule. But it can still lead."[47] In that critical quest, Obama's attempt to create a carefully calibrated US foreign policy for an emerging "post-American" world – a "post-American" foreign policy – has been important but not, as either the president's supporters hoped or his opponents feared, as yet successful or transformative. But, ironically, although the president has thus far failed either to bring about wholesale change and renewal to US foreign policy or to confirm that the US can lead from the rear as well as from the front, Obama has nonetheless hastened that post-American world into being.

As Zakaria argued back in 2008, "the rise of the rest" does not by definition imply that in departing from – for Americans, at least – a congenial era of unipolar US dominance "we are entering an anti-American world."[48] Nonetheless, four years later under Barack Obama's leadership, it is apparent that even where America's interests align closely with those of other states – from traditional allies such as Israel, the UK and Japan to the fragile and faltering Faustian pacts with Saudi Arabia and Pakistan – American "partnerships" of varying closeness and effectiveness around the globe appear increasingly transactional, acrimonious and conditional. As the former US ambassador to Saudi Arabia, Charles (Chas) Freeman, aptly put it, "After a brief, unipolar moment at the end of the Cold War, regional powers around the world are now essentially stepping forward to assert themselves and, in effect, pushing the United States aside or ignoring us altogether. No American has seen anything like that in our lifetimes."[49]

The foreign policy changes achieved by President Obama during 2009–12 have thus seen the president make a substantial contribution to recalibrating the contours of America's international relations in consequential ways. But, with his foreign policy facing the profound limits of engagement on multiple fronts, not to mention the substantial resistance at home to both his domestic and global agendas, Obama's fractious Washington appears destined to play a diminished and declining role on the world stage for several years to come. Contrary to the subtitle of *The Audacity of Hope*, the American Dream has not been reclaimed. Even restoring America's fiscal solvency, much less American greatness, remains a decidedly distant goal; less a matter of "yes we can" than "no, we probably can't." In leading from behind, the slow but steady advance of the post-American world may yet yield the arrival of an increasingly unmanageable one. What perhaps is equally of concern is that it may not be so much anti-American as much as indifferent to a downsized America unable to arrest its steady decline into an unexceptional mediocrity. That represents a change that Americans, and the West more broadly, may yet wish to reject rather than believe in.

Notes

Chapter One

1 Richard Wolffe, *Renegade: The Making of Barack Obama* (London: Virgin Books, 2009), 20.

2 Quoted in Helene Cooper, "On the world stage, Obama issues an overture," *New York Times* April 2, 2009, at http://www.nytimes.com/2009/04/03/world/europe/03assess.html?ref=us.

3 Christopher Caldwell, "Leaders for our time: do crises demand craziness?", *Financial Times* September 3–4, 2011, 11.

4 Michael Hirsh, "The Decider?", *National Journal* July 30, 2011, 37.

5 The underemployment rate combines those unemployed Americans with those in part-time work who are seeking, or would accept, full-time employment.

6 The US Census Bureau recorded 46.2 million Americans in 2010 below the poverty line, of $22,314 for a family of four and $11,139 for an individual. That amounted to 15.1 percent of the US population, the highest since 1993. See Matt Kennard and Shannon Bond, "US poverty hits record levels," *Financial Times* September 14, 2011, 10.

7 *Ibid.*

8 John R. Talbott, *Obamanomics: How Bottom-Up Economic Prosperity Will Replace Trickle-down Economics* (New York: Seven Stories Press, 2008).

9 According to Gallup, Obama's job approval in the last week of August 2011 averaged 40 percent, tying with his record-low 40 percent approval ratings for the two weeks commencing August 8. Only African Americans, Democrats and liberals gave him majority approval. See http://www.gallup.com/poll/149225/Obama-Weekly-Average-Approval-Holds-Term-Low.aspx.

10 One-fifth of Americans strongly approved of Obama's performance, according to the Rasmussen daily tracking poll, at http://www.rasmussenreports.com/public_content/politics/obama_administration/daily_presidential_tracking_poll.

11 According to a Washington Post-ABC poll conducted from August 29 to September 1, 2011, at http://www.washingtonpost.com/wp-srv/politics/polls/postabcpoll_090111.html.

12 From the Washington Post-ABC poll, *ibid.*, at http://www.washingtonpost.com/obamas-approval-ratings-skid-to-new-low-economic-stewardship-in-question/2011/09/05/gIQACwxH5J_graphic.html.

13 President Obama famously stated, in an interview with ABC's "World News" anchor Diane Sawyer on January 25, 2010, that "I'd rather be a really good one-term president than a mediocre two-term president." See Mark Mooney, "Exclusive: President Obama Would 'Rather Be Really Good One-Term President'," January 25, 2010, at http://abcnews.go.com/WN/Politics/president-obama-good-term-president/story?id=9657337.

14 The phrase is from Obama's June 2, 2008 speech in St Paul, Minnesota when he had finally won sufficient delegates to the Democratic National Convention to become the party's nominee for president. See http://www.nytimes.com/2008/06/03/us/politics/03text-obama.html.

15 There now exists an extensive literature challenging the consensus notion that American primacy is under fatal threat, whether from American decline or the

"rise of the rest." Among other valuable works, see especially: Stephen Brooks and William Wohlforth, *World Out Of Balance: international relations and the challenge of American primacy* (Princeton, NJ: Princeton University Press, 2008); Michael Mandelbaum, *The Frugal Superpower: America's Global Leadership in a Cash-Strapped Era* (New York, Public Affairs, 2010); Carla Norrlof, *America's Global Advantage: US Hegemony and International Cooperation* (New York: Cambridge University Press, 2010); Eric S. Edelman, *Understanding America's Contested Primacy* (Washington, DC: Center for Strategic and Budgetary Assessments, 2010); Josef Joffe, "The Default Power," *Foreign Affairs* 88 (2) 2009, 21–35; Robert J. Lieber, "Persistent Primacy and the Future of the American Era," *International Politics* 46 (2/3) 2009, 119–39; and Robert J. Lieber, "Staying Power and the American Future: Problems of Primacy, Policy, and Grand Strategy," *The Journal of Strategic Studies* 34 (4) 2011, 509–530.

16   Fareed Zakaria, *The Post-American World* (New York: Allen Lane, 2008), 4–5.

17   "Remarks by the President in State of Union address," January 25, 2011, at http://www.whitehouse.gov/the-press-office/2011/01/25/remarks-president-state-union-address.

18   "Address by the President to a Joint Session of Congress," September 8, 2011, at http://www.whitehouse.gov/the-press-office/2011/09/08/address-president-joint-session-congress.

19   Adam Quinn, "The art of declining politely: Obama's prudent presidency and the waning of American power," *International Affairs* 87 (4) 2011, 803–24.

20   Stanley A. Renshon, *National Security in the Obama Administration: Reassessing the Bush Doctrine* (New York: Routledge, 2010).

21   For an excellent elaboration of the distinction, see Paul McCartney, "American Nationalism and US Foreign Policy from September 11 to the Iraq War," *Political Science Quarterly* 119 (3) 2004, 399–424.

22   See Gary C. Jacobson, "Polarization, Public Opinion, and the Presidency: the Obama and Anti-Obama Coalitions," Chapter 5 in Bert A. Rockman, Andrew Rudalevige and Colin Campbell (eds.), *The Obama Presidency: Appraisals and Prospects* (Washington, DC: CQ Press, 2012), 94–122.

23   According to Gallup, Americans' political ideology at the mid-year point of 2011 looked similar to 2009 and 2010, with 41 percent self-identifying as conservative, 36 percent as moderate, and 21 percent as liberal, at http://www.gallup.com/poll/148745/Political-Ideology-Stable-Conservatives-Leading.aspx.

24   "If," in Rudyard Kipling, *Selected Poems* (London: Penguin, 1993), 134–5.

25   Fareed Zakaria, *The Post-American World* (New York: Allen Lane, 2008).

26   Barack Obama, "A World That Stands as One," Berlin, Germany, July 24, 2008, at: http://www.spiegel.de/international/germany/0,1518,567920,00.html.

27   Barack Obama, *The Audacity of Hope* (New York: Crown Publishers, 2006), 279.

28   Inderjeet Parmar, "American power and identities in the age of Obama," *International Politics* 48 (2–3) 2011, 153–63, at 154.

29   Quoted in Paul Steinhauser, "Obama: my presidency would unleash a 'transformation'," CNN.com, 27 July, http://articles.cnn.com/2007-07-27/politics/obama.black.votes_1_affirmative-action-presidential-forum-obama?_s=PM:POLITICS.

30   Jonathan Alter, for example, records that in the middle of 2009, Obama's popularity in ten nations was higher than in the US: Kenya, 94 percent; Germany, 93 percent; France, 91 percent; Canada, 88 percent; Nigeria, 88 percent; Britain, 86 percent; Japan, 85 percent; South Korea, 81 percent; India, 77 percent; Brazil, 76 percent; US, 74 percent. See Jonathan Alter, *The Promise* (London: Simon

and Schuster, 2010), 224. Other selected surveys over 2009–11 are mentioned in subsequent chapters.

31   *Hardball with Chris Matthews*, MSNBC, December 10, 2009. Quoted in Windsor Mann (ed.), *The Quotable Hitchens: from Alcohol to Zionism* (Cambridge, MA: Da Capo Press, 2011), 207.

32   According to Gallup polls, at http://www.gallup.com/poll/1726/Presidential-Ratings-Issue-Approval.aspx.

33   James Traub, "The Two Obamas," at http://www.foreignpolicy.com/articles/2010/08/06/the_two_obamas?page=0,0.

34   Stephen Walt, "Obama is zero for four and Republicans are sitting pretty," at http://walt.foreignpolicy.com/posts/2010/07/30/obama_is_zero_for_four_and_republicans_are_sitting_pretty%20.

35   Quoted in James Kitfield, "The 13th Crisis," *National Journal* August 7, 2010, 10–18, at 15.

36   Cited in Con Coughlin, "Cameron has given up on Afghanistan," *The Spectator* July 31, 2010, 12–13, at 13.

37   Quoted in Ryan Lizza, "The consequentialist," *New Yorker* May 2, 2011, 55.

38   Giles Whittell, "America lost more than lives on that fateful day," *The Times* September 10, 2011, 10–11.

39   Jeffrey Sachs, "The great failure of globalization," *Financial Times* August 18, 2011, 11.

40   Stanley A. Renshon, *Barack Obama and the Politics of Redemption* (New York: Routledge, 2012); David Remnick, *The Bridge: The Life and Rise of Barack Obama* (London: Picador, 2010); Richard Wolffe, *Renegade: The Making of Barack Obama* (London: Virgin Books, 2009); David Mendell, *Obama: From Promise to Power* (New York: Amistad, 2007); Shelby Steele, *A Bound Man: Why We Are Excited About Obama and Why He Can't Win* (New York: The Free Press, 2007); John K. Wilson, *Barack Obama: This Improbable Quest* (London: Paradigm Publishers, 2008); Jerome R. Corsi, *The Obama Nation: Leftist Politics and the Cult of Personality* (New York: Simon and Schuster, 2008); Martin Dupuis and Keith Boeckelman, *Barack Obama: the New Face of American Politics* (London: Praeger, 2008); Dinesh D'Souza, *The Roots of Obama's Rage* (New York: Regnery, 2010).

41   Larry J. Sabato (ed.), *The Year of Obama: How Barack Obama Won the White House* (New York: Longman, 2010); Kevin J. McMahon, David M. Rankin, Donald W. Beacher and John Kenneth White, *Winning The White House, 2008* (New York: Palgrave Macmillan, 2009); Daniel J. Balz and Haynes Bonner Johnson, *The Battle For America, 2008: The Story of an Extraordinary Election* (Viking Books, 2009); Carl Pedersen, *Obama's America* (Edinburgh: Edinburgh University Press, 2009); John Heilemann and Mark Halperin, *Race of a Lifetime: How Obama Won The White House* (London: Viking, 2010); Ian Leslie, *To Be President: Quest for the White House 2008* (London: Politico's Press, 2009); Chuck Todd, Sheldon Gawiser, and Ana Maria Arumi, *How Barack Obama Won: A State-by-State Guide to the Historic 2008 Presidential Election* (New York: Vintage Books, 2009); David Plouffe, *The Audacity To Win: the Insider Story and Lessons of Barack Obama's Historic Victory* (New York: Viking Press, 2009).

42   Martin S. Indyk, Kenneth G. Lieberthal and Michael E. O'Hanlon, *Bending History? Barack Obama's Foreign Policy* (Washington DC: Brookings Institution Press, 2012); Jonathan Alter, *The Promise: President Obama, Year One* (London: Simon and Schuster, 2010); Stanley A. Renshon, *National Security In The Obama Administration: Reassessing the Bush Doctrine* (New York: Routledge, 2010);

David E. Sanger, *The Inheritance: the world Obama confronts and the challenges to American power* (London: Bantam Press, 2009); Bob Woodward, *Obama's Wars: The Inside Story* (London: Simon and Schuster, 2010).

43 Barry Libert and Rick Fault, *Barack, Inc.: Winning Lessons of the Obama Campaign* (Upper Saddle River, NJ: FT Press, 2009), 4.

44 See, in particular: Steven W. Hook and James M. Scott (eds.), *US Foreign Policy Today: American Renewal?* (Washington, DC: CQ Press, 2011); and Bert A. Rockman, Andrew Rudalevige and Colin Campbell (eds.), *The Obama Presidency: Appraisals and Prospects* (Washington, DC: CQ Press, 2012).

45 Tariq Ali, *The Obama Syndrome: Surrender at Home, War Abroad* (London: Verso, 2010).

46 Dinesh D'Souza, *The Roots of Obama's Rage* (New York: Regnery, 2010).

47 See in particular: Joseph S. Nye, *The Paradox of American Power: Why the World's Only Superpower Can't Go It Alone* (New York: Oxford University Press, 2002); and Joseph S. Nye, *Soft Power: The Means to Success in World Politics* (New York: Public Affairs, 2004).

Chapter Two

1 Carl Pedersen, *Obama's America* (Edinburgh: Edinburgh University Press, 2009), 169.

2 Quoted in Ryan Lizza, "The Consequentialist: How the Arab Spring remade Obama's foreign policy," *The New Yorker* May 2, 2011, 44–55, at 46.

3 Quoted in Windsor Mann (ed.), *The Quotable Hitchens: from Alcohol to Zionism* (Cambridge, MA: Da Capo Press, 2011), 206.

4 John Kenneth White, "The Foreign Policy Election That Wasn't," Chapter 3 in Kevin J. McMahon, David M. Rankin, Donald W. Beacher and John Kenneth White, *Winning The White House, 2008* (New York: Palgrave Macmillan, 2009), 45–57.

5 Larry J. Sabato (ed.), *The Year of Obama: How Barack Obama Won the White House* (New York: Longman, 2010).

6 David Brady, Morris Fiorina and Douglas Rivers, "The Road to (and from) the 2010 Elections: what happened to the president and his party?", *Policy Review* no. 165 2011, at http://www.hoover.org/publications/policy-review/article/64061; Gary C. Jacobson (2009), "The 2008 Presidential and Congressional Elections: Anti-Bush Referendum and Prospects for a Democratic Majority," *Political Science Quarterly* 124 (1), 1–30; William Jacoby, "Policy attitudes, ideology and voting behaviour in the 2008 Election," *Electoral Studies* 29 (4) 2010, 557–568; Alan I. Abramowitz, "Transformation and polarization: The 2008 presidential election and the new American electorate," *Electoral Studies* 29 (4) 2010, 594–603; and Larry J. Sabato (ed.) (2009), *The Year of Obama: How Barack Obama Won the White House* (New York: Longman, 2010).

7 Of particular note are two recent influential monographs: Robert P. Saldin, *War, The American State, and Politics Since 1898* (Cambridge: Cambridge University Press, 2011); and Peter Trubowitz, *Politics and Strategy: Partisan Ambition and American Statecraft* (Princeton, NJ: Princeton University Press, 2011).

8 Robert P. Saldin, "Foreign Affairs and the 2008 Election," *The Forum* 6 (4) 2008, article 5, 1, at: http://www.bepress.com/forum/vol6/iss4/art5.

9 Kurt M. Campbell and Michael O'Hanlon, *Hard Power: The New Politics of National Security* (New York: Basic Books, 2006), 29.

10 http://www.nytimes.com/2008/06/03/us/politics/03text-obama.html?pagewanted=4

11 Quoted in David Nakamura, "Obama offers 2012 election supporters change they can believe in – next term," *Washington Post* August 26, 2011, at http://www.washingtonpost.com/politics/obama-offers-2012-election-supporters-change-they-can-believe-in–next-term/2011/08/25/gIQAJz9AhJ_story.html?hpid=z2.

12 David Remnick, *The Bridge: The Life and Rise of Barack Obama* (Oxford: Picador, 2011), 552. 22,500 people were polled in twenty-two countries. See "All Countries in BBC World Service Poll Prefer Obama to McCain," BBC World Service Poll, at http://www.worldpublicopinion.org/pipa/pdf/sep08/BBCPresidential_Sep08_pr.pdf.

13 Fouad Ajami, "The Foreign Policy Difference," *The Wall Street Journal* September 10, 2008, A15.

14 *Ibid.*

15 Fareed Zakaria, "Obama the Realist," *The Washington Post* July 21, 2008, A15.

16 Eli Lake, "Contra Expectations," *The New Republic* July 30, 2008, 16–18.

17 Jerome R. Corsi, *The Obama Nation: Leftist Politics and the Cult of Personality* (New York: Simon and Schuster, 2008), 279.

18 Martin Dupuis and Keith Boeckelman. *Barack Obama: the New Face of American Politics.* (London: Praeger, 2008), 81.

19 *Ibid.*, 82.

20 *Ibid.*, 84.

21 *Ibid.*, 86.

22 David Mendell, *Obama: From Promise to Power* (New York: Amistad, 2007), 303.

23 *Ibid.*, 320.

24 Charles Krauthammer, "Obama's Altitude Sickness," *The Washington Post* September 12, 2008.

25 Ryan Lizza, "The Consequentialist," *ibid.*, 44.

26 Dupuis and Boeckelman, *ibid.*, 100.

27 John K. Wilson, *Barack Obama: This Improbable Quest* (London: Paradigm Publishers, 2008), 160.

28 Mendell, *ibid.*, 306.

29 *Ibid.*, 323.

30 Mendell, *ibid.*, 331.

31 Mendell, *ibid.*, 311.

32 Dupuis and Boeckelman, *ibid.*

33 Barack Obama, *The Audacity of Hope: Thoughts on Reclaiming the American Dream* (New York: Crown Publishers, 2006), 303.

34 Obama, *ibid.*, 304.

35 *Ibid.*, 309.

36 *The Economist*, "The hard road ahead," August 23, 2008, 9.

37 Kurt M. Campbell and Michael O'Hanlon, *Hard Power: The New Politics of National Security* (New York: Basic Books, 2006), 241–45.

38 Ajami, *ibid.*

39 Samuel P. Huntington, *Who Are We? America's Great Debate* (New York: The Free Press, 2004), 263.

40 Richard Holbrooke, "The Next President: Mastering a Daunting Agenda," *Foreign Affairs* 87 (5) 2008, 2–24, at 3.

41 Carl Pedersen, *Obama's America* (Edinburgh: Edinburgh University Press, 2009), 170.

42 "Exit Polls: President, National Exit Poll," CNN, at http://www.cnn.com/
    ELECTION/2008/results/polls#val=USP00p6.

43 Bruce Stokes, "Trading Gibes," *National Journal* July 26, 2008, 36–40.

44 Gerard Barker, "American Revolution," *Standpoint* issue 2 (July 2008), 34–37.

45 Shelby Steele, *A Bound Man: Why We Are Excited About Obama and Why He
    Can't Win* (New York: The Free Press, 2007).

46 Simon Jenkins, "Obama's Offer: an end to US stupidity," *The Sunday Times*
    August 31, 2008, 16.

47 Krauthammer, *ibid.*

48 Quoted in David Nakamura, "Obama offers 2012 election supporters change
    they can believe in – next term," *Washington Post* August 26, 2011, at
    http://www.washingtonpost.com/politics/obama-offers-2012-election-
    supporters-change-they-can-believe-in–next-term/2011/08/25/gIQAJz9AhJ_story.
    html?hpid=z2.

49 Obama, *ibid.*, 293.

Chapter Three

1   President Carter interviewed on *60 Minutes*, CBS. Cited in *National Journal*
    September 25, 2010, 70.

2   Victor Davis Hanson, *How The Obama Administration Threatens Our National
    Security* (New York: Encounter Books, 2009), 40.

3   Quoted in Ryan Lizza, "The Consequentialist: How the Arab Spring remade
    Obama's foreign policy," *The New Yorker* May 2, 2011, 44–55, at 55.

4   Robert Kaplan, "Libya, Obama, and the triumph of realism," *Financial Times*
    August 29, 2011, 9; Fareed Zakaria, "The post-imperial presidency," *Newsweek*
    December 5, 2009, http://www.newsweek.com/2009/12/04/the-post-imperial-
    presidency.html.

5   Colin Dueck, *Hard Line: The Republican Party and US Foreign Policy Since
    World War II* (Princeton, NJ: Princeton University Press, 2010), 303.

6   Michael Tomasky, "Do conservatives know what they're embracing?", December 11,
    2009, http://www.guardian.co.uk/commentisfree/michaeltomasky/2009/dec/11/
    conservatives-obama-nobel-speech.

7   John Podhoretz, "Barack the neo-con," *New York Post* September 1, 2010,
    http://www.nypost.com/p/news/opinion/opedcolumnists/barack_the_neocon_
    brsZZIP4IIEMbYsUR9w5wI; Walter Russell Mead, "W Gets A Third Term in
    the Middle East," August 22, 2011, at http://blogs.the-american-interest.com/
    wrm/2011/08/22/w-gets-a-third-term-in-the-middle-east/.

8   Tony Blankley, "Obama the isolationist?", *National Review* June 23, 2010,
    http://www.nationalreview.com/articles/243316/obama-isolationist-tony-blankley.

9   Glenn Hastedt, "Presidents, Advisers and, Future Directions of American Foreign
    Policy," in Steven W. Hook and James M. Scott (eds.), *US Foreign Policy Today:
    American Renewal?* (Washington, DC: CQ Press, 2012), 16–35, at 31.

10 Stephen Walt, "Is America addicted to war?", *Foreign Policy*, at http://www.
    foreignpolicy.com/articles/2011/04/04/is_america_addicted_to_war.

11 Daniel W. Drezner, "Does Obama Have a Grand Strategy? Why We Need
    Doctrines in Uncertain Times," *Foreign Affairs*, 90 (4) 2011, 57–68.

12 Fareed Zakaria, "Stop searching for an Obama Doctrine," *Washington Post*
    July 6, 2011, at http://www.washingtonpost.com/opinions/stop-searching-for-
    an-obama-doctrine/2011/07/06/gIQAQMmI1H_story.html.

13 Ryan Lizza, "The Consequentialist," *ibid.*, 55.

14 *Ibid.*

15 Fareed Zakaria, *The Post-American World* (London: Allen Lane, 2008).

16 Statement of Senator Hillary Rodham Clinton, Nominee for Secretary of State, Senate Foreign Relations Committee, January 13, 2009, at http://foreign.senate.gov/testimony/2009/ClintonTestimony090113a.pdf.

17 Barack Obama, Inaugural Address, January 20, 2009, at http://whitehouse.gov/blog/inaugural-address/.

18 *America's Place in the World 2009*, Pew Research Center/Council on Foreign Relations (December 2009), 3–4.

19 "Most Americans Name Just Five Countries That the US Should Defend Militarily," *Rasmussen Report*, September 8, 2010, at http://www.rasmussenreports.com/public_content/politics/current_events/ally_enemy/most_americans_name_just_five_countries_that_u_s_should_defend_militarily.

20 "Just 11% Say US Should Be World's Policeman," *Rasmussen Report* June 17, 2011, at: http://www.rasmussenreports.com/public_content/politics/current_events/ally_enemy/just_11_say_u_s_should_be_world_s_policeman.

21 David E. Sanger, *The Inheritance: The World Obama Confronts and the Challenges to American Power* (London: Bantam Press, 2009), 448.

22 Wolffe, *ibid.*, 328.

23 Zbigniew Brzezinski and Brent Scowcroft, *America and the World: conversations on the future of American foreign policy* (New York: Basic Books, 2008), 2.

24 Gideon Rachman, "2011, the year of global indignation," *Financial Times* August 30, 2011, 9.

25 The most prominent case for non-polarity is Richard Haass, "The Age of Non-polarity," *Foreign Affairs* 87 (3) 2008, 18–43.

26 *National Security Strategy May 2010*, 11, at http://www.whitehouse.gov/sites/default/files/rss_viewer/national_security_strategy.pdf.

27 For a fuller discussion of the distinction, see Kenneth M. Pollack, Daniel L. Byman, Martin Indyk, Suzanne Maloney, Michael E. O'Hanlon and Bruce Riedel, *Which Path to Persia? Options for a New American Strategy Toward Iran* (Washington DC: Brookings Institution Press, 2009), Part One.

28 Thomas Wright, "Strategic Engagement's Track Record," *The Washington Quarterly* 33 (3) 2010, 35–60.

29 *National Security Strategy May 2010*, 9, at http://www.whitehouse.gov/sites/default/files/rss_viewer/national_security_strategy.pdf.

30 Miles E. Taylor, "Obama's National Security Strategy under the Microscope," *World Politics Review* June 1, 2010; http://www.worldpoliticsreview.com/articles/5656/obamas-national-security-strategy-under-the-microscope.

31 Hillary Clinton, "Remarks on the Obama Administration's National Security Strategy," The Brookings Institution, Washington DC, May 27, 2010, at http://www.state.gov/secretary/rm/2010/0S/142313.htm.

32 Cited in "Global Strategic Review," "Global Security Governance and the Emerging Distribution of Power," Geneva, Switzerland, September 10–12, 2010, *IISS News* September 2010.

33 *Ibid.*

34 Wright, *ibid.*, 39.

35 NSS 2010, 3.

36 Henry R. Nau, "Obama's Foreign Policy – The Swing Away From Bush: how far to go?", *Policy Review* no. 160, April/May 2010 at http://www.hoover.org/publications/policy-review/article/5287.

37   NSS 2010, 11.
38   Dueck, *ibid.*, 303. See also, Colin Dueck, "The Accommodator: Obama's Foreign Policy," *Policy Review* 169 (October 2011).
39   Inderjeet Parmar, "American power and identities in the age of Obama," *International Politics* 48 (2/3) 2011, 153–163, at 154–55.
40   Quoted in Lizza, "The Consequentialist," *ibid.*, 47.
41   The reference was to Doris Kearns Goodwin, *Team of Rivals: The Political Genius of Abraham Lincoln* (New York: Simon and Schuster, 2005).
42   Quoted in Lizza, "The Consequentialist," *ibid.*, 47.
43   Kurt M. Campbell and Michael E. O'Hanlon, *Hard Power: The New Politics of National Security* (New York: Basic Books, 2006), 241–245.
44   Stephen J. Wayne, *Personality and Politics: Obama For and Against Himself* (Washington, DC: CQ Press, 2012), 112–13.
45   http://www.whitehouse.gov/blog/NewBeginning
46   Gregorio Bettiza and Christopher Phillips, "Obama's Middle East Policy: Time to Decide," *Obama Nation? US Foreign Policy One Year On* (London: LSE IDEAS, 2010), 11–15, at 12.
47   Quoted in Ronald Brownstein, "A Dangerously Downward Spiral," *National Journal* September 18, 2010, 68.
48   Jon Cohen and Michael D. Shear, "Poll shows more Americans think Obama is a Muslim," *Washington Post* August 19, 2010, at http://www.washingtonpost.com/wp-dyn/content/article/2010/08/18/AR2010081806913.html.
49   Scott Wilson, "Obama's outreach toward Muslims is limited at home," *Washington Post* September 5, 2011, at: http://www.washingtonpost.com/politics/obamas-outreach-toward-muslims-is-limited-at-home/2011/08/22/gIQAySL74J_story.html?hpid=z2.
50   *Constrained Internationalism: Adapting to New Realities – Results of a 2010 National Survey of Public Opinion* (Chicago: Chicago Council on Global Affairs, 2010), 13.
51   Nico Hines, "President Obama pledges to scour world for terrorist cells," *The Times* December 29, 2009, at http://www.timesonline.co.uk/tol/news/world/us_and_americas/article6970323.ece.
52   April 4, 2009 News Conference, Palaiz de la Musique et Des Congres, Strasbourg, France, at http://www.whitehouse.gov/the_press_office/News-Conference-By-President-Obama-4-04-2009/.
53   Shelby Steele, "Obama and the Burden of Exceptionalism," *Wall Street Journal* September 1, 2011, at http://online.wsj.com/article/SB10001424053111904787404576532623176115558.html?mod=googlenews_wsj.
54   James W. Ceaser, "The Unpresidential President," *The Weekly Standard* August 2, 2010, at http://www.weeklystandard.com/articles/unpresidential-president?page=4.
55   Michael D. Shear, "Obama Pulls Up a Chair at George Will's House," *Washington Post* (blog) January 13, 2009, at http://voices.washingtonpost.com/44/2009/01/13/obama_pulls_up_a_chair_at_geor.html?wprss=the-trail.
56   Richard M. Skinner, "George W. Bush and the Partisan Presidency," *Political Science Quarterly* 123 (4) 2008–09, 605–22.
57   Charles Krauthammer, "Decline is a choice: the new liberalism and the end of American ascendancy," *The Weekly Standard* October 19, 2009, vol. 15 no. 5, at http://www.weeklystandard.com/Content/Public/Articles/000/000/017/056lfnpr.asp.
58   Interview, former senior Republican official in the Pentagon, the Hudson Institute, Washington DC, April 8, 2011.

59 John Bolton, "The Post-American Presidency," *Standpoint* no. 14 July/August 2009, 42–45, at 42.

60 Quoted in Charles A. Kupchan, "Enemies Into Friends: How the United States Can Court Its Adversaries," *Foreign Affairs* 89 (2) 2010, 120–134, at 121.

61 David Nakamura and Philip Rucker, "Romney, Perry criticize Obama's foreign policy as weak," *Washington Post* August 30, 2011, at: http://www.washingtonpost.com/politics/romney-perry-criticize-obamas-foreign-policy-as-weak/2011/08/30/gIQAhTthqJ_story.html?hpid=z1.

62 *Ibid.*

63 See, for example: Charles Krauthammer, "Obama's Policy of Slapping Allies," *Washington Post* April 2, 2010, at www.washingtonpost.com/wp-dyn/content/article/2010/04/01/AR2010040102805.html; and Robert Kagan, "Obama's Year One, Contra," *World Affairs Journal* (January/February 2010), at http://www.worldaffairsjournal.org/articles/2010-JanFeb/full-Kagan-JF-2010.html.

64 Mitt Romney, *No Apology: The Case for American Greatness* (New York: St Martin's Press, 2010), 25.

65 Romney, *ibid.*, 22.

66 Stephen J. Wayne, *Personality and Politics*, 113.

67 Quoted in Glenn Kessler, "Rice meets with Obama, then defends his administration's approach," *Washington Post* October 15, 2010, at: http://www.washingtonpost.com/wp-dyn/content/article/2010/10/15/AR2010101506018.html?hpid=topnews. Of course, many in the contemporary conservative movement and Republican Party regard Rice as a RINO ("Republican In Name Only").

68 April 4, 2009 News Conference, Palaiz de la Musique et Des Congres, Strasbourg, France, at: http://www.whitehouse.gov/the_press_office/News-Conference-By-President-Obama-4-04-2009/.

69 Address by the President to a Joint Session of Congress, September 8, 2011, at http://www.whitehouse.gov/the-press-office/2011/09/08/address-president-joint-session-congress.

70 Peter Trubowitz, *Politics and Strategy: Partisan Ambition and American Statecraft* (Princeton, NJ: Princeton University Press, 2011), 147.

71 Gary C. Jacobson, *A Divider, Not a Uniter: George W Bush and the American People* (New York: Longman, 2010).

72 http://www.whitehouse.gov/blog/inaugural-address/

73 Peter Trubowitz, *Politics and Strategy*, 147.

74 Walter Russell Mead, "The Carter Syndrome," *Foreign Policy* no. 177, January/February 2010, 58–64.

75 *Arab Spring Fails To Improve US Image* (Pew Global Attitudes Project), May 17, 2011, at http://pewglobal.org/2011/05/17/arab-spring-fails-to-improve-us-image/.

76 *Arab Attitudes, 2011* (Arab American Institute Foundation), at http://www.aaiusa.org/reports/arab-attitudes-2011.

77 "Ten years on," *The Economist* September 3, 2011, 9.

Chapter Four

1 "Remarks by the President in Address to the Nation on the Way Forward in Afghanistan and Pakistan," US Military Academy, West Point, New York, at http://www.whitehouse.gov/the-press-office/remarks-president-address-nation-way-forward-afghanistan-and-pakistan.

2 Quoted in Bob Woodward, *Obama's Wars: The Inside Story* (New York: Simon and Schuster, 2010), 364.

3 Quoted in "On the brink: America and Pakistan," *The Economist* October 9, 2010, 72.

4 The figures are according to iCasualties.org, which tracks casualties. Quoted in Matthew Green and James Politi, "Kerry defiant after helicopter attack," *Financial Times* August 8, 2011, 6.

5 Figures from CBS News and www.icasualties.org. Cited in Giles Whittell, "America lost more than lives on that fateful day," *The Times* September 10, 2011, 10–11, at 10.

6 Obama described the operation as "one of the greatest intelligence and military operations in our nation's history." Whether the targeted killing really stood comparison with the War of Independence, World Wars One and Two or the Korean War was perhaps questionable. But the risky decision to conduct a raid rather than a drone or cruise missile strike, with all its attendant dangers, and the very fact of its operational success – in contrast with the notorious failure of Jimmy Carter's attempted rescue of the US hostages in Iran and Bill Clinton's "Black Hawk Down" experience in Somalia – added substantially to Obama's stock of political capital and his standing as Commander-in-Chief.

7 C. Christine Fair, "Lashkar-e-Tayiba and the Pakistani State," *Survival* 53 (4) 2011, 29–52. See also Jeffrey Goldberg and Marc Ambinder, "Nuclear Negligence," *National Journal* November 5, 2011, 16–24, wherein Islamabad's attempts to hide their nuclear weapons from a potential Washington seizure – including transporting them in trucks, thereby making them more vulnerable to seizure by jihadist groups – are outlined in frightening detail.

8 In an August 2007 campaign speech, Obama warned that "If we have actionable intelligence about high-value terrorist targets and President Musharraf won't act, we will." See Jeff Zeleny, "Obama Calls for US to Shift Focus on Terrorism," *New York Times* August 1, 2007. The stone-age reference was the warning issued to Pakistan's intelligence director by then US Deputy Secretary of State Richard Armitage: "Be prepared to be bombed. Be prepared to go back to the Stone Age." Quoted in Pervez Musharraf, *In The Line Of Fire: A Memoir* (London: Simon and Schuster, 2006), 201.

9 Adrian Guelke, "Redefining the Global War on Terror?", in *Obama Nation: US Foreign Policy One Year On* (London: LSE IDEAS, 2010), 7–10, at 9.

10 Victor Davis Hanson, *How The Obama Administration Threatens Our National Security* (New York: Encounter Books, 2009), 5.

11 Barack Obama, Inaugural Address, January 20, 2009, at http://whitehouse. gov/blog/inaugural-address/.

12 Stephen Chan, *The End of Certainty: Towards a New Internationalism* (London: Zed Books, 2010), 316.

13 American Civil Liberties Union, "Establishing a New Normal: National Security, Civil Liberties, and Human Rights Under the Obama Administration: an 18-Month Review" (ACLU, July 2010). See also: Paul Street, *The Empire's New Clothes: Barack Obama in the Real World of Power* (London: Paradigm Publishers, 2010).

14 James D. Boys, "What's so extraordinary about rendition?", *The International Journal of Human Rights* 15 (4) 2011, 589–604, at 590.

15 Richard Jackson, "Culture, identity and hegemony: continuity and (the lack of) change in US counterterrorism policy from Bush to Obama," *International Politics* 48 (2–3) 2011, 390–411. For a similar emphasis on how little in counter-terrorism policy altered under Obama, see Trevor McCrisken, "Ten years on: Obama's war on terrorism in rhetoric and practice," *International Affairs* 87 (4) 2011, 781–801.

16 Jack Goldsmith, "The Cheney Fallacy: Why Barack Obama Is Waging a More Effective War on Terror Than George W. Bush," *The New Republic*, May 18, 2009, at www.tnr.com/story_print.html?id=1e733cac-c273-48e5-9140-80443ed1f5e2.

17 State of the Union address, January 29, 2002.

18 NATO press conference, April 4, 2009, at http://whitehouse.gov.

19 Speech to the joint session of Congress, September 20, 2001, at http://archives.cnn.com/2001/US/09/20/gen.bush.transcript/.

20 NATO press conference, April 4 2009, at http://whitehouse.gov.

21 Imtiaz Gul, *The Most Dangerous Place: Pakistan's Lawless Frontier* (London: Penguin Books, 2010).

22 Cheney, for example, declared on accepting the "Keeper of the Flame" award from the Center for Security Policy on October 21, 2009, that "The White House must stop dithering while America's armed forces are in danger." See Woodward, *Obama's Wars*, 247.

23 "Remarks by the President in Address to the Nation on the Way Forward in Afghanistan and Pakistan," US Military Academy, West Point, New York, at http://www.whitehouse.gov/the-press-office/remarks-president-address-nation-way-forward-afghanistan-and-pakistan.

24 "Remarks by the President in Address to the Nation on the Way Forward in Afghanistan and Pakistan," US Military Academy, West Point, New York, at http://www.whitehouse.gov/the-press-office/remarks-president-address-nation-way-forward-afghanistan-and-pakistan.

25 Alter, *The Promise*, 391.

26 Michael Hastings, "The Runaway General," *Rolling Stone*, July 8–22, 2010, 91–97, 120–121, at 120.

27 Quoted in Peter Baker, "For Obama, Steep Learning Curve as Chief in War," *The New York Times* August 28, 2010.

28 Michael O'Hanlon, "Staying Power: The US Mission in Afghanistan Beyond 2011," *Foreign Affairs* 89 (5) 2010, 63–79, at 64.

29 Cited in Paul Kennedy, "A Time to Appease," *The National Interest* no. 108 (July/August) 2010, 7–17, at 16.

30 Gideon Rachman, "Somali lessons for Afghanistan," *Financial Times* July 27, 2010, 11.

31 According to a Gallup poll, at http://www.gallup.com/poll/141836/Issues-Obama-Finds-Majority-Approval-Elusive.aspx.

32 *Constrained Internationalism: Adapting to New Realities* (Chicago: Chicago Council on Global Affairs), 70.

33 Cited in "Henry Kissinger talks to Simon Schama," *FT Weekend Magazine*, May 21–22 2011, 14–19, at 19.

34 Ahmed Rashid, *Descent Into Chaos: The world's most unstable region and the threat to global security* (New York: Penguin Books, 2008), 416.

35 March 27, 2010 remarks of the presidency, at www.whitehouse.gov.

36 Alter, *The Promise*, 364.

37 Aqil Shah, "Getting the Military Out of Pakistani Politics," *Foreign Affairs* 90 (3) 2011, 69–82, at 80.

38 http://english.aljazeera.net/focus/2009/08/2009888238994769.html

39 "US intensifies drone strikes in Pakistan," *Strategic Comments* Volume 16, Comment 36, October 2010 (London: International Institute for Strategic Studies).

40 "Banyan: the insanity clause," *The Economist* May 7, 2011, 60.

41 For an authoritative account of this in relation to Pakistan's nuclear weapons program, see Adrian Levy and Catherine Scott-Clark, *Deception: Pakistan, the*

United States and the Global Nuclear Weapons Conspiracy (London: Atlantic Books, 2007).

42   David Pilling, "Pakistan, the state that has refused to fail," *Financial Times* October 21, 2010, 19.

43   International donors committed $495 per person affected by the Haiti earthquake in the first ten days following the disaster, which compared to just $3.20 per person affected in the first days following the July 2010 flooding in Pakistan. See Paul Peachey, "Poor Response to Pakistan Aid Appeals Frustrates Charities," *Independent* August 13, 2010.

44   *Constrained Internationalism: Adapting to New Realities* (Chicago: Chicago Council on Global Affairs), 71.

45   Alter, *The Promise*, 347.

46   See: Peter Baker, "For Obama, Steep Learning Curve as Chief in War," *The New York Times* August 28, 2010; and Bob Woodward, *Obama's Wars* (New York: Simon and Schuster, 2010).

47   In the article, Obama had been described as "uncomfortable and intimidated" in an initial Pentagon meeting with senior military officials; Vice-President Biden was derided; Jim Jones was referred to as a "clown" who was "stuck in 1985;" and Richard Holbrooke was described as a "wounded animal." See Hastings, "The Runaway General," *ibid.*

48   David Ignatius, "Petraeus rewrites the playbook in Afghanistan," *Washington Post*, October 19, 2010, at http://www.washingtonpost.com/wp-dyn/content/article/2010/10/18/AR2010101803596.html?hpid=opinionsbox1.

49   Quoted in Ahmed Rashid, "Once again US Afghan policy is hobbled by divisions," *Financial Times* September 20, 2011, 13.

50   *Ibid.*

51   See Michael O'Hanlon, "Staying Power: The US Mission in Afghanistan Beyond 2011," *Foreign Affairs* 89 (5) 2010, 63–79.

52   Quoted in Hastings, "The Runaway General," *ibid.*, 93.

53   Adrian Levy and Catherine Scott-Clark, *Deception: Pakistan, the United States and the Global Nuclear Weapons Conspiracy* (London: Atlantic Books, 2007), 9.

54   Quoted in Aryn Baker, "Frenemies," *Time* May 23, 2011, 16–22, at 18.

55   Obama BBC Interview with Andrew Marr, May 22, 2011. Quoted in Anushka Asthana and Michael Evans, "President seeks to strengthen 'special relationship' with joint security link," *The Times* May 23, 2001, 6.

56   Quoted in Anushka Asthana and Michael Evans, "President seeks to strengthen 'special relationship' with joint security link," *ibid.*

57   Francis Elliott and Zahid Hussain, "Doctor is latest victim in fall-out from bin Laden raid," *The Times* September 2, 2011, 39.

58   Seth Jones, "Pakistan's Dangerous Game," *Survival* 49 (1) 2007, 15–32, at 28–9.

59   See, for example: C. Christine Fair, "Lashkar-e-Tayiba and the Pakistani State," *Survival* 53 (4) 2011, 29–52; and Anatol Lieven, "Military Exceptionalism in Pakistan," *Survival* 53 (4) 2011, 53–68.

60   Quoted in James Kitfield, "The Wilderness of Mirrors," *National Journal* July 16, 2011, 48.

61   Cited in Anushka Asthana and Michael Evans, "President seeks to strengthen 'special relationship' with joint security link," *ibid.*

62   Tony Blair, *A Journey* (London: Hutchinson, 2010), 675.

63   Blair, *ibid.*, 673.

64   Alter, *The Promise*, 393.

65   Quoted in Woodward, *Obama's Wars*, 354.

66 Institute for International Strategic Studies, *Strategic Survey 2010: The Annual Review of World Affairs* (Abingdon: Routledge, 2010).

67 Hillary Synnott, "After the Flood," *Survival* 52 (5) 2010, 249–256, at 255.

68 *Ibid.*, 252.

69 Quoted in Peter Bergen, "The slow death of Al-Qaeda," *The Sunday Times* News Review September 4, 2011, 6.

70 The dimensions of a potential collapse of the Pakistani state are graphically outlined in Andrew F. Krepinevich, "The Collapse of Pakistan," Chapter 1 in his *7 Deadly Scenarios: A Military Futurist Explores War in the Twenty-first Century* (New York: Bantam Books, 2010).

Chapter Five

1   http://www.whitehouse.gov/the-press-office/president-barack-obamas-inaugural-address

2   Jeffrey Goldberg, "The Point Of No Return," *The Atlantic* September 2010.

3   Karim Sadjadpour, "The Source of Iranian Conduct," *Foreign Policy* no. 182, 2010, 85–87, at 85.

4   Ray Takeyh, "The end of an era in Iran," *Washington Post* September 18, 2011, at http://www.washingtonpost.com/opinions/the-end-of-an-era-in-iran/2011/09/16/gIQAc5sYdK_story.html?hpid=z3.

5   Quoted in James Kitfield, "Kings and Opportunists," *National Journal* July 23, 2011, 24–31, at 30.

6   Barack Obama, "Renewing American Leadership," *Foreign Affairs* 2007, 2–16, at 8.

7   Speech to AIPAC, June 4, 2008.

8   Robert Baer, *The Devil We Know: Dealing With the New Iranian Superpower* (New York: Three Rivers Press, 2008).

9   Colin Dueck, *Hard Line: The Republican Party and US Foreign Policy Since World War II* (Princeton: Princeton University Press, 2010), 314–15.

10 Ali Ansari, "The Revolution Will Be Mercantilized," *The National Interest* no. 105, 2010, 50–60.

11 Robert Kagan, "Obama's Iran realism," *The Guardian,* June 17, 2009, at http://www.guardian.co.uk/commentisfree/cifamerica/2009/jun/17/obama-iran-realism-diplomacy.

12 "Surprisingly" in the sense that the president clearly has unusual qualities. As a senior Pentagon official told me: "An Arab foreign minister was hosting Ahmedinajad on a visit to his country. He recollected to me that the first thing, according to their intelligence, that the president does each morning is to ask whether anyone has seen the return of the Hidden Imam overnight." Interview, senior civil servant, the Department of Defense, Washington DC, June 12, 2008.

13 *Comprehensive Iran Sanctions, Accountability, and Divestment Act of 2010* (US Public Law 111–195), Section 401(a)(2), at http://frwebgate.access.gpo.gov/cgi-bin/getdoc.cgi?dbname=111_cong_public_laws&docid=f:publ195.111.pdf.

14 UN Security Council Resolution 1929 (2010), at http://www.iaea.org/NewsCenter/Focus/IaeaIran/unsc_res1929-2010.pdf.

15 Quoted in Giles Whittell and Alexandra Frean, "Ahmadinejad goes on the offensive at UN as Clinton calls for regime change," *The Times* September 20, 2010, 29.

16 Najmeh Bozorgmehr, "Iranians braced for end of subsidies," *Financial Times* October 21, 2010, 16.

17   Glenn Kessler, "Iran, trying to skirt sanctions, attempts to set up banks worldwide," *Washington Post* October 20, 2010, at http://www.washingtonpost.com/wp-dyn/content/article/2010/10/20/AR2010102006139.html?hpid%3Dtopnews.

18   Robert E. Hunter, "Rethinking Iran," *Survival 52* (5) 2010, 135–156, at 149–50.

19   Michael Scott Doran, "The Heirs of Nasser: Who Will Benefit From the Second Arab Revolution?", *Foreign Affairs* 90 (3) 2011, 17–25, at 20.

20   Dueck, *Hard Line, ibid.,* 315.

21   States in violation of their Non-Proliferation Treaty obligations, such as Iran, were excluded from the assurance of no US first-use nuclear strikes.

22   Quoted in Giles Whittell and Alexandra Frean, "Ahmadinejad goes on the offensive at UN as Clinton calls for regime change," *ibid.,* 29.

23   Arab states in the Gulf embarked on a $123 billion purchase of US arms to increase their deterrent capacity against Iran in 2010–11. See Roula Khalaf and James Drummond, "Gulf in $123bn US arms spree," *Financial Times* September 21, 2010, 1.

24   Roula Khalaf, "Riyadh, a rogue state and riches for the US defense industry," *Financial Times* September 21, 2010, 8.

25   Amir Taheri, "Why they want to cut off the snake's head," *The Times* November 30, 2010, 22.

26   Tom Coghlan, "Arabs urged US to bomb Iran," *The Times* November 29, 2010, 1.

27   James Kitfield, 'Kings and Opportunists', *ibid.,* 27.

28   Cited in Amitai Etzioni, "Can a Nuclear-Armed Iran Be Deterred?," *Military Review* May–June 2010, 117–125, at 117.

29   *Constrained Internationalism: Adapting to New Realities* (Chicago: Chicago Council on Global Affairs), 45.

30   *Ibid.,* 45–6.

31   A minor media controversy ensured when John McCain was caught singing the chorus, to the tune of the Beach Boys' *Barbra Ann,* of Vince Vance and the Valiants' *Bomb Iran* (first released in 1980 but re-issued in 1987). The song is available through iTunes.

32   Etzioni, "Can a Nuclear-Armed Iran Be Deterred?," *ibid.*

33   Jennifer Rubin, "Obama doubles down at AIPAC," *Washington Post* May 22, 2011, at http://www.washingtonpost.com/blogs/right-turn/post/obama-double-downs-at-aipac/2011/03/29/AFhx9C9G_blog.html?hpid=z4.

34   Anna Fifield, "US and Iraq make slow progress on relationship," *Financial Times* September 15, 2011, 8.

35   Editorial, "Planning for a follow-on force in Iraq," *Washington Post* September 14, 2011, at http://www.washingtonpost.com/opinions/planning-for-a-follow-on-force-in-iraq/2011/09/13/gIQAPsOySK_story.html?hpid=z3.

36   Tariq Ali, *The Obama Syndrome: Surrender at Home, War Abroad* (London: Verso, 2010), 56–7.

37   Elaheh Rostami-Povey, *Iran's Influence: A Religious-Political State and Society in Its Region* (London: Zed Books, 2010), 226–227.

38   Stephen F. Hayes and Thomas Jocselyn, "The Iran Connection," *The Weekly Standard* December 13, 2010, at http://www.weeklystandard.com/articles/iran-connection_520695.html?page=1.

39   On a June 2008 visit to Washington, I asked one senior Bush administration official about the diplomatic outreach to Iran that had occurred over the second term and how this squared with the "axis of evil." His explanation was the "Rasputin-like hold that Secretary Rice has over the president." The administration's refusal to bomb Syria's nuclear plant, despite Dick Cheney's

arguing for this, perhaps adds some credence to this interpretation (the Israelis destroyed the North Korean-built plant in 2007).

40 Ali M. Ansari, *Confronting Iran: The Failure of American Foreign Policy and the Roots of Mistrust* (London: Hurst and Company, 2006), 241.

41 Quoted in Sadjadpour, *ibid.*, 86.

42 Cited in Etzioni, *ibid.*, 117–118.

43 Andrew Parasiliti, "After Sanctions, Deter and Engage Iran," *Survival* 52 (5) 2010, 13–20, at 19.

44 Dana H. Allin and Steve Simon, *The Sixth Crisis: Iran, Israel, America and Rumors of War* (New York: Oxford University Press, 2010), 165.

Chapter Six

1 http://www.whitehouse.gov/blog/inaugural-address/

2 "Barack Hussein Bush," editorial, *Wall Street Journal* June 5, 2009, at: http://online.wsj.com/article/SB124416109792287285.html.

3 Avi Shlaim, *Israel and Palestine: Reappraisals, Revisions, Refutations* (London: Verso, 2010), 283.

4 Aaron David Miller, *The Much Too Promised Land: America's Elusive Search for Arab-Israeli Peace* (New York: Bantam Books, 2008), 78.

5 Joe Klein, "Q and A: Obama on His First Year in Office," *Time* January 21, 2010, http://www.time.com/time/politics/article/0,8599,1955072-6,00.html.

6 Flynt Leverett and Hillary Mann Leverett, "The Dispensable Nation," *Foreign Policy* May 20, 2011, at http://www.foreignpolicy.com/articles/2011/05/20/ the_dispensable_nation.

7 Robert Kaplan, "Libya, Obama and the triumph of realism," *Financial Times* August 29, 2011, 9.

8 International Institute for Strategic Studies, "United States: Broken Consensus," *Strategic Survey 2011: The Annual Review of World Affairs* (Abingdon: Routledge, 2011), 139–159, at 153.

9 See: Edward Luttwak, "The Middle of Nowhere," *Prospect* no. 134 (May 2007); and Michael Scheuer, *Marching Toward Hell: America and Islam After Iraq* (New York: Free Press, 2008).

10 See in particular Kenneth Pollack, *A Path Out of the Desert: A Grand Strategy for America in the Middle East* (New York: Random House, 2008).

11 Michael Scott Doran, "The Heirs of Nasser: Who Will Benefit From the Second Arab Revolution?", *Foreign Affairs* 90 (3) 2011, 17–25.

12 http://www.whitehouse.gov/blog/NewBeginning

13 John J. Mearsheimer and Stephen M. Walt, *The Israel Lobby and US Foreign Policy* (London: Allen Lane, 2007), 4.

14 David Horowitz and Jacob Laskin, "Obama and the war against Israel, part II." *National Review*, June 22, 2010 at http://article.nationalreview.com/436748/ obama-and-the-war-against-israel-part-ii/david-horowitz-jacob-laksin.

15 Inderjeet Parmar, "American power and identities in the age of Obama," *International Politics* 48 (2–3) 2011, 153–63, at 156. Obama had pressured Netanyahu to apologize for the deaths caused by the Israeli raid on the Turkish ship, but the Prime Minister refused to so, under pressure from his Foreign Minister, the right wing and religious parties in his coalition.

16 Quoted in James Kitfield, "Frozen," *National Journal* May 14, 2011, 44.

17 "The Wrath of Abbas," *Newsweek* April 24, 2011, at http://www.newsweek.com/2011/04/24/the-wrath-of-abbas.html.

18   "Remarks by the President at the AIPAC Policy Conference 2011," at
     http://www.whitehouse.gov/the-press-office/2011/05/22/remarks-president-
     aipac-policy-conference-2011.

19   "Remarks by the President at the AIPAC Policy Conference 2011," at http://www.
     whitehouse.gov/the-press-office/2011/05/22/remarks-president-aipac-policy-
     conference-2011.

20   Benny Morris, "Exposing Abbas," *The National Interest*, at http://nationalinterest.
     org/commentary/exposing-abbas-5335.

21   Quoted in Carole Cadwalladr, "Man with a mission," *The Observer* The New
     Review September 11, 2011, 8–11, at 10.

22   Jeffrey Goldberg, "Robert Gates Thinks That Netanyahu Is an Ungrateful Ally,"
     The Atlantic September 6, 2011, at http://www.theatlantic.com/international/
     archive/2011/09/robert-gates-thinks-that-netanyahu-is-an-ungrateful-ally/244570/.

23   Khaled Elgindy, "Palestine Goes to the UN: Understanding the New Statehood
     Strategy," *Foreign Affairs* 90 (5) 2011, 102–113, at 112.

24   Daniel Byman, "Terrorism After the Revolutions: How Secular Uprisings Could
     Help (or Hurt) Jihadists," *Foreign Affairs* 90 (3) 2011, 48–54, at 50.

25   Philip Stephens, "A choice of minefields for Obama," *Financial Times* May 20,
     2011, 13.

26   Shadi Hamad, "The Rise of the Islamists: How Islamists Will Change Politics, and
     Vice Versa," *Foreign Affairs* 90 (3), 40–47.

27   Confidential conversation with the American head of an Arab American
     organization, London, February 9, 2010.

28   Michael Scott Doran, "The Heirs of Nasser: Who Will Benefit From the Second
     Arab Revolution?", *Foreign Affairs* 90 (3) 2011, 17–25, at 17.

29   Ryan Lizza, "The Consequentialist," *The New Yorker* May 2, 2011, 44–55, at 52.

30   Dina Shehata, "The Fall of the Pharaoh: How Hosni Mubarak's Reign Came to
     an End," *Foreign Affairs* 90 (3) 2011, 26–32.

31   *Ibid.*, 31.

32   Cited in Ronald Brownstein, "After Mubarak," *National Journal* February 5,
     2011, 15.

33   Benny Morris, International Institute for Strategic Affairs, London, June 14, 2001,
     at http://www.iiss.org/events-calendar/2011-events-archive/june-2011/professor-
     benny-morris-on-israels-security-and-the-arab-spring/.

34   Cited in Ronald Brownstein, "After Mubarak," *National Journal* February 5, 2011, 15.

35   *Ibid.*

36   "Henry Kissinger," Interview, *The Times* Magazine May 14, 2011, 28–35, at 35.

37   *Ibid.*, 35.

38   E.J. Dionne, "Obama can't win for winning in Libya," *Washington Post* August
     24, 2011, at http://www.washingtonpost.com/opinions/obama-cant-win-for-
     winning-in-libya/2011/08/24/gIQArKsdbJ_story.html?hpid=z3.

39   Anne-Marie Slaughter, "Why the Libya sceptics were proved badly wrong,"
     Financial Times August 25, 2011, 9.

40   *Ibid.* Slaughter's comments also appear rather at odds with her previous statement
     that, "On issues like whether to intervene in Libya there's really not a compromise
     and consensus ... You can't be a little bit realist and a little bit democratic when
     deciding whether or not to stop a massacre." Quoted in Ryan Lizza, "The
     Consequentialist," *The New Yorker* May 2, 2011, 55.

41   "Gates speech on the NATO Strategic Concept," February 23, 2010, at http://
     www.cfr.org/publication/21518/gates_speech_on_the_nato_strategic_concept_
     february_2010.html.

42 James Blitz, "Gates Presses Nato Allies to March in Step," *Financial Times* June 10, 2011, at http://www.ft.com/cms/s/o/246bcb58-939f-11eo=922e-00144feab49a. html#axzz1P06OaAtL.

43 In the House of Representatives, a coalition of anti-war Democrats and Republicans opposed US intervention. Ultimately, Dennis Kucinich (D-OH) and Justin Amash (R-MI) introduced an amendment on July 7, 2011 to the Department of Defense Appropriations Bill for 2012 "to prohibit the use of funds for the use of military force against Libya." Following intense debate, the amendment was defeated 199–229; the anti-Libya camp gathered fifty-one more Democrat and Republican votes than Kucinich had obtained for an earlier resolution in June to withdraw US troops from Libya. The House then approved an amendment to the bill by Tom Cole (R-OK) to prohibit assistance to Libyan rebels (with the aim of interrupting all funding of Libyan operations). The Cole amendment passed 225–201, with forty-eight Democrats voting in favor.

44 "Libya win unlikely to convince war-weary US Congress," *IISS Strategic Comments* vol. 17, comment 29, August 2011.

45 http://www.washingtonpost.com/opinions/shameful-us-inaction-on-syrias-massacres/2011/04/22/AFROWsQE_story.html

46 "Remarks by the President on the Middle East and North Africa," May 19, 2011, at http://www.whitehouse.gov/the-press-office/2011/05/19/remarks-president-middle-east-and-north-africa.

47 Quoted in Catherine Philp, "Obama calls for regime change in Syria," *The Times* August 19, 2011, 6.

48 "EU 'to adopt Syrian oil embargo on Friday'," AFP release, September 1, 2011, at http://www.google.com/hostednews/afp/article/ALeqM5jeLakxjNbRtm6rvKMXV O367FPrYw?docId=CNG.659090a76bc9935377426243e3cd3b3f.af1.

49 Quoted in Ed Husain, "Assad need not feel threatened by Gaddafi's fate," *Financial Times* August 24, 2011, 11.

50 Shadi Hamad, "The Rise of the Islamists: How Islamists Will Change Politics, and Vice Versa," *Foreign Affairs* 90 (3) 2011, 46.

51 James Zogby, *Arab Voices: What They Are Saying To Us, And Why It Matters* (New York: Palgrave Macmillan, 2010), 191.

52 In the Libyan case, for example, the overthrow of Qaddafi saw revelations in a cache of documents that the United Kingdom and the US had developed very close relations with the colonel's regime, including intelligence-sharing and the rendition of terror suspects to Tripoli. See Michael Peel and James Blitz, "UK aided rendition to Libya," *Financial Times* September 5, 2011, 1.

53 Pew Research Center, Pew Global Attitudes Project, *Obama's Challenge in the Muslim World: Arab Spring Fails to Improve US Image*, May 17, 2011.

54 Marc Lynch, "America and Egypt After the Uprisings," *Survival* 53 (2) 2011, 31–41.

55 Adam B. Kushner, "Beyond Our Reach," *National Journal* February 5, 2011, 16–22, at 22.

56 Lynch, "America and Egypt After the Uprisings," 40.

57 Aaron David Miller, "The Virtues of Folding," *Foreign Policy* May 30, 2011, at http://www.foreignpolicy.com/articles/2011/05/30/the_virtues_of_folding?page=0,0.

58 Reuel Marc Gerecht and Mark Dubowitz, "Obama, American Liberator?", *The Washington Post* September 1, 2011, at http://www.washingtonpost.com/ opinions/obama-american-liberator/2011/09/01/gIQA3e5HvJ_story.html?hpid=z2.

59 Lee Smith, "Obama Adopts the Freedom Agenda," *Weekly Standard* May 30, 2011 at http://www.weeklystandard.com/articles/obama-adopts-freedom-agenda_567618. html.

60 Walter Russell Mead, "W Gets A Third Term in the Middle East," August 22, 2011, at http://blogs.the-american-interest.com/wrm/2011/08/22/w-gets-a-third-term-in-the-middle-east/.

61 *Constrained Internationalism: Adapting to New Realities* (Chicago: Chicago Council on Global Affairs), 72.

62 Paul Starobin, "The Israel Divide," *National Journal* January 16, 2010.

63 Quoted in Joby Warrick and Scott Wilson, "UN showdown over Palestinian statehood tests limits of US influence," *Washington Post* September 15, 2011, at http://www.washingtonpost.com/politics/un-showdown-over-palestinian-statehood-tests-limits-of-us-influence/2011/09/15/gIQATBTlVK_story.html.

64 Quoted in James Kitfield, "Kings and Opportunists," *National Journal* July 23, 2011, 24-31, at 27.

Chapter Seven

1 http://www.iiss.org/conferences/global-strategic-review/global-strategic-review-2010/plenary-sessions-and-speeches-2010/keynote-address/henry-kissinger/

2 Quoted in David Pilling, "Hillary's charm offensive in China's backyard," *Financial Times* July 28, 2011, 11.

3 Michael Sheridan, "Bullish China tries to test Obama's nerves," *Sunday Times* News Review, August 28, 2011, 4.

4 Quoted in Leslie Hook, "China tells US to 'live within means'," *Financial Times* August 8, 2011, 2.

5 Michael Schiffer and Gary Schmitt, "Keeping Tabs on China's Rise," in Derek Chollet, Tod Lindberg and David Shorr (eds.), *Bridging The Foreign Policy Divide: Liberals and Conservatives Find Common Ground on 10 Key Global Challenges* (New York: Routledge, 2008), 103–123, at 103.

6 US National Intelligence Committee, *Global Trends 2025: A Transformed World* (NIC, 2008).

7 *Military and Security Developments Involving the People's Republic of China 2011* (Washington, DC: Department of Defense, 2011), at http://www.defense.gov/pubs/pdfs/2011_CMPR_Final.pdf.

8 Matt Kennard, "Chinese Might," *Financial Times* August 25, 2011, 4.

9 Michael Schiffer and Gary Schmitt, "Keeping Tabs on China's Rise," *ibid.*, 120–121.

10 Michael Mandelbaum, *The Frugal Superpower: America's Global Leadership in a Cash-Strapped Era* (New York: Public Affairs, 2010), 112.

11 A November 3, 2010 speech by the president. See Thomas L. Friedman and Michael Mandelbaum, *That Used To Be Us: What Went Wrong with America – and How It Can Come Back* (London: Little, Brown, 2011).

12 Remarks by the President in State of the Union Address, January 25, 2011, at http://www.whitehouse.gov/the-press-office/2011/01/25/remarks-president-state-union-address.

13 Address by the President to a Joint Session of Congress, September 8, 2011, at http://www.whitehouse.gov/the-press-office/2011/09/08/address-president-joint-session-congress.

14 Among a vast literature, see in particular: C. Fred Bergsten, Bates Gill, Nicholas R. Lardy, and Derek Mitchell, *China: The Balance Sheet* (New York: Public Affairs, 2006); Eric S. Edelman, *Understanding America's Contested Primacy* (Washington, DC: Center for Strategic and Budgetary Analysis, 2010); Aaron L. Friedberg,

A Contest for Supremacy: China, America, and the Struggle for Mastery in Asia (New York: Norton, 2011); Henry Kissinger, *On China* (New York: Allen Lane, 2011); Mark Leonard, *What Does China Think?* (Philadelphia, PA: Public Affairs, 2008); Constantine C. Menges, *China: The Gathering Threat* (Nashville, TN: Nelson Current, 2005); Gary J. Schmitt (ed.), *The Rise of China: Essays on the Future Competition* (New York: Encounter Books, 2009), Michael D. Swaine and Ashley J. Tellis, *Interpreting China's Grand Strategy* (Santa Monica, CA: RAND Corporation, 2000); and Minxin Pei, *China's Trapped Transition: The Limits of Developmental Autocracy* (Cambridge, MA: Harvard University Press, 2006).

15 Peter Dombrowski, "Renewing US National Security Policy: something old, something new," in Steven W. Hook and James M. Scott (eds.), *US Foreign Policy Today: American Renewal?* (Washington, DC; CQ Press, 2011), 94–111, at 108.

16 Peter Trubowitz, *Politics and Strategy: Partisan Ambition and American Statecraft* (Princeton, NJ: Princeton University Press, 2011), 148.

17 G. John Ikenberry, "The Rise of China and the Future of the West," *Foreign Affairs* 87 (1) 2008, 23–37, at 24.

18 *Ibid.*, 25.

19 *Ibid.*, 30.

20 John J. Mearsheimer, *The Tragedy of Great Power Politics* (New York: W.W. Norton, 2001), 4.

21 Robert Kagan, *The Return of History and the End of Dreams* (New York: Atlantic Books, 2008), 30–31.

22 *Ibid.*, 36.

23 Kerry Brown, "China: between global responsibilities and internal transitions," in Robin Niblett (ed.), *America and a Changed World: A Question of Leadership* (Oxford: Wiley-Blackwell, 2010), 145–61.

24 Stefan Halper, *The Beijing Consensus: How China's Authoritarian Model Will Dominate the Twenty-First Century* (New York: Basic Books, 2010), 208.

25 Susan Shirk, *China: Fragile Superpower* (Oxford: Oxford University Press, 2007), 255.

26 *Ibid.*, 261.

27 *Ibid.*, 268.

28 Niall Ferguson, *Civilization: The West and the Rest* (New York: Penguin Books, 2011).

29 Lanxin Xiang, "True Conservatives," *Survival* 53 (4), 197–202, at 202.

30 Robert Kagan, "Ambition and Anxiety: America's competition with China," in Gary J. Schmitt (ed.) *The Rise of China: Essays on the Future Competition* (New York: Encounter Books, 2009), 1–23, at 22.

31 James Steinberg, Deputy US Secretary of State, 2009–2011, quoted in Michael Hirsh, "Affairs of State," *National Journal* July 23, 2011, 8.

32 Xinhua news agency, quoted in Leslie Hook, "China tells US to 'live within means'," *Financial Times* August 8, 2011, 2.

33 "76% See China as Bigger Economic Threat Than Military One," *Rasmussen Report* April 28, 2011, at http://www.rasmussenreports.com/public_content/politics/current_events/china/76_see_china_as_bigger_economic_threat_than_military_one.

34 Quoted in David Pilling, "Hillary's charm offensive in China's backyard," *Financial Times* July 28, 2011, 11.

35 *Ibid.*

36 Aaron L. Friedberg, *A Contest for Supremacy: China, America, and the Struggle for Mastery in Asia* (New York: Norton, 2011).

37   Remarks at the Shangri-La Dialogue, the 10th IISS Asia Security Summit, June 3–5, 2011, quoted in *IISS News*, July 2011, 2.

38   *IISS News* July 2011, 4.

39   *Military and Security Developments Involving the People's Republic of China 2011* (Washington, DC: Department of Defense, 2011), at http://www.defense. gov/pubs/pdfs/2011_CMPR_Final.pdf.

40   Quoted in Leo Lewis and Michael Evans, "Beijing hits back at Pentagon fear of its naval power," *The Times* August 26, 2011, 43.

41   Gates, at the Shangri-La Dialogue, June 3–5, 2011, quoted in *IISS News*, July 2011, 7.

42   Brahma Chellaney, "Water is the new weapon in Beijing's armoury," *Financial Times* August 31, 2011, 11.

43   Ben Bland and Girija Shivakumar, "Beijing flexes muscles in South China Sea," *Financial Times* September 1, 2011, 6.

44   Richard C. Bush and Michael E. O'Hanlon, *A War Like No Other: The Truth about China's Challenge to America* (Hoboken, NJ: John Wiley and Sons Inc., 2007), 99.

45   Michael Mandelbaum, *The Frugal Superpower: America's Global Leadership in a Cash-Strapped Era* (New York: Public Affairs, 2010), 117.

46   Richard McGregor and Kathrin Hille, "US poised to unveil Taiwan arms deal," *Financial Times* September 20, 2011, 5.

47   Gary J. Schmitt, "Facing Realities: Multilateralism for the Asia-Pacific Century," in his *The Rise of China: Essays on the Future Competition* (New York: Encounter Books, 2009), 91–111, at 109.

48   Confidential interview, member of a Washington think tank, Madrid, Spain, May 2, 2010.

49   Randall L. Schweller & Xiaoyu Pu, "After Unipolarity: China's Visions of International Order in an Era of US Decline," *International Security* 36 (1) 2011, 41–72.

50   George Walden, *China: A Wolf in the World?* (London: Gibson Square, 2008), 254.

51   Andrew J. Nathan, "What China Wants: Bargaining with Beijing," *Foreign Affairs* 90 (4) 2011, 153–58, at 158.

52   Quoted in Ryan Lizza, "The Consequentialist," *The New Yorker*, May 2, 2011, 44–55, at 49. For a detailed rebuttal of the Haass view and a restatement of administration policy, see Hillary Clinton, "America's Pacific Century," *Foreign Policy* no. 189 (2011), 56–63.

53   Mayang A. Rahawestri, "Obama's Foreign Policy in Asia: More Continuity than Change," *Security Challenges* 6 (1) 2010, 109–20, at 110.

Chapter Eight

1   National Intelligence Council, *Global Trends 2025: A Transformed World* (November 2008), 31, at http://www.dni.gov/nic/NIC_2025_project.htm.

2   Quoted in Maria Tsvetkova, "Putin says US is 'parasite' on global economy," *Reuters* August 1, 2011, at: http://www.reuters.com/article/2011/08/01/ us-russia-putin-usa-idUSTRE77052R20110801.

3   Daniel Deudney and G. John Ikenberry, "The Unravelling of the Cold War Settlement," *Survival* 51 (6), 39–62, at 41.

4   Quoted in Neil Buckley, "A democratic deficit," *Financial Times* August 19, 2011, 7.

5   Luke Harding, "Wikileaks cables condemn Russia as 'mafia state'," *The Guardian* December 1, 2010, at http://www.guardian.co.uk/world/2010/dec/01/wikileaks-cables-russia-mafia-kleptocracy.

6   Michael Mandelbaum, *The Frugal Superpower: America's Global Leadership in a Cash-Strapped Era* (New York: Public Affairs, 2010), 125.

7   Edward Lucas, *The New Cold War: Putin's Russia and the Threat to the West* (New York: Palgrave Macmillan, 2008), 13.

8   Quoted in Charles Clover, "Gorbachev sees Russia's rulers as 'worse version of communist party'," *Financial Times* August 18, 2011, 5.

9   Jeffrey Tayler, "Russia is Finished," *The Atlantic* May 2001, at http://www. theatlantic.com/doc/200105/tayler.

10   Dmitri Trenin, *Post Imperium: Russia and Its Neighbors* (Washington, DC: Carnegie Endowment for International Peace, 2010).

11   Stephen Kotkin. *Armageddon Averted: The Soviet Collapse, 1970–2000* (New York: Oxford University Press, 2008).

12   Barack Obama, "Renewing American Leadership," *Foreign Affairs* 86 (4) 2007, 2–16, at 8–9.

13   "Obama, Medvedev to Reset Ties with Arms Pact," *Reuters* April 1, 2009, at http://www.reuters.com/articlae/idUSL194925620090401.

14   "Remarks by the President at the New Economic School Graduation," Gostinny Dvor, Moscow, Russia, July 7, 2009, at www.whitehouse.gov/the_press_office/ remarks-by-the-president-at-the-new-economic-school-graduation.

15   "Remarks by President Obama," Hradcany Square, Prague, Czech Republic, April 5, 2009, at www.whitehouse.gov/the_press_office/Remarks-By-President-Barack-Obama-In-Prague-As-Delivered.

16   Personal interview, former US undersecretary for policy, the Department for Defense, Washington DC, April 6, 2011.

17   Mark Fitzpatrick, "A Prudent Decision on Missile Defense," *Survival* 51 (6) 2010, 5–12, at 9.

18   Stephen G. Rademaker, "This is no way to approve the New START Treaty," *Washington Post* August 20, 2010, at www.washingtonpost.com/wp-dyn/content/ article/2010/09/19/AR2010081905214.html.

19   Department of Defense, "Nuclear Posture Review Report" April 2010, at http://www.defense.gov/npr/docs/2010%20nuclear%20posture%20review%20 report.pdf.

20   Bob Graham and Jim Talent, *Prevention of WMD Proliferation and Terrorism Report Card* (January 2010), 2.

21   See, for example, Robert Kagan, "New START: Too modest to merit partisan bickering," *Washington Post*, July 30, 2010, at http://www.washingtonpost.com/ wp-dyn/content/article/2010/07/29/AR2010072904902.html.

22   Robert Joseph and Eric Edelman, "New START: Weakening Our Security," *National Review* May 10, 2010, at http://www.nationalreview.com/articles/229704/ new-start-weakening-our-security/robert-joseph.

23   Giles Whittell, "NATO draws up military plans to defend Eastern Europe against Russian aggression," *The Times* December 7, 2010, 5.

24   James Sherr, "Russia: managing contradictions," in Robin Niblett (ed.), *America and a Changed World: A Question of Leadership* (Oxford: Wiley-Blackwell, 2010), 168.

25   Eugene Rumer and Angela Stent, "Russia and the West," *Survival* 51 (2) 2009, 91–104, at 102.

26   Charles Clover and Christian Oliver, "North Korea seeks allies in Russia talks," *Financial Times* August 25, 2011, 4.

27   Isabel Gorst, "Washington to buy Russian arms," *Financial Times* May 31, 2011, 10.

28   Quoted in Daniel Vajdic, "Moscow to Annex South Ossetia as US-Russia Reset Crumbles?", *The American* August 5, 2011, at http://blog.american.com/2011/08/moscow-to-annex-south-ossetia-as-u-s-russia-%E2%80%9Creset%E2%80%9D-crumbles/.

29   Quoted in Ariel Cohen, "Russian Reset a Cold War Restart," August 8, 2011, *The National Interest* online, at http://nationalinterest.org/commentary/russian-reset-cold-war-restart-5717.

30   Bobo Lo, *Axis of Convenience: Moscow, Beijing and the New Geopolitics* (Washington, DC: Brookings Institution Press, 2008).

31   John Thornhill, "Russia's past is no sign of its future," *Financial Times* August 26, 2011, 9.

32   See Mary Buckley, "Anti-Americanism in Russia," Chapter 6 in Brendon O'Connor, *Anti-Americanism: History, Causes, Themes; Volume 3: Comparative Perspectives* (Oxford: Greenwood World Publishing, 2007), 103–29.

33   Quoted in Isabel Gorst, Charles Clover and Ed Crooks, "Exxon secures Arctic deal," *Financial Times* August 31, 2011, 1.

Chapter Nine

1   http://blogs.wsj.com/washwire/2010/09/23/transcript-of-obamas-remarks-to-the-un-general-assembly/

2   Tony Blair, *A Journey* (London: Hutchinson, 2010), 676.

3   Speech to the American Enterprise Institute. Quoted in Gary Schmitt and Thomas Donnelly, "Enough," *The Weekly Standard* June 6, 2011, at http://www.weeklystandard.com/articles/enough_571610.html?page=1.

4   Quoted in David Nakamura, "Obama offers 2012 election supporters change they can believe in – next term," *Washington Post* August 26, 2011, at http://www.washingtonpost.com/politics/obama-offers-2012-election-supporters-change-they-can-believe-in–next-term/2011/08/25/gIQAJz9AhJ_story.html?hpid=z2.

5   Quoted in Richard McGregor and Daniel Dombey, "Foreign policy adviser steps out of the shadows," *Financial Times* May 24, 2011, 9.

6   John Mueller, "Questing For Monsters To Destroy," in Melvyn P. Leffler and Jeffrey W. Legro (eds.), *In Uncertain Times: American Foreign Policy after the Berlin Wall and 9/11* (Ithaca, NY: Conrell University Press, 2011), 129–30.

7   Georg W. F. Hegel, *The Philosophy of Right*, translated with notes by T. M. Knox (Oxford: The Clarendon Press, 1967).

8   Stanley A. Renshon, *National Security in the Obama Administration: Reassessing the Bush Doctrine* (New York: Routledge, 2010).

9   Ryan Crocker, "Dreams of Babylon," *The National Interest* no. 108 (July/August) 2010, 18–23, at 22–23.

10   Barack Obama, Inaugural Address, January 20, 2009, at http://whitehouse.gov/blog/inaugural-address/.

11   Sean A. Wilentz, *The Age of Reagan: A History, 1974–2008* (New York: Harper, 2008).

12   Inderjeet Parmar (ed.), "American power and identities in the age of Obama," *International Politics* 48 (2–3) 2011, 153–63.

13 "The United States: Obama's New Balance," *Strategic Survey 2010: The Annual Review of World Affairs* (London: International Institute for Strategic Studies), 83–100, at 85.

14 *Ibid.*, 99.

15 Michael J. Doyle, "Between freedom and fear: explaining the consensus on terrorism and democracy promotion in US foreign policy," *International Politics* 48 (2–3) 2011, 412–33.

16 Colin Dueck, *Hard Line*, p. 301.

17 Michael Mandelbaum, "Foreign Policy as Social Work," *Foreign Affairs* 75 (1) 1996, 16–32.

18 Michael Mandelbaum, *The Frugal Superpower: America's Global Leadership in Cash-Strapped Era* (New York: Public Affairs, 2010).

19 George Schultz, *Turmoil and Triumph: My Years as Secretary of State* (New York: Charles Scribner's Sons, 1993), 648–49.

20 James M. Lindsay, "George W. Bush, Barack Obama and the future of US global leadership," *International Affairs* 87 (4) 2011, 765–79, at 779.

21 Robert D. Puttnam, "Diplomacy and Domestic Politics: The Logic of Two-Level Games," *International Organization*, 42 (Summer 1988), 427–460.

22 Clive Crook, "Time to be bold, Mr President," *Financial Times* September 5, 2011, 11.

23 Dueck, *ibid.*, 303.

24 George C. Edwards III, *The Strategic President: Persuasion and Opportunity in Presidential Leadership* (Princeton, NJ: Princeton University Press, 2009).

25 B. Dan Wood, *The Myth of Presidential Representation* (New York: Cambridge University Press, 2009). As Tim Lynch pointed out to me, this is especially ironic in Obama's case, since his record as a US senator saw him rated as one of the most liberal Democrats in the US Congress. His claims to bipartisanship were largely based on style rather than substance.

26 See: Ron Suskind, *Confidence Men: Wall Street, Washington and the Education of a President* (New York: Harpers, 2011); and Andrew Rudalevige, "Rivals, or a Team? Staffing and Issue Management in the Obama Administration," in Bert A. Rockman, Andrew Rudalevige and Colin Campbell (eds.), *The Obama Presidency: Appraisals and Prospects* (Washington, DC: CQ Press, 2012), 171–97.

27 While Obama has at times downplayed America's unique qualities, at others he has championed them, not least in using his own election as proof of the special place of the US. Obama also gave considerably more emphasis to American exceptionalism in the second half of his presidency, beginning with the State of the Union address of 2011.

28 Personal interview, Washington DC, April 10, 2011.

29 The episode, "Marge In Chains," is from the fourth series of the cartoon. The plot features the citizens of Springfield rioting after having to settle for a statue of Jimmy Carter rather than Abraham Lincoln. On July 15, 1979, Carter gave a nationally televised address in which he identified what he believed to be a "crisis of confidence" among the American people. This has come to be known as his "malaise" speech, even though he did not use the word "malaise" anywhere in the text.

30 Zbigniew Brzezinski, "From Hope to Audacity: Appraising Obama's Foreign Policy," *Foreign Affairs*, 89 (1) 2010, 16–30, at 28.

31 Quoted in David Ignatius, "Obama's foreign policy: big ideas, little implementation," *Washington Post*, October 17, 2010, at: http://www.washingtonpost.com/wp-dyn/content/article/2010/10/14/AR2010101406505.html?hpid=opinionsbox1.

32 Related to me by former US ambassador and Undersecretary of State for Policy in the US Defense Department, Eric S. Edelman.

33 Bronwen Maddox, "Trouble is brewing in Uncle Sam's backyard," *The Times*, August 16, 2011, 21.

34 See Abraham F. Lowenthal, Theodore J. Piccone and Laurence Whitehead (eds.), *Shifting The Balance: Obama and the Americas* (Washington, DC: Brookings Institution Press, 2011).

35 "Things fall apart/the center cannot hold/Mere anarchy is loosed upon the world." From "The Second Coming." William Butler Yeats, *Collected Poems* (London: Picador, 1990), 210–11.

36 On the competing evidence for the collapse of liberal internationalism, see: Charles A. Kupchan and Peter L. Trubowitz, "Dead Center: The Demise of Liberal Internationalism in the United States," *International Security* 32 (2) 2007, 7–44; Stephen Chaudoin, Helen V. Miller and Dustin H. Tingley, "The Center Still Holds: Liberal Internationalism Survives," *International Security* 35 (1) 2010, 75–94; Charles A. Kupchan and Peter L. Trubowitz, "The Illusion of Liberal Internationalism's Revival," *International Security* 35 (1) 2010, 95–109; and Peter L. Trubowitz and Nicole Mellow, "Foreign policy, bipartisanship and the paradox of post-September 11 America," *International Politics* 48 (2–3) 2011, 164–87.

37 James Kitfield, "Worse Than They Feared," *National Journal* August 6, 2011, 40.

38 *Ibid.*

39 See Trevor McCrisken, "Past is Present: Bush and the Future of Republican Party Foreign Policy," Chapter 16 in Joel Aberbach and Gillian Peele (eds.), *Crisis of Conservatism? The Republican Party, the Conservative Movement, and American Politics After Bush* (New York: Oxford University Press, 2011), 357–78.

40 Peter Baker, "Strange Brew: Does the Tea Party have a foreign policy?", *Foreign Policy* no. 181 (September/October) 2010, 38–40, at 38. For a useful and concise analysis of how the GOP may be becoming the "party of Less" abroad in relation to the 2012 elections, see also James Traub, "The Elephants in the Room," *Foreign Policy* no. 189 (2011), 79–84.

41 A. James Reichley, "The Future of the Republican Party," Chapter 4 in Joel Aberbach and Gillian Peele (eds.), *Crisis of Conservatism? The Republican Party, the Conservative Movement, and American Politics After Bush* (New York: Oxford University Press, 2011), 68–88, at 85. A typology of conservative foreign policy positions is offered in Timothy J. Lynch, "The McBama National Security Consensus and Republican Foreign Policy," in the same volume, at 345.

42 Quoted in Aamer Madhani, "More Emphasis on Foreign Policy?", *National Journal* September 18, 2010, 44.

43 Ignatius, *ibid.*

44 Philip Stephens, "No, 9/11 did not change the world," *Financial Times* September 2, 2011, 11.

45 Daniel W. Drezner, "Does Obama Have a Grand Strategy? Why We Need Doctrines in Uncertain Times," *Foreign Affairs* 90 (4) 2011, 57–68.

46 "Lexington: 9/11 plus nine," *The Economist* September 11, 2010, 48.

47 G. John Ikenberry, "The Future of the Liberal World Order," *Foreign Affairs* 90 (3) 2011, 56–68, at 68.

48 Fareed Zakaria, *The Post-American World* (New York: Allen Lane, 2008), 5.

49 Quoted in James Kitfield, "Kings and Opportunists," *National Journal* July 23, 2011, 24–31, at 29.

Bibliography

1. Books and Chapters

Ali, Tariq. *The Obama Syndrome: Surrender at Home, War Abroad* (London: Verso, 2010).

Allin, Dana H. and Steve Simon. *The Sixth Crisis: Iran, Israel, America and Rumors of War* (New York: Oxford University Press, 2010).

Alter, Jonathan. *The Promise: President Obama, Year One* (London: Simon and Schuster, 2010).

Ansari, Ali M. *Confronting Iran: The Failure of American Foreign Policy and the Roots of Mistrust* (London: Hurst and Company, 2006).

Baer, Robert. *The Devil We Know: Dealing With the New Iranian Superpower* (New York:Three Rivers Press, 2008).

Balz, Daniel J. and Haynes Bonner Johnson. *The Battle for America, 2008: The Story of an Extraordinary Election* (Viking Books, 2009).

Bergsten, C. Fred, Bates Gill, Nicholas R. Lardy and Derek Mitchell. *China: The Balance Sheet* (New York: Public Affairs, 2006).

Blair, Tony. *A Journey* (London: Hutchinson, 2010).

Brooks, Stephen and William Wohlforth. *World Out Of Balance: international relations and the challenge of American primacy* (Princeton, NJ: Princeton University Press, 2008).

Brzezinski, Zbigniew and Brent Scowcroft. *America and the World: conversations on the future of American foreign policy* (New York: Basic Books, 2008).

Buckley, Mary. "Anti-Americanism in Russia," chapter 6 in Brendon O'Connor (ed.), *Anti-Americanism: History, Causes, Themes; Volume 3: Comparative Perspectives* (Oxford: Greenwood World Publishing, 2007), 103–29.

Bush, Richard C. and Michael E. O'Hanlon. *A War Like No Other: The Truth about China's Challenge to America* (Hoboken, NJ: John Wiley and Sons Inc., 2007).

Campbell, Kurt M. and Michael O'Hanlon. *Hard Power: The New Politics of National Security* (New York: Basic Books, 2006).

Chan, Stephen. *The End of Certainty: Towards a New Internationalism* (London: Zed Books, 2010).

Corsi, Jerome R. *The Obama Nation: Leftist Politics and the Cult of Personality* (New York: Simon and Schuster, 2008).

D'Souza, Dinesh. *The Roots of Obama's Rage* (New York: Regnery, 2010).

Dombrowski, Peter. "Renewing US National Security Policy: something old, something new," in Steven W. Hook and James M. Scott (eds.), *US Foreign Policy Today: American Renewal?* (Washington, DC; CQ Press, 2011), 94–111.

Dueck, Colin. *Hard Line: The Republican Party and US Foreign Policy Since World War II* (Princeton, NJ: Princeton University Press, 2010).

Dupuis, Martin and Keith Boeckelman. *Barack Obama: the New Face of American Politics* (London: Praeger, 2008).

Edwards, III, George C. *The Strategic President: Persuasion and Opportunity in Presidential Leadership* (Princeton, NJ: Princeton University Press, 2009).

Ferguson, Niall. *Civilization: The West and the Rest* (New York: Penguin Books, 2011).

Friedberg, Aaron L. *A Contest for Supremacy: China, America, and the Struggle for Mastery in Asia* (New York: Norton, 2011).

Friedman, Thomas L. and Michael Mandelbaum. *That Used To Be Us: What Went Wrong with America – and How It Can Come Back* (London: Little, Brown, 2011).

Goodwin, Doris Kearns. *Team of Rivals: The Political Genius of Abraham Lincoln* (New York: Simon and Schuster, 2005).

Gul, Imtiaz. *The Most Dangerous Place: Pakistan's Lawless Frontier* (London: Penguin Books, 2010).

Halper, Stefan. *The Beijing Consensus: How China's Authoritarian Model Will Dominate the Twenty-First Century* (New York: Basic Books, 2010).

Hanson, Victor Davis. *How The Obama Administration Threatens Our National Security* (New York: Encounter Books, 2009).

Hastedt, Glenn. "Presidents, Advisers and Future Directions of American Foreign Policy," in Steven W. Hook and James M. Scott (eds.), *US Foreign Policy Today: American Renewal?* (Washington, DC: CQ Press, 2012), 16–35.

Hegel, Georg W. F. *The Philosophy of Right*, translated with notes by T. M. Knox (Oxford: The Clarendon Press, 1967).

Heilemann, John and Mark Halperin. *Race of a Lifetime: How Obama Won The White House* (London: Viking, 2010).

Hook, Steven and James M. Scott (eds.). *US Foreign Policy Today: American Renewal?* (Washington, DC: CQ Press, 2011).

Huntington, Samuel P. *Who Are We? America's Great Debate* (New York: The Free Press, 2004).

Indyk, Martin S., Kenneth G. Lieberthal and Michael E. O'Hanlon, *Bending History? Barack Obama's Foreign Policy* (Washington DC: Brookings Institution Press, 2012).

Jacobson, Gary C. *A Divider, Not a Uniter: George W Bush and the American People* (New York: Longman, 2010).

————. "Polarization, Public Opinion, and the Presidency: the Obama and Anti-Obama Coalitions," Chapter 5 in Bert A. Rockman, Andrew Rudalevige & Colin Campbell (eds.), *The Obama Presidency: Appraisals and Prospects* (Washington, DC: CQ Press, 2012), 94–122.

Kagan, Robert. *The Return of History and the End of Dreams* (New York: Atlantic Books, 2008).

————. "Ambition and Anxiety: America's competition with China," in Gary J. Schmitt (ed.), *The Rise of China: Essays on the Future Competition* (New York: Encounter Books, 2009), 1–23.

Kipling, Rudyard. *Selected Poems* (London: Penguin, 1993).

Kissinger, Henry. *On China* (New York: Allen Lane, 2011).

Kotkin, Stephen. *Armageddon Averted: The Soviet Collapse, 1970–2000* (New York: Oxford University Press, 2008).

Krepinevich, Andrew F. *7 Deadly Scenarios: A Military Futurist Explores War in the Twenty-first Century* (New York: Bantam Books, 2010).

Leonard, Mark. *What Does China Think?* (Philadelphia, PA: Public Affairs, 2008).

Lowenthal, Abraham F., Theodore J. Piccone and Laurence Whitehead (eds.). *Shifting The Balance: Obama and the Americas* (Washington, DC: Brookings Institution Press, 2011).

Leslie, Ian. *To Be President: Quest for the White House 2008* (London: Politico's Press, 2009).

Levy, Adrian and Catherine Scott-Clark. *Deception: Pakistan, the United States and the Global Nuclear Weapons Conspiracy* (London: Atlantic Books, 2007).

Barry Libert and Rick Fault. *Barack, Inc.: Winning Lessons of the Obama Campaign* (Upper Saddle River, NJ: FT Press, 2009).

Lo, Bobo. *Axis of Convenience: Moscow, Beijing and the New Geopolitics* (Washington, DC: Brookings Institution Press, 2008).

Lucas, Edward. *The New Cold War: Putin's Russia and the Threat to the West* (New York: Palgrave Macmillan, 2008).

Lynch, Timothy J. "The McBama National Security Consensus and Republican Foreign Policy," Chapter 15 in Joel Aberbach and Gillian Peele (eds.), *Crisis of Conservatism? The Republican Party, the Conservative Movement, and American Politics After Bush* (New York: Oxford University Press, 2011), 335–56.

McCrisken, Trevor. "Past is Present: Bush and the Future of Republican Party Foreign Policy," Chapter 16 in Joel Aberbach and Gillian Peele (eds.), *Crisis of Conservatism? The Republican Party, the Conservative Movement, and American Politics After Bush* (New York: Oxford University Press, 2011), 357–378.

Mandelbaum, Michael. *The Frugal Superpower: America's Global Leadership in a Cash-Strapped Era* (New York: Public Affairs, 2010).

Mann, Windsor (ed.). *The Quotable Hitchens: from Alcohol to Zionism* (Cambridge, MA: Da Capo Press, 2011).

Mearsheimer, John J. *The Tragedy of Great Power Politics* (New York: W.W. Norton, 2001).

Mearsheimer, John J. and Stephen M. Walt. *The Israel Lobby and US Foreign Policy* (London: Allen Lane, 2007).

Mendell, David. *Obama: From Promise to Power* (New York: Amistad, 2007).

Menges, Constantine C. *China: The Gathering Threat* (Nashville, TN: Nelson Current, 2005).

Miller, Aaron David. *The Much Too Promised Land: America's Elusive Search for Arab-Israeli Peace* (New York: Bantam Books, 2008).

Mueller, John. "Questing For Monsters To Destroy," in Melvyn P. Leffler and Jeffrey W. Legro (eds.), *In Uncertain Times: American Foreign Policy after the Berlin Wall and 9/11* (Ithaca, NY: Cornell University Press, 2011), 129–30.

Musharraf, Pervez. *In The Line Of Fire: A Memoir* (London: Simon and Schuster, 2006).

McMahon, Kevin J., David M. Rankin, Donald W. Beacher and John Kenneth White. *Winning The White House, 2008* (New York: Palgrave Macmillan, 2009).

Norrlof, Carla. *America's Global Advantage: US Hegemony and International Cooperation* (New York: Cambridge University Press, 2010).

Nye, Joseph S. *The Paradox of American Power: Why the World's Only Superpower Can't Go It Alone* (New York: Oxford University Press, 2002).

————. *Soft Power: The Means to Success in World Politics* (New York: Public Affairs, 2004).

Obama, Barack. *The Audacity of Hope: Thoughts on Reclaiming the American Dream* (New York: Crown Publishers, 2006).

Pedersen, Carl. *Obama's America* (Edinburgh: Edinburgh University Press, 2009).

Pei, Minxin. *China's Trapped Transition: The Limits of Developmental Autocracy* (Cambridge, MA: Harvard University Press, 2006).

Plouffe, David. *The Audacity To Win: the Insider Story and Lessons of Barack Obama's Historic Victory* (New York: Viking Press, 2009).

Pollack, Kenneth M., *A Path Out of the Desert: A Grand Strategy for America in the Middle East* (New York: Random House, 2008).

Pollack, Kenneth M., Daniel L. Byman, Martin Indyk, Suzanne Maloney, Michael E. O'Hanlon and Bruce Riedel. *Which Path to Persia? Options for a New American Strategy Toward Iran* (Washington, DC: Brookings Institution Press, 2009).

Rashid, Ahmed. *Descent Into Chaos: The world's most unstable region and the threat to global security* (New York: Penguin Books, 2008).

Reichely, A. James. "The Future of the Republican Party," Chapter 4 in Joel Aberbach and Gillian Peele (eds.), *Crisis of Conservatism? The Republican Party, the Conservative Movement, and American Politics After Bush* (New York: Oxford University Press, 2011), 68–88.

Remnick, David. *The Bridge: The Life and Rise of Barack Obama* (London: Picador, 2010).

Renshon, Stanley A. *National Security In The Obama Administration: Reassessing the Bush Doctrine* (New York: Routledge, 2010).

————. *Barack Obama and the Politics of Redemption* (New York: Routledge, 2012).

Rockman, Bert A., Andrew Rudalevige and Colin Campbell (eds.). *The Obama Presidency: Appraisals and Prospects* (Washington, DC: CQ Press, 2012).

Romney, Mitt. *No Apology: The Case for American Greatness* (New York: St Martin's Press, 2010).

Rostami-Povey, Elaheh. *Iran's Influence: A Religious-Political State and Society in Its Region* (London: Zed Books, 2010).

Rudalevige, Andrew. "Rivals, or a Team? Staffing and Issue Management in the Obama Administration," in Rockman, Bert A., Andrew Rudalevige and Colin Campbell (eds.), *The Obama Presidency: Appraisals and Prospects* (Washington, DC: CQ Press, 2012), 171–97.

Sabato, Larry J. (ed.). *The Year of Obama: How Barack Obama Won the White House* (New York: Longman, 2010).

Saldin, Robert P. *War, The American State, and Politics Since 1898* (Cambridge: Cambridge University Press, 2011).

Sanger, David E. *The Inheritance: the world Obama confronts and the challenges to American power* (London: Bantam Press, 2009)

Scheuer, Michael. *Marching Toward Hell: America and Islam After Iraq* (New York: Free Press, 2008).

Schiffer, Michael and Gary Schmitt. "Keeping Tabs on China's Rise," in Derek Chollet, Tod Lindberg and David Shorr (eds.), *Bridging The Foreign Policy Divide: Liberals and Conservatives Find Common Ground on 10 Key Global Challenges* (New York: Routledge, 2008), 103–123.

Schmitt, Gary J. (ed.), *The Rise of China: Essays on the Future Competition* (New York: Encounter Books, 2009).

————. "Facing Realities: Multilateralism for the Asia-Pacific Century," in his *The Rise of China: Essays on the Future Competition* (New York: Encounter Books, 2009), 91–111.

Shirk, Susan. *China: Fragile Superpower* (Oxford: Oxford University Press, 2007).

Shlaim, Avi. *Israel and Palestine: Reappraisals, Revisions, Refutations* (London: Verso, 2010).

Schultz, George. *Turmoil and Triumph: My Years as Secretary of State* (New York: Charles Scribner's Sons, 1993).

Steele, Shelby. *A Bound Man: Why We Are Excited About Obama and Why He Can't Win* (New York: The Free Press, 2007).

Street, Paul. *The Empire's New Clothes: Barack Obama in the Real World of Power* (London: Paradigm Publishers, 2010).

Suskind, Ron. *Confidence Men: Wall Street, Washington and the Education of a President* (New York: Harpers, 2011).

Swaine, Michael D. and Ashley J. Tellis. *Interpreting China's Grand Strategy* (Santa Monica, CA: RAND Corporation, 2000).

Talbott, John R. *Obamanomics: How Bottom-Up Economic Prosperity Will Replace Trickle-down Economics* (New York: Seven Stories Press, 2008).

Todd, Chuck, Sheldon Gawiser, and Ana Maria Arumi. *How Barack Obama Won: A State-by-State Guide to the Historic 2008 Presidential Election* (New York: Vintage Books, 2009).

Trenin, Dmitri. *Post Imperium: Russia and Its Neighbors* (Washington, DC: Carnegie Endowment for International Peace, 2010).

Trubowitz, Peter. *Politics and Strategy: Partisan Ambition and American Statecraft* (Princeton, NJ: Princeton University Press, 2011).

Walden, George. *China: A Wolf in the World?* (London: Gibson Square, 2008).

Wayne, Stephen J. *Personality and Politics: Obama For and Against Himself* (Washington, DC: CQ Press, 2012).

White, John Kenneth. "The Foreign Policy Election That Wasn't," Chapter 3 in Kevin J. McMahon, David M. Rankin, Donald W. Beacher and John Kenneth White, *Winning The White House, 2008* (New York: Palgrave Macmillan, 2009), 45–57.

Wilentz, Sean. *The Age of Reagan: A History, 1974–2008* (New York: Harper, 2008).

Wilson, John K. *Barack Obama: This Improbable Quest* (London: Paradigm Publishers, 2008).

Wolffe, Richard. *Renegade: The Making of Barack Obama* (London: Virgin Books, 2009).

Wood, B. Dan. *The Myth of Presidential Representation* (New York: Cambridge University Press, 2009).

Woodward, Bob. *Obama's Wars: The Inside Story* (London: Simon and Schuster, 2010).

Yeats, William Butler. *Collected Poems* (London: Picador, 1990).

Zakaria, Fareed. *The Post-American World* (New York: Allen Lane, 2008).

Zogby, James. *Arab Voices: What They Are Saying To Us, And Why It Matters* (New York: Palgrave Macmillan, 2010).

2. Journal and Newspaper Articles

Abramowitz, Alan. "Transformation and polarization: The 2008 presidential election and the new American electorate," *Electoral Studies* 29 (4) 2010, 594–603.

Ajami, Fouad. "The Foreign Policy Difference," *The Wall Street Journal* September 10, 2008, A15.

Ansari, Ali. "The Revolution Will Be Mercantilized," *The National Interest* no. 105, 2010, 50–60.

Asthana, Anushka and Michael Evans. "President seeks to strengthen 'special relationship' with joint security link," *The Times*, May 23, 2001, 6.

Baker, Aryn. "Frenemies," *Time* May 23, 2011, 16–22.

Baker, Gerard. "American Revolution," *Standpoint*, issue 2 (July 2008), 34–37.

Baker, Peter. "For Obama, Steep Learning Curve as Chief in War," *The New York Times* August 28, 2010.

————. "Strange Brew: Does the Tea Party have a foreign policy?", *Foreign Policy* no. 181 (September/October) 2010, 38–40.

Bergen, Peter. "The slow death of Al-Qaeda," *The Sunday Times* News Review September 4, 2011, 6.

Bland, Ben and Girija Shivakumar. "Beijing flexes muscles in South China Sea," *Financial Times* September 1, 2011, 6.

Bolton, John. "The Post-American Presidency," *Standpoint* no. 14, July/August 2009, 42–45.

Boys, James D. "What's so extraordinary about rendition?", *The International Journal of Human Rights* 15 (4) 2011, 589–604.

Bozorgmehr, Najmeh. "Iranians braced for end of subsidies," *Financial Times* October 21, 2010, 16.

Brownstein, Ronald. "A Dangerously Downward Spiral," *National Journal*, September 18, 2010, 68.

———. "After Mubarak," *National Journal* February 5, 2011, 15.

Brzezinski, Zbigniew. "From Hope to Audacity: Appraising Obama's Foreign Policy," *Foreign Affairs*, 89 (1) 2010, 16–30.

Buckley, Neil. "A democratic deficit," *Financial Times*, August 19, 2011, 7.

Byman, Daniel. "Terrorism After the Revolutions: How Secular Uprisings Could Help (or Hurt) Jihadists," *Foreign Affairs* 90 (3) 2011, 48–54.

Cadwalladr, Carole. 'Man with a mission', *The Observer* The New Review September 11, 2011, 8–11.

Caldwell, Christopher. "Leaders for our time: do crises demand craziness?", *Financial Times* September 3–4, 2011, 11.

Chaudoin, Stephen, Helen V. Miller and Dustin H. Tingley. "The Center Still Holds: Liberal Internationalism Survives," *International Security* 35 (1) 2010, 75–94.

Chellaney, Brahma. "Water is the new weapon in Beijing's armoury," *Financial Times* August 31, 2011, 11.

Clinton, Hillary. "America's Pacific Century," *Foreign Policy* no. 189 (2011), 56–63.

Clover, Charles. "Gorbachev sees Russia's rulers as 'worse version of communist party'," *Financial Times* August 18, 2011, 5.

Clover, Charles and Christian Oliver. "North Korea seeks allies in Russia talks," *Financial Times* August 25, 2011, 4.

Coghlan, Tom. "Arabs urged US to bomb Iran," *The Times*, November 29, 2010, 1.

Coughlin, Con. "Cameron has given up on Afghanistan," *The Spectator* July 31, 2010, 12–13.

Crocker, Ryan. "Dreams of Babylon," *The National Interest* no. 108 (July/August) 2010, 18–23.

Crook, Clive. "Time to be bold, Mr President," *Financial Times* September 5, 2011, 11.

Deudney, Daniel and G. John Ikenberry. "The Unravelling of the Cold War Settlement," *Survival* 51 (6), 39–62.

Doran, Michael Scott. "The Heirs of Nasser: Who Will Benefit From the Second Arab Revolution?", *Foreign Affairs* 90 (3) 2011, 17–25.

Doyle, Michael J. "Between freedom and fear: explaining the consensus on terrorism and democracy promotion in US foreign policy," *International Politics* 48 (2–3) 2011, 412–33.

Drezner, Daniel W. "Does Obama Have a Grand Strategy? Why We Need Doctrines in Uncertain Times," *Foreign Affairs* 90 (4) 2011, 57–68.

Dueck, Colin. "The Accommodator: Obama's Foreign Policy," *Policy Review* 169 (October 2011).

Economist, The. "The hard road ahead," August 23, 2008, 9.

———. "On the brink: America and Pakistan," October 9, 2010, 72.

———. "Lexington: 9/11 plus nine," September 11, 2010, 48.

————. "Banyan: the insanity clause," May 7, 2011, 60.

————. "Ten years on," September 3, 2011, 9.

Elgindy, Khaled. "Palestine Goes to the UN: Understanding the New Statehood Strategy," *Foreign Affairs* 90 (5) 2011, 102–113.

Elliott, Francis and Zahid Hussain. "Doctor is latest victim in fall-out from bin Laden raid,"*The Times* September 2, 2011, 39.

Etzioni, Amitai. "Can a Nuclear-Armed Iran Be Deterred?", *Military Review* May–June 2010, 117–125.

Fair, C. Christine. "Lashkar-e-Tayiba and the Pakistani State," *Survival* 53 (4) 2011, 29–52.

Fifield, Anna. "US and Iraq make slow progress on relationship," *Financial Times* September 15, 2011, 8.

Fitzpatrick, Mark. "A Prudent Decision on Missile Defense," *Survival* 51 (6) 2010, 5–12.

Goldberg, Jeffrey. "The Point Of No Return," *The Atlantic* September 2010.

Goldberg, Jeffrey and Marc Ambinder, "Nuclear Negligence," *National Journal* November 5, 2011, 16–24.

Gorst, Isabel. "Washington to buy Russian arms," *Financial Times* May 31, 2011, 10.

Gorst, Isabel, Charles Clover and Ed Crooks. "Exxon secures Arctic deal," *Financial Times* August 31, 2011, 1.

Green, Matthew and James Politi. "Kerry defiant after helicopter attack," *Financial Times* August 8, 2011, 6.

Haass, Richard. "The Age of Non-polarity," *Foreign Affairs* 87 (3) 2008, 18–43.

Hamad, Shadi. "The Rise of the Islamists: How Islamists Will Change Politics, and Vice Versa," *Foreign Affairs* 90 (3) 2011, 40–47.

Hastings, Michael. "The Runaway General," *Rolling Stone*, July 8–22, 2010, 91–97, 120–121.

Hirsh, Michael. "Affairs of State," *National Journal* July 23, 2011, 8.

————. "The Decider?", *National Journal* July 30, 2011, 37.

Holbrooke, Richard. "The Next President: Mastering a Daunting Agenda," *Foreign Affairs* 87 (5) 2008, 2–24.

Hook, Leslie. "China tells US to 'live within means'," *Financial Times* August 8, 2011, 2.

Hunter, Robert E. "Rethinking Iran," *Survival* 52 (5) 2010, 135–156.

Husain, Ed. "Assad need not feel threatened by Gaddafi's fate," *Financial Times* August 24, 2011, 11.

Ikenberry, G. John. "The Rise of China and the Future of the West," *Foreign Affairs* 87 (1) 2008, 23–37.

————. "The Future of the Liberal World Order," *Foreign Affairs* 90 (3) 2011, 56–68.

International Institute for Strategic Studies. "Global Strategic Review: Global Security Governance and the Emerging Distribution of Power," Geneva 10–12 September 2010, *IISS News* September 2010.

Jackson, Richard. "Culture, identity and hegemony: continuity and (the lack of) change in US counterterrorism policy from Bush to Obama," *International Politics* 48 (2–3) 2011, 390–411.

Jacobson, Gary C. "The 2008 Presidential and Congressional Elections: Anti-Bush Referendum and Prospects for a Democratic Majority," *Political Science Quarterly* 124 (1) 2009, 1–30.

Jacoby, William. "Policy attitudes, ideology and voting behaviour in the 2008 Election," *Electoral Studies* 29 (4) 2010, 557–568.

Jenkins, Simon. "Obama's Offer: an end to US stupidity," *The Sunday Times* August 31, 2008, 16.

Joffe, Josef. "The Default Power," *Foreign Affairs* 88 (2) 2009, 21–35.

Jones, Seth. "Pakistan's Dangerous Game," *Survival* 49 (1) 2007, 15–32.

Kaplan, Robert. "Libya, Obama, and the triumph of realism," *Financial Times* August 29, 2011, 9.

Kennard, Matt. "Chinese Might," *Financial Times*, August 25, 2011, 4.

Kennard Matt and Shannon Bond. "US poverty hits record levels," *Financial Times* September 14, 2011, 10.

Kennedy, Paul. "A Time to Appease," *The National Interest* no. 108 (July/August) 2010, 7–17.

Khalaf, Roula. "Riyadh, a rogue state and riches for the US defense industry," *Financial Times*, September 21, 2010, 8.

Khalaf, Roula and James Drummond. "Gulf in $123bn US arms spree," *Financial Times* September 21, 2010, 1.

Kitfield, James. "The 13th Crisis," *National Journal* August 7, 2010, 10–18.

———. "Frozen," *National Journal* May 14, 2011, 44.

———. "The Wilderness of Mirrors," *National Journal* July 16, 2011, 48.

———. "Kings and Opportunists," *National Journal* July 23, 2011, 24–31.

———. "Worse Than They Feared," *National Journal* August 6, 2011, 40.

Krauthammer, Charles. "Obama's Altitude Sickness," *The Washington Post* September 12, 2008.

Kupchan, Charles A. "Enemies Into Friends: How the United States Can Court Its Adversaries," *Foreign Affairs* 89 (2) 2010, 120–134.

Kupchan, Charles A. and Peter L. Trubowitz. "Dead Center: The Demise of Liberal Internationalism in the United States," *International Security* 32 (2) 2007, 7–44.

———. "The Illusion of Liberal Internationalism's Revival," *International Security* 35 (1) 2010, 95–109.

Kushner, Adam B. "Beyond Our Reach," *National Journal* February 5, 2011, 16–22.

Lake, Eli. "Contra Expectations," *The New Republic* 30 July 2008, 16–18.

Lewis, Leo and Michael Evans. "Beijing hits back at Pentagon fear of its naval power," *The Times* August 26, 2011, 43.

Lieber, Robert J. "Persistent Primacy and the Future of the American Era," *International Politics* 46 (2/3) 2009, 119–39.

———. "Staying Power and the American Future: Problems of Primacy, Policy, and Grand Strategy," *The Journal of Strategic Studies* 34 (4) 2011, 509–30.

Lieven, Anatol. "Military Exceptionalism in Pakistan," *Survival* 53 (4) 2011, 53–68.

Lindsay, James M. "George W. Bush, Barack Obama and the future of US global leadership," *International Affairs* 87 (4) 2011, 765–79.

Lizza, Ryan. "The Consequentialist: How the Arab Spring remade Obama's foreign policy," *New Yorker* May 2, 2011, 44–55.

Luttwak, Edward. "The Middle of Nowhere," *Prospect* no. 134 (May) 2007.

Lynch, Marc. "America and Egypt After the Uprisings," *Survival* 53 (2), 31–41.

McCartney, Paul. "American Nationalism and US Foreign Policy from September 11 to the Iraq War," *Political Science Quarterly* 119 (3) 2004, 399–424.

McCrisken, Trevor. "Ten years on: Obama's war on terrorism in rhetoric and practice," *International Affairs* 87 (4) 2011, 781–801.

McGregor, Richard and Daniel Dombey. "Foreign policy adviser steps out of the shadows," *Financial Times* May 24, 2011, 9.

McGregor, Richard and Kathrin Hille. "US poised to unveil Taiwan arms deal,"
 Financial Times September 20, 2011, 5.

Maddox, Bronwen. "Trouble is brewing in Uncle Sam's backyard," *The Times* August
 16, 2011, 21.

Madhani, Aamer. "More Emphasis on Foreign Policy?", *National Journal* September
 18, 2010, 44.

Mandelbaum, Michael. "Foreign Policy as Social Work," *Foreign Affairs* 75 (1) 1996,
 16–32.

Mead, Walter Russell. "The Carter Syndrome," *Foreign Policy* no. 177 (January/
 February) 2010, 58–64.

Nathan, Andrew J. "What China Wants: Bargaining with Beijing," *Foreign Affairs* 90
 (4) 2011, 153–58.

O'Hanlon, Michael. "Staying Power: The US Mission in Afghanistan Beyond 2011,"
 Foreign Affairs 89 (5) 2010, 63–79.

Obama, Barack. "Renewing America's Leadership," *Foreign Affairs* 86 (4)
 2007, 2–16.

Parasiliti, Andrew. "After Sanctions, Deter and Engage Iran," *Survival* 52 (5) 2010,
 13–20.

Parmar, Inderjeet. "American power and identities in the age of Obama," *International
 Politics* 48 (2–3) 2011, 153–63.

Peachey, Paul. "Poor Response to Pakistan Aid Appeals Frustrates Charities,"
 Independent August 13, 2010.

Peel, Michael and James Blitz. "UK aided rendition to Libya," *Financial Times*
 September 5 2011, 1.

Philp, Catherine. "Obama calls for regime change in Syria," *The Times* August 19,
 2011, 6.

Pilling, David. "Pakistan, the state that has refused to fail," *Financial Times* October
 21, 2010, 19.

———. "Hillary's charm offensive in China's backyard," *Financial Times* July 28,
 2011, 11.

Puttnam, Robert D. "Diplomacy and Domestic Politics: The Logic of Two-Level
 Games," *International Organization* 42 (Summer 1988), 427–460.

Quinn, Adam. "The art of declining politely: Obama's prudent presidency and the
 waning of American power," *International Affairs* 87 (4) 2011, 803–24.

Rachman, Gideon. "Somali lessons for Afghanistan," *Financial Times* July 27,
 2010, 11.

———. "2011, the year of global indignation," *Financial Times* August 30, 2011, 9.

Rahawestri, Mayang A. "Obama's Foreign Policy in Asia: More Continuity than
 Change," *Security Challenges* 6 (1) 2010, 109–20.

Rashid, Ahmed. "Once again US Afghan policy is hobbled by divisions," *Financial
 Times* September 20, 2011, 13.

Rumer, Eugene and Angela Stent. "Russia and the West," *Survival* 51 (2) 2009,
 91–104.

Sachs, Jeffrey. "The great failure of globalization," *Financial Times* August 18,
 2011, 11.

Sadjadpour, Karim. "The Source of Iranian Conduct," *Foreign Policy* no. 182 2010,
 85–87.

Schama, Simon. "Henry Kissinger talks to Simon Schama," *FT Weekend Magazine*
 May 21–22, 2011, 14–19.

Schweller, Randall L. and Xiaoyu Pu. "After Unipolarity: China's Visions of International
 Order in an Era of US Decline," *International Security* 36 (1) 2011, 41–72.

Shah, Aqil. "Getting the Military Out of Pakistani Politics," *Foreign Affairs* 90 (3) 2011, 69–82.

Shehata, Dina. "The Fall of the Pharaoh: How Hosni Mubarak's Reign Came to an End," *Foreign Affairs* 90 (3) 2011, 26–32.

Sheridan, Michael. "Bullish China tries to test Obama's nerves," *Sunday Times* News Review, August 28, 2011, 4.

Skinner, Richard M. "George W. Bush and the Partisan Presidency," *Political Science Quarterly* 123 (4) 2008–09, 605–22.

Slaughter, Anne-Marie. "Why the Libya sceptics were proved badly wrong," *Financial Times* August 25, 2011, 9.

Starobin, Paul. "The Israel Divide," *National Journal* January 16, 2010.

Stephens, Philip. "A choice of minefields for Obama," *Financial Times* May 20, 2011, 13.

————. "No, 9/11 did not change the world," *Financial Times* September 2, 2011, 11.

Stokes, Bruce. "Trading Gibes," *National Journal* July 26, 2008, 36–40.

Synnott, Hillary. "After the Flood," *Survival* 52 (5) 2010, 249–56.

Taheri, Amir. "Why they want to cut off the snake's head," *The Times* November 30, 2010, 22.

Thornhill, John. "Russia's past is no sign of its future," *Financial Times* August 26, 2011, 9.

Traub, James. "The Elephants in the Room," *Foreign Policy* no. 189 (2011), 79–84.

Trubowitz, Peter L. and Nicole Mellow. "Foreign policy, bipartisanship and the paradox of post-September 11 America," *International Politics* 48 (2–3) 2011, 164–87.

Whittell, Giles and Alexandra Frean. "Ahmadinejad goes on the offensive at UN as Clinton calls for regime change," *The Times* September 20, 2010, 29.

Whittell, Giles. "NATO draws up military plans to defend Eastern Europe against Russian aggression," *The Times* December 7, 2010, 5.

————. "America lost more than lives on that fateful day," *The Times* September 10, 2011, 10–11.

Wright, Thomas. "Strategic Engagement's Track Record," *The Washington Quarterly* 33 (3) 2010, 35–60.

Xiang, Lanxin. "True Conservatives," *Survival* 53 (4), 197–202.

Zakaria, Fareed. "Obama the Realist," *The Washington Post* July 21, 2008, A15.

Zeleny, Jeff. "Obama Calls for US to Shift Focus on Terrorism," *New York Times* August 1, 2007.

3. Reports, Polls, and Electronic Media

American Civil Liberties Union. "Establishing a New Normal: National Security, Civil Liberties, and Human Rights Under the Obama Administration: an 18-Month Review" (ACLU, July 2010).

Arab American Institute Foundation. *Arab Attitudes, 2011*, at: http://www.aaiusa.org/reports/arab-attitudes-2011

Bettiza, Gregorio and Christopher Phillips. "Obama's Middle East Policy: Time to Decide," *Obama Nation? US Foreign Policy One Year On* (London: LSE IDEAS, 2010), 11–15.

Blankley, Tony. "Obama the isolationist?", *National Review* June 23 2010, http://www.nationalreview.com/articles/243316/obama-isolationist-tony-blankley

Blitz, James. "Gates Presses Nato Allies to March in Step," *Financial Times*, June 10 2011, http://www.ft.com/cms/s/o/246bcb58-939f-11eo=922e-00144feab49a. html#axzz1P06OaAtL. http://blogs.wsj.com/washwire/2010/09/23/transcript-of-obamas-remarks-to-the-un-general-assembly/

Brady, David, Morris Fiorina and Douglas Rivers. "The Road to (and from) the 2010 Elections: what happened to the president and his party?", *Policy Review* no. 165 2011, at http://www.hoover.org/publications/policy-review/article/64061

Brown, Kerry. "China: between global responsibilities and internal transitions," in Robin Niblett (ed.), *America and a Changed World: A Question of Leadership* (Oxford: Wiley-Blackwell, 2010), 145–61.

Ceaser, James W. "The Unpresidential President," *The Weekly Standard* August 2, 2010, at http://www.weeklystandard.com/articles/unpresidential-president?page=4

Chicago Council on Global Affairs. *Constrained Internationalism: Adapting to New Realities – Results of a 2010 National Survey of Public Opinion* (Chicago: Chicago Council on Global Affairs, 2010).

Clinton, Hillary. Nominee for Secretary of State, Senate Foreign Relations Committee, January 13 2009, http://foreign.senate.gov/testimony/2009/ClintonTestimony090113a.pdf

————. "Remarks on the Obama Administration's National Security Strategy," The Brookings Institution, Washington DC, May 27, 2010, http://www.state.gov/secretary/rm/2010/0S/142313.htm

Cohen, Ariel. "Russian Reset a Cold War Restart," August 8, 2011, *The National Interest* online, at: http://nationalinterest.org/commentary/russian-reset-cold-war-restart-5717

Cohen, Jon and Michael D. Shear. "Poll shows more Americans think Obama is a Muslim," *Washington Post* August 19, 2010, at http://www.washingtonpost.com/wp-dyn/content/article/2010/08/18/AR2010081806913.html

Comprehensive Iran Sanctions, Accountability, and Divestment Act of 2010 (US Public Law 111-195), Section 401(a)(2), at http://frwebgate.access.gpo.gov/cgi-bin/getdoc.cgi?dbname=111_cong_public_laws&docid=f:publ195.111.pdf

Cooper, Helene. "On the world stage, Obama issues an overture," *New York Times* April 2, 2009, http://www.nytimes.com/2009/04/03/world/europe/03assess. html?ref=us. http://www.cnn.com/ELECTION/2008/results/polls#val=USP00p6. http://archives.cnn.com/2001/US/09/20/gen.bush.transcript/. http://www.cfr.org/publication/21518/gates_speech_on_the_nato_strategic_concept_february_2010. html

Department of Defense. "Nuclear Posture Review Report" April 2010, at http://www.defense.gov/npr/docs/2010%20nuclear%20posture%20review%20report.pdf

Dionne, E.J. "Obama can't win for winning in Libya," *Washington Post* August 24, 2011, at http://www.washingtonpost.com/opinions/obama-cant-win-for-winning-in-libya/2011/08/24/gIQArKsdbJ_story.html?hpid=z3

Edelman, Eric S. *Understanding America's Contested Primacy* (Washington, DC: Center for Strategic and Budgetary Assessments, 2010).
http://www.gallup.com/poll/141836/Issues-Obama-Finds-Majority-Approval-Elusive.aspx
http://www.gallup.com/poll/149225/Obama-Weekly-Average-Approval-Holds-Term-Low.aspx
http://www.gallup.com/poll/1726/Presidential-Ratings-Issue-Approval.aspx
http://www.gallup.com/poll/148745/Political-Ideology-Stable-Conservatives-Leading.aspx

Gerecht, Reuel Marc and Mark Dubowitz. "Obama, American Liberator?",
    The Washington Post September 1, 2011, at: http://www.washingtonpost.com/
    opinions/obama-american-liberator/2011/09/01/gIQA3e5HvJ_story.html?hpid=z2
Goldberg, Jeffrey. "Robert Gates Thinks That Netanyahu Is an Ungrateful Ally,"
    The Atlantic September 6, 2011, at http://www.theatlantic.com/international/
    archive/2011/09/robert-gates-thinks-that-netanyahu-is-an-ungrateful-
    ally/244570/
Goldsmith, Jack. "The Cheney Fallacy: Why Barack Obama Is Waging a More
    Effective War on Terror Than George W. Bush," *The New Republic*, May 18, 2009,
    at www.tnr.com/story_print.html?id=1e733cac-c273-48e5-9140-80443ed1f5e2.
    http://www.google.com/hostednews/afp/article/ALeqM5jeLakxjNbRtm6rvKMXV
    O367FPrYw?docId=CNG.659090a76bc9935377426243e3cd3b3f.af1
Graham, Bob and Jim Talent. *Prevention of WMD Proliferation and Terrorism Report
    Card* (January 2010).
Guelke, Adrian. "Redefining the Global War on Terror?", in *Obama Nation: US
    Foreign Policy One Year On* (London: LSE IDEAS, 2010), 7–10.
Harding, Luke. "Wikileaks cables condemn Russia as 'mafia state'," *The Guardian*
    December 1, 2010, at: http://www.guardian.co.uk/world/2010/dec/01/wikileaks-
    cables-russia-mafia-kleptocracy
Hayes, Stephen F. and Thomas Jocselyn. "The Iran Connection," *The Weekly
    Standard* December 13, 2010, at http://www.weeklystandard.com/articles/iran-
    connection_520695.html?page=1
Hines, Nico. "President Obama pledges to scour world for terrorist cells', *The
    Times* December 29 2009; http://www.timesonline.co.uk/tol/news/world/us_and_
    americas/article6970323.ece
Horowitz, David and Jacob Laskin. "Obama and the war against Israel, part II,"
    National Review, June 22 2010 at http://article.nationalreview.com/436748/
    obama-and-the-war-against-israel-part-ii/david-horowitz-jacob-laksin
Ignatius, David. "Obama's foreign policy: big ideas, little implementation,"
    Washington Post, October 17, 2010, at http://www.washingtonpost.com/wp-dyn/
    content/article/2010/10/14/AR2010101406505.html?hpid=opinionsbox1
————. "Petraeus rewrites the playbook in Afghanistan," *Washington Post*,
    October 19, 2010, at http://www.washingtonpost.com/wp-dyn/content/
    article/2010/10/18/AR2010101803596.html?hpid=opinionsbox1
International Institute for Strategic Affairs. *Strategic Survey 2010: The Annual Review
    of World Affairs* (Abingdon: Routledge, 2011).
————. *Strategic Survey 2011: The Annual Review of World Affairs* (Abingdon:
    Routledge, 2011).
————. "US intensifies drone strikes in Pakistan," *IISS Strategic Comments* vol. 16,
    comment 36, October 2010.
————. "Libya win unlikely to convince war-weary US Congress," *IISS Strategic
    Comments* vol. 17, comment 29, August 2011. http://www.iiss.org/events-
    calendar/2011-events-archive/june-2011/professor-benny-morris-on-israels-
    security-and-the-arab-spring/
Joseph, Robert and Eric Edelman. "New START: Weakening Our Security," *National
    Review* May 10, 2010, at http://www.nationalreview.com/articles/229704/
    new-start-weakening-our-security/robert-joseph
Kagan, Robert. "Obama's Iran realism," *The Guardian*, June 17, 2009, at http://
    www.guardian.co.uk/commentisfree/cifamerica/2009/jun/17/obama-iran-realism-
    diplomacy

Kagan, Robert. "Obama's Year One, Contra," *World Affairs Journal* (January/February 2010), at http://www.worldaffairsjournal.org/articles/2010-JanFeb/full-Kagan-JF-2010.html

Kagan, Robert. "New START: Too Modest to merit partisan bickering," *Washington Post*, July 30, 2010, at http://www.washingtonpost.com/wp-dyn/content/article/2010/07/29/AR2010072904902.html

Kessler, Glenn. "Rice meets with Obama, then defends his administration's approach," *Washington Post* October 15, 2010, at http://www.washingtonpost.com/wp-dyn/content/article/2010/10/15/AR2010101506018.html?hpid=topnews

————. "Iran, trying to skirt sanctions, attempts to set up banks worldwide," *Washington Post* October 20, 2010, at http://www.washingtonpost.com/wp-dyn/content/article/2010/10/20/AR2010102006139.html?hpid%3Dtopnews

Klein, Joe. "Q and A: Obama on His First Year in Office," *Time* January 21, 2010, at http://www.time.com/time/politics/article/0,8599,1955072-6,00.html

Krauthammer, Charles. "Decline is a choice: the new liberalism and the end of American ascendancy," *The Weekly Standard* October 19 2009, vol. 15 no. 5, at http://www.weeklystandard.com/Content/Public/Articles/000/000/017/056lfnpr.asp

————. "Obama's Policy of Slapping Allies," *Washington Post* April 2, 2010, at www.washingtonpost.com/wp-dyn/content/article/2010/04/01/AR2010040102805.html

Leverett Flynt and Hillary Mann Leverett. "The Dispensable Nation," *Foreign Policy* May 20, 2011, at http://www.foreignpolicy.com/articles/2011/05/20/the_dispensable_nation

Mead, Walter Russell. "W Gets A Third Term in the Middle East," August 22, 2011, http://blogs.the-american-interest.com/wrm/2011/08/22/w-gets-a-third-term-in-the-middle-east/

Miller, Aaron David. "The Virtues of Folding," *Foreign Policy* May 30, 2011, at http://www.foreignpolicy.com/articles/2011/05/30/the_virtues_of_folding?page=0,0

Mooney, Mark. "Exclusive: President Obama Would 'Rather Be Really Good One-Term President'," January 25, 2010, at http://abcnews.go.com/WN/Politics/president-obama-good-term-president/story?id=9657337

Morris, Benny. "Exposing Abbas," *The National Interest*, at http://nationalinterest.org/commentary/exposing-abbas-5335

Nakamura, David. "Obama offers 2012 election supporters change they can believe in – next term," *Washington Post* August 26, 2011, at http://www.washingtonpost.com/politics/obama-offers-2012-election-supporters-change-they-can-believe-in--next-term/2011/08/25/gIQAJz9AhJ_story.html?hpid=z2

Nakamura, David and Philip Rucker. "Romney, Perry criticize Obama's foreign policy as weak," *Washington Post* August 30, 2011, at http://www.washingtonpost.com/politics/romney-perry-criticize-obamas-foreign-policy-as-weak/2011/08/30/gIQAhTthqJ_story.html?hpid=z1

National Security Strategy May 2010, at http://www.whitehouse.gov/sites/default/files/rss_viewer/national_security_strategy.pdf

Nau, Henry R. "Obama's Foreign Policy – The Swing Away From Bush: how far to go?", *Policy Review* no. 160 (April/May) 2010, at http://www.hoover.org/publications/policy-review/article/5287. http://www.nytimes.com/2008/06/03/us/politics/03text-obama.html

"The Wrath of Abbas," *Newsweek*, April 24, 2011, at http://www.newsweek.com/2011/04/24/the-wrath-of-abbas.html

Obama, Barack. "A World That Stands as One," Berlin, Germany, July 24, 2008.

————. Inaugural Address, January 20, 2009, at http://whitehouse.gov/blog/
    inaugural-address/

Pew Global Attitudes Project. *Arab Spring Fails To Improve US Image*, May 17, 2011,
    at http://pewglobal.org/2011/05/17/arab-spring-fails-to-improve-us-image/

Pew Research Center/Council on Foreign Relations. *America's Place in the World
    2009* (December 2009).

Podhoretz, John. "Barack the neo-con," *New York Post* September 1, 2010, at
    http://www/nypost.com/p/news/opinion/opedcolumnists/barack_the_neocon_
    brsZZIP4IIEMbYsUR9w5wI.

Rademaker, Stephen G. "This is no way to approve the New START Treaty,"
    Washington Post August 20, 2010, at www.washingtonpost.com/wp-dyn/content/
    article/2010/09/19/AR2010081905214.html.

    http://www.rasmussenreports.com/public_content/politics/current_events/ally_enemy/
        most_americans_name_just_five_countries_that_u_s_should_defend_militarily.

    http://www.rasmussenreports.com/public_content/politics/current_events/china/76_
        see_china_as_bigger_economic_threat_than_military_one.

    http://www.rasmussenreports.com/public_content/politics/current_events/ally_
        enemy/just_11_say_u_s_should_be_world_s_policeman.

    http://www.rasmussenreports.com/public_content/politics/obama_administration/
        daily_presidential_tracking_poll.

    http://www.reuters.com/articlae/idUSL194925620090401.

Rubin, Jennifer. "Obama doubles down at AIPAC," *Washington Post* May 22, 2011,
    at http://www.washingtonpost.com/blogs/right-turn/post/obama-double-downs-at-
    aipac/2011/03/29/AFhx9C9G_blog.html?hpid=z4

Saldin, Robert P. "Foreign Affairs and the 2008 Election," *The Forum* 6 (4) 2008, at
    http://www.bepress.com/forum/vol6/iss4/art5

Schmitt, Gary J. and Thomas Donnelly. "Enough," *The Weekly Standard* June 6, 2011,
    at http://www.weeklystandard.com/articles/enough_571610.html?page=1

Shear, Michael D. "Obama Pulls Up a Chair at George Will's House," *Washington
    Post* (blog) January 13, 2009, at http://voices.washingtonpost.com/44/2009/01/13/
    obama_pulls_up_a_chair_at_geor.html?wprss=the-trail

Sherr, James. "Russia: managing contradictions," in Robin Niblett (ed.), *America and a
    Changed World: A Question of Leadership* (Oxford: Wiley-Blackwell, 2010), 162–84.

Smith, Lee. "Obama Adopts the Freedom Agenda," *Weekly Standard* May 30, 2011 at
    http://www.weeklystandard.com/articles/obama-adopts-freedom-agenda_567618.
    html. http://www.spiegel.de/international/germany/0,1518,567920,00.html

Steele, Shelby. "Obama and the Burden of Exceptionalism," *Wall Street Journal*
    September 1, 2011, at http://online.wsj.com/article/SB1000142405311190478 7404
    576532623176115558.html?mod=googlenews_wsj

Steinhauser, Paul. "Obama: my presidency would unleash a 'transformation'," July
    27, 2007, at http://articles.cnn.com/2007-07-27/politics/obama.black.votes_1_
    affirmative-action-presidential-forum-obama?_s=PM:POLITICS

Takeyh, Ray. "The end of an era in Iran," *Washington Post* September 18, 2011, at
    http://www.washingtonpost.com/opinions/the-end-of-an-era-in-iran/2011/09/16/
    gIQAc5sYdK_story.html?hpid=z3

Tayler, Jeffrey. "Russia is Finished," *The Atlantic* May 2001, at http://www.theatlantic.
    com/doc/200105/tayler

Taylor, Miles E. "Obama's National Security Strategy under the Microscope," *World
    Politics Review* June 1, 2010 at http://www.worldpoliticsreview.com/articles/5656/
    obamas-national-security-strategy-under-the-microscope

Tomasky, Michael. "Do conservatives know what they're embracing?", December 11, 2009, at http://www.guardian.co.uk/commentisfree/michaeltomasky/2009/dec/11/conservatives-obama-nobel-speech

Traub, James. "The Two Obamas," at http://www.foreignpolicy.com/articles/2010/08/06/the_two_obamas?page=0,0

Tsvetkova, Maria. "Putin says US is 'parasite' on global economy," *Reuters* August 1, 2011, at http://www.reuters.com/article/2011/08/01/us-russia-putin-usa-idUSTRE77052R20110801

United Nations. UN Security Council Resolution 1929 (2010), at: http://www.iaea.org/NewsCenter/Focus/IaeaIran/unsc_res1929-2010.pdf

US Department of Defense. *Military and Security Developments Involving the People's Republic of China 2011* (Washington, DC: Department of Defense, 2011), at http://www.defense.gov/pubs/pdfs/2011_CMPR_Final.pdf

US National Intelligence Committee, *Global Trends 2025: A Transformed World* (NIC, 2008).

Vajdic, Daniel. "Moscow to Annex South Ossetia as US-Russia Reset Crumbles?", *The American* August 5, 2011, at http://blog.american.com/2011/08/moscow-to-annex-south-ossetia-as-u-s-russia-%E2%80%9Creset%E2%80%9D-crumbles/

Wall Street Journal. "Barack Hussein Bush," editorial, *Wall Street Journal* June 5, 2009, at http://online.wsj.com/article/SB124416109792287285.html

Walt, Stephen. "Obama is zero for four and Republicans are sitting pretty," at http://walt.foreignpolicy.com/posts/2010/07/30/obama_is_zero_for_four_and_republicans_are_sitting_pretty%20

————. "Is America addicted to war?", *Foreign Policy* at http://www.foreignpolicy.com/articles/2011/04/04/is_america_addicted_to_war

Warrick, Joby and Scott Wilson. "UN showdown over Palestinian statehood tests limits of US influence," *Washington Post* September 15, 2011, at http://www.washingtonpost.com/politics/un-showdown-over-palestinian-statehood-tests-limits-of-us-influence/2011/09/15/gIQATBTlVK_story.html

Editorial, "Planning for a follow-on force in Iraq," *Washington Post* September 14, 2011, at http://www.washingtonpost.com/opinions/planning-for-a-follow-on-force-in-iraq/2011/09/13/gIQAPsOySK_story.html?hpid=z3.

http://www.washingtonpost.com/opinions/shameful-us-inaction-on-syrias-massacres/2011/04/22/AFROWsQE_story.html

http://www.washingtonpost.com/wp-srv/politics/polls/postabcpoll_090111.html.

http://www.washingtonpost.com/obamas-approval-ratings-skid-to-new-low-economic-stewardship-in-question/2011/09/05/gIQACwxH5J_graphic.html.

http://www.whitehouse.gov/blog/inaugural-address/

"Remarks by President Obama," Hradcany Square, Prague, Czech Republic, April 5, 2009, at www.whitehouse.gov/the_press_office/Remarks-By-President-Barack-Obama-In-Prague-As-Delivered.

http://www.whitehouse.gov/the-press-office/2011/05/22/remarks-president-aipac-policy-conference-2011

http://www.whitehouse.gov/the-press-office/remarks-president-address-nation-way-forward-afghanistan-and-pakistan.

http://www.whitehouse.gov/the_press_office/News-Conference-By-President-Obama-4-04-2009/

http://www.whitehouse.gov/the-press-office/remarks-president-address-nation-way-forward-afghanistan-and-pakistan. www.whitehouse.gov/the_press_office/remarks-by-the-president-at-the-new-economic-school-graduation.

http://www.whitehouse.gov/blog/NewBeginning

http://www.whitehouse.gov/the-press-office/2011/01/25/remarks-president-state-union-address.

http://www.whitehouse.gov/the-press-office/2011/05/19/remarks-president-middle-east-and-north-africa

http://www.whitehouse.gov/the-press-office/2011/09/08/address-president-joint-session-congress.

"Remarks by President Obama," Hradcany Square, Prague, Czech Republic, April 5, 2009, at www.whitehouse.gov/the_press_office/Remarks-By-President-Barack-Obama-In-Prague-As-Delivered.

http://www.whitehouse.gov/the-press-office/2011/05/22/remarks-president-aipac-policy-conference-2011.

http://www.whitehouse.gov/the-press-office/remarks-president-address-nation-way-forward-afghanistan-and-pakistan.

http://www.whitehouse.gov/the_press_office/News-Conference-By-President-Obama-4-04-2009/.

http://www.whitehouse.gov/the-press-office/remarks-president-address-nation-way-forward-afghanistan-and-pakistan. www.whitehouse.gov/the_press_office/remarks-by-the-president-at-the-new-economic-school-graduation.

http://www.whitehouse.gov/blog/NewBeginning.

http://www.whitehouse.gov/the-press-office/2011/01/25/remarks-president-state-union-address.

http://www.whitehouse.gov/the-press-office/2011/05/19/remarks-president-middle-east-and-north-africa.

http://www.whitehouse.gov/the-press-office/2011/09/08/address-president-joint-session-congress

Wilson, Scott. "Obama's outreach toward Muslims is limited at home," *Washington Post* September 5, 2011, at: http://www.washingtonpost.com/politics/obamas-outreach-toward-muslims-is-limited-at-home/2011/08/22/gIQAySL74J_story.html?hpid=z2. http://www.worldpublicopinion.org/pipa/pdf/sep08/BBCPresidential_Sep08_pr.pdf

Zakaria, Fareed. "The post-imperial presidency," *Newsweek* December 5, 2009, at http://www.newsweek.com/2009/12/04/the-post-imperial-presidency.html

————. "Stop searching for an Obama Doctrine," *Washington Post* July 6, 2011, at http://www.washingtonpost.com/opinions/stop-searching-for-an-obama-doctrine/2011/07/06/gIQAQMmI1H_story.html

Index